International Purchasing and Management

Professor Alan E. Branch

FCIT, FIEx, FILT

International Business/Shipping Consultant

Examiner in Export Practice/Shipping/International Marketing;
Visiting Lecturer Cardiff University/Reading University/Plymouth
University/Leicester University/London City College/Rennes
International School of Business France

Fellow Chartered Institute of Transport and Fellow Institute of Export

THOMSON

LEARNING™

Australia • Canada • Mexico • Singapore • Spain • United Kingdom • United States

THOMSON

LEARNING

International Purchasing and Management

Copyright © 2001 Alan Branch

Business Press is a division of Thomson Learning. The Thomson Learning logo is a registered trademark used herein under license.

For more information, contact Thomson Learning, Berkshire House, 168–173 High Holborn, London, WC1V 7AA or visit us on the World Wide Web at: http://www.thomsonlearning.co.uk

British Library Cataloguing-in-Publication Data
A catalogue record for this book is available from the British Library

ISBN 1–86152–511–7

Typeset by LaserScript, Mitcham, Surrey
Printed in Singapore by Markono Print Media Pte Ltd

Contents

Preface

This book, the first title to be published in this field, has been written at the request of many people. Readers, both business executives and academics across the world, of my eleven titles on international trade, require a publication to provide an overall understanding to purchasing goods and services overseas on a cost effective basis. This involves the competitive buyers' contract as well as embracing the international distribution arrangements including despatching the goods from the supplier to the buyer. In effect, the process of formulating a product specification; finding a reliable quality overseas supplier in an acceptable international environment; evaluating any risk areas; negotiating a purchase having regard to the culture/protocol of the supplier culture; formulating the delivery terms having regard to Incoterms 2000; arranging the trade finance reflecting the most advantageous international options; processing the international consignment from the supplier's premises to the importer's address featuring carriers' arrangements, insurance and all the customs arrangements and associated documentation. Hence, the book focuses on the essential and strategic elements of buying overseas.

The book is written in a simple language with a strategic and pragmatic focus on international purchasing aided by case studies. It reflects the best practice code and enables the buyer to secure the best and most practical deal on a value added basis. This includes not only the product specification but also the growing importance of logistics and electronic commerce (e-commerce) in the conduct of buying goods overseas.

Successful overseas buying can only be achieved through complete professionalism. Accordingly, the book extols this ideology and features the following 15 chapters: Rationale of international purchasing; Market research and selection; Overseas culture and market environment; Buying strategy and planning; Logistics and globalization; Negotiating the contract (two chapters); Import finance; Import documentation; International physical distribution and management strategy (two chapters); Cargo insurance; Import customs practice; Processing the imported consignment; and International purchasing facilitation. In addition there are two appendices containing useful trade addresses and a list of international buyer's terms and abbreviations plus a further reading section. The book is an essential *aide mémoire* to the discerning international buyer operating within the business plan of the company and buying under the most favourable terms having regard to the product specification and international environment. The emphasis has been given to product development and empathy with the overseas supplier and encouraging competitive tendering both of the product and delivery terms in a global environment. It contains many useful hints. In short, it focuses on the strategic profitable development of an international purchasing policy.

The book is not only ideal for the practising international buyer but also for students in colleges of higher education and universities throughout the world. This includes degree level undergraduates studying International Business, International Purchasing, International Marketing, International Management, International Physical Distribution and International Logistics. Moreover, it is suitable for students taking professional examinations sponsored by one of the numerous institutes such as the Chartered Institute of Purchasing and Supply, the Institute of Export, the Chartered Institute of Marketing, the Chartered Institute of Logistics and Transport and the British International Freight Association. It will also prove a popular title for Chambers of Commerce, Trade Associations and Training Agencies conducting short courses and seminars on International Purchasing.

The book focuses strongly on management techniques and strategy, albeit on a pragmatic but thoroughly professional basis. It will prove popular with universities and business schools who continue to expand their International Trade/Management degree portfolio and require publications written in a lucid style which provide a pragmatic yet professional approach to the subject. This includes Diploma courses in Management Studies and BTEC Higher National Certificate and Diploma courses. The book is also suitable for International Purchasing courses held in Malaysia, Hong Kong, Malta, Thailand, Singapore, Australia, USA, India and Saudia Arabia.

Finally, I would like to acknowledge with grateful thanks the generous secretarial help from Mr and Mrs Splarn and as always my dear wife Kathleen in proofreading. This trio has provided encouragement, forebearance and above all complete professionalism to produce such a title.

A E Branch
19 The Ridings
Emmer Green
Reading
Berkshire
England RGH 8XL

May 2001

Acknowledgements

I am greatly indebted to the various organizations listed below for their enthusiastic assistance, especially the British Standards Institute.

Arthur Andersen
Baltic and International Maritime Council
Barclays Bank Plc
British Standards Institution
Export Master Systems Ltd
Felixstowe Dock and Railway Company
GE SeaCo Services Ltd
Hapag Lloyd
HM Customs and Excise
HSBC Trade Services
International Chamber of Commerce
International Standardization Organization
Lloyd's Register of Shipping
Lloyd's Register Quality Assurance
London Metal Exchange
P&O Nedlloyd
PricewaterhouseCoopers
Simpler Trade Procedures Board
Willis Corroon Cargo Ltd
World Trade Organisation

Dedication

To my wife Kathleen and our children David and Anna who have brought so much happiness and fulfilment in our lives

Books by the same author:

Export Practice and Management
Elements of Shipping
Maritime Economics Management and Marketing
Shipping and Air Freight Documentation for Importers and Exporters
International Purchasing and Management
Elements of Port Operation and Management
Dictionary of Shipping International Business Trade Terms and Abbreviations
Dictionary of Commercial Terms and Abbreviations
Dictionary of English-Arabic Shipping/International Trade/Commercial Terms and Abbreviations
Dictionary of Multi lingual Commercial/International Trade/Shipping Terms in English French German Spanish

1

Rationale of international purchasing

Introduction

Today we live in a global market which has undergone a massive reconstruction and diversification towards a changing product/goods sector (see Table 1.1). Moreover, the change is still rampant in many segments of the global market, much facilitated by the expanding development of cyberspace on a transnational basis and foreign inwards capital investment.

It is no longer the case that industrial products are manufactured from indigenous resources involving numerous componentized units produced and assembled in one single country. The tendency is to design the product in country A and assemble it in country A or B, relying on many imported componentized parts from a range of countries. This operation is complex and the object of this book is to focus on the professional techniques and methodology of buying overseas emphasizing a strategic focus to ensure the buyer obtains a competitive product and focuses on the consumer's and industry's needs.

The key to buying overseas is the availability of a product specification, market access, formulating a negotiating position to obtain the product at the right price and being distributed ideally in the logistic environment.

International purchasing is a very high profile international business. It is driven by many elements including technology, marketing, cyberspace opportunities, logistics, finance, innovation, social/economic well-being and wealth creation. Overall, it is a fast moving market – accelerated today with the internet – with an emphasis on purchasing value added products to satisfy the consumer/industrial needs found in a competitive market.

Hence, there is a paramount need for all those involved in the conduct of international purchasing to be completely professional. This book aims to realize this objective and it is primarily written for the student/undergraduate or business person, for example a buying executive who has limited knowledge or experience of overseas buying and the essential and strategic elements coupled with the international environment in which goods are purchased. This book will focus on all the various stages starting with the rationale of the company business to buying overseas, the selection process, the negotiation, product specification/ standards to the final distribution and payment arrangements. Particular emphasis will be given to the risk areas and the international environment of international trade. The competitive environment and the benefits to the importer of product/component sourcing overseas in a competitive global situation will be highlighted. It will reflect future trends, including logistics, and will focus on the need to buy overseas and gain a value added benefit for the importer's company product and profile. With the foregoing aspects in mind, the book will include the benefits of buying overseas, market research and supplier selection, overseas culture and environment, buying strategy and planning, quality control and standards, logistics and distribution, negotiation of the contract, import finance and documentation and customs. The book contains numerous case studies.

Overall, the book is written in a simple but lucid style and reflects the author's experience in international trade spanning 40 years, embracing not only the work environment and consultancy on a worldwide scale in the industry itself, but also as a lecturer and chief examiner at home and overseas, involving overseas governments and multinational industries. This book treats the subject on the basis that international trade must be developed on a profitable basis and that this is realized only through complete professionalism at all levels.

Basically, there are three major trading areas in the world: Europe, incorporating the expanding European Union and its single market, North America incorporating NAFTA and the Far East which incorporates ASEAN, China and Japan.

An analysis of the growth in world merchandise trade by selected region in 1998–99 (Table 1.1) and growth in the value of world merchandise trade by region 1998–99 (Table 1.2) is given and merits close study. The main driving force in the world economy remains trade and investment. Service trade will continue to grow faster than goods trade, and goods trade and investment will continue to grow faster than trade.

Importers worldwide are now focusing their attention on developing a global strategy in their search for competitive, quality products at lower prices. This is the result of greater competition and the consumer yearning for a wider product range at the point of sale. This embraces all the elements in the overseas buying process in a changing marketplace. Overall, it requires complete professionalism at all levels – a feature extolled in this book.

An example of a global strategy can be found in Greece at a manufacturer of clothes for a number of global brand names. The actual fabrics are bought from Italy, Morocco and Egypt whilst the labour input and production are undertaken in a province of Athens. Hence, by relying on imported cloth from close Mediterranean countries, the organization adds value to the product and enhances its competitiveness through the Greek workforce. Moreover, Greece is a member of the EU, part of the single market with free access to 14 state markets.

TABLE 1.1 Leading exporters and importers in world merchandise trade, 1999
(Billion dollars and percentage)

Exporters	Value	Share	Annual percentage change 1998	1999	Importers	Value	Share	Annual percentage change 1998	1999
United States	695.0	12.4	−1	2	United States	1059.9	18.0	5	12
Germany	540.5	9.6	6	0	Germany	472.6	8.0	6	0
Japan	419.4	7.5	−8	8	United Kingdom	320.7	5.5	2	2
France	299.0	5.3	5	−2	Japan	310.7	5.3	−17	11
United Kingdom	268.4	4.8	−3	−2	France	286.1	4.9	7	−1
Canada	238.4	4.2	0	11	Canada	220.2	3.7	3	7
Italy	230.8	4.1	1	−5	Italy	216.0	3.7	3	0
Netherlands	204.1	3.6	4	2	Netherlands	188.9	3.2	5	1
China	194.9	3.5	1	6	Hong Kong, China	181.7	3.1	−12	−3
Belgium-Luxembourg	184.1	3.3	6	3	retained imports a	29.2	0.5	−30	−20
					Belgium-Luxembourg	169.4	2.9	7	2
Hong Kong, China	174.8	3.1	−7	0	China	165.7	2.8	−1	18
domestic exports	22.2	0.4	−10	−10	Mexico	148.2	2.5	14	13
Korea, Rep. of	144.2	2.6	−3	9	Spain	145.0	2.5	8	9
Mexico	136.7	2.4	6	16	Korea, Rep. of	119.7	2.0	−35	28
Taipei, Chinese	121.6	2.2	−9	10	Taipei, Chinese	111.0	1.9	−8	6
Singapore	114.6	2.0	−12	4	Singapore	111.0	1.9	−23	9
domestic exports	68.6	1.2	−13	8	retained imports a	65.0	1.1	−31	18
Spain	109.4	2.0	5	0	Switzerland	80.1	1.4	5	0
Malaysia	84.5	1.5	−7	15	Australia	69.0	1.2	−2	7
Sweden	84.5	1.5	2	0	Sweden	68.2	1.2	4	0
Switzerland	80.6	1.4	4	2	Austria	67.8	1.2	5	0
Russian Fed. b	74.3	1.3	−16	0					
Ireland	69.6	1.2	20	8	Malaysia	65.5	1.1	−26	12
Austria	62.0	1.1	7	−1	Brazil	51.8	0.9	−7	−15
Thailand	58.4	1.0	−5	7	Thailand	50.6	0.9	−32	18
Australia	56.1	1.0	−11	0	Ireland	45.6	0.8	14	2
Saudi Arabia	50.5	0.9	−35	27	Poland	44.8	0.8	11	−5
Indonesia	48.5	0.9	−9	−1	India	44.6	0.8	3	4
Brazil	48.0	0.9	−4	−6	Denmark	43.3	0.7	4	−6
Denmark	47.8	0.9	−1	−1	Russian Fed. b	41.1	0.7	−20	−30
Norway	44.9	0.8	−18	13	Turkey	39.2	0.7	−5	−15
Finland	41.5	0.7	6	−4	Portugal	37.6	0.6	5	2
Total of above c	4927.0	87.8	–	–	Total of above c	4976.0	84.7	–	–
World c	**5610.0**	**100.0**	**−2**	**3**	**World c**	**5875.0**	**100.0**	**−1**	**4**

a Retained imports are defined as imports less re-exports.
b Includes trade with the Baltic States and the CIS.
c Includes significant re-exports or imports for re-export.

Reproduced courtesy WTO.

TABLE 1.2 Leading exporters and importers in world trade in commercial services, 1999 (Billion dollars and percentage)

Exporters	Value	Share	Annual percentage change		Importers	Value	Share	Annual percentage change	
			1998	1999				1998	1999
United States	251.7	18.8	2	5	United States	182.3	13.7	8	10
United Kingdom	101.4	7.6	7	2	Germany	127.2	9.5	3	2
France	79.3	5.9	5	−6	Japan	113.9	8.5	−9	3
Germany	76.8	5.7	3	−3	United Kingdom	81.4	6.1	11	4
Italy	64.5	4.8	0	−3	Italy	62.7	4.7	7	0
Japan	59.8	4.5	−9	−3	France	59.2	4.4	5	−9
Spain	54.1	4.0	12	11	Netherlands	46.5	3.5	4	0
Netherlands	53.1	4.0	3	3	Canada	37.1	2.8	−4	5
Belgium-Luxembourg	37.6	2.8	6	4	Belgium-Luxembourg	35.5	2.6	8	4
Hong Kong, China	35.4	2.6	−10	3	China	32.1	2.4	−4	–
Austria	32.6	2.4	9	3	Spain	30.9	2.3	13	12
Canada	32.4	2.4	2	7	Austria	29.5	2.2	6	−2
Switzerland	27.2	2.0	5	5	Korea, Rep. of	26.7	2.0	−19	14
China	26.6	2.0	−2	–	Ireland	23.5	1.8	32	18
Korea, Rep. of	25.0	1.9	−6	5	Taipei, Chinese	23.2	1.7	−4	0
Singapore	22.9	1.7	−40	25	Sweden	22.8	1.7	11	5
Sweden	18.0	1.3	1	2	Hong Kong, China	22.4	1.7	−2	−2
Australia	17.2	1.3	−13	9	Singapore	19.3	1.4	−7	8
Denmark	16.0	1.2	6	8	Australia	18.0	1.3	−8	6
Turkey	16.0	1.2	21	−31	India	17.3	1.3	16	22
Taipei, Chinese	14.8	1.1	−2	−11	Denmark	16.2	1.2	13	5
Thailand	14.1	1.1	−16	8	Switzerland	15.7	1.2	8	3
Norway	13.7	1.0	−3	−2	Norway	15.4	1.2	4	2
India	13.2	1.0	24	19	Thailand	13.9	1.0	−31	17
Mexico	11.6	0.9	6	−3	Mexico	13.7	1.0	7	9
Malaysia	10.8	0.8	−24	–	Malaysia	13.0	1.0	−24	–
Greece	10.5	0.8	6	–	Indonesia	12.7	0.9	−28	8
Israel	10.3	0.8	8	14	Russia Fed.	11.7	0.9	−14	−27
Poland	9.8	0.7	21	−10	Brazil	11.6	0.9	9	−26
Russian Fed.	9.7	0.7	−9	−25	Israel	10.7	0.8	5	12
Total of above	1165.0	87.1	–	–	Total of above	1145.0	85.9	–	–
World	**1340.0**	**100.0**	**0.0**	**1.5**	**World**	**1335.0**	**100.0**	**0.5**	**2.5**

Reproduced courtesy WTO.

Advantages and rationale of buying overseas

The decision to buy overseas does require a strategic vision to be adopted within the company to ensure that the product(s) bought accords with the company's business plan and reflects its production/assembly/product and its standards/

logistic/customer needs. The product specification must be market research driven and comply with the legislative environment together with acceptable quality and standards controls.

The main reasons for importing are:

(a) to obtain raw materials, components or finished goods which are not available in the buyer's country – maybe because the buyer needs them for the business or has identified a market for a particular overseas product;
(b) to obtain goods or materials from a source which is the cheapest available or of the highest quality/standard for a given price.

Advantages of buying overseas are detailed below.

1. Lower prices. This may be due to low labour costs, quality control and more efficient production technology. Exchange rate levels can play a decisive role. Overall, the total delivered price must be considered ideally based on CIP or DDU terms (see pages 288–290).
2. Product availability. The goods may not be available in the buyer's country or those that are available may be of inferior quality. To source overseas enables the buyer's product range/standard to be much increased/improved, thereby enhancing the competitiveness of the company's products.
3. A further area of improved importer's competitiveness is realized by the product's added value. It may be through design, quality/standards, durability, efficiency, technology, multi-user capability.
4. It enables a wider choice of supplier's products to be considered and bears the cost and risk of transfers: all the research and development costs and associated capital investment risks are borne by the exporter. It may be developed jointly (buyer/seller) with the seller taking the investment risks.
5. Emerging from the previous item is an added benefit to the buyer that his or her investment expenditure on development is much reduced with its attendant risk. Accordingly, the importer can concentrate on product specification/standard and quality in accord with market research findings and focus on customer needs. The onus of developing a competitive product is thus transferred to the global suppliers' market. Such an outsourcing strategy enables the buyer to evaluate continuously the supplier's market and select the most acceptable supplier. It presents an opportunity to switch suppliers as circumstances dictate.
6. Outsourcing products permits immediate availability and no lead time in product development and production. Again, it enables the buyer to keep ahead of the market and not be constrained by domestic design and production delays.
7. Successful businesses have a strategic plan and focus. The availability of cyberspace resources enables the buyer to keep up-to-date with product development and availability. Moreover, it enables pricing and delivery factors to be under constant review together with assembly and distribution location. The adoption of third country assembly or distribution points is

(d) Activating the contract within the buyer's supply chain network relative to the date, place of delivery, quantity, funding arrangements with the buyer's issuing bank (see pages 135–7) and processing import and customs documentation in accordance with the contract of sale, Incoterms 2000, UCP 500 and Documentary Collections.

(e) Managing the supply chain (see also item d) – a logistic operation – in accordance with the delivery date, involving the collection of the goods from the supplier's premises perhaps in the form of a container to an ICD or seaport; clearance through customs at the importer's ICD or seaport premises; loading the container on to the vessel for its destination seaport and subsequent transhipment at the container hub on to a feeder service; unloading at the seaport for despatch to customs clearance and raising of any import duty at the seaport, ICD or buyer's premises. Maintaining liaison with the Issuing Bank regarding payment arrangements and loan provision.

(f) Tracking the cargo throughout the transit using on-line computer access.

(g) Taking delivery of the goods and undertaking any product evaluation – transit delays, damage claims, payment arrangements including currency, import customs clearance, etc.

(h) Developing an after care strategy whereby the product is continuously reviewed for any subsequent orders or necessary modifications and, for regular suppliers, initiating continuous dialogue and establishing empathy with the supplier.

The foregoing methodology will be explained in depth as we progress through the book and will vary with each contract.

Factors influencing international trade

As we start to progress through the twenty-first century, the discerning overseas buyer must have an appreciation of why nations trade and we will consider this now. There are numerous reasons why nations trade with one another; and there are differences in taste, preferences and consumption patterns to be satisfied. This applies, for example, to the importation of consumer goods, clothing and foodstuffs. It manifests itself through culture and it is stimulated by travel and education. Consumer choice and the ever widening range of products is leading retailers to adopt a global focus to satisfy his or her clients' needs. This is driving the growing import market through price and fashion especially in the developed countries of Europe and North America.

Production costs differ by country being influenced by labour costs, technology, volume of production, transportation and product costs. Lack of mobility is a major factor. Some products and resources can only be utilized where they are located or found, for example minerals. Economies of scale vary by product/service, both internally and externally within an economy. Finally, differences arise in factor endowments, which extend to differences in both qualities and quantities as well as variations in climatic conditions. Let us consider foodstuffs: the climatic conditions in a country enable a range of crops to be grown which in turn enables other countries across the world to import such products given an adequate infrastructure and quality control standard with a competitive pricing structure. The ISO maritime container (see pages 202–16) has provided new opportunities for major supermarkets (food chains) to import a range of foodstuffs in quality condition from distant markets.

The benefits from the development of international trade are numerous, including making a wider range of goods/services available to a larger market. It permits wider consumer choice and higher levels of consumer satisfaction. Lower production costs through economies of scale and technology contribute to lower prices to the end consumer. The electronics market is an example of an area where research and development is continuous and costly. Moreover, such investment is worldwide; likewise production plants and consumers become ubiquitous through competitive pricing. The importer, by buying into such a market, enables his or her consumer to benefit from a greater choice of the latest technology at the point of sale.

International trade increases competition and prevents the monopolistic control of the home market by local producers. It provides a stimulus to economic growth, developing technology and raising living standards. Importation provides wealth to the economy and opportunities arise to exchange ideas and develop the infrastructure of a country or region and its resources as found in FTZs and Economic Zones (see page 187). Many importers adopt a re-export strategy. Goods, particularly components, are imported to form a finished manufactured unit and are re-exported as a composite unit. Vehicle manufacture is conducted on this basis as are many electronic consumer goods. The methodology which is complex and immune from import duty through inward processing relief is fully explained on page 265. Trade also develops beneficial links between countries and encourages tourism and education. Many importers have visited a country as a tourist, sampled a local product and returned home to become the import agent for that particular company.

The rapid growth in international trade and specialization raises the question of the economic reasons for trade. The key to this question lies in the theory of comparative advantage: a nation can raise its standards and real income by specializing in the production of those commodities or services in which it has the highest productivity or comparative advantage. The benefits of specialization may also be affected by transport costs of the goods and raw materials which have to be transported around the world. The cost of transport will narrow the limits between which it will prove profitable to trade.

Extending the principle of comparative advantage a little further, where a country has 'absolute advantage' in the production of two or more products, it is still beneficial to trade. For example, the USA may have a higher output per worker (or per unit output) than the rest of the world both in steel and computers. However, it might still benefit the USA to engage in trade – exporting computers (in which it is relatively more productive) and importing steel (in which it is relatively less productive). Similarly, a country will gain by trading with the USA, even if it is absolutely less efficient in the production of a range of goods. It is unrealistic to believe that a country has no comparative advantage in anything.

To conclude our review of absolute advantage, a country with no absolute advantage should concentrate on the products and/or services which bring the least comparative advantage; for a country having no absolute advantage in all lines of production, it would still be worthwhile to enter into trade provided there are comparative advantages in certain commodities. In such circumstances, the country should concentrate on the products which bring the greatest comparative advantage. Trade will not take place, however, if there is no comparative advantage.

In examining the theory of comparative advantage it should be remembered that it assumes free trade which limits the benefits from specialization. Additionally, the theory ignores foreign exchange difficulties, national and international standards and it fails to take transportation and logistic costs into account, where increasing costs can wipe out gains from trade; it assumes a constant cost of production and free mobility of the factors of production; and finally it assumes full employment and flexibility in the economy. A rigid state controlled economy allows partial specialization. Such constraints must be considered when examining the theory of comparative advantage in any trade strategy.

International trade can disadvantage some countries. For example, it lowers the standard of living in a poor country as the specialized industries, such as those with high technology, may not generate enough jobs and unemployment results. Countries specializing in agriculture may face persistent adverse terms of trade which will result in an adverse balance of payments situation. Moreover, backward countries may become dumping grounds for obsolete products. International trade increases monopoly and this can be abused. Finally, international trade transmits slumps and booms between countries and this is particularly serious in economic terms when a slump hits a poor country with limited resources. An example of a country transformed from an agricultural to an industrial/service sector is Malaysia which hitherto relied on its rubber and timber commodity markets.

International trade overview and trends

To the international buyer embarking on his or her first experience of buying overseas, it is important to have a brief overview of the international trade environment and its trends.

(a) The process of buying overseas is becoming more complex. Training is desirable and hopefully this book will contribute to the reader's ability to conduct and execute successful overseas business ventures.

(b) Import regulation and technical constraints and national and international standards are tending to become more extensive (see page 91). Moreover, they can change quickly without little notice to the trade, particularly in the seller's country.

(c) Governments are taking a keener interest in trade with more emphasis being placed on trade facilitation.

(d) The role of international agencies such as ICC, WTO and UNCTRAL are becoming more dominant primarily with a view to develop more business confidence in the conduct of trade. Examples include Incoterms 2000 (page 288) and UCP 500 (page 128) initiated by the ICC.

(e) Companies are having to become more internationally focused to remain competitive and are therefore outsourcing many of their supplies overseas. Moreover, joint ventures and mergers and acquisitions are on the increase with parties to the agreement being situated in different countries.

(f) Major contracts awarded to consortia result in extensive subcontract work on an international scale.

(g) International distribution embracing logistics, just in time and supply chain management is on the increase. Overseas buyers are fast becoming logistically focused, especially for larger companies relying on a continuous flow of a range of products, such as a supermarket retailing a range of consumer goods.

(h) The rapid expansion of cyberspace with its global focus is stimulating international purchasing as the discerning international entrepreneur probes the Internet for a product supplier. Communication through 'e-' and 'm-' commerce is accelerating negotiation and communication.

(i) The global village concept is fast expanding, stimulating competition and resulting in fewer major players – see item (e).

(j) The influence of customs unions and economic blocs is very much on the increase with a continuous expansion of the number of countries featured therein. For example, EU membership may rise from 15 states in 2000 to 21 in the next few years.

(k) Processing the imported consignment remains complex but computer technology is facilitating the technique, especially through on-line computer access with the carrier, banker, customs, port authority and freight agent.

(l) Exchange rate levels continue to be a risk area, but many options exist to lessen the problem (see page 151).

(m) Money laundering remains a major problem.

The foregoing analysis is subject to continuous change as we operate in a fast moving global market.

An overview of import regulations

The overseas buyer must be familiar with import regulations. These are extensive and subject to continuous change. However, an overview is given now, and will be developed as we progress through the book.

One must be aware that international purchasing involves the interface of four contracts: the contract of finance (Chapter 8); the contract of carriage (Chapter 9); the contract of insurance (Chapter 12) and finally the contract of sale and purchase (Chapter 6).

The rationale of the existence of overseas trade regulation and of national and international standards is wide ranging and the salient issues are detailed below.

(a) To build up and sustain business confidence as found in Incoterms 2000 and UCP 500 (see page 128) sponsored by the International Chamber of Commerce.

(b) To regulate and control trade flows through government controlled import regulations (see below).

(c) To reduce the risk of fraud, particularly money laundering and misappropriation of funds. This embraces the pre-shipment inspection of goods as developed by WTO (pages 177–80).

(d) To adopt uniform standards and regulations as extolled by the WTO (page 257).

(e) Related to item (d) is the need to have national and international product standards (see page 16). This also embraces uniform product standards in economic blocs, as found in the European Union and apply to all member states (see page 314). Allied to this point is the role of patents.

(f) Many importers, in order to comply with import regulations, test the product for safety, pollution, emission and quality prior to importation, whereupon a quality certificate of national standards of compliance is issued. This is to maintain adequate national standards. This is particularly relevant in Japan and the USA for consumer and industrial goods.

(g) To reduce the risk of plant and livestock disease and maintain health and hygiene standards, imported products must be duly certificated (pages 177 and 190). This includes live animals, plants and foodstuffs.

(h) To stabilize a country currency through exchange control regulations usually controlled by the central bank on behalf of the government. This is practised widely by less developed countries which do not have a convertible currency and trade through the US dollar.

Given below is a list of import regulations, and technical and financial constraints.

(a) The import licensing system controls and restricts the quantity and value of specified products. Details are available from the trade department in the buyer's country.

(b) Import tariff. This is an import duty raised on a range of goods. It may extend from 10 to 100 per cent. It is designed to restrict imports and protect indigenous manufacturers in areas such as agricultural, automobiles and range of consumer goods. The overseas buyer must be very conscious of the level of import duty as it will increase the domestic price. It can be avoided for re-exported goods through inward processing relief (page 265).

(c) Quota system. This regulates the quality or value of goods imported and reflects a bilateral trade agreement.

(d) Financial controls. This includes exchange controls, prior import deposits, and is usually based on import value and credit restrictions. It is practised widely in less developed countries.

(e) Restrictive customs procedures resulting in onerous and lengthy import procedures. This includes product valuation, inspection, documentation, health and safety regulations, permits and licences. This is practised widely in less developed countries.

(f) Product requirements featuring national and international standards, packaging, labelling, marking, product testing and product specification. The international buyer can check out these details with the trade association or government trade department.

(g) The payment cycle in international trade is lengthened and this needs to be reflected in the buyer's pricing strategy. It focuses on the time between placing an order for goods and receipt of cash in respect of their subsequent resale. The buyer may be purchasing finished goods for stock or to fulfil pre-sold orders. Alternatively, the goods may be raw materials for re-manufacture or components requiring assembly. Season peaks, long transit times and lengthy credit terms all add to the demands on the international buyer.

(h) Countervailing duty. Such duties are imposed on imports to counter the effects of export subsidies used by an exporting country.

(i) Discriminatory government and procurement strategies usually favouring the local national source of supply.

This list should not be regarded as exhaustive as individual countries or different economic blocs and customs unions have their own import regulations and technical constraints. Hence, the need for the international purchaser to check out the regulations before embarking on an import strategy.

Company business plan

The business plan or programme covers a period of 3–5 years and features the company's intentions, policies and objectives, identifying annually by service, product or activity the predicted level of income, expenditure and capital investment.

Import regulations and technical or financial constraints is a strategic part of business planning. Many companies now see importing as part of the product sourcing discipline, designed to improve the product specification standards and satisfy customer needs. The impact of importing can be summarized as follows.

(a) Production and assembly cost benefits.

(b) Lower investment capital and risk as all the development and research cost is borne by the supplier.

(c) Greater flexibility, as the overseas buyer can switch suppliers to keep up-to-date in terms of technology and competitive pricing.

(d) The company can become more logistically focused with all the inherent benefits it offers. See item (g).

(e) The working capital will become larger as the payment cycle is longer (see page 150).

(f) Company resources will be more targeted on marketing including product acceptance and development and less focused on technical research and production or assembly technology, particularly if a finished product is purchased. Much depends on the product. For example, car production relies on a high percentage of imported componentized units requiring extensive skills in assembly, production and logistics. In contrast, a garment manufacturer will focus on design and production whilst their overseas supplier will concentrate on the fabric quality and texture.

(g) Human resources need to be focused on higher quality personnel with an international buying focus, language proficiency and international logistics – factors not usually found in indigenous manufacture where there is no export strategy and reliance is completely on the domestic market. This requires a new strategic vision. Two main criteria have to be satisfied: first there needs to be an integrated network of professionals throughout all the countries concerned to ensure the smooth passage of imported goods and secondly there has to be a high level of specialist expertise and knowledge relating to the multitude of laws, conventions and regulations inherent in the conduct of the international environment. Moreover, personnel must be computer literate as transparency of data communication must be evident at all times between the buyer and seller in the supply chain.

(h) Cash management is more complex in international trade as it involves purchases in both world trading currencies and non-convertible currencies. It is a risk area and requires special management skills, hedging techniques or other alternatives.

Recommended reading

- WTO *Focus* – latest issues available from Media Division of the WTO.
- International banks on currency management.
- *International Financial Outlook* available from Barclays Bank Plc.

2

Market research and selection

Determining product specification

The management culture of a company will be a critical factor in the manner in which a product/service specification is determined and negotiations conducted. It will be influenced by the market environment and by market research. The product will fall into one of two divisions: industrial and consumer.

Industrial products

The industrial market is usually of high capital value, is focused on industrial needs such as production and is identified with a specific efficiency/production criteria, for example in the case of an industrial crane which will have a specified lifting capacity or an industrial plant which will have to be able to handle a specified number of units per hour. It may, alternatively, be a 'one off' purchase. A high priority is its efficiency, reliability, technology and durability. Price is a significant factor but greater efficiency and durability will justify a higher price. However, industrial product pricing is usually inelastic and has relatively few buyers. Computer technology features strongly in industrial products as it can reduce the labour operating cost input. Additionally, the industrial unit may be multi-user designed to perform a function previously requiring two or three units.

A maintenance and servicing contract may also be involved in the purchase contract, together with spares. An example is the contract to supply London Underground with 106 trainsets for the Northern Line including a 20 year guarantee that trains will be available for service. Alstom – a leading Anglo-French global manufacturer in engineering which got the contract was also responsible for much of the trackside equipment and took over the line's maintenance depots. Additionally, training was to be given to the buyer's technical maintenance team.

Industrial product negotiations will be engineering and technically focused, involving professional qualified personnel. Negotiations with the preferred supplier may be spread over several months and involve detailed discussion on the specification content. It is likely that the specification may be improved possibly through a joint technical development embracing the buyer and seller. Overall, the negotiations can be lengthy and very detailed. The role of cyberspace involving conferencing and e- and m-commerce is becoming commonplace. The buyer, however, is still likely to visit the seller's premises to evaluate prototypes and conduct discussions.

Industrial suppliers tend to be geographically centred – usually in fully developed and/or industrialized countries.

The number of major industrial manufacturers seems to be in decline at the start of the twenty-first century through mergers and acquisitions. It is not a fast moving market as is found in consumer goods.

Consumer products

In contrast the consumer product is found in a fast moving market, with a large number of suppliers, very elastic pricing geared to volume, relatively low capital value, many buyers. It is a very competitive market.

Buyers of consumer products tend not to be professionally qualified in the same way as a civil engineer or a chemist require skills or knowledge which reflects the consumer's needs – often their knowledge base is consumer market research driven. Fashion, technology, design and a cost–benefit analysis of the product are critical elements and should include non-price areas such as warranty, after sales, servicing, spares and consumer friendly service. The environments in which the product will operate are critical, together with cultural aspects. Negotiations do not tend to be as lengthy as those for industrial products. Likewise, the relationship between consumer, buyer and seller is not as intense but often involves little interaction and a minimum of negotiation.

Overall, a major change has emerged in the consumer market at the end of the 1990s which is logistically and cyberspace driven. Department stores are increasingly relying on sourcing their goods overseas in low labour cost countries where personnel are technically trained and have access to good quality raw materials. These countries are served by a good global international container or multi-modal infrastructure distribution chain network. Hence, the consumer market is focused on the logistics operator's task to ensure that goods are manufactured to a saleable quality, are transported safely and cost effectively and are delivered on time.

National and international standards of product specification

Product specification

The process of determining the product specification is a critical one and requires continuous evaluation in line with market expectations and needs. It will be determined by technology, the legal environment involving national and international quality standards, pricing strategy, competitiveness, patents, the product life cycle, value added benefit, political environment, operating environment, design, culture, fashion, the warranty offered by the supplier, spares availability and product access and availability. Most importantly, it is stressed that the ingredients of the product specification will vary by buyer and seller.

Quality does not always mean best: it means the right or appropriate quality for the product function. We do not need to over specify the materials or products we wish to acquire: such over specification will result in abortive expenditure and time wasting.

Getting the specification right is fundamental in obtaining the quality of goods required. If the specification is not explicit from the outset, then the supplier is reduced to taking part in some kind of guessing game to work out what it is the buyer wants or needs. Hence, an organization needs to use an approach which is unambiguous, easily understood, easily transmitted and as compact as possible. If this is not readily achieved problems arising from the seller misinterpreting the buyer's requirements are far from uncommon. Hence, the need to audit the specification thoroughly with all interested parties with special focus on national and international standards.

Overall, there are five elements in the product specification which encompass all the features discussed above in the analysis of industrial and consumer products.

1. The tasks of the technical specification and the marketing element tend to be undertaken simultaneously. The technical specification of the goods or services is the 'core element' in the purchasing process and must be zero error rated. It includes value added cost analysis; the supplier audit and competence including ISO 9000 accreditation (see page 26), management culture, logistic and computer focus; the supplier selection process; CE marking to pan-European products; product quality and compliance with national and international standards and the brand image of the supplier. The service sector will focus on delivery of the service and the quality of the human resource.

   A further aspect is the import duty the technical specification will attract. The process of importing a complete product in comparison with a componetized unit needs to be evaluated. Substantial import duty tariff cost savings may be realized with the componetized unit in comparison with the complete product (see page 264). Also, import duty will be avoided for goods re-exported under the pre-planned inwards processing relief scheme (IPR see page 265).

2. The marketing ingredient embraces the terms and conditions of the contract negotiated between the supplier and the buyer. This includes the search for a suitable supplier or range of acceptable suppliers in accordance with company strategy, perhaps taking into account the supplier's ISO 9000 accreditation (page 19). This will entail accessing trade association directories, Internet

websites, data banks, Government agencies, trade exhibitions directories and visits, both at home and overseas; and networking. The search for a suitable supplier may have political constraints. Evaluation of the supplier quotation should embrace all its elements: technical, financial, specification, delivery time scale and quality standards compliance. Negotiations may take months for a large industrial contract such as a ship, aircraft, an irrigation scheme or a communication project.

3. The financial element reflects the funding arrangements including pricing strategy and budgets (buyer funding). The payment cycle and range of options is described in Chapter 8. A bank loan may be required. A risk analysis needs to be undertaken and provision made to minimize such risk including insurance. It may involve stage payments as required with a ship and negotiating a mortgage with a bank. High value capital projects such as railway equipment, aircraft, ships, power stations and mass transit systems involve the supplier subcontracting much of the work and the buyer complying to a payment programme which may extend the buyer's gearing situation, hence the need for professional financiers to be involved in the funding negotiation.

4. The logistics time scale concerns the supply programme of the materials order; deliveries to the materials requirement planning; or supply of the finished product. The goods or services involved may be component parts for a car production or assembly plant; a departmental store responding to customer demand for garments; raw materials for a manufacturing plant; supply of foodstuffs or wine for a festive occasion or a computer office setting up a high tech network to continuously receive patient records following consultations with a doctor. Logistics have become an important element in international trade today (see Chapter 5).

5. The administrative element is one of coordination. It embraces the import documentation processing and auditing payments to the supplier.

Today, a company involved in international trade will have a project manager for a major overseas purchase who would then be the Executive in charge and coordinate all the above activities. Usually this role is entrusted to the logistics division which drives the contract and is planning focused.

BSI and ISO

Buyers who source overseas and have requirements which involve detailed technical specifications and who wish to eliminate both financial and technical risk and uncertainty, should use services, both national and international, which are registered to a universally recognized level of quality. This is a pre-requisite for trading to take place. In the United Kingdom the relevant body is the British Standards Institution. Whenever overseas suppliers are asked to quote for a technical product, the identification of the relevant standards, approvals and regulations, the meeting of consumer association requirements and the comparison between foreign and domestic and/or transnational standards where they exist, should be done by a professional, qualified expert.

The BSI was founded in 1901 and incorporated by Royal Charter in 1929. In 1979, BSI was the first to publish a quality standard, BS 5750. In 1987, BS 5750 was adopted by the International Standards Organisation as ISO 9000. In 1994 the harmonized standard was renamed BS EN ISO 9000. Today more than 70 000 organizations worldwide have registered to ISO 9000. Any kind of organization can apply for ISO 9000 registration, whether they be a manufacturer; service industry retailer; charity; educational, professional or public sector body.

ISO 9000 has been adopted by more than 70 countries as well as the European Union which has incorporated the series without modification as European Standards. The ISO 9000 series of standards is recognized internationally as a benchmark for measuring quality in a trade context.

The ISO 9000 series provides guidelines for quality management within an enterprise – or indeed within any organization – and quality assurance models for use between that entity and its customers or public. Unlike many standards that present technical specifications for a particular product, material or process, the ISO 9000 contains generic guidelines for quality systems within manufacturing industries or service organization in any sector.

Companies seeking ISO 9000 qualification are required to define their work practices, provide the related documentation, maintain standards, undertake the task or work effectively and monitor the system learning from observation, experience and initiating improvements and changes on an ongoing basis. The benefits of registration embrace greater responsibility, accountability and quality consciousness amongst staff; better use of time and resources; greater consistency and traceability of product or services, less wastage through product or service failure, continual improvements in quality and efficiency and finally improved profit. Moreover, it enhances the company market appeal to its trading partners and customers. This results in wider market opportunities, increased customer satisfaction and improved customer loyalty.

ISO 9000 provides concrete answers to some of today's major business preoccupations. First, the removal or erosion of protected markets is making it imperative for companies to ensure the optional quality of their products or services if they are to survive in open competition. ISO guidelines also allow a company to implement a quality management· system based on the best international practices and provides a framework for continuous improvements. Secondly, few firms today are totally independent of suppliers and subcontractors. In business-to-business relationships, a company that applies ISO 9000 to itself can promote this fact to create confidence amongst its business partners, such as an overseas buyer. The latter may then forgo costly and time-consuming inspection of the goods or services he or she orders from that company because of the confidence generated by the ISO 9000 quality management system that the supplier operates. Finally, proof of conformance with an ISO 9000 quality assurance model to ISO 9000 quality assurance procedures can be presented by an exporting company to the importer as an 'international visa' of quality. Hence, by offering a coherent, globally recognized alternative to multiple, national assessments of quality, ISO 9000 contributes to the development of open markets.

BSI registrations are renewed annually and the benefits from a trader's viewpoint include better customer satisfaction, improved profits, increased competitiveness and efficiency, less waste and duplication of work, fewer errors, cost savings, better motivated employees, better use of time and resources, improved communications and customer confidence, wider market opportunities and continuous improvements. Overall, ISO 9000 standards add value to the company product and service and allow the international entrepreneur to adopt a strategy of competing on quality and not on price.

It is often assumed that legal requirements overseas will be the same as at home. People think the same of subsidiary regulations and requirements, standards, approval or certification schemes and other practices. The fact is that there is a very good chance that the requirements and practices overseas will be different.

Much of English law is based on the common law principle, where custom and practice are enshrined in precedent. The way the law is administered can also affect the style of the law overseas. For example the 'it shall be safe' type of law does not always need to be specific if the system allows for subsidiary regulations to cover particular issues and competent inspectors and examiners are available locally to administer the requirements.

Many countries take this approach, which the buyer must recognize in negotiations with the seller, for example, in France the system relies heavily on codified law more centrally enforced. This is published in a wide range of Ministerial Decrees, Arrêtés, Régles, etc., some of which contain detailed requirements for the performance of products. In addition, in this sort of system, legal responsibilities for performance is often vested in the manufacturer or designer – a form of product liability. This frequently means that insurance companies and trade groups, who are actively involved in producing standards and codes of practice and ensuring compliance with them, are brought into the negotiations.

Prime examples of technical requirements in legislation occur in the USA where there are over 30 pertinent standards produced by a number of standards bodies and trade associations applicable to a range of goods from household and industrial ladders to swimming pools and Jacobs ladders. Overall, there are more than five pages of mandatory requirements for ladders in the USA contained in the Code of Federal Regulations and which prescribe dimensions, materials and use.

A further complication can arise in countries with a federal system of government such as Germany or the USA. Here, some of the federal law and regulations are enforced on a national basis, but a number of them allow the state authorities to modify the federal requirements.

There are two other matters related to the laws of the land. The first is that it is fairly common for third party certification of a wide range of products to be a legal requirement. Secondly, laws and regulations produced by a country are directly related to the particular experiences in that country. These differences in laws and regulations are going to be around for a long time. They are based on the historical and regional characteristics of the countries concerned, as well as their legal systems. The laws and regulations themselves will often contain technical requirements which affect products and equipment. International and European (EU) standardization solves some of these difficulties but problems still remain.

Although there is now much more international harmonization activity, there are still many national standards that differ in some way from those of other countries. Additionally, what is contained in a single standard in the UK may be covered by four or five standards in another country because its standards – and hence procedures – are slightly different.

Furthermore, although national standards authorities similar to BSI exist in most countries today, they do not all cover the same range of activities and the role of other organizations, such as trade and professional bodies, vary across industry sectors and countries.

In Germany, for example, although the Deutsches Institut für Normung (DIN), the German national standards authority, is a strong body, there are other organizations actively producing standards and codes of practice. Verband Deutscher Elektrotechniker (NDE), the Association of German Electrical Engineers, produces standards, many of which are recognized as having national status, whether or not they have been adopted by the national standards authority. It is estimated that in the USA there are more than 400 organizations in addition to the American National Standards Institute (ANSI) that are actively involved in the preparation of standards and similar documents.

In general, there will be standards related to manufactured products in most countries. These standards will probably differ in some respects unless they have been the subject of international or European harmonization – and even here differences can still arise.

As with laws and regulations, countries' approaches to standards can reflect their history. Algeria, for example, works largely, but not exclusively, to French standards although this is changing. Australia and New Zealand have moved from almost automatic adoption of British Standards to writing their own standards to meet their specific needs and conditions.

There are two main types of product certification:

(a) Independent third party certification: certification of conformity to requirements which is undertaken by an organization independent of the manufacturer seeking certification. An example is the kite-mark scheme operated by the BSI.
(b) Self-certification: the manufacturer or producer takes responsibility for certifying conformity of the product to the applicable criteria.

Additionally, there is quality certification whereby a manufacturer is certified as being capable of producing goods on a consistent basis. This type of quality management system will apply not just to the production process but to processing customer complaints, sources of supply, etc. and is based on a consistency of procedure. Many organizations make the use of a quality management system a contractual condition for suppliers. In a large number of countries it was, and still is, a legal requirement that goods be certified. In the EU the number of products affected has been considerably reduced – emerging from the Single Market Entity EU concept – but many customers, whether individuals or organizations, still look for the certification marks they have grown accustomed to seeing on the products they buy. What was once a legal requirement has become a commercial necessity for new products competing against established ones.

Any certification system needs a standard or specification to certify against. Where new products or materials are used for which there is no standard, special procedures have to be developed.

There are many different certification schemes and they vary in their requirements and methods of operation. Schemes exist for both components and complete assemblies and can therefore involve more than one approval or testing authority. These authorities can be government departments, trade associations, insurance organizations or private companies. The schemes can involve site visits and usually strict adherence to administrative procedures. Sometimes it is the manufacturer who obtains certification. Alternatively, it may be an agent or subsidiary legally constituted in the country concerned.

A common problem in certification procedures is the detailed information required by some certification authorities, which can be far more extensive than is required in the UK. In Germany and Japan, forms must be completed meticulously for there to be any chance of a smooth passage through the certification procedure.

Similarly, what the manufacturer may consider to be minor changes to the product line after approval can lead to serious difficulties if these are not made known to and accepted in advance by the certification authority involved. It is this need for certification – and the time, effort and cost associated with it – that can catch out the unsuspecting supplier.

For some products, such as boilers and pressure vessels, compulsory certification or approval is an almost universal requirement, either to national codes or to a widely recognized code such as that produced by the American Society of Mechanical Engineers (ASME). Final approval for a pressure vessel is given in France by Direction Inter departmentale de l'Industrie (DII) – a government department; in Germany by Technischer Überwachungs – Verein (TÜV) – an independent testing and inspection organization; and finally in the USA by ASME – a professional organization.

The situation for certification of electrical equipment varies widely. For example, in the USA one of the major approval and test authorities is Underwriters Laboratories (UL), a private insurance based organization. For products or equipment covered by a UK scheme, approval becomes virtually compulsory if wide penetration of the market is planned, because it is required by the insurers, the major retail outlets and frequently by labour unions if their members are to use the equipment. In Germany electrical equipment must comply with the Equipment Safety Law; approval by VDE or TÜV to VDE and DIN VDE standards is the usual way of demonstrating this compliance. This is not to be confused with CE marking which applies to electrical equipment operating only within certain voltage limits.

The problems relating to laws, standards and certification requirements are probably the most widespread and obvious technical obstacles to trade, which we will now briefly examine.

Suppliers may tend to avoid a potentially lucrative market because of product liability considerations, especially in countries renowned for being litigious. It is true that product liability by the producer is at its most fearsome when it is based on the concept of 'strict liability' by the producer for injuries and damage attributable to a defective product. However, the criteria for judging defectiveness can vary from one jurisdiction to another, and are generally based on the level of safety the user is reasonably entitled to expect in the particular circumstance. It is not difficult to see the role of insurance companies becoming more significant in some markets as far as product liability is concerned. They will be setting criteria for aspects of quality control and testing which may well constitute obstacles to trade in the future.

Another difficult area is quantities and units. Hitherto it was a major problem but today the differences between metrological practices – particularly those relating to units of measurement – are being progressively eliminated as more and more countries adopt the harmonized metric system. While leading trading nations like the USA and the UK continue to be in a transitional stage, problems will remain.

Even in the long term it should be borne in mind that not all 'metric' countries have precisely the same system. Although all national metric systems are based on the International System (SI), some non-SI units remain in use. One notable area of differing national practices is dual scale markings (e.g. SI and non-SI units). Some countries permit this practice although it can be conditional on SI marking being the larger; others do not allow dual scales.

Patents and trade marks are not usually an obstacle to trade, but they can present something of a problem in the context of conformity certification systems. Many such systems tie the validity of 'type certification' or 'type approval' to continuing production of the same product and the criteria may well include retaining a particular trade or brand mark. A change of trade or brand mark, perhaps to permit the supplier to market through two or more major 'own brand' retail organizations, may necessitate a formal amendment to the certification documents. Such trade or brand marks may also be significant in establishing the identity of the 'producer' for product liability purposes and any change may require formal revision or amendment to the insurance documents by the supplier. An example is motor vehicle emission control legislation in the USA and the EU. This has resulted in vast sums of R&D funds being devoted to emission control technology and in the patenting of many different solutions to the problem. A manufacturer may develop a technically viable solution, but it is unlikely to be commercially viable if another company has beaten them to the world's patent offices. It should be noted that in the EU one patent office serves all the member states.

Finally, it should be appreciated that new technical regulations tend to focus the attention of R&D departments throughout the industrial world on a specific need.

International Standardization Organization

The ISO (International Standardization Organization) is a worldwide federation of national standards bodies, at present comprising 132 members, one in each country. Of these 87 are member bodies entitled to participate and exercise full voting rights within the ISO and 36 correspondent members. Additionally, there are nine subscriber members representing countries with very small economies. The ISO is based in Geneva, Switzerland.

The mission of the ISO is to promote the development of standardization and related activities in the world with a view to facilitating the international exchange of goods and services and to developing cooperation in the spheres of intellectual, scientific, technological and economic activity. The ISO's work results in international agreements which are published as International Standards.

Standards are documented agreements containing technical specifications or other precise criteria to be used consistently as rules, guidelines or definitions of characteristics to ensure that materials, products, processes and services are fit for their purpose. For example, the format of the credit cards, phone cards and 'smart' cards that have become common place is derived from an ISO International Standard. Adhering to the standard, which defines such features as an optimal thickness (0.76 mm) means that cards can be used worldwide. Hence, international standards contribute to making life simpler and to increasing the reliability and effectiveness of the goods and services we use.

Industry-wide standardization is a condition existing within a particular industrial sector when the large majority of products or services conform to the same standards. It results from consensus agreements reached between all economic players in that industrial sector – suppliers, users and often governments. They agree on specifications and criteria to be applied consistently in the choice and classification of materials, the manufacture of products and the provision of services. The aim is to facilitate trade, exchange and technology transfer through the following:

(a) enhanced product quality and reliability at a reasonable price;
(b) improved health, safety and environmental protection and reduction of waste;
(c) greater compatibility and inter-operability of goods and services;
(d) simplification of improved usability;
(e) reduction in the number of models and thus reduction in costs;
(f) increased distribution efficiency and ease of maintenance.

Moreover, users have more confidence in products and services that conform to International Standards. Assurance of conformity that can then be provided by manufacturer's declarations, or by audits carried out by independent bodies.

The existence of non-harmonized standards for similar technologies in different countries or regions can contribute to 'technical barriers to trade'.

International standardization is now well established for very many technologies in such diverse fields as information processing and communications, textiles, packaging, distribution of goods, energy production and utilization, shipbuilding, banking and financial services.

Today's free market economies increasingly encourage diverse sources of supply and provide opportunities for expanding markets. On the technology side, fair competition needs to be based on identifiable, clearly defined common references that are recognized from one country to the next and from one region to another. An industry-wide standard, internationally recognized, developed by consensus among trading partners, serves as the language of trade.

No industry operating globally can claim to be completely independent of components, products, rules of application, etc. that have been developed in other sectors. Bolts are used in aviation and for agricultural machinery; welding plays a role in mechanical and nuclear engineering, and electronic data processing has penetrated all industries. Environmentally friendly products and processes, and recyclable and biodegradable packaging are pervasive concerns. The computer industry offers a good example of technology that needs to be quickly and progressively standardized at a global level. The ISO's OSI (Open Systems Interconnection) is the best known series of International Standards in this area. Full compatibility among open systems fosters healthy competition among producers and offers real options to users since it is a powerful catalyst for innovation, improved productivity and cost cutting.

Standardization programmes in completely new fields are now being developed. Such fields include advanced materials, the environment, life sciences, urbanization and construction. In the very early stages of new technology development, applications can be imagined but functional prototypes do not exist. Here the need for standardization is in defining terminology and accumulating databases of quantitative information.

Development agencies are increasingly recognizing that a standardization infrastructure is a basic condition for the success of economic policies aimed at achieving sustainable development. Creating such an infrastructure in developing countries is essential for improving productivity, market competitiveness and a global market.

The technical work of the ISO is highly decentralized and is carried out by a hierarchy of some 2700 technical committees, subcommittees and working groups. In these committees, qualified representatives of industry, research institutes, government authorities, consumer bodies and international organizations from all over the world come together as equal partners in the resolution of global standardization problems.

The major responsibility for administering a standards committee is accepted by one of the national standard bodies that make up the ISO membership and which are detailed below.

ANSI	American National Standards Institute
API	American Petroleum Institute
ASME	American Society for Mechanical Engineers
BSI	British Standards Institution
CEN	European Committee for Standardisation
CSA	Canadian Standards Association
DIN	Deutches Institut Für Normung
DEMKO	Danmarks Elektriska Material-Kontral
JIS	Japanese Industrial Standard
ICEMA	Nv Tot Keuring Van Electrotechnische Materialen
MITI	Ministry of International Trade and Industry (Japan)
NATO	North Atlantic Treaty Organisation
SAE	Society of Automotive Engineers
SEMKO	Svenska Elektriska Material-Kontrallan Stalten

ISO standards are developed according to the following principles:

(a) *Consensus*: the views of all interested parties are taken into account: manufacturers, vendors and users, consumer groups, testing laboratories, governments, engineering professions and research organizations.
(b) *Industry worldwide*: global solutions to satisfy industries and customers worldwide.
(c) *Voluntary*: international standardization is market driven and is therefore based on the voluntary involvement of all interested parties in the marketplace.

There are three main phases in the ISO development process:

1. The need for a standard is usually expressed by an industry sector which communicates this need to a national member body. The latter proposes the new work item to the ISO as a whole. Once the need for an international standard has been recognized and formally agreed, the first phase involves definition of the technical scope of the future standard. This phase is usually carried out in working groups which comprise technical experts from countries interested in the subject matter.
2. Once agreement has been reached on which technical aspects are covered in the standard, a second phase is entered into during which countries negotiate the detailed specifications within the standard. This is the consensus-building stage.
3. The final phase comprises formal approval of the resulting draft international standard (the acceptance criteria stipulate approval by two-thirds of the ISO members who have participated actively in the standard development process, and approval by 75 per cent of all members who vote) following which the agreed text is published as an ISO International Standard.

Most standards require periodic revision. Several factors combine to render a standard out of date: technological evolution; new methods and materials; new quality and safety requirements. To take account of these factors, the ISO has established the general rule that all ISO standards should be reviewed at intervals of not more than five years. Sometimes it is necessary to revise a standard earlier. To accelerate the establishment process (handling of proposals, drafts, comment reviews, voting, publishing, etc.) the ISO makes use of information technology and programme management methods.

Overall, there are nine technical sectors: generalities, infrastructures and sciences; health, safety and environment; engineering technologies; electronics, information technology and telecommunications; transport and distribution of goods; agriculture and food technology; materials technologies; construction; and special technologies. At the close of the twentieth century, a total of 12 524 International Standards and standards type documents were published, of which 961 were approved in 1999.

The ISO collaborates closely with the International Electrotechnical Commission (IEC). An agreement reached in 1976 defines each institution's responsibilities: the IEC covers the field of electrical and electronic engineering, all other subject areas being attributable to the ISO. When necessary, attribution of responsibility for work programmes to the ISO or IEC is made by mutual agreement. In specific cases of mutual interest, joint technical bodies or working groups are set up. Common working procedures ensure efficient coordination and the widest possible global application. The ISO and IEC are not part of the United Nations (UN), but have many technical liaisons with specialized UN agencies, including the International Telecommunication Union, the World Health Organisation, the Food and Agriculture Organisation and the International Atomic Energy Agency.

The ISO maintains close working relations with regional groups of standards bodies. In practice the members of such groups are also members of ISO and the principle is generally accepted that ISO standards are taken as the basis for whatever standards are required to meet the particular needs of a given geographical region.

The ISO and CEN (European Committee for Standardisation) have defined procedures for the development of standards that will be acceptable both as European Standards and as International Standards.

Finally, it should be noted that there are several thousand standards and technical regulations in use throughout the world containing special requirements for a particular country or region. ISONET, the ISO information network, exists to provide a worldwide network of national standards information centres which have cooperatively developed a system to provide rapid access to information about the standards, technical regulations and testing and certification activities currently used in different parts of the world.

CE marking – European Union

CE marking is a legal requirement for trade within Europe. Hence, manufacturers selling their products within the European Union must display CE marking on their products and/or packaging and accompanying literature.

The CE marking on the product is the manufacturer's declaration that the product complies with the EU directive and may be legally offered for sale in the manufacturer's own country. CE marking requirements are not uniform across all directives and may be varied for different products within a directive. The requirements range from a manufacturer's declaration, up to a full Notified Body assessment of the product and manufacturing controls such as for medical devices, gas appliances, etc.

Each country within the European Union has its own laws and regulations that manufacturers must comply with in the interests of the environment and consumer safety and protection. These laws differ from country to country making it difficult for a manufacturer wishing to market products across Europe. The new approach directives (pan-European laws) are designed to solve this problem.

The directives set out the essential requirements for products, written in general terms, which must be met before the product can be offered for sale in any country belonging to the EEA (European Economic Area) including the UK.

A directive does not come into force immediately after it is passed by the European legislative system. There is often a limited 'transition period'. During this period a manufacturer can voluntarily apply CE marking to a product that conforms to the directive, but is not legally required to do so until the end of the transition period. There are no further concessions after that point.

Where more than one directive applies to a product, there may be different transition periods and points at which the directives become legal requirements. In this case, CE marking may be applied only for those directives already in force, provided this is clearly stated. However, it may well be simpler and cheaper for a manufacturer to comply with both legal and transitional directives at the same time.

Where a directive requires independent assessment of products or systems, this must be done by an organization that has been nominated by a government and has been notified to the European Commission. These are appointed by government departments or agencies. Some directives call for a technical construction file evaluation to be carried out by a 'Notified Body'.

The BSI is a Notified Body under a number of directives and one of the very few Notified Bodies able to offer all of the services required by the directives embracing standards identification: technical file evaluation; initial type testing; quality system assessment; factory production control system assessment; EC certificate issue; and surveillance of product and quality system or factory production control.

The CE marking process embraces eleven stages:

(a) identify the directives relevant to the product;

(b) identify the entry route of the product into the EC;

(c) determine the dates by which action must be taken;

(d) identify if there are relevant harmonized European Standards;

(e) check that no other purely national requirements still exist in countries where the product may be sold;

(f) determine that the product complies with the essential requirements of the directives, taking appropriate measures to comply or identify existing data and test reports;

(g) identify whether independent assessment of the product's conformity, or some aspects of it, is required from a notified body;

(h) continue to work closely with a notified body to complete any testing and assessment measures required, ensuring that the appropriate Conformity Assessment Procedures are met;

(i) prepare the declaration of conformity and the required supporting evidence (if applicable);

(j) maintain technical files and any other reports by the Directive(s);

(k) apply CE marking correctly on the product and/or its packaging and accompanying literature.

Process of sourcing potential suppliers

There is a wide range of ways to identify a suitable buyer.

(a) Attending a trade exhibition. This enables the buyer to gauge the level of competition, prices, technology and provides an opportunity to meet the personnel on the stand. Also, it enables the buyer to study and evaluate a range of exhibitors and their products/services and make valid comparisons.

(b) Attending a sales conference or seminar. This may extend to several days while speakers deliver papers on areas of current interest and development. It also enables networking to take place.

(c) Identifying suppliers in a trade directory. Such directories may be issued by Trade Associations, Government, International Agencies, Professional Institutes, Country's/National Chambers of Commerce, Importers Associations and private companies. Many such sources now have direct access through the Internet.

(d) Journals, newspapers and magazines are a good source of supplier information. Also, they contain articles on recent developments and future trends.

(e) Major suppliers circulate to their loyal buyers house magazines and sales bulletins. Also delegates at sales conferences and hospitality events are likely to receive or obtain promotional material.

(f) The Internet is a fast growing aid to identifying suitable global suppliers. Moreover, e- and m-commerce communication is instantaneous and global with few cultural barriers and no national boundaries.

(g) Government, chambers of commerce/trade associations arrange inward trade missions. This involves existing and potential buyers visiting, as a group, a specific country to meet exporters. Alternatively, an outward mission embraces exporters visiting a country to meet potential buyers or selecting an import agent. The inward and outward trade delegations are often government assisted. Both large and small importers are involved.

(h) Trade Ministers during their visits overseas tend to promote their country's products and put buyers in touch with suitable suppliers. This can extend to special promotions such as a Danish Week held in a Rotterdam department store to promote Danish consumer goods including foodstuffs.

(i) The Commercial Attaché of the embassies will have details of potential suitable suppliers in their country.

(j) Business clubs offer endless networking opportunities together with meeting guest speakers and attending seminars.

Selection of the overseas supplier

Having established a list of potential overseas sources, the next stage will normally be to issue an enquiry which clearly and unambiguously indicates what is required. The following is a list of areas which will needs adequate evaluation to determine costs, risks, logistical focus and acceptability.

(a) The supplier selection is a crucial decision. The following factors are relevant and may allow a short list of three to be drawn up:
   (i)   a credit rating undertaken by an independent company such as Dun and Bradstreet,
   (ii)   national and international standards accreditation of products ISO 9001,
   (iii) the company's position in the marketplace – market leader or laggard,
   (iv) major existing importers,
   (v)   qualifications of directors and the quality of management and the workforce,
   (vi) any litigation pending with clients,
   (vii) any awards received by the company,
   (viii) is the company computer and logistically focused?,
   (ix) company membership of any trade or professional association,
   (x)   experience of manufacturing on producing the required product (companies which comply precisely with the product specification/ service should be considered),
   (xi) value added benefit offered by the company product – quality, high tech, warranty, design, spares, training, servicing and general competitiveness (this may extend to the funding arrangement and any finance package available),
   (xii) product availability and delivery time scale,

(xiii) evaluation of the production and manufacturing systems, embracing organization, planning, management/documentation, manufacturing plant, production procedures/instructions, inspection procedures/instructions, process parameters, final inspection, sampling instructions, quality and inspection status, training of the workforce, documentation/registration and corrective measures, and product testing.

(xiv) a visit to the manufacturing plant could embrace the foregoing areas,

(xv) the company's last three annual reports.

(b) Meeting the directors, managers and workforce.

(c) Determining a general overview of the company and its management culture.

(d) Conducting a product audit to determine the degree to which a company succeeds in having a zero failure rate in its production lines in accordance with the quality standards specified.

(e) Process audit a programmed investigation to measure the extent to which the (technical) processes are capable of meeting the required standards.

(f) Systems audit – a comparison of the quality system to the external standards (see page 98).

(g) Take any opportunity to further improve the specification and if practicable have sample for evaluation or have access to working models such as an earlier buyer.

(h) An increasing number of suppliers develop, jointly with the buyer, the product to reflect the buyer's environment. This involves several visits to the supplier's premises and the final cost will include development and maybe innovation.

(i) The degree of subcontracting and quality control and availability.

(j) A range of existing buyers which the buyer may visit or contact to screen their evaluation of the supplier. An increasing number of buyers have two overseas suppliers to combat the risk of any liquidation of the supplier or any unforeseen event. Conversely, one supplier may have a constraint on production capacity to cope with seasonal surges. Again, a second supplier may be desirable.

(k) Some buyers invite selected suppliers to give a presentation or demonstration of their product.

(l) Currency. What currency should be used – the buyer's or the seller's currency or a third currency such as the US dollar? The buyers currency ensures no risk to the buyer with all the risk transferred to the sellers. Conversely, using the sellers currency ensures no risk to the seller but all the risk being transferred to the buyer. The euro currency – operative in twelve EU countries – eliminates all currency risk undertaken in the Eurozone (see Chapter 8).

(m) The geographical location of the supplier and/or the place of supply. The buyer's address may be different from the point of supply. The point of supply will be the determining factor in import tariff duty terms and likewise in freight cost. A strategic focus is required on the supply source. Do we need a developed or underdeveloped market?

In a developed market, such as the G7 members, there will be a good infrastructure and a technically trained workforce. Convertible stable currencies are more likely with a politically stable government. However, labour costs will be relatively high. A developed market may have a regulated economy, as in France or Germany, or a deregulated market, as found in the USA and the UK. Conversely, the less developed country will have a less stable currency, which trades through the US dollar, poor infrastructure and low labour costs with limited technical skills.

Other factors to consider are a near or distant market and membership of a customs union or economic bloc. The EU single market encourages transnational EU state business as no trade barriers exist. The goods and services may flow freely across international borders with no customs impediment. Bi- or multi-lateral trade agreements exist globally which offer preferential customs duty between the two countries or trading groups to encourage trade.

(n) The international distribution network (see Chapters 10 and 11). The product may need to be transported by sea, air or via multi-modalism or a combined transport system involving, perhaps a container shipment of furniture from Malaysia to Europe embracing road, sea and rail. Overseas buyers need to examine very closely the available transport services and their cost, efficiency, frequency and transit time. Countries which have no access to a global container network are seriously disadvantaged in their export market development.

(o) Which Incoterm 2000 to use (see Chapter 14). Buyers are encouraging quotations on a delivered-basis, covering the transit to the frontier point. DAF, or destination point, CIP, DDU or DDP. This enables a valid comparison to be made irrespective of the sourcing country and reflects the cost of the goods plus the transport cost to the buyer's nominated destination address in the overall tender price. Alternatively, the buyer may wish to collect the goods from the seller's factory, EXW and make his or her own transport arrangements.

(p) The payment arrangements (see Chapter 8). This may be via open account, documentary credits or bill exchange. Financing the trade cycle needs careful evaluation by the buyers.

(q) The supplier's quotations need very careful evaluation. The specification must be unambiguous. Likewise, supporting data such as drawings and references to any specific standards or instructions should be checked out. The unit of measure should ideally be metric.

(r) The collection address could be different from the ordering address.

(s) The total cost needs careful evaluation (see Chapter 4). The following elements will feature: product price, transportation, insurance, documentation, customs clearance, import duty, VAT, currency (risk), forwarding agent's commission, bank charges, packaging, interest on capital goods in transit and so on.

The criteria of the final choice will vary by product and buyer's circumstances. Price is a dominant factor but other areas will also have an impact, especially the delivery time. Competition risk analysis should be conducted – currency and political aspects, product availability, language, value added benefit, convenience of the supplier location and management culture and finally the brand image of the supplier. A visit to the seller facilitates a better evaluation and determines whether a good working relationship can be developed.

One must stress in conclusion to this chapter that the buyer must approach each supplier's country on an individual basis and have paramount consideration of the international (ISO) and national (BSI) standards. Further, each product must be thoroughly researched. Ideally it is best to visit the supplier's country and formulate a good relationship. Sufficient time should be spent on determining the product specification and ensuring it complies to national and international standards.

Recommended reading

- British Standards Institution publications.
- International Standards Organisation publications.
- Department of Trade and Industry publications.

Note

Extracts from British Standards and BSI material in this chapter and throughout the book are reproduced with the permission of BSI under licence number 2000SK/0525. Complete copies of British Standards can be obtained by post from BSI Customer Services, 389 Chiswick High Road, London W4 4AL.

3

Overseas culture and market environment

The development of a successful international purchasing strategy is based on a sound understanding of the similarities and differences that exist in the various countries around the world. Hence the need for the overseas buyer to research fully the seller's market. In this chapter we will examine cultural and social issues and also look at some of the major markets of the world with a cultural focus. This will enable the buyer to understand the business environment of the seller's market and thereby adopt successful negotiating skills. Many overseas buyers fresh to the business undergo a culture briefing and learn the seller's language to conversational level.

Culture

Culture has been defined as 'the configuration of learned behaviour and results of behaviour whose component elements are shared and transmitted by members of a particular society'. The various aspects of a society's culture pose many challenges to the overseas buyer. We shall consider some of these aspects in more detail.

1. Cultural differences: the 'in one, in all' principle can be applied to cultural as well as economic groupings. 'Culture' is usually taken to imply such adornments of a civilization as music, art and language, but we shall adopt a wider definition here to embrace these and many other things. We will define a society's culture as everything about which human beings conform, resulting in a distinctive way of life for its people.
2. Material culture: this includes all artefacts, that is all physical objects which are made, such as pottery, paintings, houses, roads, dams and airports. Material culture is a useful guide to a society's standard of living. The term 'standard of living' is not to be confused with 'quality of life' – indeed, the two are often in opposition to each other.
3. Education: a highly educated population is easier to communicate with and usually quite sophisticated. Educated populations are more likely to have a

higher standard of consumption and be more discerning on product choice development together with knowledge of the product service. Moreover, the workforce is likely to be well trained with high literacy standards. Market research data will be extensive and reliable.

4. Religion: characteristic attitudes and taboos often result from religion, which extends to food and people's attitudes to a whole range of products from deodorants to alcoholic drinks. It embraces philosophical systems, beliefs and norms. Rifts within societies are often along religious lines, and must be respected in conducting business overseas. There are also implications for business practice: Muslims regard Fridays as their Sabbath, and, for example, other religions so regard Saturday or Sunday. Additionally, colour has different meanings in different countries – white for mourning in China and orange has political significance in Northern Ireland. This must be borne in mind when presenting gifts.

5. Social organization, customs and roles: the social fabric and structure are changing in many countries through the influence of education, investment, travel, communication, the Internet and technology. This change is driven by the younger generation. Social organization represents the way in which society organizes itself and is particular how that society thinks about kinship, social institutions, interest groups and status groups such as clubs. Overall, a new era of networking and a changing business environment is emerging. In developed countries, 'career wives' are a common feature – an increasing number occupying the professions. This is resulting in smaller families or childless couples who opt to develop their careers and not raise a family. 'Convenience goods' is the marketeer's watchword here, since the traditional household caterer now no longer has the time, or the inclination, for such tasks. Take-away food, microwave ovens and many other products owe a lot of their success to the increase of working wives and the first generation in their profession. Overall, a new life style is generated for the professional family who consequently have different expectations, for example house ownership rather than living in rented accommodation.

Social groupings occur around activities such as sailing, music, business clubs, horse riding, rambling or embroidery – each offering its own networking opportunities. In less developed societies, these groupings are not so common as they are in the West. Moreover, many families live in agricultural communities, are on lower incomes and have lower living standards.

6. Language: while English is becoming the international business language of the world, and is spoken by a quarter of the world's population as a first or second language, there are also some 2700 other languages, not including dialects. Language can either be a great cultural pitfall or an opportunity in international marketing. The overseas buyer can communicate in the seller's language or a third language acceptable to both the seller or buyer. This affects not only normal business negotiations and communication, but also

'marketing communication'. The problem becomes acute where legal documents and the seller's advertising material have to be translated for international purchasing use. In many cases, not only the words but also the underlying concepts have to be translated, and this can only be done effectively by a member of the indigenous population. There are many examples of brand name 'howlers' resulting from insufficient research into the meanings they might convey in a foreign language. The marketeer communicating in the buyer's language generates confidence, integrity and commitment to the buyer which augurs well for business opportunities and development and also for protocol.

7. Aesthetics: the term 'aesthetics' refers to ideals of beauty and good taste in art, music, architecture and so forth, and products and product support material should have designs which appeal to local tastes. Some Chinese advertising for medical products, for example, would be found too explicit for the UK, and the standard of public taste exhibited on Japanese television causes Westerners to blanch, in spite of the refinement found in other aspects of Japanese culture. This is not to say that one country's aesthetics are inferior to another's – but the differences must be taken into account. Local aesthetics have a strong appeal to the local populace but can be unacceptable or have less cogency for an overseas culture. It is important that the aesthetics of a country, region or religion are respected.

8. Ethics and mores: ethics is all about perception – the customer's expectation and experiences of the product/service are identified in the brand image of the company. Companies with a strong brand usually retain the brand when a merger or acquisition takes place. The buyer's expectation of the brand, and therefore of the social and business ethics associated with it vary considerably around the world. One aspect of business ethics that needs to be mastered is the expectation in many countries that business incentives such as bribes will be issued as a matter of course: they may be essential in some cultures to secure an order. Mores relate to moral matters, and generally derive from religion. They may restrict or prohibit the use of particular products: for example, the marketing of contraceptives to the unmarried – this latter constraint is now being eliminated as the World Health Organisation advocates birth control and raising health standards in less developed and emerging markets.

9. Political systems: these are unique to particular societies and have many implications for overseas buying and negotiating and for market access. The buyer must keep in touch with the ideology of governments since an increasing number are privatizing former state industries and developing mixed economies with limited state control or ownership and more control in the private sector, as found in China. Widespread privatization is having considerable social and economic implications and is encouraging more inwards investment, thereby raising the competitiveness of particular industries or service sectors through modernization and capital investment.

Political systems in host countries need very careful examination where the buying strategy involves the setting-up of revenue-earning assets overseas featuring inwards investment and product/service outsourcing. Local attitudes regarding the employment of nationals of the host country, levels of taxation, ownership of equity and repatriation of profits may be particularly contentious and may differ according to local political factions. Also, there is the prospect of nationalization. The prevailing orthodoxy will be reflected in current legislation, but there may be a strong minority who would change things if they were elected. In extreme cases, an asset might even be expropriated. The formulation of trading blocs is tending to open up markets and encourage trade on a low-risk basis. Political stability favours more commitment by the importer. International banks such as Barclays provide regular up-dated country reports for over 100 countries which feature both the economic and political environment.

10. Protocol: basically protocol concerns how to present oneself. It extends to dress code, mannerisms, language, body language, propriety, discretion, non-verbal messages, codes of behaviour when conducting negotiations and the decision-making process. An important aspect is to respect national protocol and never discuss trade and politics together. Again, a culture briefing is desirable prior to the inexperienced buyer visiting the seller's country to conduct negotiations.

11. Economic systems: these are usually the outcome of political stances of one kind or another and may create problems in internal dealings. A major complication in negotiating deals in controlled economies, for example, is that orders are placed with the state organization and the export team are not free to negotiate a deal with the visiting overseas buyer.

12. Legal systems: these tend to reflect the broad political aims of the country. Legal systems feature trade barriers; market access; multi- and bi-lateral trade agreements; economic, customs and trade blocs; and the commercial legal environment. It extends to membership of any International Convention.

13. Management culture: this embraces the manner and protocol in which the company conducts its business overseas and also the company structure; in particular the decision maker and the influencers and the overall decision-making process. It also reflects the company business plan objectives and constraints in dealing with any particular country, company or product overseas.

Cultural comparisons by country

The 13 areas of culture that we have examined are, in practice, closely interwoven in ways which affect the buyer or the seller. Problems of cultural adaptation will be highlighted when personal contacts are made, especially when the buyer visits the seller's country and becomes involved in negotiations. These problems will be felt most acutely by expatriate staff. We will now examine a number of contrasting economies/cultures.

Japanese culture

Statistics: area 370 000 km^2; population 127 million; per capita GDP US$32 000. The key to understanding the Japanese culture and protocol is through the concept of a group which is tightly knit and pervades every aspect of life. Confucian principles of social order mean that an emphasis on hierarchy according to status and age and rigid codes of behaviour exists in Japan. Ethnically, the population is extremely homogeneous and very nationalistic, having one language. Buddhism and Shintoism are the main religions. Family and traditional values permeate the culture. Family size is almost invariably one or two children. Japanese society is very chauvinistic. Company and family are the most important groups and loyalty is very strong.

Overall, company ranks above family – but this is changing with the younger generation – above individuals and the emphasis is on long-term development. Japanese businessmen are very honest, but decision making is a long drawn-out collective process – and once a decision is made it is not rescinded.

Japanese etiquette is one of the most elaborate and complex in the world. One-to-one meetings are rare; usually, four persons is the norm. Punctuality is essential and a fairly smart, stylish and conservative dress is expected. There is a strict code of propriety as regards business cards which are seen as being as important as the person him- or herself, and must be accorded the same respect. Place your card in your back pocket and you could lose the deal. The Japanese traditionally put their family name first and the name of the company must be introduced before your own. If you can do a formal bow it helps, but many Japanese expect foreigners to shake hands and follow this practice themselves. Seating etiquette demands the guest sits furthest from the door. Meetings will always start off with pleasantries, no matter what the time constraints. In conversation an interest in Japanese culture is appreciated; the Second World War is a taboo subject.

The Japanese have a deep sense of propriety and discretion. They pay a lot of attention to non-verbal messages. Be tentative about gestures, as even blowing your nose loudly in front of others is considered rude. Try not to slouch – the line of the back is an indication of character to the Japanese. A Japanese smile in business meetings is often from a reluctance to say 'no' and avoiding eye contact is seen as polite. The full force of eyes is seen as a 'knife in one's hand'.

Gift giving is part of social communication in Japan. It is very rude to refuse a gift, but they are given in the spirit of reciprocity. The number of items given is significant – four of anything means death and for auspicious occasions odd numbered items should be given but nine suggests suffering.

If you go to a restaurant, you will be expected to take your shoes off and leave them pointing towards the door. Don't help yourself to food or drink in

Japan and don't stick your chopsticks into the rice like flagpoles – this is done when the Japanese symbolically offer a bowl of rice to the dead. Conversation is not at a premium during meals and if offered sake from your hosts glass, accept it graciously – it is an honour.

The Japanese seem to be most honest and open when drinking, which you will experience if doing business there. For a nation so self-disciplined, it may come as a surprise that people do not give a second thought about getting roaring drunk and being quite loud and bawdy.

Japan has a homogeneous market which is very nationalistic about its own manufactured products. It exports a very wide range of consumer and industrial products – ideal for the overseas buyer to target. Distribution networks are based on very tight relationships between customers and suppliers. The common pattern in any product distribution system in Japan is for there to be a middleman – the wholesaler – often acting as agent for the foreign supplier. The number of buyers is nearly always greater for consumer products than for industrial goods, although for some of the latter, there are also many buyers.

American culture

Statistics: area 3 717 796 sq miles; population 273 million; per capita GDP US$32 000.

The USA has a large and diversified economy with a broad base of natural and human resources and a well-developed physical and technical infrastructure. Buoyed by a steady flow of immigrant labour and a large domestic market, it remains a global leader in technological innovation and product dissemination. US multinationals dominate many industries and US trends, particularly in financial services, and have a profound impact on virtually all the economies of the world.

The USA has a material culture and Protestantism is the dominate religion. It has a pluralistic society with room for many individual aspirations and high individualism.

The USA is an ideal market for procurement, with major exports in manufactured goods, machinery and transport equipment, chemicals, food and a wide range of manufactured goods. It has an active Chamber of Commerce in most countries of the world promoting US products and facilitating bi-lateral trade. The market is highly competitive and overseas buyers are urged to visit the market once their own market research and pre-planning has been completed. The American market is logistically driven and very high tech with computer literacy evident across the industrial and consumer spectrum in 50 states.

Chinese culture

Statistics: area 9 579 000 km^2; population 1239 million; per capita GDP US$800.
What immediately stands out about China is its huge size in terms of its population, land area and economic resources. China's population of 1.2 billion is

equivalent to a fifth of the world's population and the economic and political logistics of feeding, clothing, housing, educating and providing jobs and medical care for so many people are complex and demanding and exert a considerable strain on China's budgetary resources.

The size of the domestic market permits economies of scale in production even in the absence of export markets. Moreover, the considerable surplus of cheap labour confers on China an advantage in the production and export of labour-intensive manufacturing products – making it an attractive market for procurement. China is endowed with significant reserves of energy, minerals and agricultural resources, access to which eases the pressure on the balance of payments by minimizing the need to import these products and allowing rapid rates of industrial growth. Moreover, the emphasis latterly placed on education and training has boosted productivity levels and facilitated a faster application of modern industrial technologies.

Following the 'open door' policy initiated in the late 1970s the economy has undergone some major structural changes as a direct result of a series of pragmatic and well coordinated economic and financial reforms. The reforms have been prioritized and staggered, with efforts concentrated first in restructuring the agricultural sector, then progressing to the town and village enterprises, manufacturing industries and subsequently to foreign trade and foreign investment. China's industrial strategy has focused on the rapid development of the Special Economic Zones in the coastal regions, with foreign finance, foreign technologies and foreign management practices playing a key role.

Attention is now focused on reforming the state-owned enterprises, banking systems and the stock and foreign exchange markets. China also recognizes the need to speed up the reform of the legal, fiscal and accounting institutional framework in order to establish a greater degree of transparency, consistency, predictability and a level playing field.

Despite the rapid rates of economic growth and improvements in general living standards, China remains a poor country with the bulk of the population still engaged in farming and earning considerably less than the urban population. In addition there are also wide income inequalities between the inefficient state-owned enterprises and the town and village enterprises and foreign joint ventures. This situation is being exacerbated by rising levels of unemployment and underemployment and the flood of millions of unskilled migrant agricultural labourers to congested urban centres.

The opening up of China as a trading destination has been accompanied by an increase in distribution services from major shipping lines, airlines, express carriers and freight forwarders. Additionally, the country is investing in its transport infrastructure. With so many major destinations along China's seaboard, many of the shipping services call at ports such as Shanghai or Hong Kong. Feeder services are then used to reach other, smaller ports around China. Air transport has developed similarly.

Russian culture

Statistics: area 17 075 400 sq km; population 147 million; per capita GDP US$1900.

The Russian culture is emerging from a system of federal communism with state objectives uppermost to an open market economy. Religion is predominantly Orthodox. The social organization is primarily monolithic with limited possibilities for exploiting individual life styles in marketing. Consumers yearn for technical products but demand is limited as no buying power exists. Moreover, the consumer product range is limited due to mismanagement of the economy. Aesthetics is frowned upon where it is creating numerous difficulties in marketing communications. Advertising is found only in major cities. TV ownership and the number of students attending universities compares very unfavourably with the developed markets of, for example, the USA and France. Russia is not a materialistic, throw-away, fashion-conscious society like the USA as the economic environment and purchasing power are limited.

Russia is rich in energy resources with major deposits of petroleum, coal, peat and natural gas. It also has significant deposits of aluminium, copper, iron ore, lead, phosphate rock, nickel, magnesium, gold and diamonds. Exports are dominated by raw materials, with petroleum, petroleum products, natural gas, minerals and metals accounting for about 60 per cent of the total. Hence, Russia is highly susceptible to world price movements in primary products.

Russia had achieved a great deal in the period following the dissolution of the USSR in 1991 when it adopted policies to enable it to become a market economy up until the sudden dismissal of the Kiriyenko Government in 1998. There followed a period of economic and financial turmoil. There has been a massive disruption to production brought about by the collapse of central planning, the break-up of traditional trade and payments systems and increasing economic imbalances. As a consequence, since the beginning of the 1990s there has been a substantial decline in real GNP while barter trade (counter trade see page 148) has become an important feature of the economy. Weak political resolve has also undermined structural reform efforts while policy execution has been extremely poor. The link between the economy and politics or crony capitalism remains a serious threat to the functioning of the nascent market economy. Many observers believe that fundamental reforms are needed – particularly in the tax collection system which leaves the government short of revenue – before the economy can truly prosper again.

Russia, at the start of the twenty-first century, is entering a new era under President Vladimir Putin and is now experiencing a degree of economic stability following the later years of President Boris Yeltsin's authority of economic mismanagement and the misuse of constitutional power. The economy is forecast to grow following a rise in industrial production and a relatively tight monetary policy. A financial aid package from the IMF has been rescheduled which will allow improved economic growth and further restructuring of the economy moving from a state controlled market to a market-driven free economy.

The private sector accounted for an estimated 70 per cent of officially recorded GDP in 1998. As part of the privatization programme, leading domestic banks acquired major stakes in some of Russia's largest companies in return for lending the Government funds to help finance the budget deficit. Banks are now major corporate owners, adding to the predominance of monopoly structured industries, imposing minimal corporate discipline on managers.

Russia remains a market of great potential for companies willing to take a long-term view for procurement: research the market thoroughly and proceed with caution.

Malaysian culture

Statistics: area 329 293 km^2; population 22.0 million; per capita GDP US$3,300. This country has been transformed from a commodity and agricultural country to a newly industrialized market under a national economic plan. About half of the population are Malays with a further 35 per cent Chinese and 15 per cent Indian. These three different races have different religions, languages, customs, taboos and aesthetics. Malaysia is therefore better treated as three markets with differential buying complications and opportunities.

European Union – culture and strategic focus

The European Union (EU) is the wealthiest market in the world with a population of 370 million people and 15 member states as shown in Table 3.1.

It must be stressed the EU is a single market embracing 15 states each with different cultures and languages, retaining their international borders and frontier points, but permitting freedom of movement of goods and services. Moreover, greater financial stability has emerged through the development of the euro currency ensuring transparency of pricing. The euro brand product permits common standards but permits local national taste, fashion or design to be retained. Overall, the EU strives to have unified economic and monetary policies and encourages cross border business and the elimination of national prejudices over product/service choice. Some countries like France tend to retain their national preference to buy French goods whilst the UK and Germany tend to have more of an open market and a less nationalistic attitude. The younger generation generally tend to be less nationalistic. The buyer must focus closely and continuously on sourcing within the EU. It is advantageous for the buyer to be bi- or multi-lingual: an ability to converse in English, French, German or Spanish when negotiating in the seller's country is highly beneficial.

A broad strategic and cultural analysis of buying within the EU – the Single Market – may be summarized as follows.

1. Overall, the population has a high literacy level with a good standard of living. It has a Westernized Mediterranean/Scandinavian culture and market

TABLE 3.1 European Union states, 1998/9

State	Area (km^2)	Population (m)	Per capita GDP (US $)
Austria	84 000	8.072	26 250
Belgium	30 518	10.2	23 945
Denmark	43 093	5.310	32 900
Federal Republic of Germany	357 868	82.020	26 039
Finland	337 030	5.2	24 938
France	543 965	58.970	24 400
Greece	131 957	10.50	11 420
Irish Republic	68 895	3.7	22 980
Italy	301 300	58.0	20 170
Luxembourg	2 586	0.4	39 068
Netherlands	41 160	15.6	23 108
Portugal	91 831	9.96	10 720
Spain	504 748	39.4	14 052
Sweden	449 790	8.85	25 840
UK	244 755	59.0	20 870

profile with high expectations of long-term growth in a stable environment of low inflation.

2. The EU has strong buying power with a rising living standard. Over 50 per cent of the trade is pan-European. The 15 states primarily exercise a non-nationalistic prejudice in consumer choice, based on the value added concept and personal taste and preference. The younger age segment especially favours a wide product source range based on their particular needs.

3. One patent office exists to serve the 15 states. Hence once a product is patented goods can be sold throughout the market with no market entry impediment.

4. Emerging from item (3) suppliers can distribute the product throughout the 15 states without any impediment. Hence, the procurement executive can source a product as soon as the patent has been granted. This is particularly advantageous for products with a short life cycle as it enables the importer to remain competitive as the buyer can source products throughout the EU as soon as they are patent registered.

5. Ease of access throughout the market in terms of capital flow and distribution of goods with no customs impediment coupled with the euro, operative in twelve states (see page 155), enables the procurement executive to access and source the EU with confidence, competitiveness and no political risk. Hence products manufactured in Germany, France, the UK and Italy each have free access to all the other states with no trade barriers or customs duties.

6. A unified integrated transport system exists with no impediment of movement at frontier points. Moreover, carriers documentation and liability

are common throughout the EU. An increasing number of rail freight services are now operating Trans-European services on dedicated schedules. Professional standards are high and the major European seaports are advanced in computer logistics and multi-modalism, offering competitive rates and transits to inland industrial and commercial centres and to industrial and free trade zones. A major proportion of the industrial and consumer goods are distributed by road with a gross tonnage of 44 tonnes thereby taking advantage of the extensive motorway network providing a door to door service. An increasing number of companies sourcing goods throughout Europe and outside the EU such as Sweden, Switzerland, Turkey may use the LIC system (see page 270).

7. As indicated in item (5) product sourcing throughout the pan-euro zone eliminates financial risk in terms of currency risk fluctuations and price stability. The euro is further evidence of an integrated financial European Union.

8. The EU encourages businesses to expand as competition drives down prices and to reduce cost in all sectors of their business. Companies adopt a policy of continuously reviewing their position in the market place in sourcing, production distribution and profitability and also adopt strategies through merger and acquisition to improve their financial performance and market position. This involves rationalizing production, outsourcing components and centralizing R&D and control and administration. Moreover, freedom of capital movement is permitted throughout the EU which encourages such strategies. Such business ingredients stimulates the buyer to examine continually product sourcing throughout the EU to secure the most competitive product both in terms of cost and value added benefit.

9. The market is high tech in all areas including production and communication embracing the latest technology, EDI-paperless trading, the Internet (see page 108). It greatly facilitates communication/negotiation through video conferencing and develops the logistics environment. This includes supply chain management with hub centres performing the assembly and distribution and spoke centres supplying the componetized units.

10. The market is well served with market research data which enable the buyer to identify potential suppliers. Many of the data are on the Internet and, in addition, the EU and major trading associations produce a wide range of market reports and analysis. Specialist agencies also exist in all the member states.

11. Mobility of labour is a key factor in the EU where personnel are able to take up employment in any of the 15 states. However, tax systems and the social structure do vary by state.

12. Overall the EU is an open market with no exchange controls.

13. Low inflation is one of the key factors aligned to the convergence strategy applied rigidly through the 12 member states forming the euro zone (see page 155).

14. A common product specification exists – the euro brand – of the core product (see page 42) with unified standards, especially in the area of health and safety. This reduces design and production costs through economies of scale realized through value sales. Again there is a price benefit to the procurement executive. Goods can be customized to meet the buyer's specification in terms of language, packaging, size, local operating needs, colour and capacity. The metric system prevails throughout the EU.

15. The market is easy to visit with a common ideology of doing business in an environment of stability, high standards, growth and technology. It has a highly developed transport network with road and rail ideal for shorter distances and air being more favourable for longer passenger journeys.

To the buyer, the EU is an area of opportunity and integrated trans EU business. Buyers must focus on it seriously if they are to develop their business. Companies should feature the EU in their business plans. Adaptability, total commitment, complete professionalism and, above all, ongoing product sourcing analysis and research coupled with determination reflects the culture to succeed. Creative thinking, empathy with the seller and well thought out strategies and planning all contribute to becoming a successful entrepreneur. Full use should be made of market research data which should include e-commerce and the Internet.

Market environment

In examining the overseas market environment the overseas buyer must focus on the following aspects.

1. Who are the main players in the global market and what are their profiles? An analysis is desirable. In particular buyers should consider their market share, their financial resources, their position in the market, whether they are a leading player or laggard, their future plans and nature of the business in which they operate.

2. Accessibility to the market and the political and legal environment are key factors. This embraces market stability and the infrastructure serving the market.

3. Product availability embracing national and international standards coupled with added value are all decisive elements. Overall, this embraces product quality.

4. Is the market computer and logistically literate and, overall, are the suppliers flexible and adaptable in meeting the buyer's needs?

5. Product cost and specification are key areas in the market environment. This embraces exchange rates stability.

6. Whether the market is fully developed, an underdeveloped LDC or developing should be assessed. Fully developed markets tend to be high tech and capital intensive with a fully trained workforce, high labour costs and high GDP.

Conversely the LDC is agriculturally driven and often a commodity focused economy with low labour costs and low levels of technology. Moreover, LDC's currencies are usually non-convertible with volatile fluctuations correlated to the seasonal performance of its commodities in the global marketplace.

7. Does the market offer inwards investment opportunities to enable the buyer to establish a joint venture, merger and acquisition or industrial transplant. Multinational companies tend to switch their manufacturing and assembly plants from one country to another, based on the strategic criteria of cost, infrastructure, labour resources, access to markets, technology, logistics and general competitiveness. Governments and the local financial environment including employment law, taxation and industrial grants will feature in the evaluation. Also consider whether the supplier is located in an economic or free trade zone (see page 187).

8. The geographical location and membership of an economic bloc may have a role to play.

9. The perceived benefits of the market. France is well known for its wine, the Netherlands for its cheese, Switzerland for watches, Japan for its electronics and Germany for its high tech heavy engineering.

The market environment is one of accelerating change. Moreover, consumer and industrial taste and preferences are changing. Cyberspace and the Internet are also playing a decisive role. The procurement executive must correlate these changes and product sources to meet industrial and consumer needs.

Recommended reading

- Barclays Bank Country reports.
- Barclays Bank Economic Review.
- East European Trade Council – *East Europe Bulletin*.
- *The European* – EU paper, published quarterly.
- *Financial Times*.

4

Buying strategy and planning

As the growth of international trade continues, the professional standards of buying overseas rises. In many situations such company involvement has arisen due to force of circumstances and has not resulted from any preconceived policy. The end result is sometimes that the company's resources are not always used cost effectively nor are the strategies well conceived. Hence, senior management must devote adequate time and energy to effective planning and the evolvement of sound realizable strategies.

When a company is committed to a policy of buying overseas, it must earmark adequate resources in terms of personnel, finance and accommodation for production, assembly and storage. Such data will feature in the company's budget. Personnel should be professionally qualified in the area of international business with sound linguistic, negotiating and product knowledge skills. Additionally, the executive must be culturally focused with logistic and high-tech computer skills. Furthermore, the buyer must have a good technical knowledge of the product sought and all the ingredients of the overseas contract embracing finance, Incoterms 2000, import duty and documentation.

The buyer must take a keen interest in the supplier's product and company and technical development to ensure it is competitive in the marketplace and cost effective to buy. Regular visits should be exchanged. Company policy on product sourcing overseas requires continuous review in terms of suppliers, price, technical development, general competitiveness and the market environment. Market research should play a major role. The important area is planning.

International purchasing strategy and planning

Planning is the processing of regulating and coordinating activities on a time basis together with the resources necessary to carry out these activities in order to achieve set objectives. Essentially it is a management function and has a strategic focus. Planning is especially important for the complex and diverse process of international purchasing. It yields the following benefits.

(a) Planning defines objectives which will relate to current and future strategic aims and the encourages commitment of all personnel to a common vision of the future as featured in the plan.

(b) Planning has a control function over all the resources in the plan.

(c) Overall, planning and logistics have a synergy essential to the international purchasing process.

(d) Planning measures performance by individual and all the elements of the international supply chain including the supplier.

(e) It minimizes cost and maximizes profit. This is realized through a critical analysis of the planned route to the objective thereby achieving the value added benefit concept focus on each element of the plan.

(f) International purchasing planning involves all the ingredients of the company's business and enables a fusion to be sought.

(g) Planning develops a more competitive business and enables the contributors to have a common objective with complete transparency.

(h) Buying overseas encompasses business units within the buyer's company the decision maker and suppliers units plus supply chain resources operating in a changing international market embracing exchange rates, product availability, transportation costs and import duty.

(i) International purchasing planning will feature current and future market trends. This represents important elements in the control and monitoring elements of the plan execution as detailed in item (h).

(j) Planning stimulates both lateral and horizontal thinking within the buyer's company and a proactive approach rather than a reactive one. As the situation becomes more complex, managers become more focused in their thinking. Additionally, decisions are taken more quickly.

(k) Decisions are taken on a rational and systematic basis aided by reliable market research data.

(l) Good international purchasing planning raises standards and performance quality and develops a benchmark strategy.

(m) International purchasing planning can facilitate the integration of the short-term action and control measures with the long-term strategies.

(n) Effective planning encourages a strategic focus and an analysis of all the ingredients in the decision-making process.

(o) Finally, the development of the Internet websites, e- and m-commerce and other forms of computer technology have all contributed to facilitating international purchasing planning with no culture or global boundaries.

International purchasing planning

Import planning is the process whereby the company must decide which strategy to adopt in relation to its products or services and the options available and the resources which will need to be allocated within the company in order to put the strategy into effect. It is the establishment of objectives and the formulation, evaluation and selection of the policies, strategies, tactics and action required to achieve these objectives. The strategic focus will be found in the company's business plan. It will reflect the company's strategy in both the short- and long-term.

Overall, the company will focus on the following areas to optimize a viable international purchasing strategy.

1. Company resources: these embrace human resources, capital availability, cash flow, both short- and long-term, production and assembly capacity and so on.
2. Market situation: the company's short- and long-term forecast. Where is the company going? A key factor is competition both on product specification, servicing of the product and the product life cycle. New players may emerge in the market whilst others lapse due to lack of capital to fund new technology or product development. Buying overseas provides immediate access to high-tech products and avoids the lengthy process and capitalization of developing the latest generation of product.
3. Pricing is a key factor: many companies source overseas because of a price advantage, which could not be matched if the buyer opted to manufacture and develop it. Currency variation and distribution costs can fluctuate, changing the economics of the buying strategy (see page 151).
4. Companies today are driven by a logistics focus (see page 70). It applies to all aspects of ordering, stock management, production and assembly planning, supplier lead times, delivery schedules and distribution. Basically, it is managing the supply chain in accordance with the marketing plan identifying the sales forecast. Overseas product pricing and international distribution costs are key areas where financial improvements are continuously sought through logistics planning.
5. Quality control is a very critical area in the buyer's product specification. It requires continuous monitoring, regular discussions and visits to the supplier's premises where possible.
6. The use of third parties is widely used in international purchasing. Cost benefits may be secured by buying from distributors, agents or importers rather than direct from the manufacturer. In some situations one may entrust it to an international logistic operator who has continuous access to a range of acceptable suppliers.
7. Communication technology through the Internet, e-commerce, cyberspace, facsimile and telephone has transformed the exchange of data. Modern methods of communication enable both the supplier and the buyer together with all parties to the international distribution network to have regular contact and transparency of information. This greatly facilitates the formulation of a purchasing information and control system.
8. The product specification is a key area in the planning process. Not only must the specification comply with international and national legal standards together with the end user's requirements, but also focus on the buyer's decision whether to opt for standardization or non-standardization. It also

determines the import duty level (see page 264). Much depends on costs, customer needs, competition and the value added benefit.

9. Buying overseas offers endless opportunities not usually available in domestic sourcing. One option is third country assembly and distribution. This offers a lower overall cost: tax advantages, reduced transport costs (as the assembly plant is closer to the supplier), lower labour costs, end product closer to the buyer's market and customer and greater flexibility. An example arises in the port of Rotterdam distriparks where oriental companies have set up assembly plants in the port environs to serve all 15 European States and countries outside the EU in areas such as foodstuffs, electrical goods and industrial products. Countries featuring in the scheme include Malaysia, China, South Korea, India, Singapore and Japan. The strategy also features in other countries, especially in the USA under Free Trade Zones (see page 187).

10. The method of payment and the options available and costs.

11. The country risk factor: Dun and Bradstreet provide a comparative, cross border assessment of the risk of doing business in a country. Essentially the indicator seeks to encapsulate the risk that countrywide factors pose to the predictability of political, commercial, macroeconomic and external risk. Political risks embrace internal and external security situations, political competency and consistency and other such factors that determine whether a country fosters an enabling business environment. The commercial risk incorporates the sanctity of the contract, judicial competence, regulatory transparency, the degree of systematic corruption and other such factors that determine whether the business environment facilitates the conduct of commercial transactions. The third macroeconomic risk reflects the inflation rate, fiscal deficit, money supply growth and all such macroeconomic factors which determine whether a country is able to deliver sustainable economic growth and a commensurate expansion in business opportunities. Finally external risk reflects the current account balance, capital flows, foreign exchange reserves, size of external debt and all such factors that determine whether a country can generate enough foreign exchange to meet its trade and foreign investment liabilities.

12. Investment buying covers a wide range of goods. It may be wine for onward sale several years later. The buyer pays no duty until released from the bond and this arrangement is pre-planned between the buyer and customs. Other examples include antiques, machinery, services and installations including commercial and residential property. Adequate market research is essential, particularly exchange rates, nationalization of foreign assets, taxation and local legislation. Penalties may be high on resale to overseas clients.

13. Buying services is a growth market. This is driven by efficiency and global communication permitting routine administrative and back office work such as telephone helplines, paper pushing and data processing to be transferred overseas. India and China have a vast reservoir of highly educated workers who can be paid much less than their counterparts in developed industrial

markets such as the USA, Germany, France and the UK. Not only are the labour costs substantially lower, but also the office rental and ancillary costs. British Airways has been one of the pioneers in taking the back office functions overseas to Bombay, India. Other areas in the course of outsourcing include pharmaceuticals, market research, the finance, banking and insurance sectors. In the USA, a group of medical practitioners outsource their medical resources to India. Key areas in planning are adequate staff training, control, reliability of data input, regular audit confidentiality and an acceptable management culture in the overseas office. Regular visits and daily conferences over the satellite network are essential.

14. Buying maintenance, repair and operating supplies. This is a large market and is volume focused, with a high degree of specification but irregular consumption. It requires pre-planning with customs on inwards processing relief (IPR). The IPR need is eradicated for such work being undertaken within the EU.

15. Outsourcing. The process of buying products overseas and assembly in a third country is a growth market (see page 90). It requires very extensive planning and monitoring and control systems. Basically it is logistically driven.

Aligned to a viable international purchasing strategy is the need to focus on resource planning with an emphasis on materials, components, pricing and profit planning, focusing particularly on customs. We will examine resource and materials planning first.

The company resources of the buyer must be fully utilized to maximize efficiency and profitability. Also, customers must not be frustrated through non-availability of the product due to poor planning emerging from under production and a misjudged market forecast. Impatient customers will buy elsewhere if the product is not available promptly at the point of sale.

Hence, in devising the materials and the components master plan, one must rely totally on the company's marketing plan and all its constituents parts. The marketing plan may comprise a range of consumer products, each product having a series of sizes, design, etc. This will be further segregated into the weekly sales forecast. It will embrace a sales plan, a turnover plan, planned stocks of finished products and production and international purchasing plans being fully integrated. The resource plan will quantify the resources required – labour, materials, plant availability – all embracing the manufacturing process to execute the plan efficiency. It will take account of plant and its infrastructure capacity limits, storage capacity for the materials and components, plant flexibility and testing and control systems. Contingency master plans are essential, especially when relying on overseas sourcing and disruption to the international supply chain. Overall, the master plan will be logistically driven. A good example of a materials and components plan is a car plant which is volume focused relying on many components of domestic and international suppliers. Likewise in the industrial field of shipbuilding, where each vessel is specially designed for its trade, only 20 per cent of the structure is fabricated in the shipyard and the residue is sourced domestically and internationally – primarily the latter. This involves a very extensive logistics operation.

Pricing and profit planning is a key area in purchasing strategy. The buyer's objective of the 'right product at the right price' is unlikely to be attained in the absence of customs planning. This risk is minimized when goods are purchased and consumed in a free trade area such as the European Union. Goods bought outside a free trade area and involving the merchandise crossing international boundaries are subject to customs controls and to duty payment. For example, a UK buyer would not be subject to any import duty payment for any goods bought and manufactured or produced within any of the 15 states. However, a buyer situated in the UK, Germany or Italy buying goods outside the European Union such as the USA, Japan, Peru, Canada, India and Thailand would be subject to import duty payment. However, when the goods have entered the UK, Germany and Italy and duty has been paid and cleared and released by customs, the goods may enter free circulation within the 15 states and no duty payment arises.

Hence, any sourcing decision involving import duty payment must take account of the following considerations:

(a) materials and components imported for use in export products may be relieved of import duty (inwards processing relief, see page 265);
(b) buying materials in the country to which the products will be exported may result in the customer paying less duty;
(c) it may be possible to suspend duty on imported goods which are not available from Community (EU) sources (see page 269);
(d) low manufacturing costs overseas may be outweighed by high duties whilst tariff preferences may mitigate high prices.

As stressed earlier, the availability of duty reliefs and other customs planning opportunities can have a material effect on the relative economics of buying inside and outside the EU. It is the landed price which counts, not necessarily the commercial price. The solution is to make cost effective sourcing decisions and to obtain duty reliefs and suspensions.

The customs value of imported goods is a fundamental factor in determining the price at which the goods are bought and sold and the profit which they realize. Companies which conclude contracts with their suppliers or customers or set transfer prices without regard to customs values risk incurring either excessive duty liabilities or penalties. The key to customs effective pricing is to ensure that the total consideration for imported goods is kept to the minimum consistent with both commercial objectives and the requirements of the valuation regulations bearing in mind the following points:

(a) additional payments to the supplier of imported goods (such as royalties, licence fees, research and development and design, tooling and engineering costs) may attract duty if not suitably structured;
(b) some other payments may be excluded or deducted from the price of imported goods, thereby reducing their duty liability;

(c) in certain circumstances, the actual price will not constitute an acceptable basis for paying duty and an alternative method of valuation must therefore be found.

For multinational companies there is the potential conflict between the optimum customs and tax treatment of transfer prices. Transfer pricing is the process of a multinational company or entity undertaking inter-company transactions of goods and services and in the process thereof determining the transfer price of such goods and services. In such situations involving transactions across 'international frontiers' within the corporate family of the multinational company or entity, the goods/services are subject to customs duties, currency risk, foreign exchange controls and so on. Transfer pricing (see page 60) presents the multinational with the opportunity to manipulate and adjust the transfer price to further the goods and aims of the carrier. Unrealistic transfer prices can result in excessive duty liabilities and partial disallowances for tax purposes whilst prices which are acceptable to the revenue authority may not meet the minimum level for customs purposes. Injudicious year-end and other retrospective price adjustments can also create customs problems and may even invalidate the original transfer prices.

The solution to the foregoing is for the buyer to structure international transactions in order to pay the minimum duty; to draw up customs effective agreements with foreign suppliers and customers and to determine the optimum transfer pricing arrangements for both customs and corporation tax purposes.

Optimizing a viable international purchasing strategy can be said to be driven by five aspects:

(a) a marketing focus to become more competitive in price, specification and closer to the end user needs;
(b) a logistic function based on supply chain management;
(c) a strategic focus to improve market share, improve profitability, more emphasis on a company position in the marketplace and a stronger focus on the company's long-term objectives and the route to those objectives – one of which may be to place more reliance on sourcing overseas and less on the domestic market;
(d) a financial approach which identifies each element of the business as a profit centre otherwise alternatives are sought;
(e) administration which seeks to focus on a departmentalized approach rather than an integrated approach.

Today it is a combination of a strategic approach, driven by a marketing price orientation with an integrated focus on logistics and finance. The administrative departmentalized focus is of little relevance in today's global market environment.

Problems associated with international purchasing and international logistics

As we progress through the early part of the twenty-first century the pace of change will accelerate as the international trading pattern unfolds. China will become a major trading power; Europe will become further integrated as EU membership expands; North and South America will become a trading bloc; and the Far East will be a stronger, more vibrant and economically sustainable trading resource. Hence, the enterprising international overseas buyer must be vigilant for new outsourcing opportunities.

Associated with this trading development is the shorter product life cycle, the shorter time scale to design new models such as many consumer goods, the added value benefit from buying overseas, the tendency to have multi-user consumer products, thereby enabling the product to have more than one use; the continuing increase in the article assortment requiring manufacturing to carry an ever-increasing range as found in the car industry; the increasing power of the consumer through consumer associations representing a balance of power moving away from the manufacturer; the rapid expansion of international logistics resulting in companies restructuring their production facilities on a global scale; companies tending to focus more on export driven trade to increase their sales volume, spread their market risk and lower their unit cost; and the development of e-commerce, Internet use and computer technology. Overall, the calibre of management will have to rise to cope with these developments as more and more companies rely on overseas sourcing for their products. Many such companies when the product is assembled or processed re-export the goods on a pre-planned inwards processing relief customs arrangement basis (see page 265).

In the light of the foregoing, detailed below are the problems associated with international purchasing and international logistics.

(a) The supplier may go into liquidation. It may be prudent to have more than one supplier, preferably in another country.
(b) The political situation in the supplier's country may make it untenable to trade without severe risk.
(c) Currency variation. Either the buyer's or seller's currency may change to such an extent that it is no longer viable for the buyer to trade in that country. A possible solution is to use a third currency.
(d) Incorrect product specification or if the buyer changes the specification to comply with new national or international standards or quality controls making it difficult or impossible for the supplier to comply.
(e) Frequent changes in the materials planning may disrupt the delivery schedule with suppliers. This may result in cancellation of the supplier's contract and resourcing with another supplier. The key factor when selecting a supplier is having the flexibility to meet the buyer's needs and prioritize the delivery schedule.
(f) Poor management in the buyer's company. Lack of coordination between marketing, international purchasing and production personnel. The solution is to have an international purchasing control module.
(g) Unreliable data in the master, marketing production, materials or resource plans and an absence of any transparency interface.

(h) Inadequate customs planning resulting in high import duty levels (see page 264) and the buyer's failure to opt for a third country assembly or distribution centre with a lower overall cost distribution–duty–assembly (see page 196).

(i) The absence of any contingency plan to cope with unforeseen events.

International purchasing funding options

The growth in international trade has greatly increased both the demand for trade finance and the degree of sophistication with which it is delivered. Today there is a much greater choice of financial solutions for importers to consider when developing an international trading strategy.

Organizing the finance is an important part of a well-defined strategy and a key contributor to success in international trade. Indeed the availability of finance can be a major factor in securing new business as it provides the flexibility to offer competitive terms to overseas trading partners.

There are usually several possible solutions to any financing problem, each dependent upon the chosen payment mechanism and other criteria. This includes: the terms of trade, assessment of the risks, the supplier requirements, fluctuations in exchange rates, credit availability and the cost. It is prudent to examine alternative markets and suppliers and invite competitive tenders to enable a comparison to be made and a focus on more or less favourable financial trading terms. For example, to trade within the euro zone may prove more beneficial than to trade outside it.

It is important to bear in mind that the supplier and buyer are equal partners in the export sales contract, both in its terms and funding of the purchase. They have equal negotiating strengths. Situations will vary, however, according to the market conditions. The Far East currency crisis towards the end of the 1990s demonstrated the weak position of a supplier with a depreciating currency and exporters anxious to secure overseas orders to maintain a positive cash flow. Hence, the buyers were in a strong position to negotiate a very competitive price and favourable funding option.

Buyers must take up a strong strategic position in negotiating the funding option. An analysis of the availability of the funding options available associated with each payment method is required. Companies able to fund in-house incur lower costs than when relying on import loan facilities. Financial planning for overseas supply sourcing encourages efficiency within the company and enables more competitive pricing of any end user customer pricing. For example a product assembled in the buyer's country containing 80 per cent of imported components and funded within the importer company's financial resources will incur lower costs than a competing product relying on loan capital.

The choice of payment method will involve the following elements.

(a) As mentioned earlier, the range of financial options.

(b) The usual contract terms adopted in the exporter's or supplier's country.

(c) How quickly payment is required by the supplier.

(d) The political situation in the supplier's and buyer's countries.

(e) Availability and cost of foreign currency to the importer or buyer, that is exchange control regulations.

(f) Whether the cost of any credit can be arranged by the supplier (exporter) or buyer (importer).

(g) Exporter risk – problems in producing the correct documentation and failure to supply goods in accordance with the sales contract.

(h) Importer risk – non-payment of invoices, delayed payment of invoices and insolvency of the buyer.

(i) Availability and cost of foreign currency to the importer or buyer.

(j) Funding resources of the importer.

(k) Country risk – political and economic instability, transfer risk, hostilities and import and export regulations.

(l) Transportation risk – risk associated with the mode of transport, for example marine risks and storage facilities in ports.

(m) Foreign exchange risk – fluctuating exchange rates affecting pricing and profit.

The importance and significance of each element will vary by market and political conditions.

Every company's trade cycle is unique, although there will be elements (e.g. purchasing, manufacturing, shipping, credit, etc.) which are common to them all. Each stage in a trade cycle places different demands on a company's finances but a key component in determining the overall level of working capital required for any business is the time taken between the start of the cycle (i.e. ordering the goods or raw materials) and receipt of payment for corresponding sales of finished products.

The terms of trade and risk inherent at each stage of a particular trade cycle need to be structured by the buyer to ensure working capital is available for the different stages in the cycle. Seasonal peaks, long transit times and lengthy credit terms, or staged payments all add to the demands on the buyer.

Small to medium-sized companies are often under capitalized. Moreover, an increasing number of importers are being asked to hold onto stock for their customers who require just-in-time deliveries. This ties up working capital and can create cash flow problems within a company, generating a need for an import loan available from a bank or venture capitalist. The loan will provide flexibility to take a period of extended credit undisclosed to the seller whilst allowing optimum payment terms to be offered. This allows the importer time to sell the goods and realize the proceeds before having to repay the loan.

This form of finance can be arranged where payment for the imported goods is being made via documentary credit or bills for collection. It is common for the underlying transaction to be settled on a 'sight' basis with the goods being consigned to the order of the bank. By offering to settle import bills immediately, importers may be able to negotiate better terms or prices with their suppliers.

Where credit is still taken from the supplier, the facility can be used to meet the importer's obligation on the maturity date of a term bill and provide finance for an extended period to match sales receipts.

Where goods are consigned to the order of the bank, they can be warehoused in the bank's name for an agreed period and may be drawn by the importer from time to time (against cash payment). Where immediate possession of the goods is required, for example to fulfil orders already received, the goods may be released to the importer 'in trust' for an agreed period, at the end of which payment would be required. In either case, the agreed period would take account of the importer's usual terms of trade and would commence from the date of the bank's payment in settlement of the underlying transaction.

Import loans usually cover individual shipments of goods and may be arranged in all major currencies, with fixed or variable interest linked to the base rate for the currency. Interest is usually payable at maturity of the loan, although variable rate loans have the advantage of being able to be repaid early without penalty, for example if the subsequent sale proceeds were received earlier than anticipated.

A recent development to aid the supplier in funding export opportunities is to provide funds or loans against the import invoice up to 90 per cent of its sales ledger value. This provides much needed cash flow to the exporter to actually execute the order.

A number of trade financing options are listed below and will be discussed in greater detail in Chapter 8.

(a) The fastest method of making an international payment is to remit funds through the secure inter-bank computer network known as SWIFT (Society of Worldwide Interbank Financial Telecommunication) or telex or cable. Payment instructions provided to the bank should include the beneficiary's full banking details as this will ensure the earliest possible receipt of funds.
(b) Debtors own cheque. This is not a very satisfactory method from the creditor's point of view.
(c) International bankers draft. This would be a draft drawn by the buyer's bank on its correspondent bank in the exporter's country. This is ideal for non-priority, low value payments or for those which are to be accompanied by documentation such as invoices.
(d) Mail transfer (MT). This is the most common method of payment. The debtor instructs his or her bank to request its corresponding bank in the exporter's country to pay the specific amount to the exporter. Mail payments are either sent by mail or SWIFT.

Open account

If the relationship between the buyer and seller is good, then it may be agreed to trade on 'open account' terms. This means the seller will despatch the goods directly to the buyer, send him or her an invoice and await remittance of payment from the buyer as in domestic trading. There are four ways to execute an open account payment, most of which also apply to advance payments.

Advance payments represent the least secure method for the importer who has to face several risks including goods that may never be shipped; goods that may be shipped late; the wrong goods being shipped; problems with documentation and cash flow pressure on the exporter.

Documentary credits

Documentary credits are one of the most popular methods for selling international trade transactions because they offer security to both buyer and seller. Moreover, they are honoured through the international banking system. The supplier wants security of payment; the buyer wants an assurance that payment will only be made after despatch of the specified goods. In some countries, particularly LDC, settlement by documentary credit is mandatory. The documentary credit is in the form of a letter of credit: it may be (a) irrevocable; (b) a confirmed irrevocable; or (c) revocable.

Documentary collections

Documentary collections are those which include shipping and commercial documentation such as a bill of exchange, a bill of lading, invoices and insurance documents. These are submitted to the exporter's bank and then forwarded to the importer's bank for release to the importer against acceptance or payment in accordance with the terms set out in the remitting bank collection order. It is common practice to defer presentation, payment or acceptance until arrival of the carrying vessel.

The documentary collection may take the form of documents against acceptance. In this situation the documents are released to the importer against their acceptance of a term bill payable at a fixed or determinable future date. A further method is documents against payment or cash against documents. In either case the collection is payable upon presentation (at sight) and documents released to the buyer against payment of the amount due. CAD terms are used when a collection order does not contain a bill of exchange. For the buyer there are few risks associated with bills for collection. However, unlike a documentary credit, shipment schedules and documentation cannot be controlled and if payment has been made against a D/P or CAD collection, the importer runs the risk that the goods shipped may be of inferior quality.

Trading within international groups

The influence of the multinational industry is tending to increase and today represents some 70 per cent of world trade. It is being driven by a variety of circumstances.

(a) Mergers and acquisitions.

(b) The drive by consumers to have more competitive prices through volume sales, economies of scale, outsourcing of products, components, service and warranty, product specification.

(c) The need to have a flatter organizational structure and have a greater focus on the consumer through a decentralized regional management structure.

(d) To take full advantage of satellite communication, e-commerce and computer technology. Global online sales are very much on the increase.

(e) To embrace an international logistics strategy.

(f) To formulate an international marketing strategy with a shorter time scale for new product design and formulation in an era where the product life cycle is much shorter whilst shelf life of food products is tending to be lengthened by technology.

(g) To examine and develop every opportunity to reduce costs through taxation, transfer pricing (page 60), import duty level (page 264), inwards processing relief (page 265), lateral importing, third country assembly, avoidance of domestic tax liabilities, avoidance of foreign tax, customs tariff product specification, inwards investment strategy and continuing improvement through the hub and spoke container logistic supply chain.

In the light of the foregoing, features of the multinational industry (MNI) may be briefly summarized as follows:

(a) high profile with enormous capital resources and production potential;

(b) very professional qualified workforce of high calibre;

(c) high tech, logistically and computer-equipped and focused workforce;

(d) strong negotiating power with many MNIs having an annual turnover in excess of the GNP of some less developed countries;

(e) enormous resources available for research and development;

(f) customer focused, with a strong empathy with the market needs;

(g) strong, marketing focused management culture;

(h) budget driven;

(i) decision making can be slow, but with decentralization found in subsidiaries the process today is quicker.

Today many MNIs have their headquarters in the USA, Europe or Japan with subsidiaries in key volume generated profit markets. This might be a region such as Europe or an individual country. There are fiscal advantages plus opportunities to build empathy with the market. Production and distribution can be closer to the market with associated cost and supply chain advantages (see page 83).

Pricing within international groups is based on optimized corporate pricing strategies. It is a complex issue and the buyer must prepare adequately prior to any negotiations. This includes studying the MNI annual report, identifying the company organization structure and key personnel together with decision makers, the position in the marketplace, product range and value added benefit, non-price areas (warranty and brand image), any networking data, terms of sale and future developments.

Transfer pricing, a feature of MNIs in international markets, tends to alienate governments. It has been defined as the process of a multinational company or entity undertaking inter-company transactions of goods and services, and in the process thereof determining the 'transfer price' of such goods and services. In such situations when transactions cross 'international frontiers' within the corporate family of the multinational company, the goods/services are subject to customs duties, currency risks, foreign exchange controls and so on. Transfer pricing presents the multinational with an opportunity to manipulate and adjust the transfer price to further the aims of the enterprise. In short, it is concerned with the pricing of goods sold within a corporate family. The transactions involved are from one division to another, to a foreign subsidiary, or to a partner in a joint venture agreement. The key factor is that whilst these transfer prices are internal to the company, they are important externally because goods being transferred from country to country must be valued for cross border taxation and import duty purposes.

The MNI with its subsidiaries or divisions is usually a profit centre whose object is to maximize profit through market pricing strategies. Hence, goods transferred from one division to another would be transferred at a high price to maximize profit margins. Conversely, a subsidiary may sell to a foreign subsidiary in an LDC at a low price to gain market penetration in a country where buying power is low. There are three methods of transfer pricing.

1. Transfer at cost with no profit margin and immunity from corporate taxation on such a transaction. This enables the overseas subsidiary – the buyer – to charge a market price to achieve a sales budget performance. Import duty would be lower due to the lower transfer price, and similarly corporation taxation applicable to the goods sold. The level of corporation tax may be lower than the exporter's country. A further benefit may arise if the foreign subsidiary price is low; it may abstract business from the higher priced domestically produced goods.
2. Transfer at arms length when the international division price is at parity with any buyer outside the company. Such a strategy is based on market conditions and not on profit.
3. Transfer at cost plus a realistic profit margin. The profit may be split between the production and the international divisions. This involves an agreement mechanism between divisions.

Other factors involved in transfer pricing include creating barriers to entry through low pricing and discouraging competitors who could not sustain such price levels. Additionally, there is the avoidance of domestic tax liabilities, the avoidance of foreign tax, lower sales and VAT and lower import duty.

The overseas buyer operative in an environment of trading within a international group requires a well-devised strategy. Transfer pricing is an area where profit objectives, managerial motivations and government/trading blocs –

EU regulations – interact. Moreover, it does involve the fusion of strategy devised by accountants, lawyers, tax advisers, customs, banks and divisional managers.

Commodity markets

Commodity markets embrace both industrial materials and foodstuffs. They include oil, aluminium, zinc, copper, vegetable oilseeds, rubber, cotton, lead, wool, cocoa, soya beans, coffee, sugar, maize and wheat. They represent a substantial volume of international trade.

Before the advent of today's organized commodity exchanges, the world's trade in basic raw materials developed in several centres in different parts of the world. At the time there was no way of avoiding the risk inherent in owning a commodity. Producers of raw materials could sell only to merchants or to the converters involved in processing the raw commodity; the merchants and converters were in the same position in that they too could only sell when their customers want to buy. Thus none of those involved in the chain of events leading to the sale of finished goods to the final customer could protect himself against loss due to prices falling during the period of ownership. Planning was extremely unreliable. For example, a fabricator making a product with a substantial quantity of copper incorporated in it would not be able to plan sales in any useful way. The sales would follow the price of copper, falling when the price was high and vice versa.

Subsequently, organized markets evolved for the purpose of providing traders with a means of avoiding the market risk. The first of these was in Chicago, the centre of the US grain trade. It became effective in 1865, 17 years after its formation. Today there are organized markets in many countries including the USA, Canada, Holland, Japan and the UK.

The factors driving the variation in the world price of commodities are numerous but in the main they reflect the impact of economic cycles and international trade cycles. The latter has four elements: peak, decline, trough and growth.

Factors determining world commodity prices include inflation, strikes, production quotas, an unstable political environment, anti-pollution legislation, collusion by buyers or sellers, stock levels, exchange rate fluctuation, international agreements and conventions, natural disasters, climatic conditions, new technology, infrastructure, adequacy of investment feeding new technology and methodology, logistics and changes in production and distribution.

An examination of the various commodities identifies particular features. Oil price levels, for example, are determined by a complexity of factors which are not easily discernable to allow any prediction of trends. OPEC controls one-third of the market and determines prices primarily on a production quota system as agreed by their members. The quotas reflect market conditions. Saudi Arabia produces 10 per cent of the world's oil and through its production variation, influences price. The non-OPEC producers include the USA and the North Sea oilfields which are outside any direct control strategy, but prices move in accordance with market conditions. Oil futures traders who make prices in Brent crude at London's International Petroleum Exchange also influence the market. Industrial demand, inventory stock levels and seasonal demand play a major role. For example a mild winter in the northern hemisphere can reduce global demand by 0.5 mbd from the norm, while a harsh winter can increase it by a similar magnitude. New technology is continuously being developed favouring the shallow maritime field. Overall, global industrial production has a major impact on the global demand for oil. Also one must recognize that high oil prices are inflationary and have an adverse effect on the economies of LDCs with no oil production resources. They can also depress global trade. The International Energy Association (IEA) produces market forecasts of oil production.

Industrial materials and foodstuffs

Each transaction undertaken on the commodity market places an obligation involving the delivery of a specific quantity and quality of the commodity at, or by, a specified point of time in the future. However, an obligation to buy can be countered by an obligation to sell at the same date of delivery with the difference between the two prices being settled in cash.

Industrial commodity market prices – particularly for non-ferrous metals – are driven by demand which, in turn, are related to growth in world industrial production. Hence, a resurgence in demand through increased industrial activity yields an improvement in prices. In regard to copper and aluminium higher energy charges and rising alumina costs contribute to rising prices. In the copper market new mining and smelting capacity based on the expansion of low cost, solvent-extraction/electro winning (SXEW) projects continues to lower the average production cost. Natural rubber producers are examining the formulation of a minimum export price and market intervention strategy following the failure of the International Natural Rubber Organization (INRO) price support scheme. In the fibres sector demand and over production/stock piling influences price levels.

In the foodstuffs sector a surplus of demand over supply and a burdensome level of global stocks can depress prices. This may apply to grain, cocoa, coffee and sugar from time to time. The variation in wheat production globally and weather conditions are crucial factors. This applies also to soya beans. Coffee production is very vulnerable to frost, as has been found in Brazil. The Association of Coffee Producing Countries have agreed a new export retention strategy in an effort to support prices.

Finally, one must be conscious that the foodstuff markets in some sectors are subject to continuous improvement in terms of agricultural technology, management and distribution.

To summarize, there are basically four groups of people found in the commodity market. These include the buyer who is keen to ensure that the commodity maintains its price in the selling process; the trader who may be the buyer or seller earning commission in the process; the producer who may be engaged in oil, coffee or cocoa; and finally the speculators who are also buyers and sellers with the sole objective of securing gain from the transaction.

For the market to be effective there must be political stability, stable liquid currency, a good transport infrastructure serving the production, a location preferably by sea, an economically-sized production plant and liquidity of both buyer and seller. The latter point causes problems from time to time in commodity producers in LDCs which experience volatility in their currency movement due to a variety of reasons (see page 151).

The main commodity markets are Comex in New York, Nymex, the New York mineral exchange, the Chicago Board of Trade, the Baltic Exchange, the International Petroleum Exchange and the London Metal Exchange which we will now examine.

London Metal Exchange

The London Metal Exchange (LME) is the world's premier non-ferrous metals market. It has an international membership and more than 95 per cent of its business comes from overseas. The LME trades in futures and traded options contracts for copper, primary aluminium, zinc, nickel, lead, tin, aluminium alloy and silver with specifications fine-tuned to best serve industry. In 2000 it had an annual turnover value of some US$2500 billion.

The LME futures and traded options contracts are available for the six major primary non-ferrous metals. In addition, it offers contracts for secondary aluminium as well as for silver, which is both an industrial metal and a precious metal. The LME also operates futures and traded options contracts based on an index (LMEX) of the six primary contracts.

The LME's future and traded options contracts provide ideal hedging tools for the world of metals. The prices discovered each business day through the Exchanges open outcry trading sessions are taken as reference prices that are relied upon across the world.

Details of world annual production of the foregoing eight traded commodities are:

Copper	14 million tonnes	Silver	529 million troy ounces
Lead	6 million tonnes	Nickel	1 million tonnes
High grade Primary Aluminium	23.6 million tonnes	Zinc	8.2 million tonnes
Aluminium Alloy	7.5 million tonnes	Tin	0.24 million tonnes

Overall, the LME is a trade-based market, and the founding of its metals contracts on tangible deliveries cements that link: every contract is presumed to be a physical contract. To meet this physical aspect large stocks of metal are held in warehouses approved but not owned by the LME at selected locations around the world. Currently there are over 350 approved warehouses in some 42 locations covering the USA, Europe, and the Middle and the Far East.

Delivery of LME contracts is in the form of LME warrants, which are bearer documents entitling the holder to take possession of a specified tonnage of a specified metal at a specified LME approved warehouse. Each LME warrant is for one lot of metal and states its brand, the exact tonnage, the shape and the location. Warrants are issued by the warehouse companies on receipt of metal as soon as they are satisfied that the metal conforms to the specifications covering quality, shape and weight as defined by the special contract rules of the LME and is of a brand or production of a producer named in the LME approved list. In 1999 the LME introduced an electronic transfer system, SWORD, for the handling of warrants. Only a small percentage of LME contracts result in a delivery, as the vast majority of contracts prove to be hedging contracts bought or sold back before falling due. As a result, deliveries that do take place, either in or out of the warehouse, strongly reflect the physical market demand and supply and the LME's daily stock reports play a major part in the assessment of prices quoted by market makers.

Basically there are two types of contracts traded on the LME – Exchange Contracts and Clients Contracts. Exchange Contracts are contracts between clearing members on the LME. Client Contracts are contracts between customers and ring dealing members, associate broker clearing members or associate broker members.

All LME contracts are between the parties acting as principals. This prevents any party entering an LME contract as agent for someone else but does not prevent an agent effecting a contract between two parties if the resulting LME contract is between an LME member and a disclosed customer each acting as a principal.

LME members may act both in the capacity of market maker and broker. Customer orders may be filled directly from a member's 'book' or filled by the member after it has bought/sold metal in the LME market.

The LME operates via two distinct trading mechanisms, open outcry and inter-office.

1. Open outcry. During open outcry ring and kerb sessions, the majority of customer business will be transacted based upon the prices achieved in those ring and kerb sessions. Customers can follow market activity by listening to the simultaneous floor commentary provided by members and/or by monitoring quoted and traded prices disseminated via the LME vendor feed system (VFS). The VFS publishes real-time prices traded during ring and kerb times on price vendor information services such as Reuters.

2. Inter-office. Inter-office trading is conducted by telephone or other electronic means. On contacting an LME member, customers will usually be provided with the member's current bid–ask quote. The customer may choose to trade on this quote, or choose to call another member in an attempt to improve the previous quote, or wait and watch for price movements on the LME vendor feed system, or leave an order with a member using one of the following terms or a combination (e.g. 'at best ring 1').

The following order styles do not represent all possible methods of order execution but an overview of the situation.

(a) Ring. Customer orders are not traded directly in the rings or kerbs, so an order using the term 'in/on/during the ring/kerb' will be executed on the basis of the prices traded/quoted during the particular session. A member who undertakes to match a price traded in the ring/kerb is not necessarily undertaking that it will trade during the ring/kerb. If a customer trades in the prevailing market quote proffered in ring/kerb their executor is not necessarily obliged to effect an Exchange Contract at the same price. This can lead to situations where the customer has traded at the prevailing market quote, without that same price trading in open outcry across the floor of the Exchange.

(b) Market. In normal circumstances a market order is one executed on a timely basis at the prevailing market price. The market during ring/kerb times is defined by activity within the ring/kerb. During inter-office trading the market is harder to determine. The main indication of the market price during inter-office sessions can be seen on the LME's VFS. However, these quotes represent indicative prices and may not be available to all parties.

(c) Best. Order styles on the LME using the word 'best' confer some discretion upon the members when executing the order. The extent of the discretion is fixed by the terms of the order. This type of order is distinct from 'best execution' as defined by the Financial Services Authority. Best orders may be executed both on rings/kerbs and inter-office. Inter-office trades rely upon the members' skill in determining the level of the market at any particular time. Best orders received during ring/kerb times may not result in the customer receiving the 'best' price achieved during the session if the price improves after the member has booked the metal intended to fill the order.

(d) Close. Most orders placed 'on the close' are for either the close of the second ring (official LME prices) or the second ring kerb (closing prices). Both these prices are demonstrable because of the publication of official and closing prices. In all circumstances, customers and members need to agree the style of execution, that is bid–ask, mean or traded price. Members may not always be able to guarantee execution (price or volume) due to prevailing market conditions.

(e) Open customers placing orders to trade on the opening of a market session must provide clear instructions to the LME members, which indicate how this order should be activated. Customers will also need to inform their executor of their requirements if the executor is unable to fill the order basing the 'opening' price in its entirety due to market constraints such as insufficient supply/demand.

(f) Resting orders. When placing resting orders such as 'good till cancelled' ('GT', or any derivations thereof) or stop loss orders, customers should ensure that they are in agreement with their executor's definition of the 'trigger' point of the order. It is possible for a customer not to receive a 'fill' on a resting order despite the 'trigger' point being 'touched'. This could be due to a number of circumstances such as order priority, illiquidity, prevailing market conditions, etc. Whatever the reason the executor should be able to provide the customer with a full explanation of why it was unable to fill the order.

We will now examine a hedging example which provides a focus on how manufacturers can use LME contracts to protect their profit against price fluctuations of raw materials.

A simple average price hedge – The physical contract

On 16 August an aluminium rolling mill agrees a fixed price contract with a car manufacturer for 550 tonnes of sheet to be delivered in December at a price of $1895 per tonne (this is based on the LME price currently being quoted for December of $1700 plus $195 production and delivery costs and profit margin).

The aluminium required to fulfil the car manufacturer's order is needed in the mill in November and will be bought from a regular supplier on the basis of the LME average official cash settlement price of the month prior to the month of shipment.

The first thing is to identify the risk involved and the pricing period to which it refers. The mill has sold to the car manufacturer at a fixed price, but the buying-in price for the aluminium is unknown. This means the profit written into the contract is subject to price fluctuations and the mill is at risk. It therefore needs to buy forward, using LME contracts, in order to protect its profit against this risk.

The pricing period for the physical purchase is October, the month prior to the metal reaching the rolling mill. We must construct a hedge that will mimic the LME Official Monthly Average Settlement Price for October, since that will be the basis on which the mill will be charged for the aluminium. To achieve this it needs to have a position of equal tonnage for every trading day in October. A calendar for the relevant period is shown in Table 4.1.

As today's date is 16 August, the end of October is less than three months away, so every working day is a tradable prompt date.

TABLE 4.1 Calendar of October and November working days

	October				*November*	
Monday	28	5	12	19	26	2
Tuesday	29	6	13	20	27	3
Wednesday	30	7	14	21	28	4
Thursday	1	8	15	22	29	5
Friday	2	9	16	23	30	6
Saturday	3	10	17	24	31	
Sunday	4	11	18	25	1	

The LME's two-day arrangement of cash to prompt means that the first trading day in October (Thursday 1 October) will have a cash settlement price set for the 5 October prompt date. Similarly, when the last day in October (Friday 30 October) is included in the monthly average, it will refer to a prompt date of Tuesday, 3 November. So the original hedge will have to be transacted for prompt dates in the period 5 October to 3 November. There are 22 prompt days in this period. Conveniently, the tonnage is 550 tonnes of aluminium, which equates to 22 lots (i.e. 22 × 25 tonnes).

Having clarified the set of prompt dates required, and the amount for each day, the instruction from the mill to its LME broker is, 'buy one lot for each prompt date from 5 October to 3 November'.

Typically, the broker will give the mill one contract for 22 lots, rather than 22 separate contracts (one for each day), using the average price obtained from the individual deals, say $1680. This is not only simpler, but it also saves some transactions costs.

The hedge is now in place, and can be left in place until the beginning of October, at which time the broker must start to 'unwind' it. On 1 October the broker is instructed to sell back one cash lot each day from 1 October to 30 October at the close of the second morning ring. By 30 October all 22 lots have been sold. Since each trade has been done at the same price as will be used for the day's Official Settlement Price, the official average for the month will have been achieved. The hedge is lifted, and the mill has avoided exposure to any price volatility over the August to November interval.

Trimming hedge

Has the rolling mill achieved a perfect hedge? Not quite. The London Metal Exchange announces the Official Monthly Average Settlement Price at the end of each month, but this will not be exactly the same price in this case as the average of the prices at which the hedge was lifted. This is because the price achieved when selling the hedged position would have been the bid price. The LME Official Settlement Price is always the offer price. So the hedge will be imperfect to the extent of the spread between the bid and offer prices, but this is a minor inaccuracy in the overall picture. It could have been taken into account in the original quotation to the car manufacturer since bid-offer spreads are quite stable.

Table 4.2 shows the result of this hedge with a price rise using realistic prices in a contango market.

As we can see, the net additional profit is equal to the contango between the quotation period for the purchase (October) and the quotation period for the sale (December) at the time of placing the hedge, less the bid–offer spread at the time of lifting the hedge. The contango of $20 would have been a known factor when pricing the physical sales contract, and would have been taken into account.

It doesn't matter whether the price rises or falls, the result would be the same, which is the whole point of the hedge – to achieve a known and acceptable result.

TABLE 4.2 Average hedge, price rise

Date	Action	LME 'account'	Physical 'account'
16 Aug	Contracts to sell 550 tonnes physical metal, delivery Dec Hedge Buys one lot/day LME for delivery 5 Oct to 3 Nov	@ $1680.00 av. per tonne	@ $1895.00 per tonne
1–30 Oct	Sells one lot for each business day LME for cash delivery	@ $1752.64 av. per tonne	
early Nov	Buys 550 tonnes physical metal, delivery Nov @ Oct Official		
	Av. price	_____	$1754.20 per tonne
		+$72.64	+$140.80
	So, combining the two	=$213.44	

This net figure of $213.44 per tonne is made up of:

Initial production costs and profit margin	+195.00
Favourable contango (Oct/Dec)	+20.00
Bid–offer spread	− 1.56
Net:	+ 213.44

As mentioned initially, straightforward figures have been used to clarify the method used to achieve an average-price hedge. Things are rarely that simple. First, what if the pricing months are far forward so that only the third Wednesday of the month is a tradable date when placing the hedge? Secondly, what if the number of lots to be hedged is not divisible by the number of days?

These difficulties can be overcome by the development of average price books by brokers.

It would be useful at this point to examine The London Metal Exchange 'Vendor Feed System' (LMEVFS). It is the primary vehicle for providing price and other information on each of the eight metals traded on the LME. It provides a real-time data feed to over 40 information quote vendors who provide prices, stocks, turnovers and other relevant information to over 20 000 user screens around the world.

The LMEVFS provides a fast and reliable means of distributing data to market users. Those who conduct business in the metals market such as brokers, industrial clients, traders, banks, private investors and other market participants are provided with the price transparency they need via information quote vendors.

All LME contracts, futures and options are cleared by the London Clearing House (LCH) whose systems provide the LMEVFS with intra-day, end-of-day and previous day turnover figures, evening evaluation prices and daily open interest volumes. Daily warehouse stock figures from LME approved listed warehouses are published each morning.

To summarize our review of the LME, it must be stressed that it is in the van of change driven by technology. In October 2000 it was announced that the LME was going to demutualize embracing screen-based electronic trading for the first time. This new system is called LME Select. This is against a background of peak investment in the financial services sector in all areas of technology. For exchanges, the pace is rapid as ECNs (electronic communication networks) are becoming the favoured way of matching buyers and sellers.

LME has the world's largest liquidity in the non-ferrous contracts and traded options exchange. Open outcry is much respected by market users as a transparent way of determining a world reference price. The market is well regulated and low cost and the telephone market allows 24-hour a day trading on a global basis.

In February 2001 The London Metal Exchange (LME) members began a live trading on LME Select, the Exchange's new screen trading system. Thirty three member firms are connected to the system and for the first time accredited traders will be able to execute trades via the screen in addition to open outcry in the ring and the traditional telephone market.

More than 325 traders from member firms have been accredited to use the system and the feedback has been very positive. Traders have been impressed by the fucntionality of LME Select and the versatility with which it can be adapted to their individual needs. The LME website www.lme.c.uk tracks current developments.

Recommended reading

- *BP Statistical Review* – World Energy.
- WTO *Media Focus*.
- *Pipeline*, IPE Magazine published quarterly.
- *Ringsider*, London Metal Exchange, magazine.
- *Barclays Commodities Survey*, Barclays Bank, monthly.
- International Energy Association publications.
- Farmer, D. and A.J. van Weele (1995) *Gower Handbook of Purchasing Management*, 2nd edn, Gower Publishing.
- LME select screen trading system.

5

Logistics and globalization

Role of logistics

The procurement manager today must have a good knowledge of the fundamentals of logistics. Logistics can be broadly defined as the time related positioning of resources ensuring that materials, people, operational capacity and information are in the right place at the right time in the right quantity and at the right quality and cost. Hence, the process of delivering a container from A to B is not logistics – it is transport – just one element in the logistics plan.

As we progress into the early stages of the twenty-first century, the international purchasing manager must devise a strategy to process the order to reflect the logistic international environment. Today the trend is greater complexity in the logistics task reflecting the increased product range, shorter product life cycle, marketplace growth, and the range of supply/demand channels. Hence, an international logistics plan must be devised in consultation with all parties to the supply chain. Overall, it is forecast during the period 2001–3 that the demand for international logistics will rise 20 per cent annually.

The world today is a single integrated marketplace in which supply chain efficiency has become a competitive necessity. Manufacturers or suppliers and buyers have sought cost savings and service improvements to enhance their competitiveness by supplying larger markets with fewer production and distribution centres. This is also driven by an increasing number of mergers and acquisitions and operating alliances. Hence, a global logistic strategy must be devised identifying the degree of centralized management, manufacturing and distribution whilst at the same time meeting the needs of the local market and achieving economies of scale through standardization.

Additionally, one must bear in mind that world markets are not homogeneous and local needs must be customized in product specification. It is a question of standardization versus adaptation. Furthermore, logistics demands a high level of coordination to control the complex logistic global supply chain, otherwise higher costs may result.

Central to logistics in its true sense is the concept of supply chain management. The chain in, say, consumer goods production starts with raw materials, their sourcing and delivery, through manufacturing to distribution of the finished goods to the consumer. With production quality and efficiency levelling up around the world and global sourcing and distribution becoming easier even for quite modestly sized enterprises, companies are finding that logistics management has become a critical function in differentiation, profitability and even survival. Place, time and value – these are the fundamental elements in logistics management. Along the supply chain, transport and inventory are intermediate links where costs can be squeezed out, performance raised and value added. Although the ideas have been around for a long time they have only been raised to an art form, and indeed a science in its own right, in the last decade. The reason for that is the exponential development of information technology – because information and its use are the key to unlocking the benefits in logistics management.

The multinational industry or company is now logistically driven and managers must be logistically literate. This has placed new demands on the logistics industry and, in order to meet these demands, a new industry of global supply chains services is developing quickly. The gains that can be made from inventory reduction due to quick response and just-in-time have been the basis of widespread industry reform. It is realized through production rationalization and centralized inventories.

Logistics is a corporate function and a strategic part of business planning particularly in the area of procurement. Global brands and companies now dominate most markets. Hence, the strategic focus is to develop the business through market extension and penetration, coupled with seeking cost reduction through economies of scale in purchasing, production and through focused and manufacturing and/or assembly operations. Many companies now see logistics management as part of a sourcing and business planning designed to improve customer service and sales performance. The buyer adopts a policy of sourcing overseas to become more competitive in both price and product range and quality. Moreover, service industries are outsourcing to reduce cost and take advantage of satellite communication and the Internet. For a logistics operation to be successful on an international scale, two main criteria have to be satisfied: there needs to be an integrated network of professionals throughout all countries concerned to ensure the smooth passage of goods; and secondly there has to be a high level of specialist expertise and knowledge relating to the multitude of laws, conventions, product quality controls and regulations inherent in the conduct of the international trade environment. A further point, transparency of data communication, must be evident at all times between parties in the supply chain. This embraces the progress of the consignment throughout its international transit. The trend in the past decade has been for international companies to rationalize their business by integrating production, sales and marketing across international frontiers. Their suppliers have followed suit and in the logistics industry there has been a strong move towards creating international networks either through merger and acquisition or through confederations of independent professionals. Hence, there is no established pattern of international logistics networks at present. Each logistics company will have its own particular type of network with its own strengths suitable for some types of customers and not others.

The demand-focused international trade industry increasingly relies on satellite production and encourages suppliers to have shorter product life cycles through fashion, technology advancement, legal environment and in the food industry develop a longer shelf life, again through technology. All these factors help to drive logistics in a shrinking world of global sourcing.

Few industries have changed more dramatically than international distribution in the past decade. The impact of logistics has turned transport on its head. An activity long regarded as a self-defining but unavoidable cost centre is now seen as a means of reducing inventory, cutting cost, improving customer service and added value benefits. Hence, buyers and sellers have the tools by which they can become more efficient, customer focused, profitable and develop a quicker response rate to competition and customer needs. The many small firms that do not need a customized logistical service can call on the integrators (see page 217). Led by a handful of mainly US owned multinationals, these companies have been winning a market share as their operational ambitions have been extended.

Similarly, information technology systems have equipped transport providers to upgrade their services to improve utilization and yield. Whether, it is the transport industry, the port industry, international rail freight or air transport, the current common denominator is to aim for the optimum use of capacity and resources irrespective of whether the equipment is a container gantry crane or a Boeing 747 freighter. In the container operation field, major container lines give a shipper or consignee the ability to track his or her container from the start to the finish of its journey. But in the real world delays occur. To be able to know 24 hours a day the precise location of the container that may be altering its estimated time of arrival or route, is a tremendously powerful tool for adjusting other elements in business procurement. At the other end of the scale, deciding on behalf of a European wide supermarket chain how many distribution centres it should build and where they should be located to optimize the delivery operation is a complex numerical evaluation aided by computer analysis. The key to it is the infrastructure. A country, region or continent with a good infrastructure, such as Europe and North America, lends itself to a logistically focused strategic environment, whereas the subcontinent does not have the facility for the efficient distribution of international routed goods.

Logistics suppliers may be classified as follows in order of priority:

(a) one stop shop suppliers;
(b) express carriers;
(c) regional contractors;
(d) consolidated shipment carriers;
(e) domestic contractors.

Emerging from the foregoing, an increasing number of businesses are outsourcing part or all of their international distribution management with enormous financial benefit and customer satisfaction. Shipping lines such as P&O, Nedlloyd and CSX/Sea Land have logistics subsidiaries to bid for this third party business.

The number of multinationals are becoming fewer whilst their share of world trade is increasing and approaching the 70 per cent level. Such expansion is being driven by the multinationals adopting a logistics strategy which stipulates quality of service and the medium-sized and small firms are simply having to comply. Consequently medium-sized and small companies are changing their organizational structure and focus and the former shipping departments are becoming part of a larger customer service organization. Multinationals have built partnerships with their logistics suppliers. Large companies sourcing their materials on a global basis insist on dealing with a logistics company with a worldwide network. Major buyers are looking to reduce inventory, improve operational performance and enhance customer service.

Logistics generate a competitive advantage in the marketplace and achieve cost reduction. Moreover, it introduces a logistics management culture into a company which in turn raises the quality of service and can be further improved by adding value to the service through a variety of options (see page 75). The key to it is adaptation and transparency whereby all parties in the supply chain have complete integrity through the continuous exchange of data.

An analysis of the logistics needs a European focused procurement company would be as set out below.

European companies require a European service from logistics service providers. They do not want:

(a) a plethora of service providers when they are consolidating;
(b) to manage distribution at a national level when they are operating at European level;
(c) different computer systems throughout Europe when they have introduced European-wide integrated systems;
(d) varying reporting methods and measures in different markets.

European companies do not need:

(a) a single service provider operating in all markets and geographies;
(b) assets owned and managed by the same company in all markets.

They do need:

(a) a single management interface for all European operations;
(b) a common standard of measures and reports provided centrally by the European logistics service managers;
(c) a single systems interface giving visibility of stock movements and locations;
(d) a common billing standard;
(e) a single agreement.

It is agreed that logistics service providers must meet this challenge and must also provide the following:

(a) a consistently high standard in the basic services of transport and warehousing;
(b) a visionary approach with new ideas, concepts and approaches;
(c) access to best practice from different sectors and national approaches;
(d) a clear chain of command, with 'national' and 'locations operations' treating all customers as 'ours' and not treating some as 'theirs' and therefore as second class.

The global and European logistics services market it is predicted will undergo 'a significant change' in the next few years. These changes could include:

(a) more mergers and acquisitions to reduce excess capacity and increase scope and opportunity;
(b) joint ventures between different types of service providers;
(c) joint ventures and operating networks across European and global markets;
(d) a move to provide chain management services with 'basics' such as transport and warehousing outsourced;
(e) joint ventures between logistics and other service providers, including systems houses and consulting groups;
(f) joint ventures between logistics service companies and niche market clients.

A key factor in international logistic management is the channel of distribution (see chapter 11). The degree to which the channel is simple or complex will depend on the nature of the goods and the channel strategy. A channel of distribution which involves numerous stages is likely to add considerably to the final price of the goods as each intermediary adds a percentage for profit. Hence, determining the channel of distribution strategy for a logistics operation is one of the most important factors in the whole process. It must reflect the need to maximize sales opportunities, achieve high levels of customer service, minimize cost and ensure accurate information flows. Many companies use a third party logistics specialist.

Warehousing and storage systems play a decisive role in international logistics. It does include the FTZ and distriparks (see page 187) as found in seaports and their environs. It epitomizes the role of the modern seaport today as the trading centre. Effective warehouse management does ensure a smooth level of supply to customers. Additionally, it does yield the following benefits: economies of scale permitting long production runs and bulk cargo shipments; the ability to build up stocks in anticipation of seasonal or new product demand; improved customer service by, for example, the quick replacement of faulty goods or components; it facilitates break bulk and other assembly operations as found in distriparks and FTZ for onward shipment to customers; and finally it provides a secure and good environment to protect goods from damage, deterioration and pilferage internationally. Logistically-focused warehouse management is found in the ports of Singapore, Dubai and Rotterdam where goods are assembled, processed and packaged for distribution to an international market. All the warehouses in these ports are computer controlled.

Global logistics operators

Few logistic suppliers can justify the claim to provide just-in-time deliveries on a global basis. One such operator is Geo Logistics who handles a Taiwanese high-tech manufacturing giant Lite On, manufacturing CD ROMs and computer monitors. It is a partnership that draws on Geo Logistics' ability to add value, to provide a global IT track and trace system, to drive down capital cost by minimizing the time the product is held in stock and, in Europe, to act as Lite On's fiscal representative. A key feature is the presence of Geo Logistics' office in Taiwan to enable close contact with Lite On, which minimizes problems caused by the six-hour time difference between Taipei and Europe. The Taiwan office works closely with the Geo Logistics branches in the USA and across the Asia–Pacific area. Overall, the Company moves to the USA several hundred container movements a year together with a substantial volume of air freight.

In Europe the bulk of Lite On's product range is distributed from a warehouse at Breda in the Netherlands. Other depots are found in Frankfurt and Dusseldorf. An inventory system enables Lite On to track and trace consignments from its factory in Taiwan to the customer – the buyer. While it is usual for logistics specialists to adapt their computer systems to those of their clients, the reverse has happened between Lite On and Geo Logistics, with the shipper adjusting its system to make it compatible with that of its logistics provider.

Most of the CD ROMs and monitors reach the Breda warehouse in containers via the Port of Rotterdam. As it needs to be flexible enough to provide same day delivery, Geo Logistics works with a number of preferred road hauliers. Air couriers and dedicated vehicles are used to deliver urgent consignments. A feature of the operation is the value added service provided. At the Breda warehouse the product is tested and labelled and technical alterations are made where necessary. The warehouse staffs' duties embrace administration; distribution; customs clearance; incoming containers; product testing assembly and related services.

Future plans for the Breda operation embrace the setting up of a multi-vendor European hub. The hub is considered a key element in supply chain management and enhances JIT, vendor-managed inventory and vendor-consigned inventory. The inventory is consolidated at a single facility close to the end user's assembly or distribution point. The end user is able to withdraw stock on an as-needed basis. This enables the end user to have greater control over the product in the supply chain pipeline by reducing inventory replenishment time from days to hours. More dramatically it can drastically reduce, if not eliminate, emergency stocks and inventory carrying costs, which can represent 40 per cent of inventory value.

Multi-vendor hubs are starting to replace the more traditional warehouse and inventory management practice which normally require large and expensive stocks to be held to meet manufacturing requirements. Where many vendors are involved, products are sent to strategically located JIT warehouses where the manufacturer pulls in the components as needed, often resulting in multiple deliveries.

Geo Logistics also focuses on fiscal concessions such as VAT. Whereas VAT on imports has to be paid immediately in most EU countries, this is not the case in the Netherlands, Belgium, Denmark and the Irish Republic. The Company acts as Lite On's fiscal representative for duty and VAT for container imports from Taiwan. As its fiscal representative, Geo Logistics reports to Dutch Customs on Lite On's behalf. It is a service that volume shippers particularly appreciate since it removes a potential problem area where hours of management time can be lost.

Another leading player in the field of global logistics operation is the mega-container carrier P&O Nedlloyd Container Line. It has 600 specialist staff working in 44 offices in 19 countries spanning Europe, the Gulf, the USA, the Far East and the Indian subcontinent.

Finally, the procurement officer researching new channels to serve international markets should make full use of the Internet and e-commerce resources. There are four relevant features of electronic communication channels: information is now more widely available; the speed of getting goods to the market has increased; geographical impediments to buying have been reduced; and entry barriers lowered. Buyers selecting Internet suppliers should focus on brand consistency, maintaining customer loyalty, offering a dynamic trading system, operating a vertical organizational structure and providing a just-in-time service with a zero failure rate. Additionally, the buyer should analyse competitor suppliers on the Internet. In summary, there are six key areas sought by customers in logistic management and resources.

(a) The overseas buyer seeks strategic solutions to the problems of long distance product sourcing and movement. This is realized by matching the client's business needs to the latest techniques and expertise to formulate solutions to the problems of long distance product sourcing and movement. An example is European based departmental stores which buy a range of consumer products from the Far East. Key factors are quality control, the ability to cope with variations in consumer demand and to distribute supplies in a cost effective manner.

(b) Companies which can provide capabilities interfaced across a range of different transport modes including sea, road, rail, canal and air as found in multi-modalism.

(c) Continuous improvements in quality of service to end customers. This basically centres on customer asset management – ensuring the goods arrive in a quality condition to a prescribed schedule with zero failure rate.

(d) Improvements in profits realized through all the marketing and financial benefits inherent in the global logistic system to the user. This results in the departmental store, for example, having lower inventory costs and a wider product range which can be replenished within hours, as found in the Geo Logistic operation.

(e) Management of 'trade offs' within the supply chain. This should be calculated on the total cost trade off where the cost of long supply pipelines may outweigh the production cost saving.

(f) A fully outsourced logistic management service.

Users of the service include automotive manufacturers, high street retailers, wine and spirit users, footware, fashion, foodstuffs, garments, sports goods, computer equipment and software and electronic manufacturers.

Global logistics operators focus attention on four key areas as detailed below:

1. *Supply chain management.* This requirement may be illustrated by the leading chains sourcing their merchandise from suppliers in Europe, the Far East and the USA. The logistics operator's task is to ensure that goods of a merchantable quality are manufactured and transported safely and cost effectively and are delivered on time. This key service involves three elements:
   (a) vendor management involving the processing of customers' orders direct to their suppliers and monitoring the process as demonstrated in Geo Logistics' operation;
   (b) information featuring receipt of customers' orders via EDI download (this leads to 24-hour monitoring and reporting of status and cost down to item level);
   (c) communication permitting customers to receive advance notice of shipments which are off schedule via international e-mail links.

   The key benefits are reduced inventory levels, improved visibility of all cost to item level, improved delivery on time and clearer management responsibility. Study the supply pipe line in Figure 5.1.

2. *Delivery and customs clearance.* An example of this requirement is provided by a leading drinks company with over 50 brands worldwide. The objective is to receive and handle stock and to arrange transport and overseas shipment. The four main features of the service include:
   (a) inventory management, featuring direct data exchange to provide online reporting;
   (b) order pricing, embracing maximizing deliveries of export shipments direct to the end customer;
   (c) quality control including checking on arrival, arranging, relabelling and repacking as required;
   (d) security requires the adoption of sophisticated arrangements suitable for a high value commodity.

   The key results include delivery only when market demand dictates, secure and cost effective storage and efficient onward distribution services.

3. *Distribution management.* This is the requirement of a major sportswear company which buys/imports merchandise from suppliers in the Far East. The objective is to improve upstream process controls and maximize direct delivery to high street stores in Europe. The three main features of the service include:
   (a) quality control, embracing collecting goods from suppliers and ensuring compliance with specified quality standards;
   (b) consolidation and delivery, embracing sorting, labelling and packaging, goods to the buyer or end customer order requirements and providing

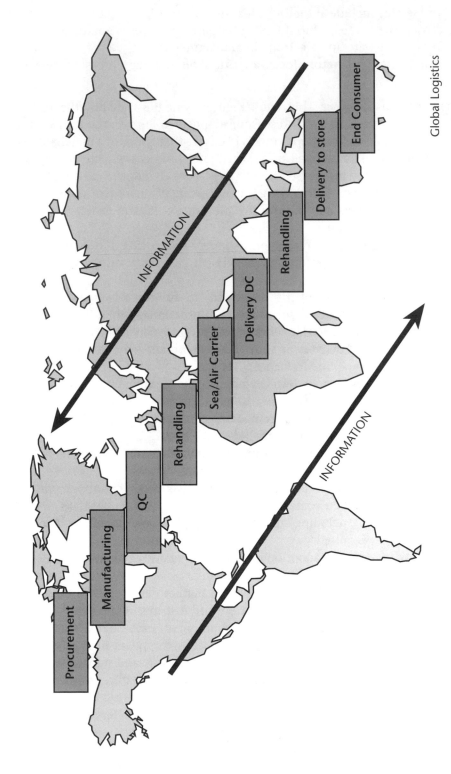

FIGURE 5.1 Global logistics supply pipe line
Reproduced courtesy P&O Nedlloyd

delivery direct to the customer. A range of options exist, including the LCL, FCL, air freight consolidation and sea/air consolidation (see page 199);

(c) information embracing full integration via EDI between the customer's or buyer's purchase order system, their financial and distribution systems and the global supply chain management system.

The ultimate results were improved supplier quality standards, reduced warehousing and handling costs and shortened order cycle times.

4. *Import logistics and outbound distribution.* This is illustrated by a manufacturer of electronic goods which sources components in the Far East for manufacture in Europe. The objective is to manage the inbound supply of components to exacting production schedules and distribute the finished products across Europe. The three main features of the service include:

(a) supply chain management embracing despatch of orders, monitoring of production, consolidation and delivery on time to the manufacturing plant;

(b) information, embracing tracking progress in the supply chain so that buyers and customers can accommodate changes to the production plan;

(c) consolidation and distribution featuring maximizing container usage to cut cost and distribution 'on time' to retailers.

Key results are proactive control of delivery schedules and reduced shipment costs from the consolidation and integration of inward and outward distribution.

Overall, the global logistics company concentrates on six core products: supply chain management; warehousing; customs clearance; air freight; consolidation; and project cargo. It will improve supply chain visibility by developing tailored processes and tracking systems. This will lead to improved buying processes and decision making, reduced stock levels and improved reaction times in delivering to end users. Overall, it will reduce supply chain costs, thus cutting lead times, creating fast-flow procedures and introducing upstream controls.

A critical area in the global supply chain is the extended and unreliable transit times. Consequently air freight features more strongly in long haul transit for many commodities.

Logistics department

The overseas buyer must be very conscious of the benefits of operating in a logistic environment and it is appropriate to evaluate the logistics department structure.

The role of the basic logistics team includes:

(a) assessing the supply chain competitiveness of the organization;

(b) creating a vision of the desired supply chain;

(c) closing the gaps between vision and the present supply chain reality;

(d) prioritizing items and appropriate resources.

The primary function performed by the logistics department within the firm includes:

(a) traffic management;
(b) warehousing;
(c) facilities location;
(d) global logistics;
(e) inventory control;
(f) order processing;
(g) packaging;
(h) purchasing;
(i) order entry;
(j) product planning;
(k) sales forecasting;
(l) general management.

The logistics department tends to exhibit both on integrated and process orientation. An integrated orientation seeks to simultaneously manage logistic flows, coordination and complexity within the organization and with external parties. A process orientation seeks efficiency, control and cost reduction. A cost analysis resource is also important for implementing a cost minimization strategy. This embraces a strategic focus to determine what is driving logistics costs, material costs, production costs, staffing patterns and inventory costs.

An important area is the development of strategic partnerships with external transportation providers, focused on long-term commitments, open communications and information sharing and the sharing of risks and rewards.

Factors contributing to the development of logistics

The international buyer is the lead player in putting pressure on the logistics operator to continuously improve and add value to the supply chain mechanism. Hence, logistics today has a major input into the strategic focus of the professional international buyer. It is therefore appropriate that we examine the factors influencing the development of global logistics. The salient ones are detailed below:

1. The development of information technology (IT) has enabled a transformation to take place in communication and data transmission opening up markets and re-focusing strategies in distribution and manufacturing outsourcing assembly. It embraces e-commerce, the Internet, on-line electronic access to the supply chain (see page 83 item 21) and satellite communication including video conferencing. It has no culture or language barriers, no time zones and is available continuously, bringing together the low and high labour cost nations and their skills for the exchange of goods and services.

2. The globalization of markets with their infrastructure embracing inter-national distribution and commercial resources and the international trade

environment has generated business confidence internationally. This includes international conventions (see page 235) and the work of the WTO which has reduced trade barriers, eliminated many subsidies and opened up markets developing the most-favoured nation (MFN) concept.

3. The accelerating development of the global container network has offered a new challenge to the global trader. It has placed a fresh focus on global distribution with an emphasis on added value in the distribution chain. Buyers are offered the option of independent software and systems as an alternative to those available from the carrier. This allows suppliers, carriers, manufacturers and retailers to make optimum routing decisions and increases the transparency of goods flows. The financial efficiency of the supply chain network is also being examined. This involves developing a product to coordinate the flow of funds more efficiently with the movement of goods thereby allowing the buyer and seller access to cheaper sources of money.

4. The continuous expansion of the integrators TNT and DHL has opened up new markets to both the manufacturing and service industries.

5. Another factor is the emergence of the mega container operator (see page 202) which exploits economies of scale and allows them to provide the 'in-house' global logistics resources such as those offered by P&O Nedlloyd.

6. The development of the free port, free trade zones and distriparks in the port environs has opened up new opportunities of trade distribution for the international entrepreneur. Such designated areas are immune from customs examination and revenue collection until the goods enter the domestic market. They enable the global trader to outsource the product and focus on such areas as the component assembly point, the packaging and distribution point, and the mixing and blending unit for powdered cargoes such as spices.

7. Value is added to the product through the global logistic network. It may be through better packaging arrangements, more outsourcing of componetized products which offer lower costs and better quality, or through blending and mixing of food products as found in the distriparks in the port of Rotterdam.

8. Companies, particularly multinationals, are being driven by their logistics departments. Moreover, MNIs now focus on a simultaneous global product launch across all markets to ensure an early cash return on capital expenditure rather than concentrating on regional launches over a period of time, for example phase one Europe, phase two North America and phase three the Far East.

9. Competition is driving the logistics operation: to remain competitive companies must adopt a global logistic strategy.

10. Satellite production demands a logistic network; it is computer driven.

11. Shorter product life cycles driven, by a fashion conscious international market and continuous technical advancement favours logistics efficiency.

12. Ongoing technological developments providing a longer shelf life for many consumer products, especially foodstuffs, needs a logistically driven distribution and sourcing mechanism.

13. The global logistic facility offers a one-stop operation and an opportunity to deal with one person – the account executive. Therefore, both the importer and exporter develop empathy with the global logistics operator on a tailor-made basis, taking full advantage of their professionalism and experience coupled with a competitively priced operation. Buyers can therefore concentrate on their core business of marketing, developing and sourcing products, finding new markets, researching production and assembly in third countries and investment.

14. The global logistics operation encourages the rationalization of distribution networks. This will accelerate as the hub and spoke system develops through the mega carrier operations.

15. There are continuing improvements in the global infrastructure, for example port modernization, FTZ, ICDs, free ports, LIC, LEC and the development of road and rail networks. There is a strong level of interfacing and integration between transport modes and the emergence of dedicated services favouring global logistics.

16. Companies – and overseas buyers – today demand responsiveness from the global operator. The discerning overseas buyer demands the 'total logistics product service'. When a trader purchases a service, the trader expects the consignment to be delivered or to be informed of delays or challenges encountered. As trade expands and companies move from a regional to a global market to exploit economies of scale, to remain competitive in price and product specification and to increase market penetration, the quality of service becomes paramount. Moreover, the global logistics operator will be able to help the buyer in planning such market expansion and provide data on the culture, the market environment, customs regulations and the best practice global logistics operation feasible. The buyer will place particular emphasis on product quality control and the quick response to changing and volatile order levels with cycles of peaks and troughs.

17. Market research confirms that only 30 per cent of changes in suppliers are motivated by a better or cheaper product. Most changes occur due to poor service quality or inadequate attention to the individual customer. This favours the mega logistics global operator.

18. The manufacturer/producer is striving to achieve a shorter production cycle facilitated by many of the ingredients offered by the logistics system. This aim is particularly important to the buyer who wishes to keep inventory stocks low, have a wider product range available to the customer and to achieve a quick order response rate.

19. The development of third party logistics contractors.

20. The continuous improvement in supply chain software. The most important concept underlying the management of supply is that of integration. This embraces the buyer's resource planning inventory management and supply chain design. Goods must be able to flow in a highly organized manner between each stage of the supply chain while at the same time achieving the

most desirable balance between the buyer's company sales and performance, inventory, import flows, customer service, total cost of product including import duty and working capital. Each supply chain will have a different set of emphases. For example, the buyer of high specification valuable goods may be more interested in speed and security than achieving the lowest cost. It is important that all parties involved in the supply chain have an agreed set of priorities. Moreover, effective transparent communication and understanding are vital to ensure that both sides know what the supply chain is designed to achieve. It is, similarly, important that logistics systems can send data to where the decisions are taken and to keep all the international business managers and sectors informed about the flow of goods. Figure 5.2 features the supply chain software. Software advances have been accelerated through the rapid globalization of manufacture and distribution.

21. The development of time sharing with the logistics contractor. This involves the contractor being linked to the buyer's own IT system – receiving orders, picking and delivery instructions, implementing them and feeding back the results for processing and evaluation.

22. Economic and trading blocs as found in Europe, North America and the Far East are continuing to develop as member states realize their benefits. Such blocs particularly favour the global logistic trader or buyer who can adopt the strategy of buying through the total logistic product service. A single price can be secured and the supply chain management benefits can be realized.

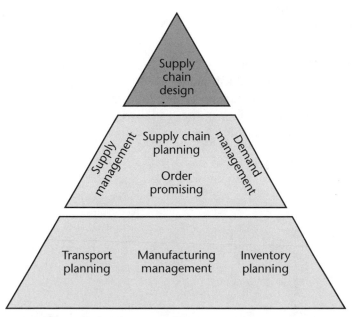

FIGURE 5.2 A focus of the supply chain software
Reproduced by courtesy of Synquest

Study of Tables 1.1 and 1.2 (pages 3–4) identifies the trading performance of countries worldwide. The overseas buyer must keep up-to-date with the development of products in such countries and which may interest his or her clients. This means continuously searching the web of such product development and sourcing availability. This ensures the buyer's products remain market leaders in terms of specification; price and value for money.

The Far East, China and Japan remain popular sourcing countries for a wide range of consumer goods including garments, white goods and electrical goods. The USA is an excellent sourcing market for high tech goods and a wide range of industrial and consumer goods. Europe is an excellent market for most consumer and industrial goods and wide variety of foodstuffs.

To conclude our analysis the specific reasons for the increasing interest in supply chain management and global logistics can be summarized as follows.

(a) *Concept*: companies are primarily concerned with reducing delivery times and improving responsiveness to buyers or customers, reflecting the shorter product life cycles they face.
(b) *Value*: equal emphasis is placed cost savings (from reduced inventory levels, economies of scale and a reduction in fixed assets) and improved service quality (through reliable delivery, improved stock availability and response times).

To achieve improvements in the management of a supply chain, keeping track of goods at all times is the key.

Recommended reading

- WTO *Media Focus*.
- Christopher, Martin (1998) *Logistics and Supply Chain Management*, 2nd edn, Financial Times Pitman Publishing.
- Institute of Logistics and Transport quarterly journal.
- *Focus Japan* and PIERJ – opportunities in Japan, JETRO, monthly.
- *Distribution Business*, monthly magazine.

6

Negotiating the contract I

E-commerce, globalization and computerization are the three major engines of change for the twenty-first century. The development of an increasingly complicated and diversified supply chain as featured in the previous chapter demands a more flexible approach. Hence, communication between the buyer and seller today relies upon excellent communication systems, not only for the on-line accessibility of discrete information, but also for direct global communication using video clip messages and on-line visual conferencing, aided by increasingly sophisticated web cameras and mobile phone technology. The ability to communicate better, faster more efficiently and economically – whether by voice or data – is a major stimulant in fast growing international trade. It encourages the buyer, in particular, to source overseas by easing market entry, access and communication. It is within the foregoing context that we will examine negotiating contracts in this and the next chapter. (see also page 108, 'Digital trade revolution').

A key factor of international buying entrepreneurial skills is contract negotiation. It involves many elements of which the principal one is adequate planning and market research to ensure that the product specification is acceptable to the end user and fully conforms to all the relevant national and international standards.

Product specification

Chapter 2 (pages 15–33) focuses on particular elements of the product specification. It is appropriate, therefore, to examine this in a wider concept within the context of the skills required by the international negotiator and the rationale behind the product specification formulation.

Commercial aspects

The commercial aspects of the product specification are driven by market research and industrial research to allow an empathetic strategy with the consumer or end user to be developed. It reflects the value added benefit the product brings to the user.

Other elements include the design, packaging, colour, and the user's environment, cultural needs and buying power. Markets in less developed countries (LDCs) have limited buying power compared with developed markets such as the USA, which need more sophisticated products of a higher specification. This raises the question of standardization versus adaptation in product acceptance. Other factors include the brand and the vendor's position in the marketplace. Major companies tend to devote a great deal of time and energy through their marketing and product development departments on devising the most acceptable product and the buyer must be fully aware of the rationale behind the product specification.

Consumer design tends to be a mass fast moving market whilst the industrial sector focuses on technical performance and reliability with a much longer life cycle spanning many years. Productivity and performance are key areas and capital cost is less significant whilst day-to-day operating costs are crucial. Industrial products focus especially on spares, training and servicing availability. An overseas buyer negotiating the purchase of a fleet of buses or tendering for a power station would focus particularly on these areas and include them in the contract price. If the negotiation is for a rollover contract using the same vehicle manufacturer there may be a trade off between the existing fleet of buses and the new ones. Innovation is a key factor in negotiation and the buyer is in a strong position to take the lead in this area.

Technical aspects

The technical aspects of products have gone to the top of the buyer's list of priorities in product choice, both in consumer and industrial sectors. High tech products reflect market leadership and the prudent buyer would be advised to look into the future investment in product development from his or her suppliers.

Quality is a key factor in product specification, including commercial, technical and legal considerations. Foodstuffs is a massive market internationally much of which is shipped in controlled temperature ISO containers (see page 202) or trucks to maintain quality. Product testing at the time of shipment and following arrival are key audit strategies to safeguard against the risk of any shipment falling below quality standards. This can apply not only to consumer products such as foodstuffs – spices, meat – but also industrial shipments such as oil. The pre-shipment inspection system has been devised to safeguard against the shipment of shoddy goods (see page 177).

Legal aspects

Compliance with legal specifications is paramount in the product specification and no deviation is acceptable (see page 24). Legislation is tending to increase as more countries achieve developed status. The ISO takes the lead in this area, but particular markets are very concerned with legal specifications, for example Japan, the USA and the EU. Suppliers should not be utilized if they cannot produce evidence of compliance with the appropriate legal specification, for example an approval certificate. This applies not only to the product specification but also to the supplier's total quality management (see pages 98–9).

Health and safety regulations also form part of the legal environment. These regulations apply particularly to foodstuffs, including packaging and handling, and also to a wide range of consumer goods, because they impact on aspects such as electronics, fire resistant properties and, safety in use, that is on general consumer product design. Industrial product designs are very much focused on safety and quality standards and the use of specific materials with minimum constituents. Customs controls on importation impose stringent inspection disciplines on a wide range of goods to ensure compliance with legal standards and require appropriate documentation, for example a Health Certificate. In the case of agricultural and animal products, the Health Certificate certifies that they comply with the relevant legislation in the exporter's country. It also responds to the importer's request to comply with health regulations and confirms that the product was in good condition at the time of inspection (see page 175).

There are also legal implications of the product specification as featured in the customs documentation at the time of importation. This determines the level of import duty which will subsequently effect the price at the point of sale, that is it will be passed on to the customer. The level of import duty is set out in the customs tariff code. The tariff includes 15 000 headings, set out in 97 chapters, broken down into sections, headings and sub-headings. It is based on the Harmonized System code (see page 258). Careful customs planning (see pages 196–8) can ensure that the correct code is being used to minimize import duty. It may be advantageous for the international buyer to order components for assembly in the importer's country rather than the complete product and thereby have a different customs duty code attracting a lower import duty tariff. The buyer should involve the supplier to explore such possibilities.

Patents limit market penetration and it is important that the appropriate patent registration has been granted. In the EU, the 15 states share one patent office. This ensures that once a patent is approved the goods may be sold in all 15 states without waiting for each individual country's approval, which may be a lengthy process frustrating speed of market entry.

Transportation

The international buyer must be very familiar with the transportation arrangements. It is desirable that discussions be conducted on routing, transit time, freight, insurance, packaging, stowage areas, together with any constraints. The latter points can influence the product specification such as whether the goods are shipped as a componentized break bulk unit or as a complete unit. By altering the packaging it may be possible to improve the utilization of the cubic capacity of the container thereby, through the reduction of broken stowage, increasing by up to 5 per cent the number of units shipped.

Similar benefits accrue when using a logistics operator who, through consolidation and other areas, may be able to reduce freight/packaging charges and speed up transit times.

The foregoing discussion demonstrates the desirability of linking product specification in terms of quantity, dimension, componentized or complete product and sourcing areas with the optimum transportation and logistics operation. Such product specification, however, cannot be varied or compromised if it would put at risk the legal accreditation and end user specification. Cost and customer satisfaction are major considerations.

Product standardization

We have already mentioned the question of product standardization versus adaptation. The overseas buyer must be very conscious of the rationale behind this argument as it will enable the buyer to have a useful input to the marketing development discussions. In such discussions the buyer will be able to reflect on what is available in the market overseas.

1. *Type of product.* Greater levels of standardization are possible with industrial products which are bought largely to specification on a high volume basis. Consumer goods are more likely to have to be adapted or customized to suit local tastes and social or economic environments.
2. *Stage of market development.* An expanding market in the rapid growth stage of the aggregate product life cycle, that is when all competitive products are jointly considered, is more likely to allow for standardization. At a more mature stage, when consumers become more selective, products need to be differentiated to attract attention. Hence, de luxe models emerge bringing added value and benefit to the product user. In the USA and Japan the de luxe model is preferred rather than the standard specification (see item (9)).
3. *Cost–benefit relationship.* Adaptation can be expensive in terms of research and development, changed production lines, shorter production runs and possible packing and packaging changes. Unless the benefits outweigh these extra costs, the company is likely to standardize on a core product but add value through local customized upgrades. For example, imported cars could have air conditioning fitted by local distributors.
4. *Legal requirements.* For example, compulsory technical standards may force modifications. Hence, the overseas buyer's company may be obliged to employ a different modification for its domestic market compared with the exported product which contains imported components. The automotive industry is a good example.
5. *Competition.* Competitors which are willing to adapt products to local needs will abstract sales from other retailers unless their lead is followed. Market research will help the product manufacturer design the product most suitable for the user, consumer or industrialist.

6. *Product support system*. This embraces servicing needs. The more variations there are, the more variations are needed in spare parts, service routines, maintenance and training. If there is an extensive support system, as with technical products, it may not be possible to afford too many variations and still remain competitive in terms of price.

7. *Physical environment*. For example, the overseas buyer sourcing components for assembly and re-export to a tropical environment may be forced to adapt the electric and electronic goods, develop plastics that do not crack and will remain colour fast under strong sunlight and which are tolerant to high or low temperatures. It also includes different consumer life styles and housing conditions. Personnel living in apartments in cities such as Paris, London, New York and Rome have small kitchens which place limits on the size of appliances. Conversely country properties tend to be larger, with space available for larger units and appliances in the kitchen. For similar reasons, in France top loader washing machines are preferred whereas in the UK front loaders are more popular.

8. *Market conditions*. There are considerable economies of scale involved in developing high volume sales. This tends to favour standardization through competitive pricing.

9. *Buying power*. The overseas buyer purchasing goods for the USA and Japanese markets will tend to opt for the top of the product range and seek customized product solutions, as the higher living standards in such markets result in more buying power compared with countries like Thailand and India.

10. *Media*. The media power which is global has an enormous impact on product awareness, especially in developed countries.

11. *Culture*. This tends to encourage product customization and is found in homogeneous markets such as Japan. It may be manifested in the form of colour, design, packaging and presentation.

12. *Green environmental issues*. This extends to food products and a wide range of consumer and industrial goods: it can also involve local environmental issues.

13. *Economic blocs and customs*. The EU strongly favours common product specification and the emergence of a euro brand.

Finally, the international buyer in his or her contribution to evolving the product specification with the marketing department or client must note the trend towards product standardization, which is due to the following reasons:

(a) markets are becoming more homogeneous;

(b) there are more identifiable common consumer requirements when considered on an international basis;

(c) companies are moving towards globalization through increased competition which is driven by lower unit product costs and ultimately a reduced product range, with an emphasis on standardization and the evolution of the global core product which can be customized locally for individual markets.

Product formulation

We will now briefly examine the product formulation in the service sector.

The process of buying services overseas or outsourcing a domestic service to an overseas market is a growth sector. As indicated earlier (page 51) the areas involved may be medical records, airline reservations or information services. Overall, the rationale of outsourcing a service must add value to the service through cost reduction, greater efficiency and market development. Outsourcing has the following features.

1. *People*. Essentially this is a resource involving a high labour content in the delivery of the service. The labour force must be well managed, have a strong empathy with the service provided, be well motivated, have received good training for the specific work environment, be adequately educated, have a good work ethic and attitude, offer a high level of productivity, be adaptable and willing to respond to opportunities, facilitate a good interface amongst various cultures and, ideally, be of good business acumen. Additionally, the workforce should have favourable global and international focus. This list of features will vary in content and emphasis according to the nature of the service and level of skill and management. This applies particularly to high tech skills such as those required for computer and logistic literacy, on-line communications and processing, e-commerce, the Internet and video conferencing. An adequately trained workforce with continuous training is desirable. There must be good compatibility between the buyer's management culture and the supplier's. The buyer's company brand image must be maintained and promoted.

2. *Process*. A key factor in the service sector is the delivery of the service in accord with the buyer's specification. A well-designed method of delivery is essential. Different cultures have different standards. Moreover, when outsourcing in a global environment there must be benchmark standards to maintain customs satisfaction. Adequate monitoring and control systems including some form of audit must be put in place. Transparency of communication between the supplier and buyer must be available at all times. The processing system must be computer focused.

3. *Physical aspects*. A range of physical features exist regarding the appearance of the delivery location. The buyer company's corporate identity must be maintained. Uniformity of standards is another key area as these may vary between locations. The total service cost will also vary to reflect currency variations and the political and economic environment.

The foregoing elements must be reflected in the selection criteria of the service supplier and contract formulation.

To conclude our analysis of the product specification it is important to bear in mind that there is a cost and innovation focus.

National and international standards

In Chapter 2 we examined national and international standards in depth. This included BSI, ISO and EU regulations. This chapter will focus on the importance of the buyer becoming familiar with and understanding the relevant national and international standards from the buyer's negotiating standpoint and the methodology recommended.

1. Buyers who source overseas and have requirements which involve detailed technical specifications and who wish to eliminate both financial and technical risk and uncertainty should use the services of the British Standards Institution. Whenever overseas suppliers are asked to quote for technical products, the identification of the relevant standards, approvals and regulations, the meeting of consumer association requirements and the comparison between foreign and domestic and/or supranational standards, where they exist, should be done by an expert.

2. Trade Association membership enables the buyer to keep up-to-date with the on going changes in national and international standards. The buyer's company should have an executive responsible for standards compliance. This position should oversee not only the domestic market but also those markets served overseas including goods bought overseas – components and materials – and re-exported. Sources of data include the Department of Trade and Industry, Embassies and Consulates, National Chambers of Commerce and the EU.

3. The International Chamber of Commerce (ICC) is another research source for standards and also for a wide range of international business activities.

4. As mentioned on page 24 the International Standardization Organization is the largest international organization for industrial and technical collaboration and standards. It produces a wide range of publications and operates through its member bodies in 135 countries. Readers are urged to contact the ISO via e-mail: central@iso.ch or on their website www http://www.iso.ch/ for further data, advice and list of publications.

   The range of ISO activity is vast and is channelled through their technical committees, which are extensive. Further details can be found in Appendix C.

5. The United Kingdom national and international standards organization is the British Standards Institute (BSI). It produces a wide range of specialist publications. As with the ISO, a multitude of areas are covered, including construction; engineering and automotive; electrical and electronic; gas and pressure equipment; environment and health and safety; quality and management and miscellaneous titles. Readers are urged to contact the BSI via e-mail: info@bsi.org.uk or on their website: www.bsi.org.uk

6. A wide range of international standardizing bodies exist and these include the following – all of them having dedicated websites. Co-operation Centre for Scientific Research relative to Tobacco, Intergovernmental Organization for International Carriage by Rail, International Air Transport Association,

International Association for Cereal Science and Technology, International Atomic Energy Agency, International Bureau for the Standardization of Man-made Fibres, International Bureau of Weights and Measures, International Civil Aviation Organization, International Commission for Uniform Methods of Sugar Analysis, International Commission on Illumination, International Commission on Irrigation and Drainage, International Commission on Radiation Units and Measurements, International Commission on Radiological Protection, International Council for Research and Innovation in Building and Construction, International Council for Standardisation in Haematology, International Council on Combustion Engines, International Dairy Federation, International Federation for Information and Documentation, International Federation for Structural Concrete, International Federation of Fruit Juice Producers, International Federation of Library Associations and Institutions, International Federation of Organic Agriculture Movements, International Gas Union, International Institute of Refrigeration, International Institute of Welding, International Labour Organisation, International Maritime Organisation, International Office of Epizootics, International Olive Oil Council, International Organisation of Legal Meteorology, International Seed Testing Association, International Silk Association, International Telecommunication Union – Radiocommunication Sector, International Telecommunication Union – Telecommunication Standardisation Sector, International Union of Leather Technologists and Chemists Societies, International Union of Pure and Applied Chemistry, International Union of Railways, International Union of Testing and Research Laboratories for Materials and Structures, International Vine and Wine Office, International Wool Textile Organisation, United Nations Education, Scientific and Cultural Organisation, World Customs Organisation, World Dental Federation, World Health Organisation, World Intellectual Property Organisation, World Meteorological Organisation.

To conclude our insight into national and international standards, it must be stressed that adequate research is required to ensure the correct specification is formulated. Contact with any of the foregoing organizations will elicit information on not only the current regulations but also those under consideration for future accreditation. The best contact is your local standard institute and/or the ISO website.

Sourcing of products

Product sourcing looks at overseas purchasing from an overall strategic level. It may be at the international, regional or global level.

The rationale of adopting a foreign buy in the procurement of materials or services has been explained in Chapter 1. A major consideration is the inability of the domestic market to supply the specific goods within the buyer's criteria.

Recent surveys identified the following reasons for buying overseas: lower price, better quality, only source available, advanced technology, consistent attitude, cooperative delivery, counter trade requirements and provision of the materials beyond the supplier's capabilities. A major factor is technology and maintaining the buyer's brand image. The key factor is for the buyer to remain or to become competitive.

Buying overseas will not necessarily produce optimum solutions in an international or global market. Other factors contributing to a company's international success include the development of an innovative product technology, the ability to move from concept to market in reduced time, world class quality levels and achieving a position near to being the lowest cost producer.

To these ends, the procurement officer will endeavour to develop supply chains throughout the world and in so doing source products which add value to the product and its sales potential. An intermediate choice may be related to the choice of one or more of the key regional blocs as the focus for the main activities.

An example is EU sourcing. Buyers situated in the EU are free to purchase goods or services within the EU with the following benefits. It is a single market with a euro brand, no customs import duty, free circulation of goods, common specification, one currency in the euro zone, good infrastructure, political stability, no trade barriers, freedom of capital flows and a very wealthy market with over 60 per cent of trade being trans European. A European manufacturer might use one of a number of strategies: source with a EU supplier who is part of a global network; source with a foreign supplier who supplies to a foreign part of the global network; source with a foreign supplier who has EU support for example R&D or maintain support for R&D in a foreign country and source there.

The buyer's market sourcing criteria selection (see page 95) would embrace company objectives and strategy, product availability and accreditation, legal and political constraints, political and economic stability, culture, the buyer's experience in the market, any long-term development in the market company management culture, membership of any economic trading bloc or customs union – ASEAN, NAFTA, EU – whether the market is open or closed, degree of infrastructure, whether international distribution is developed or underdeveloped – homogeneous or heterogeneous – whether it is a near or distant market and the total landed price.

International sourcing involves operating on a country by country basis. It evaluates countries on an individual basis and not within the context of an overall global sourcing plan. Hence, the company operates in a number of countries and adjusts its products in each at high relative cost. Much buying business is undertaken in this manner.

Regional sourcing is where a buyer sources a particular group of countries such as the EU or NAFTA. This tendency is on the increase as trading blocs and customs unions form bilateral trading agreements eliminating any trade barriers and offering preferential customs tariffs. The procurement executive should examine this sourcing resource, as substantial cost benefits many accrue.

Global sourcing looks at international purchasing from an overall strategic level. Hence, instead of the requirements of one country or plant being considered in sourcing terms as under an international purchasing practice, all plants in all countries within the firm have their requirements coordinated across the globe. The buyer has to search for commonality of requirement and achieve the best available globally to satisfy the objectives of purchasing. The global corporation operates with a resolute certainty – at low relative cost – as if the entire world – or major regions of it – were a single entity; it sells a broadly identical product globally.

Global sourcing may start with a regional focus, for example in the Americas, Europe or the Pacific Rim, and subsequently developed on the following basis:

(a) by selecting global locations for manufacturing/support operations;
(b) by developing a supply base with a corresponding global network;
(c) by developing a local supply arrangement in each location with the ability to cross trade to supply niche requirements.

Global sourcing involves integration and coordination in two respects – the internationalization of purchasing activities and the adoption of a strategic orientation for all resource management. The aim of global sourcing is to utilize purchasing potential on the worldwide level.

Global sourcing is a critical factor in a variety of competitive strategies in the following ways:

(a) supporting a global strategy by realizing economies of scale through material inputs;
(b) supporting a multinational strategy by developing potentials for differentiation and by having an active influence on quality standards;
(c) supporting a strategy concerning the general improvement of input–output relations.

Global sourcing is a growing market for a variety of reasons, as described on pages 80–4. It is logistically driven. Overall there are five stages in the progression from domestic purchasing to global procurement:

1. Stage I Domestic – domestic purchasing only.
2. Stage II Foreign buying – business units use subsidiaries or other corporate units for international sourcing assistance. It responds to a reactive strategy in common with stage I. A foreign-based subsidiary can perform a variety of functions for the domestic firm. Some of the advantages to the parent company include: knowledge of local suppliers by foreign unit; proximity to foreign suppliers; knowledge of foreign business practices and better communication skills with non-English speaking suppliers.
3. Stage III International purchasing offices established throughout the world – This involves the establishment of international purchasing offices which are usually staffed by foreign nationals reporting to a corporate procurement

office. The international purchasing office's functions include identification of foreign suppliers for company operations; tracing shipments; negotiating supply contracts; ensuring that the buyer and seller understand all communications; obtaining samples; managing technical samples; acting as the sole representative of the firm to the supplier; managing counter trade; obtaining design and engineering support and providing that a quality focus adopts a proactive strategy.

4. Stage IV Assign, design, build and sourcing responsibility to a specific business unit somewhere in the world – This strategy recognizes that within a firm one unit may have a comparative advantage in technology, manufacturing or distribution.

5. Stage V Integration and coordination of the worldwide global sourcing strategy – This involves the integration and coordination of a firm's procurement requirements. Its main objective is to maximize the buying leverage of the firm on a global basis. Business units must be committed to using common worldwide sources of supply to achieve maximum procurement benefits.

Global sourcing has become a prerequisite to competing in today's marketplace. Lower costs are no longer the only benefit of global sourcing. Many firms are finding that the pay-off increasingly comes from the availability, uniqueness and quality which adds value to the product and improves competitiveness. Global sourcing offers the potential for a lasting advantage in supremacy, penetration of growth markets and high speed.

If a firm is to achieve maximum benefit from the global coordination of procurement requirements, it must have the proper organizational structure and the commitment by management to overcome any entrenched attitudes within the firm. It must be logistically focused – see Chapter 4.

Source location and evaluation

Buying in an acceptable overseas market is a crucial decision to be taken by the procurement executive. It involves various stages which we will now examine.

1. Defining the problem. It is important that the salient requirements of the market and supplier are evaluated by the company, involving all its departments. This embraces not only the product specification but also funding market access, political stability, short- and long-term prospects, total cost, membership of any trading blocs or customs unions, visits to the market, culture, infrastructure exchange rate stability, near or distant market and total cost.

2. The next stage, as outlined in Chapter 2, is to undertake both desk and field research to answer the points raised in item (1). A visit to the supplier's website and studying country reports, such as those issued by Barclays Bank, will contribute to the evaluation. Attending trade fairs also produces good

input. Many overseas buyers use the services of Dun and Bradstreet, who monitor country risk. This company produces a monthly review on international risk and payment covering 131 countries. Additionally, it publishes 60-page country reports embracing political, economic and commercial data analysis, including changes in business risk and a detailed forecast of the country's prospects in the short- to medium-term. Visit their website at www.dunandbrad.co.uk

Key points which need close examination are as follows:

1. Trading relations with the country – long- and short-term.
2. Near markets are easier to visit and control than distant markets. Many buyers prefer to visit the supplier's production plant and discuss their particular product and see at first hand production methods and technology. Visits develop empathy and improve culture relations as well as the quality and reliability of delivery.
3. Logistically focused and computer literate markets are much favoured by the discerning buyer.
4. The country infrastructure is important. This favours developed countries in particular where goods move quickly and efficiently via a dedicated supply chain, thereby exploiting the benefits of logistics. This is particularly relevant to the hub and spoke mega container service, air freight movement, overland trucking or to airport, seaport, ICD and transit security.
5. The degree of flexibility in the market. This is embodied in its culture and response to product change and order flow, the resources available in the country to cope with increased business and whether the country is highly regulated – as in many EU states – or deregulated – as in the USA. The more regulated a country the more difficult it becomes to respond to trade opportunities.
6. Topographical features require examination in terms of channels of distribution and their impact on the supplier's product availability and reliability.
7. Financial arrangements and risk factors. The procurement officer requires a zero failure rate and quality product sourcing within the agreed logistic programmed time scale.
8. How does the country fit in with the buyer's overall global sourcing plan especially bearing in mind the criteria laid down? This is very relevant to global sourcing.
9. What are the country's main commodities and what is the country's global market share?
10. Which other buyers use the market and what is their experience of and reason for doing so?
11. The relative level of inwards and indigenous investment. Investment signifies confidence in a country and usually focuses on modernization and development.

12. Membership of an economic bloc or customs union, and/or international agencies such as WTO does encourage trade and conformity to a code of practice and international recognition.
13. High tech communication systems are essential, for example e-commerce, satellite communication, Internet and on-line computer technology.
14. Five-year economic plans feature in many countries' economic management and can indicate the way the country is moving.
15. Economic and financial reports by the OECD and the IMF and any constraints imposed on government's management of the economy.
16. Any guidance given by the Embassy/Consulate or the Foreign and Commonwealth Office.
17. Trade magazines and media data.

The foregoing analysis should not be regarded as exhaustive as different products require varying levels of emphasis on the selection criteria evaluation.

The next stage is to produce a short list of three country sources for discussion and decide on a preferred market and proceed accordingly. The task of company and country source selection tends to be conducted simultaneously.

In the long term the buyer must keep a range of markets under continuous review. The buyer's priority is to buy in those countries which produce the most value added benefit to the end user at a competitive price.

Tendering

Tendering represents an important part of the international purchasing process. A tender is an offer to sell at the price indicated and can be converted into a contract by acceptance in the form of the buyer's order. A quotation – or quote – is merely an invitation to treat, an indication of the price or conditions under which the supplier would be prepared to sell if somebody made him an offer. Following a quotation, the buyer makes an offer by placing an order, and the acceptance of this order by the supplier brings a contract into existence.

The buyer when inviting overseas suppliers to tender must bear in mind the following:

(a) the invitation must reflect the buyer's company strategy and objectives;
(b) compliance with national and international standards must be an essential part of the supplier's tenders;
(c) suppliers must ideally have quality management assurance and have the appropriate accreditation (BSI, LRQA, ISO 9000, EN 29000);
(d) the invitation must comply with any government or international regulations and conventions – code of practice – constraints;
(e) the invitation to tender must have an input from all departments not only in product specification, but also in distribution and payment terms – for example, which method of payment is preferred: documentary credits, bills

of exchange, open account (see page 142); which currency (Euro, USD), and whether either is the buyer's or seller's currency (see page 151); which Incoterm 2000: FCA, CIP or DDP (see page 285);

(f) other factors in the tender invitation include: use of the metric system; time scale of tender submission; training and manual input; guarantees/warranties; technology; time scale of delivery and any areas subject to negotiations.

The foregoing list should not be regarded as exhaustive. Much depends on the product and whether it is consumer or industrial or alternatively whether it concerns the service sector. The following is a general specification for an invitation to tender:

(a) title of specification;
(b) list of contents;
(c) foreword;
(d) description of specification;
(e) function and role of specification, i.e. medical;
(f) terminology, abbreviations, pictograms;
(g) reference to related accredited document BSI, ISO;
(h) any drawings;
(i) materials, properties, tolerances and samples;
(j) texture and finish;
(k) safety provision;
(l) training provision;
(m) warranty.

Today it is a prerequisite for the overseas buyer to select only those companies which have Total Quality Management accreditation. Therefore, companies without TQM accreditation (see page 185) are unlikely to survive in a competitive environment. Basically TQM establishes a set of guidelines for the professional management of any commercial venture. It is geared primarily towards the manufacturing industries but includes the service sector. Its objective is a reliable and consistent assurance of quality emerging from a well structured run company. The company is subject to annual inspection compliance, otherwise the accreditation lapses.

A number of approved companies can offer inspection, verification and issuance of the quality registration. These include BSI, Bureau Veritus Quality International (BVQI) and Lloyd's Register Quality Assurance Ltd (LRQA). BSI, BVQI and LRQA all comply with the International Standard, ISO 9000 and European Standard, EN 29000.

The management of quality standards globally embraces both the manufacturing and the service sector. We will examine the manufacturing sector by first taking the example of a major accreditation company, Lloyd's Register Quality Assurance Ltd (LRQA).

Quality management systems (QMS) enables a company to maximize resources while minimizing waste. Quality is a fluid concept, difficult to define and hard to measure, largely because it is so subjective. Lloyd's Register Quality Assurance is one of the world's most experienced companies in helping organizations worldwide to ISO 9000 certification. It is an accredited certification body. Certification is realized through the installation of quality management systems which not only improves efficiency but also greatly enhances status and customer.

An analysis of the benefits of quality management systems embraces the following:

(a) *Internal benefits*: improves management efficiency, planning, problem solving, supplier control, communications, ability to change, discipline and staff morale.
(b) *Internal benefits*: reduces duplicate effort, rework, waste, costs and staff turnover.
(c) *External benefits*: improves product and service, quality, customer satisfaction, repeat sales and company image.
(d) *External benefits*: reduces complaints and warranty claims.

Rapidly developing technology, increasing domestic and international competition, legislative demands and the sheer speed of economic change have resulted in a growing demand for quality management systems.

The methodology adopted by LRQA to gain ISO 9000 accreditation is as follows. It also embraces Environmental Management Systems (EMS) which comply with the international environmental management systems standard ISO 14001 or the European ECO – Management and Audit Scheme EMAS Regulation.

1. The company submits an application form specifying the nature of the business and the activities which support it. Subsequently a price is quoted, contract executed and a specific assessor from LRQA appointed.
2. The content of the documentation is analysed, reviewed and assessed; subsequently any problem areas are identified and remedied by the company. Ultimately, a mutually agreed visit schedule is agreed.
3. An in-depth document review is undertaken to ensure that a sound quality system exists on paper. It is the implementation of this system which demonstrates the company's commitment to quality. The LRQA assessors will observe the system in action and conduct any informal interviews and examinations to establish conformity with the standard.
4. On completion of the assessment, LRQA will issue a comprehensive report which will bring all aspects of the audit into perspective. This constructive overview of the company's performance details the parts of the standard which have been satisfactorily addressed and identifies areas of system deficiency or non-compliance.
5. On completion of a successful assessment, LRQA will issue a certificate of approval. It details the scope of the approval and is valid for three years subject to satisfactory maintenance of the company's quality system.

6. The system on approval is usually monitored by the LRQA at six monthly intervals. Such surveillance visits are conducted to ensure the system continues to meet the requirements of the standard and is modified to reflect any changes in the business environment.

7. The approval certificate is subject to renewal every three years when a reassessment is carried out by LRQA. This is more demanding than surveillance visits. The extent of the reassessment is determined by the Company's track record and the system maturity. Confirmation is sought that the system has not deteriorated and that all individual parts still link coherently. The visit is designed to give the Company and its customers every confidence that the company continues to meet the highest quality standards.

The LRQA covers quality assessments in: construction, paper, business services, power, food, the automotive industries, mining, quarrying, general engineering, nuclear, electronics, chemicals, oil/gas (onshore and offshore) and transportation.

For the service sector we will consider the BIS 5750 accreditation which falls into three parts. Part II is given below because of its relevance to service industries and complies with EN 29000 and ISO 9000.

(a) Clear policies and strategies to ensure quality, well-defined operational and service standards.

(b) A structured and effective management organization with specific allocation of responsibility for all aspects of quality management.

(c) A documented quality system and operational procedures.

(d) Specified methods of understanding and recording customers' service requirements and certification that those needs have been met.

(e) Timely and precise control of all documentation including procedures, standard forms, paper work systems and software. This to include the relevant communication of all revisions and amendments.

(f) Knowledge of the quality level of suppliers and evidence that this is taken into account in purchasing decisions.

(g) Establishing routines for work planning and for the execution of the basic administrative and legislative systems of the business.

(h) Management controls, performance measurement and corrective action.

(i) Clear plans and procedures for the identification and rectification of mistakes, deficiencies and causes of customer complaints.

(j) A code of conduct to cover product handling, packaging, transportation and storage whenever these activities are performed within the company.

(k) Pre-planned and structured senior management reviews of the major aspects of the quality system supported by formal routine auditing of all operational practices and procedures.

(l) Appropriately experienced and trained personnel.

(m) Records to demonstrate consistent compliance with the foregoing issues.

It must be recognized that a large volume of smaller contracts emerge from the buyer in the form of a general enquiry regarding the availability price EXW/CIP and delivery of a particular product. It may be spares, items for resale or a product batch.

For the larger contract, maybe involving a consortia, a tender system is adopted. This obtains in the public procurement business. The tender price is delivered in a sealed envelope to the principal – the buyer – and opened on a specific day. Usually the lowest tender is awarded the contract. This form of tendering is common for contracts such as railway rolling stock, ship machinery, interior design on a cruise liner, defence or medical equipment in a new hospital. The contract may span several years, have a clause relating to penalties for delays, to performance bond criteria or price indexation; it may involve staged payments which continue beyond the delivery date and have a turnkey feature. This might involve not only building a hospital but also recruiting medical staff to run and operate it for a specified period until a local workforce can take over the management. Larger contracts can also involve project forwarding.

Supplier audit

The task of analysing a supplier's creditability and a related quotation is a crucial one. Many data banks have company data with which the buyer is urged to comply. Examination of a company's annual report and its membership of trade associations can also provide useful lines of enquiry. A visit to the country to discuss potential business opportunities among a range of potential suppliers can be productive. The buyer can check out a company's credentials at any trade fair. Accreditation with ISO 9000 or EN 9000 also produces positive signs. Many buyers check out previous clients of the supplier to evaluate their management culture, adherence to contract terms, any disputes or late deliveries and general, overall performance.

A keen analytical attitude should also be taken to evaluate the supplier's quotation. It must be borne in mind that an invitation to tender does not guarantee that a particular supplier will respond. This may be for a variety of reasons, for example a full order book, required product no longer being manufactured, etc. However, it is usual for the buyer (or his or her agent) to provide some form of explanation to maintain good relations for any future business.

The simplest approach to the comparison of quotations and tenders is to establish that the supplier is reliable and that the operational requirement of the transaction, such as quality and delivery, is sustainable. This involves production capacity, professional skilled labour resources, high tech equipment, delivery time scale, transportation arrangements, total quality management accreditation, product quality compliance with national and international standards, any comparison with previous buyers and compliance with an international logistic plan, the method of payment and Incoterm used (see page 290). A visit to the supplier's premises and a study of the company's annual report will assist in many of these areas.

Detailed analysis of quotations and prices from abroad should always be closely examined and considered otherwise the opportunity presented by the supplier may be misunderstood. For example, the supplier may operate a different accounting system of plant depreciation and special tooling amortization. This may look uncompetitive at first sight, but, when analysed, may in fact offer advantages to the buyer.

A cost comparison is relatively simple when based on EXW, CIP or DDP (see page 288) price exchange rates. But many sourcing decisions involve commitments over a long period of time. In these cases the buyer will need to assess all the current overseas sources available and make a forecast of how the situation might change over time. Two factors, beyond the control of both the buyer and the seller are exchange rates and inflation which will affect both parties differently. The buyer may adopt a variety of measures to counter exchange rate and inflationary fluctuations, as detailed below.

1. Examine economic forecasts and country reports available from Barclays Bank, EIU, OECD and the EU. These also feature currency movements.
2. Exchange rate fluctuations: when buying goods in the seller's or a third currency, a currency risk arises from the fluctuations in the exchange rate in the period between prices being agreed and payment being received. Management of this exposure is essential to minimize the potential risks and maximize the profit from the underlying transactions. The technique of protecting against future exchange rate movements is called 'hedging'. The forward contract is one of the simplest hedging techniques allowing the buyer to fix the exchange rate for the purchase of a specific quantity of a currency for delivery at an agreed future date. It is a legally binding contract between the bank and the buyer, a bank credit line is required to cover the amount and period of all forward contracts at any one time. The period of a forward contract can range from one day after spot value up to five years depending on the currencies involved. Maturity of the contract can be arranged either for settlement on a specific date (fixed contract) or on or between two dates (option-dated contract) where the precise delivery date is not known. The key benefit from a forward contract is that the buyer knows in advance the exact value of future transactions in domestic currency terms. This will assist with cash flow management, budgeting, costing and pricing processes. (Other currency options exist, see page 154.)

The payment method options to be adopted by the buyer are fully explained in Chapter 8. However, settlement by documentary credit demonstrates that the seller is creditworthy, offers financial benefits to the seller which may enable the buyer to negotiate price discounts or other improved terms such as an extended trade credit. In addition, payment need only be made if the documents presented conform to the buyer's requirement, such as the pre-shipment inspection procedure (see page 177), and the buyer can manage and control the transit through document definitions and through stipulated conditions such as a 'shipped on board clean bill of lading' (see page 165). This requires the advising, or confirming, bank to process the payment only when the goods have been placed on board the vessel and the shipping company has issued a clean on board shipped bill of lading.

The buyer may also wish to have a tender guarantee, which is a document to support an initial bidder tender for a contract. Another guarantee is the performance guarantee which covers failure to fulfil contractual obligations.

The supplier audit will vary by circumstances and the focus must always be on the company's creditability, ability to deliver the contract and an analysis of their quotation.

Finally, associated with an examination of suppliers quotation is a necessity to understand the pricing strategy and interaction of the demand/supply market structure. A range of options exist and these are detailed below.

(a) Competitor oriented pricing. This focuses on the competitor's pricing structure with a view to gaining a price advantage in the marketplace and thereby win market share and increased sales.
(b) Tender price – see page 97.
(c) Cost oriented pricing. This focuses on the product cost in the formulation of the price in the marketplace. It favours the volume market, as the greater the volume of sales, the lower the unit cost, thereby permitting lower prices with increased market share penetration.
(d) Demand oriented pricing. The price is set at a level which will generate increased demand and gain long-term market share and increased sales volume.
(e) Market penetration pricing. Process of conducting a pricing strategy which will penetrate the market and thereby increase sales and/or market share.
(f) Market skimming pricing. To price a product/service at a level which will generate adequate income to fund the production investment outlay over a relatively short time scale.
(g) Satisfactory rate of return. To set a price which will achieve a specific level of return on investment.
(h) Differential pricing. To price a product/service at a level which is different in various regions or areas of the market.

The interaction of demand and supply involves different market structures. On the supply side, four types of market structures exist:

(a) *Monopolistic competition* – it features a high degree of production and each supplier endeavours to make his or her product stand out in order to create a monopoly situation.
(b) *Monopoly* – the existence of only one supplier of the product in the marketplace.
(c) *Oligopoly* – obtains when a limited number of suppliers exists and a limited product differentiation exists.

(d) *Pure competition* – reflects a transparent marketplace where the supplier and buyer have equal bargaining power in price determination. A good example is the commodity market (see page 61).

In contrast the demand structure has three types of market:

(a) *Monopsony* – where only one buyer exists and many suppliers are available from which to choose.
(b) *Oligopsony* – arises where there are a few buyers and many suppliers.
(c) *Pure competition* – identical to item (d) above.

Costing has been examined on pages 223–6 but for ease of reference we reiterate the elements which comprise the seller's or exporter's price.

(a) cost of the product;
(b) export overheads including export documentation and bank charges;
(c) packing and marking;
(d) transport costs to ICD, airport or seaport;
(e) export documentation;
(f) customs clearance – export;
(g) port handling charges – departure port;
(h) forwarding agent's commission;
(i) exporter's profit mark up;
(j) insurance cargo;
(k) air or sea freight;
(l) port handling charges – arrival port;
(m) forwarding agent's commission;
(n) import duty;
(o) VAT;
(p) customs clearance – import;
(q) warehouse charges;
(r) transport cost to buyer's premises.

The inclusion of all these elements will be determined by the Incoterm 2000 used (pages 287–302).

Finally it is important that the overseas buyer is aware of two ICC model contracts embracing the International Sale Contract and Occasional Intermediary Contract.

The ICC Model International Sale Contract is a guide for traders, importers and all parties involved in these important transactions. It provides directions to sellers and buyers of manufactured goods. The contract is divided into two parts: Specific Conditions and General Conditions.

The model contract was specifically developed for sales of manufactured goods intended for resale where the purchaser is not a consumer and where the contract is an independent transaction rather than part of a long-term supply arrangement. The ICC model is flexible enough to allow users either to incorporate only the general conditions common to all contracts, or to include the specific conditions which set out standard terms common to all contracts incorporating the ICC General Conditions of Sale. Moreover, while the model contract subjects the transaction to the United Nations Convention for the International Sale of Goods (CISG) Vienna Convention; it also, in certain circumstances, permits the parties to incorporate specific conditions of national law.

The ICC model Occasional Intermediary Contract provides guidance from all parties involved in intermediary transactions. The contract provides a unique and balanced legal platform that takes into account the interest of all parties involved in a non-circumvention and non-disclosure agreement. It also minimizes the risk of fraud and misunderstanding. The occasional intermediary, unlike the Agent, undertakes to provide certain services to the parties without any continuing obligation to develop the market. The contract sets out special conditions to define the terms that are specific to this kind of contract; the general conditions common to all transactions incorporating the ICC General Conditions for Non-circumvention and Non-disclosure agreements; defines the services to be provided by the intermediary; describes the exclusive rights of the intermediary and clarifies the intermediary undertaking not to compete.

The overseas market

A critical aspect in buying overseas is to visit the overseas market to identify or audit potential sellers. A strategic focus is required, incorporating a plan and stated objectives. Such visits must be included in the buyer's budget. In addition to their evaluative function, visits allow empathy to be developed with the exporter. It also provides opportunities for both the buyer and seller to keep in touch with market developments, embrace new technology, consider the competition, standards, legislation and consumer or industrial needs and behaviour. Overall, it bridges the two cultures and represents a form of research and intelligence gathering and provides the buyer with an opportunity to see the manufacturing process at first hand and meet the personnel in the commercial/industrial environment. It is likely that such a visit may arise from an invitation from the seller to visit the place of manufacture and discuss mutual business opportunities.

The rationale for the buyer's overseas visit may be for any of the following purposes.

(a) To attend a trade exhibition to find suitable suppliers.
(b) To feature in an outwards trade mission arranged by government, trade association or chamber of commerce to meet potential exporters.
(c) To see existing exporters and seek out new ones.
(d) To appoint an import agent and freight forwarder in the seller's country.
(e) To evaluate the market opportunities of potential sellers.
(f) To negotiate a contract.

(g) To formulate a joint venture.

(h) To attend a sales, trade conference or seminar.

(i) To view or buy property – hotels, land or residential and industrial or commodity sales and auction houses.

(j) To accept an invitation from the seller to discuss business opportunities.

The key to any overseas visit is pre-planning and adequate research of the market, its culture and protocol. Ideally buyers visiting the market for the first time should have a culture briefing (page 34). Buyers conducting their negotiations in the seller's language present a favourable image in negotiations and smooth the way to benefiting from potential business opportunities. Undertaking this kind of commitment develops the culture and business synergy which are essential in the global business environment.

Sales over the Internet are growing internationally at a rapid rate. E-commerce may produce massive growth in on-line sales. This may have an impact on reducing the growth of overseas visits as more business is done on the Web. Companies doing business on-line are confronted with a number of problems, such as orders that fail to be delivered and products put up for auction which violate social standards. The overseas visit can lessen such risk together with many other risk areas associated with the Web including company audit.

The following points are essential in planning an overseas visit.

(a) Formulate an itinerary and involve the sellers or clients closely in the schedule. Take advice on the time scale of the visit and allow time for flight delays and prolonged negotiations.

(b) If the buyer is responding to an invitation, respect the itinerary and hospitality emphasis and respond with a suitable level of entertainment and an appropriate gift. Advice should be sought if there is any doubt about what would be suitable.

(c) Conduct in-house meetings prior to and following the overseas trip. Focus particularly on product specification (page 15), import customs duty (page 264), transportation (page 232) and funding arrangements (page 126). Identify the object of the visit and conduct an audit of potential sellers such as annual reports, recent orders, risk areas as well as company structure and senior management. It is important that the buyer has appointments with key personnel in the company that is with decision makers and not with influencers.

(d) At an early stage, book flights and other travel arrangements with some degree of flexibility. Also check visa and passport requirements.

(e) Ensure that details of next kin and the itinerary plan are deposited with key personnel in the company including telephone, facsimile, website, e-commerce and m-commerce details.

(f) Hotels should be of four or five star grade and have adequate secretarial resources.

(g) The dress code should be appropriate for both business engagements and entertainment or leisure. The buyer should not engage in business dialogue during leisure engagements.

(h) Business cards, which should be double sided, reflecting both the buyer's and seller's language should be presented. Observe any protocol as found in the Japanese culture (see page 38).

(i) The buyer and his or her team must be fully briefed for the visit. A strategic negotiating plan should be devised for each visit in order to present a strong negotiating position embracing all the contractual elements (see chapter 7).

(j) The executives must be skilled in negotiation and able to prioritize key objectives.

(k) Market research is a key aspect of a successful trip. Conducting negotiations in different cultures is a challenging task and guidance can be sought by contacting other buyers who have experience of the overseas market. Also contacting the seller's overseas Embassy, Commercial Attaché, High Commissioner or Consulate may elicit some guidance or even extend to identifying suitable suppliers.

(l) The supplier's company culture must embrace logistics and computer technology.

The above list must not be regarded as exhaustive as each visit will vary, but the key to a successful trip is adequate preparation and realistic objectives. Each trip must be tailor-made to the culture, country, company and product. On return, the buyer must produce a report and circulate it to the relevant personnel and departments and conduct a debriefing meeting. An action plan should then be prepared and controlled to ensure adequate preparation.

Recommended reading

- *Purchasing Management* – A.J. Van Weele – Thomson Learning.
- *Shipping and Air Freight Documentation for Importers and Exporters* – Alan Branch – 2nd edition – Witherby & Co Ltd.
- ISO publications.
- BSI publications.
- OECD country reports/analyses.
- *The Merchants Guide 2000 edition* – P&O Nedlloyd publication.
- Barclays Bank country reports.
- Lloyd's Register Quality Assurance *Review* – monthly magazine.
- The ICC Model International Sale Contract – Manufactured goods intended for resale – ICC publication No. 556.
- The ICC Model occasional intermediary contract – non-circumvention and non-disclosure agreement – ICC publication No. 619.

7

Negotiating the contract II

Digital trade revolution

It is appropriate that we start this chapter by focusing on the digital trade revolution. This relates to the electronic transmission of all documents and data between various elements of the international supply chain. Such communication is now well underway in many companies global as it speeds up the negotiation process and is conducive to developing quick decision making. Global communication is instantaneous, through the satellite voice and video network as described on page 109. Ultimately the digital network aims to eliminate paper-based administration that is used to sell or buy across international boundaries.

In September 1999 Bolero International devised and launched a new service: bolero-net. It involves an open commercial module, a unique legal framework and complete security. The system is designed to be an internationally accepted standard and the world business community will reap considerable benefits as a result of its introduction. Electronic commerce is revolutionizing the way in which we do business internationally and the legal implications therefrom.

Driving this phenomenal growth in e-commerce is a fairly simple strategic value proposition: electronic commerce opens up an economically more efficient way of running a business. When applied effectively, e-commerce enables an international business to reduce operating costs whilst also raising the quality of their operations.

The information technology (IT) behind e-commerce was entrenched in most businesses well before the present boom in e-commerce. Briefly the trends that have made a commercial medium out of computer networking are detailed below.

1. *Simple, standardized communications*. The popularization of the Internet and in particular the World Wide Web, has resulted in two all-purpose ways of communicating electronically – the interactive Web session and e-mail, both of which transfer information according to the lower-level Internet protocol. Ten years ago, countless alternative ways of communicating electronically

caused confusion and, because they were all different, every linkage had to be agreed, supplied with special software and set up in its own peculiar way. Today, all of the alternatives are rapidly converging to Web sessions and e-mail messages and the Internet protocol is often used even for closed networks that are not part of the Internet.

2. *Data and document integration.* Formerly, structured database type data and documents had little to do with each other. Now the Web has made it commonplace to find database data embedded in documents. The old EDI technology split the data out of its business and legal context into an inflexible and complex series of rigorously codified transaction sets, the implementation of which required much expensive programming and a value added network. The Web, and particularly its newly developed ability to embed data within documents through Extensible Markup Language (XML) has proved the feasibility of a simpler, less expensive and more effective way of doing transactions.

3. *Security through cryptography.* As digital networks become larger and involved ever more strangers, ensuring the authenticity and confidentiality of information became a greater problem. Cryptographic techniques, such as digital signatures and message encryption solve these problems. They ensure, to an even greater degree than comparable paper techniques, that a message has indeed been authenticated by its signatory, has not been altered since then and is not readable by parties not privy to it.

Together, these three trends lead to more flexibility and lower start-up costs to using e-commerce. They have coincided with increasing user friendliness and ease of use. Standard Internet style networking technology is now bundled into almost every computer operating system, and the know-how for making it work is widespread. Web, and particularly XML document processing technology, is available off the shelf with particular capabilities for extracting data embedded in documents and entering it into databases. Digital signatures and encryption eliminate the high cost of value added and are a substantial improvement over the rather modest security they provided.

Technologically, the essentials for realizing the value of electronic commerce are not only available but are already technologically mature; they have been in use for some years now, in business as well as academic and test-bed environments. What tends to be less clearly established are the legal issues of e-commerce.

The international framework of commercial law has assumed that transactions are done on paper. Sometimes it requires paper formalities such as writing on paper or an ink signature. A digitally signed electronic document is functionally equivalent or better than a signed paper document but the law does not recognize this fact.

The discipline of the law looks backwards in order to look forwards. It seeks precedents from the past to devise a way into the future. Past experience in developing global commercial systems offers two proven models.

1. *Treaties among all the sovereigns.* A manifest need for greater coordination or uniformity has sometimes led governmental representatives to confer and formulate a widely acceptable approach to resolve what they all recognize as their common problems. Developing a consensus among expert representatives from various legal cultures often takes time and enacting the representatives' proposals, if that even happens, takes more time. However, many international trade issues have been resolved in this way.

2. *Contract based approaches.* In recent decades, some of the most effective worldwide legal infrastructures have been based on contractually adopted systems of rules. Bank cards and bank clearing systems rely on contracts to establish the rules of the business system, often with an overlay of national regulatory law. The rapid, worldwide proliferation of these systems occurred in much less time than would be required for international consultation and treaty making.

In the shipping business, the most common method has been the harmonization of positive law through international consultation. The Hague–Visby Rules, for example (see pages 164, 237), a major cornerstone of international shipping law, were adopted by that method. However, more recent business and technological innovations, such as electronic fund transfers and bank card payment authorizations, have moved too quickly to wait for positive legal rulings like the Hague–Visby to catch up with them. Instead they have been based on contract infrastructures.

As the e-commerce revolution makes its way into the shipping world, contractual approaches to building the supporting legal infrastructure have the advantages of being fast and flexible. However, they are subject to an overlay of national mandatory law and possibly diverging local interpretations and applications that will need to be managed over time.

Nevertheless, the necessity of rapid change and responsiveness to both technological and market forces in present times practically forecloses the viability of coordinated legislation by all sovereigns as an option, at least in the early stages.

Addressing this requirement for rapid change and legal assurance, bolero-net has underpinned it services with the world's largest legal study ever to have been conducted into electronic commerce. Conducted in 18 different jurisdictions the aim of the study was to produce a set of rules that would allow 'a functional equivalence' between the electronic and paper worlds – that is it allows for legal results similar to those that business people would expect with a paper transaction.

The result is the bolero-net Rule Book. Bolero-net's most valuable piece of intellectual property, the Rule Book is a unique multi-party contract, which will bind every user, without exception.

It is certainly clear that the electronic commerce revolution is here. Like every revolution, it was born of economic and social forces that propelled it ahead of the established law, which struggled to keep up and adapt. By creatively drawing from experience and probably using flexible, managed contractual approaches, shipping and trade can move forward with a firm legal footing into the future.

Negotiating skills

The process of concluding a purchase overseas involves many skills and each situation varies by product/service; culture; competition; language; management culture and attitudes; infrastructure and environment in the seller's country; export regulations; protocol; political structure; and so on. Personal relationships, adequate research and planning and complete professionalism are all paramount considerations. Each situation requires a different strategy and adequate preparation is essential. Overall, the buyer must work towards an objective and the negotiating route to that objective will vary by product, service and country.

The following points should be borne in mind.

(a) A negotiating plan with an objective is essential. It must be flexible and focused on the objective.

(b) Preparation embraces a wide range of areas: product specification; quantity; delivery time scale; funding strategy; Incoterms 2000 to be used; currency to be specified and payment strategy.

(c) Research the infrastructure of the supplier's country; political stability and attitudes; economic indicators; protocol; and language.

(d) Research the supplier's company: the company structure, its organization, who the decision makers are; the R&D budget; annual report analysis; current and future investment levels and projects.

(e) Check out the basis and criteria of the country and supplier's selection – see item (h).

(f) Risk areas to be identified and measures needing to be taken to minimize such risk.

(g) Buyer's team and the leader. In major contracts this would include a legal representative based in the supplier's country. The contract terms (see page 114) will identify whether the contract will be governed by English law and the arbitration procedure. The ICC guidelines are usually adhered to (see page 124).

(h) The buyer leading the negotiation will need to formulate an agenda and should hold a meeting within the company to devise a negotiating strategy position on key areas.

This final point is most important, so we will now consider some of its aspects in more detail. It is likely that the supplier will have been in contact with the senior buyer and established a relationship. The buyer in such circumstances needs to respect the protocol, be positive and enthusiastic. Agreement needs to be reached whether the negotiations are held in the buyer's, the supplier's or a third country. Guidance in visiting an overseas market is found on pages 105–7. Lengthy negotiations held over a period of months may allow the venue to be alternated.

It is likely that during the supplier's selection process samples from the supplier will have been obtained. In some cases a short list of three may have been devised and each made a presentation, before the preferred supplier was selected. The presentation will have had a question and answer session to identify key areas of mutual interest or concern. A key factor in the selection process is being able to work with the supplier's management culture in a computer logistic environment. It is usually prudent for the buyer to become familiar with the country's history and its economic and political focus. Also, trade and political issues should be treated separately and the buyer must concentrate on trade throughout the visit. The supplier is usually appreciative of the buyer's knowledge of his or her country's history and its economic and social strata and well-being. Also, a buyer's ability to conduct the negotiations in the supplier's language or a third language is much appreciated as it avoids the use of interpreters which, in addition to being expensive, can prolong the negotiations and interfere with the free flow of the dialogue and discussion. Full use must be made of the e-mail and Internet.

The time scale of the buyer's negotiation will vary considerably and can extend from several days to, in extreme situations, 2 or 3 years. Usually the capital goods market takes much longer and involves more detailed negotiations extending to both buyers and technical personnel. In a free market economy (free of government controls) the time scale is shorter and there is less bureaucracy. Most countries are keen to sell their product/services as it develops their economy and improves their wealth and employment levels together with technical skills. China is a fast expanding economy keen to sell its goods. Counter trade (see page 148) still obtains in many countries with hard currency problems and the buyer can often negotiate favourable deals on the back of a counter trade transaction from the Indian subcontinent, China, the USSR, South America, a number of African states and former Eastern Bloc countries. The contract and bureaucracy may be complex. Another area is bi-lateral trade agreements which present favourable opportunities for buyers to do business.

It is appreciated that buying is a diverse activity and given below are a number of points to consider in buying negotiations – each situation, it is stressed, will vary by circumstances.

1. Points (a) to (h) in the previous list will be undertaken prior to the start of negotiations. All members of the buyer's negotiating team should be provided with a brief prepared in-house. All such personnel should have a business card for presentation, ideally double sided – one side in the buyer's commercial international language and one in the language of the seller.

2. Greet the seller with the appropriate culture of the overseas territory which in Thailand, for example, means putting one's hands together and bowing the head. Also, use the appropriate greeting in the seller's language. This quickly establishes a favourable relationship and confirms to the seller that his or her visitor has taken the time and trouble to learn something of the culture of the country. Such information can be obtained through a cultural briefing prior

to the buyer's departure. On arrival at the host's office, accept their hospitality with regard to their national customs, such as in the form of refreshment.

3. Establish a personal relationship with members of the seller's team. It is often customary to exchange gifts, as in Japan for instance. Enquire about their hobbies, interests and family backgrounds and do not be offended if you are asked about religion and other matters which might be considered inappropriate elsewhere, especially politics. Exchange views in a cordial and diplomatic manner and endeavour to understand the basis of the seller's views having regard to the cultural environment and political situation.

4. The sellers usually open the meeting, assuming they are the host, by discussing common ground – within the pre-agreed agenda content – and establishing what you all hope the talks will accomplish. Ideally points of contention should be considered when relations between the buyer and seller have been well established.

5. When negotiating in English in an overseas territory where English is not the first language, such as the Arab States, Japan, China, etc., do not assume that the person with the best command of English is the most important member of the team. Negotiators (buyers) who address comments to this person risk insulting more senior members who do not speak English. In social and business situations address the entire team.

6. Maintain a firm posture throughout the negotiations. Casual dress is unacceptable during negotiations. The buyer must be well groomed and neatly presented, with men wearing suits appropriate to the climatic conditions. Short-sleeved presentation is not usually acceptable. It is not common to use first names at the initial meeting. To do so later is acceptable when the friendship develops.

7. Be prepared for periods of silence at the meeting and do not be in a rush to fill the gap. Silence can be a sign that the supplier's team is considering an important point; it may also be a sign of respect.

8. If the buyer's question is met with silence or an evasive response, do not pursue the point immediately. Reflect on why the question got that response, reformulate it to avoid the sticking point and ask it later – maybe at the next meeting.

9. Start each session with a review of the main points agreed in the previous session. Debrief each member of the buyer's team after every session.

10. Be aware of the seller over-selling the product with excessive praise of the product or service. For example, Japanese buyers are likely to consider hard sell tactics or aggressive confrontational behaviour as bullish.

11. Communicate clearly and avoid using idioms.

12. If negotiations stall, try to find a third party who has had success with the seller's team and in so doing, endeavour to establish what can be done to break the deadlock.

13. Do not mix business with pleasure. When negotiating teams dine together or go out for a night on the town, do not discuss business items.
14. The final stage in the negotiations is for the exporter to close the sale when the deal has been finalized. To avoid ambiguity, it is good policy for the supplier to summarize the salient points embracing any areas of controversy. This gives the buyer the opportunity to challenge any areas or points of misinterpretation.

To expand on the aforementioned aspects, the following list should not be regarded as exhaustive but as containing some important considerations:

(a) As stressed earlier, adequate planning is essential.
(b) Be professional at all times. Ensure all members of the buyer's team are competent and have authority to take decisions at the meeting(s).
(c) A company portfolio of the supplier is essential.
(d) Develop the quality of perseverance and stress continuously the salient features of the product/service required, particularly the added value elements.
(e) An acceptable personality of team members is desirable, with a quality of diplomacy and an ability to get on with the supplier.
(f) Deal with unanswered questions effectively and professionally. The buyer may wish to have product samples to test consumer reactions or may recommend modifications which could take weeks. For example, in furniture this might concern the design, colour or size; for fabrics the quality, size or design, etc.
(g) Use e-commerce and the Internet for communication purposes.

Buyers are urged to study Chapter 3 (pages 37–42) on the Russian, Chinese, US, Malay and Japanese cultures and protocols when visiting these markets.

To conclude, successful negotiation is usually realized through the most thorough preparation and professionalism at all levels. The nature of the product/ service sought coupled with the market environment will be dominant factors.

Terms and conditions of the contract

The terms and conditions of contract are taken to include standard conditions of payment terms, transport and insurance. The basis of the export business is found in the composite export sales contract drawn up by the supplier and accepted by the buyer when the order is placed. Not only does the contract feature the product specification, penalty clauses, warranty conditions and time scale, but also the delivery arrangements. These include Incoterms 2000 (see page 287), and Uniform Customs and Practice for Documentary Credits ICC publication No. 500 covering the payment and delivery arrangements (see page 128) The Incoterms define the method of delivery of the goods by the exporter and indicate what charges are included in the price; and also define the responsibilities of the parties to the contract of sale for the arrangement of insurance, shipping and packaging.

The scale of the contract will reflect its complexity from very extensive to very brief. Buyers are urged to study the range of publications available from the ICC in contract formulation (see page 125).

The buyer is responsible for ensuring that the order is being processed in accord with the contract terms and may appoint an Agent to verify this at various stages of manufacture until final despatch under the pre-shipment inspection arrangements (see page 177). Ideally the buyer and supplier must develop a good relationship to ensure that any problems are quickly resolved to the mutual benefit of both parties. Full use should be made of e-commerce and satellite communication. The export sales contract terms are likely to comply with the supplier company strategy of conditions of sale and payment terms unless any variation emerges from the discussions between the buyer and seller.

The payment terms present a number of options (see chaper 8) and it is important that the appropriate funding arrangements are put in place by the buyer in liaison with his or her bank. The payment regulations are specified in the export sales contract and may embrace the Uniform Rules for Collection ICC Publication No. 522 (see page 140).

Transport arrangement may fall in to one of the following categories, embracing the conditions of carriage as specified.

(a) Air freight – involving the air waybill document. The international air carriage of goods is subject to either the Warsaw Convention 1929 or the amended Warsaw Convention 1955.

(b) CIM International Rail consignment note. The COTIF Convention concerning international carriage by rail was signed in Berne in May 1980. It was given legal effect in the UK by section 1 of the International Transport Convention Act 1983 with effect from May 1985.

(c) CMR International Road Haulage consignment note. The convention governing the international carriage of goods by road was signed in Geneva in 1956 and enacted into the laws of the UK by the Carriage of Goods by Road Act 1965.

(d) Combined Transport document. This embraces a range of situations which have not received international approval as follows:

  (i) ICC Rules for a Combined Transport Document. This includes at various stages of its development Tokyo–Rome Rules, Tokyo Rules and TCM convention.

  (ii) UNCTAD MMO Convention. This embraces the United Nations Convention on the International Multi-Modal Transport of Goods adopted in Geneva in May 1980. It relates to the Hamburg Rules.

  (iii) UNCTAD/ICC Rules for Multi-Modal Transport Documents. These have been developed by UNCTAD/ICC and are related to the Hague–Visby Rules.

(e) Bills of lading – sea transport. This involves the Hague Rules and Carriage of Goods by Sea Acts 1924, 1971 and 1992.

The cargo insurance conditions are found in the Marine Insurance Act 1906. The new Marine Policy form and new Institute Cargo clauses were introduced in January 1982 and superseded the SG (ship goods) form adopted by Lloyd's in January 1779.

The new Marine Policy form features Institute of Cargo clauses 'A', 'B' and 'C' each with different areas of protection and exclusion. Additional Institute sets of clauses cover war, strikes, coal, frozen meat and commodity trades.

The transport conditions of carriage and cargo insurance are examined in Chapter 11.

Costing the constituents

The overseas buyer's objective is to purchase products or services in accordance with the company's strategic objective. This usually means buying at a competitive price. Hence, the buyer, in evaluating the contract, must reflect on total cost. This embraces not only the price of the goods at the factory gate but also all the other costs reflected in the landed price. The costs incurred from the factory gate include not only the items on page 104 featuring transportation, import duty, cargo insurance, etc., but also banking charges to fund the transaction and the supplier organization's ability to deal with all the import documentation complexities and transportation from the seaport, airport or ICD.

Prior to examining the cost constituents we will briefly identify the various categories of costs:

(a) Fixed costs – these remain the same even when the volume of output changes.
(b) Variable costs – these vary as the volume of output changes.
(c) Direct costs – these costs are aligned to a particular activity such as producing a particular garment.
(d) Direct labour costs – those labour costs aligned to a particular activity.
(e) Direct material costs – materials, parts and components forming part of the product or provided in the service to the customer.
(f) Indirect labour costs – employees not engaged on the product or services supplied to the customer such as maintenance, administration, etc.
(g) Indirect materials – costs derived from, for example, stationery and cleaning materials.
(h) Indirect expenses – costs incurred such as insurance, rent and energy.

Direct costs can be charged or allocated in their entirety to the product sold to the customer. However, indirect costs are those items of total cost which cannot be immediately identified with the product going to customers and are usually allocated to these items on another basis, for example if a company manufactures four car models – model A, model B, model C and model D it may allocate indirect costs to each model in the proportions 20 per cent, 15 per cent, 25 per cent and 40 per cent respectively perhaps based on each model's sales as a proportion of total sales. The total of indirect costs is usually called overheads and the total of direct costs is called the prime cost.

When conducting negotiations with the supplier the buyer will have a plan and one challenging area of analysis is the basis of the price structure. The following points are relevant.

(a) The product may be componetized and represents imported assembled items which are later re-exported as the finished product. Such items qualify for inwards processing relief (see page 265).

(b) Is the product specially designed for the buyer or is it a standard item? Design costs, special materials and plant modifications will all increase costs. Standard items could have an off-the-shelf price or be available in the international catalogue.

(c) There may be fees arising from patents, royalties and hire charges.

(d) It is reasonable to assume the higher the volume bought, the lower the production cost per unit through economies of scale which will be passed on to the buyer? Benefits will also accrue in freight charges using the FCL rather than the LCL (see page 203).

(e) The price will include a percentage to cover administration, overseas visits and miscellaneous items such as credit insurance premiums.

(f) The payment arrangements are likely to cover 90 to 180 days compared with 30 days in the domestic market. Hence, the international payment cycle is longer and will have an adverse effect on the supplier's working capital. This can be mitigated by an advance payment on the export sales acceptance contract. Another way to alleviate this problem may be factoring (see page 150). Alternatively the supplier may opt for a bank loan, the cost of which will be reflected in the price.

(g) The goods may be bought through a third party such as an import agent. The price will reflect any commission earned by the agent from the sale.

(h) Currency fluctuation is a risk area and the supplier's finance department will reflect this in the price.

(i) The supplier may insist on selling on CIP terms (see pages 299–300). This may yield a benefit to the seller who can then obtain favourable contractual insurance premiums from the insurance broker and freight forwarder embracing the sea/air/combined transport multi-modal transit. The supplier may put a mark-up on the insurance and freight quotations to offset the cost of the exporter's logistic department processing the documents and of the transit arrangements for export sales contracts.

(j) The level of profit margin devised by the supplier will probably reflect market conditions. Usually there is no parity or correlation between the domestic price and overseas – the latter could vary by country and/or region such as having one price for euro zone buyers using the euro currency.

The above list should not be regarded as exhaustive, as variations will occur by product, service or markets.

The cost constituents of the landed price of the product which are under the control of the buyer will vary considerably according to the Incoterm 2000 adopted. If the buyer wishes to have a lead price embracing all the costs of delivering the goods to the specified destination (see table 14.1 page 287) the terms CPT, CIP, DDU, CIF, CFR or DDP will be used. Conversely, if the buyer wishes to take control of the distribution arrangement either from the factory gate or inland customs depot the terms EXW, FCA, FAS or FOB would be used. All these cost elements are detailed on pages 287–290.

The buyer must become very conversant with all 13 Incoterms 2000 (see page 287) and be able to analyse the price differentiation to determine which is the most favourable in the circumstances, for example CPT versus FCA. Any such analysis made by the buyer must take full account of the import logistic department's cost of reservation, any special contract rate on the cargo insurance premium and freight for multi-modal transport.

Another cost area for the buyer to consider is the funding options. This is a complex area and is explained more fully in Chapter 8. The buyer should confer with an international bank. To alleviate the lengthened payment cycle staged payments may be arranged. A range of other options exists which innovative bankers continue to introduce.

The foregoing cost analysis must take full account of any international trade law, codes of practice and the ICC code.

Tender receipts: analysis, evaluation and acceptance

Basically, a tender is an offer to sell at the price indicated and can be converted into a contract by acceptance in the form of a buyer's order. A quotation (or quote) on the other hand, is merely an invitation to treat, an indication of the price or conditions under which the supplier would be prepared to sell if somebody made him an offer. It is not part of the contract. However, following a quotation, the buyer makes an offer by placing an order, and the acceptance of this order by the supplier, within the time scale prescribed, brings a contract into existence. Unfortunately, as with many apparently simple situations, a closer examination reveals a rather more complicated position. It is not always clear who is making an offer and where the acceptance comes from.

An enquiry to a supplier in France for a certain article might elicit a response along the lines of 'this item is available from stock at a price of euros 4000'. Perhaps the response might be 'Thank you for your enquiry; we offer to supply you with the article at a price of euros 4000'. Maybe the e-mail reply might say something like 'You can buy such an article from us at a price of euros 4000'. At first it may seem that there is not much difference between these statements. They are all quotations but they can be interpreted differently. The first response is simply a statement of fact, as it does not seem to be any kind of offer by the supplier. The second statement, on the other hand, clearly is an offer. The third statement may or may not be on offer. If it became an issue of contention between a buyer and seller then the lawyers or arbitrators with the responsibility for resolving the situation may take quite a time to decide.

The following items need scrutiny in a tender offer:

(a) the product specification and conformity with international and national standards and quality details;
(b) payment details;
(c) any constraints;
(d) arbitration;
(e) price indexation;
(f) any default conditions on contract execution;
(g) detailed analysis of tender details compared with earlier discussions;
(h) additional clauses;
(i) scrutiny of the supplier company trading conditions i.e. payment terms and how long the tender is valid;
(j) Incoterm 2000 and any variation from terms.

This list is not exhaustive.

A comparison with any ICC code should be made. Visit the ICC website (see page 122) and you may find one of their booklets useful in export contracts and tendering codes of practice. Also it should be noted that under the pre-shipment inspection (see page 177) arrangements, the agent may check out the validity of price acceptance in regard to any comparison with market conditions.

Quality procedures in an international context

Buyers have a range of options for checking the acceptability of quality procedures.

(a) The pre-shipment inspection arrangements involve the buyer-appointed agent, such as SGS, conducting regular inspections throughout the production process to ensure that the quality specification is maintained. Failure to do so may result in the agent refraining from issuing the Clean Report of Findings. This latter document may be required as a condition to process the letter of credit payment arrangement.
(b) Testing any samples.
(c) The buyer visiting the overseas production or manufacturing plant and reviewing progress. This involves testing the product and checking on quality control procedures/techniques/monitoring.

Dispute procedures, including arbitration, conciliation and the role of International Chamber of Commerce

Discerning overseas buyers with the full support of their suppliers feature the International Chamber of Commerce (ICC) Arbitration clause in their contracts. Such contracting parties wishing to have the option of resorting to ICC Arbitration in the event of a dispute with their contracting partner should specifically and clearly agree upon ICC Arbitration in their contract, or in the event of no single contractual document existing, in the exchange of correspondence which constitutes the agreement between them. The following standard arbitration clause is recommended by the ICC:

> All disputes arising in connection with the present contract shall be finally settled under the Rules of Conciliation and Arbitration of the International Chamber of Commerce by one or more arbitrators appointed in accordance with the said Rules.

The International Chamber of Commerce International Court of Arbitration is held in Paris. We will now examine the ICC Arbitration and Conciliation rules.

The ICC International Court of Arbitration is the leading body in international commercial arbitration. Founded to resolve business disputes of an international character, its strict impartiality and effectiveness are recognized everywhere. Established in 1923 as the arbitration body of the ICC, the International Court of Arbitration has pioneered international commercial arbitration as it is known today. Since its creation, the court has administered some 11 000 international arbitration cases involving parties and arbitrators from more than 170 countries and territories. Demand for its services grows year by year in line with the expansion of international trade and the rapid globalization of the world economy.

The dispute resolution mechanism developed by the ICC has been conceived specifically for business disputes in an international context. These disputes pose unique difficulties and challenges. Usually the parties will be of different nationalities with different linguistic, legal and cultural backgrounds. They may also have very different expectations as to how a dispute can be resolved reasonably and fairly. Distrust may be relatively strong accompanied by uncertainty or lack of information about the course to follow. These difficulties may be compounded by distance and the disadvantages one party may face in submitting to a procedure on the other's home ground.

For all these reasons, national courts in the country of one of the parties may not appear suitable to the other parties. The ICC has always led the way in providing international business with alternatives to court litigation.

To the buyer, arbitration offers distinct advantages and is extolled by the ICC in both the international and domestic business markets. Among the most readily available dispute resolution alternatives, arbitration is by far the most commonly used internationally. The main reasons for this are discussed below.

1. The decisions are final and binding: while several mechanisms can help parties reach an amicable settlement – for example through conciliation under the ICC Rules of Conciliation – all of them depend, ultimately, on the goodwill and cooperation of the parties. A final and enforceable decision can generally be obtained only by recourse to the courts or by arbitration. Because arbitral awards are not subject to appeal, they are much more likely to be final than the judgments of courts of first instance. Although arbitral awards may

be subject to being challenged (usually in either the country where the arbitral award is rendered or where enforcement is sought) the grounds of challenge available against arbitral awards are limited.

2. The international recognition of arbitral awards: arbitral awards enjoy much greater international recognition than judgments of national courts. More than 120 countries have signed the 1958 United Nations Convention on the Recognition and Enforcement of Foreign Arbitral Awards, known as the 'New York Convention'. The Convention facilitates enforcement of awards in all contracting states. There are several other multilateral and bilateral arbitration conventions that may also help enforcement.

3. The neutrality of the arbitral proceedings are paramount: parties can place themselves on an equal footing in five key respects: place of arbitration, language used, procedures or rules of law applied, nationality of the arbitrators and legal representation. Hence, arbitration may take place in any country, in any language and with arbitrators of any nationality. With this flexibility, it is generally possible to structure a neutral procedure offering no undue advantage to any party.

4. The specialized competence of arbitrators is an important factor: judicial systems do not allow the parties to a dispute to choose their own judges. In contrast, arbitration offers the parties the unique opportunity of designing persons of their choice as arbitrators, provided they are independent. This enables the parties to have their disputes resolved by people who have specialized competence in the relevant field.

5. Speed and economy of the proceedings: arbitration is faster and less expensive than litigation in the courts. Although a complex international dispute may sometimes take a great deal of time and money to resolve, even by arbitration, the limited scope for challenge against arbitral awards, as compared with court judgments, offers a clear advantage. Above all, it helps to ensure that the parties will not subsequently be entangled in a prolonged and costly series of appeals. Furthermore, arbitration offers the parties the flexibility to set up proceedings that can be conducted as quickly and economically as the circumstances allow. In this way, a multi-million dollar ICC arbitration was once completed in just over two months.

6. Confidentiality is paramount: arbitration hearings are not public, and only the parties themselves receive copies of the awards.

The ICC International Court of Arbitration was the initiator and leader of the movement which led to the adoption of the New York convention of 10 June 1958 on the Recognition and Enforcement of Foreign Arbitral awards. The New York Convention is the most important multilateral treaty in international arbitration. Basically, it requires courts of each contracting state:

(a) to recognize arbitration agreements in writing and to refuse to allow a dispute to be litigated before them when it is subject to an arbitration agreement;

(b) to recognize and enforce arbitral awards.

Before entering into an international arbitration agreement, check whether the states of the other contracting party, and if appropriate, of the place of arbitration, have ratified the New York Convention or have signed other multilateral treaties offering the same guarantees. Readers are encouraged to check the ICC Paris website www.iccarbitration.org e-mail arb@iccwbo.org

The ICC International Court of Arbitration ('the Court') is the world's foremost institution in the resolution of international business disputes. While most arbitration institutions are regional or national in scope, the ICC Court is truly international. Composed of members from some 65 countries and every continent, the ICC Court is the world's most widely representative dispute resolution institution.

The ICC Court is not a 'court' in the ordinary sense. As the ICC arbitration body, the Court ensures the application of the Rules of Arbitration of the International Chamber of Commerce. Although its members do not decide the matters submitted to ICC arbitration – this is the task of the arbitrators appointed under the ICC Rules – the Court oversees the ICC arbitration process and, among other things, is responsible for: appointing arbitrators; confirming, as the case may be, arbitrators nominated by the parties; deciding upon challenges of arbitrators; scrutinizing and approving all arbitral awards; and fixing the arbitrators' fees. In exercising its functions, the Court is able to draw upon the collective experience of distinguished jurists from a diversity of backgrounds and legal cultures as varied as that of the participants in the arbitral process.

The Court is assisted by a Secretariat located at ICC headquarters in Paris. The Secretariat currently has a full-time staff of 45 persons, including more than 25 lawyers of 15 different nationalities. The Secretariat closely follows all ICC cases and is available to provide assistance and information in a dozen different languages. At present, each case is followed by one of six teams headed by a Counsel. The Secretariat has state-of-the-art computerized case management and information retrieval systems which function in four different languages.

Unlike many other institutions, the ICC Court monitors the entire arbitral process, from the initial request to the final award. The ICC Rules require that, within two months of receiving the file, the Arbitral Tribunal prepare and submit to the Court a document defining its Terms of Reference. A unique feature of ICC arbitration, the Terms of Reference serve the useful purpose of bringing the arbitrators and parties together at an early stage to identify the issues they will be required to deal with and the procedural details that need to be addressed. It is also sometimes possible at that stage for the parties to reach agreement on certain outstanding issues, such as the language of the arbitration or the governing substantive law. A fact which users should not overlook is that a significant proportion of ICC arbitration cases are amicably settled at the stage of the Terms of Reference.

During the proceedings, the Court regularly reviews the progress of all pending cases, and, in the process, considers whether there are any measures that need to be taken in order, for example, to help ensure that the case advances as quickly as reasonably possible and that the proceedings are being conducted in conformity with the Rules. In this connection, the staff of the Court's Secretariat closely follow the case and receive copies of all written communications and pleadings exchanged in the arbitration proceedings.

Parties using arbitration have a choice between designating an institution, such as ICC, to administer it, or proceeding ad hoc outside an institutional framework. In ad hoc cases, the arbitration will be administered by the arbitrators themselves. However, should problems arise in setting the arbitration in motion or in constituting the arbitral tribunal, the parties may have to require the assistance of a state court, or that of an independent appointing authority such as ICC. Although institutional arbitration requires payment of a fee to the administering institution, the functions performed by the institution can be critical in ensuring that the arbitration proceeds to a final award with a minimum of disruption and without the need for recourse to local courts. The services an institution may offer are exemplified by the role of the ICC Court, which provides the most thoroughly supervised form of administered arbitration in the world. Among other things, the ICC Court will, as necessary: (i) determine whether there is a prima facie agreement to arbitrate; (ii) decide on the number of arbitrators; (iii) appoint arbitrators; (iv) decide challenges against arbitrators; (v) ensure that arbitrators are conducting the arbitration in accordance with the ICC Rules and replace them if necessary; (vi) determine the place of arbitration; (vii) fix and extend time-limits; (viii) determine the fees and expenses of the arbitrators and (ix) scrutinize arbitral awards.

One of the most important functions of the Court is the scrutiny of awards. The ICC Rules provide that the Court must approve all awards as to their form and that the Court may also, without affecting the arbitrators liberty of decision, draw their attention to points of substance. In ICC arbitration, scrutiny is a key element ensuring that arbitral awards are of the highest possible standard and thus less susceptible to annulment in the national courts than they might otherwise be. The scrutiny process provides the parties with an additional layer of protection that would not otherwise be available, since arbitral awards are generally not subject to appeal. This unique quality control mechanism makes ICC arbitration the world's most reliable arbitration system.

A practical study of the process of arbitration cannot escape the question of time limits. Legal disputes are a factor to be considered in corporate strategy, whether as a source of profits or losses. Before starting an arbitration many companies understandably want to know how long it will take before the final award is handed down. In most cases it would be unrealistic to expect that the final Award may be made in less than one year, although complex ICC arbitration proceedings have been conducted in as little as two and a half months. Adherence to time limits is monitored closely by the Court and its Secretariat. Once the arbitral tribunal has been constituted and the financial and other conditions have been met, two important time limits govern the actual proceedings – the two months already referred to for transmitting the Terms of Reference to the Court, followed by six months for rendering the final award. The Court can extend these time limits if circumstances so require. The Court follows each case by means of progress reports that are submitted to it periodically by the Secretariat. In addition, the ICC system of arbitrator remuneration is designed to encourage the efficient conduct of the arbitration as the arbitrators are not paid on an hourly or daily basis.

ICC arbitration is possible only if there is an agreement between the parties providing for it. ICC recommends that all parties wishing to have recourse to ICC arbitration include the following standard clause in their contracts:

> All disputes arising out of or in connection with the present contract shall be finally settled under the Rules of Arbitration of the International Chamber of Commerce by one or more arbitrators appointed in accordance with the said Rules.

It may also be desirable for the parties to stipulate in the arbitration clause itself: the law governing the contract; the number of arbitrators; the place of arbitration and the language of the arbitration.

Parties should also consider the possible need for special provisions in the event that arbitration is contemplated among more than two parties. In addition, the law in some countries may lay down certain requirements in respect of arbitration clauses.

In principle, parties should also ensure that the arbitration agreement is:

(a) In writing. The effectiveness of an arbitration clause first of all depends on proof of its existence. It should therefore generally be in writing. The 1958 New York Convention specifically states (Art. II) that Contracting States shall recognize arbitration agreements 'in writing'.
(b) Carefully drafted. Time and again, the Court receives requests for arbitration based on ambiguous arbitration clauses. Badly worded clauses, at the very least, cause delay. At worst, they may impede the arbitration process.

The ICC rules of Arbitration and conciliation operative from 1 January 1988 are found in ICC publication No. 581. Its contents embrace the following Rules of Arbitration of the International Chamber of Commerce articles:

(1) International Court of Arbitration; (2) Definitions; (3) Written notifications or communications: Time Limits; (4) Request for Arbitration; (5) Answer to the request – counterclaims; (6) Effect of the Arbitration Agreement; (7) General provisions; (8) Number of Arbitrators; (9) Appointment and Confirmation of the Arbitrators; (10) Multiple Parties; (11) Challenge of Arbitrators; (12) Replacement of Arbitrators; (13) Transmission of the file to the Arbitral Tribunal; (14) Place of the Arbitration; (15) Rules governing the proceedings; (16) Language of the Arbitration; (17) Applicable Rules of Law; (18) Terms of reference – procedural timetable; (19) New claims; (20) Establishing the facts of the case; (21) Hearings; (22) Closing of the proceedings; (23) Conservatory and Interim Measures; (24) Time limit of the Award; (25) Making of the Award; (26) Award by consent; (27) Scrutiny of the Award of the court; (28) Notification, deposit and enforceability of the Award; (29) Correction and interpretation of the Award; (30) Advance to cover the costs of the Arbitration; (31) Decision as to the costs of

the Arbitration; (32) Modified Time Limits; (33) Waiver; (34) Exclusion of Liability; (35) General Rule.

Statutes of the International Court of Arbitration of the ICC Articles: (1) Function; (2) Composition of the court; (3) Appointment; (4) Plenary session of the Court; (5) Committees; (6) Confidentiality; (7) Modification of the Rules of Arbitration.

International Rules of the International Court of Arbitration of the ICC Articles: (1) Confidential Character of the work of the International Court of Arbitration; (2) Participation of Members of the International Court of Arbitration in ICC Arbitration; (3) Relations between the Members of the Court and the ICC National Committees; (4) Committee of the Court; (5) Court Secretariat; (6) Scrutiny of Arbitral Awards Arbitration costs and fees.

Articles: (1) Advance costs; (2) Costs and fees; (3) Appointment of Arbitrators; (4) Scales of Administrative 'Expenses and of Arbitrator's fees'.

To conclude these two chapters on negotiation, it is stressed that the buyer should be fully conscious of the total cost of the product and correct specification and the legal environment. The buyer's legal advisor may be engaged to examine any extensive complex export sales contract or tender submission. Full use should be made of the ICC publications available as recommended below or scan a more extensive list on their Website, page 122.

Recommended reading

- International Court of Arbitration – Rules of Arbitration from 1 January 1988 and Rules of Conciliation from 1 January 1988, ICC publication No. 581.
- International Chamber of Commerce, *International Court of Arbitration Bulletin*, published twice yearly by ICC Paris.
- The ICC International Centre for Expertise (Rules from 1 January 1993) – ICC Publication No. 520.
- International Court of Arbitration – Resolving Business disputes worldwide; ICC Publication No. 800.

8

Import finance

Trade finance has become a strong bargaining point in the conduct of international trade. Both the buyer and seller are keen to adopt positions in the negotiating strategy which will reduce the financial risk and secure the best deal possible.

Buying goods overseas requires a different financial strategy compared with buying in the domestic market. The time between placing an order for goods and receipt of the cash in respect of their subsequent resale, can put a significant strain on an importer's financial resources. The importer may be purchasing finished goods for stock or to fulfil pre-sold orders. Alternatively, the goods may be raw materials for re-manufacture or components requiring assembly. Seasonal peaks, long transit times and lengthy credit terms all add to the demands on the importer. It is important that the finance to meet these fluctuations in the importer's working capital requirements is geared to the terms and method of payment agreed between buyer and seller. For example, documentary credit facilities might be required to cover the pre-shipment period, whilst post-import finance can be obtained through an import loan.

The growth in international trade has greatly increased both the demand for trade finance and the degree of sophistication with which it is delivered. There is now a much greater choice of financial solutions for buyers and sellers to consider when developing an international trade strategy. The buyer must continuously keep in touch with innovative funding facilities available through finance houses.

The documents relating to the importation of goods, import customs and cargo insurance are dealt with in Chapters 9, 13 and 12 respectively and processing the imported consignment in Chapter 14.

Selection criteria

Every company's trade cycle is unique, although there will be elements (e.g. purchasing, manufacturing, shipping, credit, etc.) which are common to them all. Each style in a trade cycle places different demands on a company's finances, but a key component in determining the overall level of working capital required for any business is the time taken between the start of the cycle (i.e. ordering goods or raw materials) and receipt of payment for corresponding sales of finished products.

Many International Trade Banks provide advice to traders (also available on their websites) to ensure that at each stage of the particular trade cycle, that a structure can be put in place to provide working capital for that stage and in consequence directly relate to the needs of the client's business. As the bulk of international trade is undertaken on terms of 180 days or less, these facilities are important considerations for the buyer.

The method of payment is specified in the contract of sale and is reflected in the export/commercial invoice. The choice of method will involve the following considerations:

(a) the range of available financing options;
(b) the funding resources of the buyer;
(c) exchange control regulations in both the buyer's and exporter's countries;
(d) exporter risk – problems in producing the correct documentation and failure to supply goods in accordance with the sales contract;
(e) foreign exchange risk – fluctuating exchange rates affecting price and profit;
(f) country risk – political and economic instability, transfer risk, war and import/export regulations;
(g) transportation risk – risk associated with the mode of transport, for example marine risks and storage facilities in ports;
(h) the political situation in the buyer's country;
(i) how quickly payment is required (time scale);
(j) the availability and cost of foreign currency to the importer/buyer;
(k) the terms of the contract of sale;
(l) the nature of the relationship between buyer and seller;
(m) whether the cost of any credit can be arranged by the supplier (exporter) or buyer (importer);
(n) importer risk – non-payment of invoices, delayed payment of invoices and insolvency of buyer.

Many of the risks can be insured against or mitigated through sound trade financial management. We will now examine the payment structure involving documentary credits (UCP 500) and documentary bills collection URC 522. This will be followed by the range of payment options available to the buyer.

There are five principal mechanisms for settling international trade debts available to the buyer: documentary credit, bill of collection, open account, advance payment and bill of exchange. The risk ladder in Figure 8.1 illustrates the way in which the payment mechanism affects the security maintained by each party.

The choice depends on many factors (see page 133). We will now examine the documentary credit (UCP 500) system to be followed by the bills for collection (URC 522) and subsequently open account, advance payment and bill of exchange.

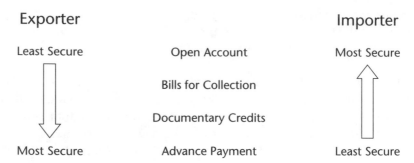

FIGURE 8.1 Risk ladder
Reproducd by courtesy of HSBC Midland Bank PLC

UCP 500 documentary credits

The successful overseas buyer takes a keen interest in the funding cycle and particularly the benefits accruing from the International Chamber of Commerce (ICC) code of practice known as 'Uniform Customs and Practice for Documentary Credits (UCP)'. This enables the buyer to control the payment and transit arrangements as payment of the goods is only made when the cargo has been shipped in accordance with the export sales contract.

The usual form of credit sought by the supplier is the 'irrevocable' credit as found in the letter of credit (L/C). This means that it cannot be cancelled or amended without the agreement of the beneficiary (the supplier) and all other parties. Such a credit, opened by a reputable bank on instructions by the buyer in a sound country, means the exporter can rely on payment being made as soon as he or she has shipped the goods and produced the documents called for in accordance with the terms of the credit. The security provided by an irrevocable credit may be further enhanced if the bank in the exporter's country (advising bank) is requested by the issuing bank to add its 'confirmation'. The exporter then has a 'confirmed irrevocable credit' and he or she need look no further than his or her own local bank for payment. With a credit which is not 'confirmed' however, the point of payment is the issuing bank (abroad), although the advising bank would usually be prepared to negotiate with recourse. The alternative to a confirmed irrevocable credit is an irrevocable letter of credit which offers less security for the seller because it can be revoked at any time before presentation of the documents. However, it does offer benefits to the buyer precisely because he or she can revoke the credit at any time before presentation of the documents. Conversely, the exporter is relying primarily on the undertaking of the overseas issuing bank to make payment.

All documentary credits must conform to the (UCP). These were developed with the assistance of banks and other interested parties, to achieve uniformity of interpretation of DC terms and conditions. The current code is defined in the 1993 revision ICC Publication No. 500. Article No. 1 confirms that UCP 500 applies to all Documentary Credits (including the extent to which they may be applicable Standby Letter(s) of Credit) where they are incorporated into the text of the credit and is binding on all parties unless otherwise expressly stipulated in the credit.

Documentary credits (DC) are completely separate transactions from the underlying commercial contracts and banks are not concerned with or bound by, the terms of such contracts. An important provision of UCP is that all DC terms and conditions should be covered by the documents called for in the credit. In DC operations, banks deal exclusively with documents and not with goods, services or other performances to which the documents relate.

Documentary credits are normally sent to the beneficiary (exporter) via an advising bank in the beneficiary's country. The advising bank may also be requested (by the issuing bank) to confirm the credit (i.e. add its own undertaking to that of the issuing bank). In such cases, the confirming bank assumes that the credit risk of the overseas issuing bank and the political risk are associated with the importing country. On an unconfirmed credit, the revising bank does not make any commitment to honour the DC; the exporter is relying primarily on the undertaking of the overseas issuing bank to make payment.

The buyer can gain additional protection through the document definitions (for example, by calling for independent inspection or quality certificates) and can control delivery schedules and other aspects of the transaction by stipulating specific conditions such as the latest shipment date. The importer is assured that payment will not be made until the issuing bank has checked that the documents are in full conformity with the DC terms and conditions.

The DC terms may provide for payment immediately upon presentation of conforming documents (sight credit) or at some future date taking account of any extended payment terms granted by the seller to the buyer (usance or acceptance credit). For usance or acceptance credits, payment is made (and the importer's account debited) at the end of the extended term (i.e. on the maturity date). However, the shipping documents are usually released to the buyer at the time they are presented to the issuing bank, enabling the goods to be collected.

Very few risks arise for the seller because the potential problem areas of the buyer and country risks can be eliminated through the addition of the 'confirmation' of the advising bank, thereby transferring the responsibility from the importer's bank overseas to a more familiar bank in the country of the exporter.

Employing a documentary credit usually works in the following way:

(a) Importer/buyer, also called the applicant, agrees terms with the seller, and initiates the documentary credit by applying to his bank to open a documentary credit in favour of a named seller specifying details of the documents required together with all the terms and conditions which are to be applied, that is expiry date, etc.

(b) Issuing/opening bank (buyer's bank) will open the documentary credit by instructing the seller's bank (or other bank in the seller's country) to advise the documentary credit to the seller.

(c) Advising/confirming bank (generally the seller's bank) will advise the documentary credit to the seller with all the details/documents required and authenticate its genuineness. The advising bank may also be the confirming bank if adding their conditional guarantee.

(d) The exporter (seller/beneficiary) receives notification that the documentary credit has been opened in their favour with all the terms and documents required in order to receive payment. Finally, the issuing bank forwards the documents to the importer and receives payment.

By using DCs, the exporter knows, usually before manufacture or shipment, the precise terms and conditions which must be met in order to obtain payment and when that payment will be received. The seller will carefully check all DC terms and conditions upon receipt. If they do not reflect the underlying commercial contract or include unacceptable conditions, amendment of the DC should be arranged prior to shipment. The seller must be able to present the correct documents and comply fully with the terms and conditions of the credit to ensure payment. Failure to do so could result in the exporter losing the protection of the credit thereby moving up the risk ladder towards bills for collection (URC 522) or open account.

Other than payment in advance, confirmed irrevocable credits are the most secure method of payment for a seller, always provided that conforming documents can be presented (see page 146).

The importer may need to issue a documentary credit weeks or months in advance of shipment to allow the exporter to purchase raw materials, manufacture the goods and organize delivery. This period (prior to presentation of documents) is often referred to as the DC 'lead time'. Documentary Credit facilities can be combined with import loan facilities (see page 143) to permit the importer to finance the centre period between purchase and sale of the goods.

The DC mechanism can also be used to provide a period of extended credit by allowing usance (term) drafts to be drawn (see page 133). Assuming confirming documents are presented, a banker's acceptance would be created under the DC extending the importer's liability up to the maturity date of the acceptance and possibly beyond the expiry date of the DC. When assessing the level of DC facilities required, importers need to consider their maximum potential period of liability i.e. the validity period plus any usance period as well as the anticipated turnover for which DCs will need to be issued.

Given below is a synopsis of the UCP contents which are constructed in article form:

A. General Provisions and Definitions
   Article 1 Application of UCP
   Article 2 Meaning of Credit
   Article 3 Credits v Contracts
   Article 4 Documents v Goods/Services/Performances
   Article 5 Instructions to Issue/Amend Credits

It is important for the buyer to realize that in formulating the import funding strategy, most exporters need to finance the period between shipment and receipt of payment. The purchase of raw materials (or finished goods) and other costs such as packaging, transportation and labour can impose considerable demands on the supplier's working capital. Turning the exports into cash provides an immediate boost to the supplier's cash flow. Documentary credits can provide access to finance without affecting the exporter's existing banking facilities. In fact, finance under certain types of documentary credit is provided without recourse, that is the paying, accepting or negotiating bank does not reserve the right to ask for its money back if payment is not received from the issuing bank.

Post-shipment finance can be provided in several ways under a DC, each depending on how the DC is payable. Finance under DC's is usually based on inter-bank rates which can show an interest advantage over other forms of finance such as bank overdrafts. Furthermore, the interest cost is fixed and calculated in the currency of the credit which may show further cost advantages.

Pre-shipment finance can be raised in two ways from a documentary credit. The simplest is for the DC terms to include a clause (known as the red clause) permitting an advance of funds to the beneficiary (exporter) prior to presentation of the shipping documents. In this way the importer directly finances the exporter. Alternatively, the supplier's bank can provide a short-term loan for a percentage of the DC value, which is repaid from the proceeds of the subsequent presentation under the DC. The existence of the DC does not, in itself, normally constitute security for such loans; a banking facility, subject to normal lending criteria would be required. The term Packing Credit Advance is generally used to describe loans of this type. A summary on post-shipment finance is given in Table 8.1.

Finally, a key point in the buyer's funding process associated with the UCP 500 is the need to complete correctly the international bank application form which creates the foundation of the buyer's documentary credit. Essentially it is an authority to debit the buyer's account which is conditional upon presentation of documents conforming to the terms and conditions laid down by the buyer and agreed with the supplier and stipulated on the letter of credit issued to the exporter. These terms and conditions should reflect the underlying commercial contract, avoid ambiguity and not be so complex as to make the transaction unworkable.

The following points cover the key areas to consider on the application form to help the buyer to establish a clear and concise instruction.

TABLE 8.1 Post-shipment finance under documentary credits

DC available by	Drafts drawn at	How financed
Confirmed DC		
Payment	Sight	Paid on presentation to confirming bank.
Negotiation	Sight	Negotiated, without recourse, on presentation to confirming bank. Exporter pays interest for the period that the confirming bank is out of funds.
Negotiation	Usance	Negotiated, without recourse, on presentation to confirming bank. Exporter pays interest for the period that the confirming bank is out of funds.
Acceptance	Usance	Accepted drafts may be discounted by the acceptor (usually the confirming bank) or sold to a bank, discount house or forfaiter.
Deferred payment	No drafts	The confirming bank will issue its undertaking to pay on the due date. Unless the DC states otherwise, the deferred payment period may only be financed outside the terms of the DC.
Unconfirmed DC		
Payment	Sight	Paid on presentation to advising bank only if sufficient funds available from the issuing bank.
Negotiation	Sight	Documents may be negotiated provided that the negotiating bank is willing to take the risk of the issuing bank. Exporter pays interest for the period that the negotiating bank is out of funds.
Negotiation	Usance	Documents may be negotiated provided that the negotiating bank is willing to take the risk of the issuing bank up to the due date. Exporter pays interest for the period that the negotiating bank is out of funds.
Acceptance	Usance	Drafts drawn on the advising bank will only be accepted if the advising bank is willing to take the risk of the issuing bank up to the due date. Once accepted, drafts may be discounted by the accepting bank or sold to a bank, discount house or forfaiter.
Deferred Payment	No drafts	The issuing bank will issue its undertaking to pay on the due date. Unless the DC states otherwise, the deferred payment period may only be financed outside the terms of the DC.

1. *Date and place of expiry and place of payment.* These are important considerations because they determine when and where documents are to be presented and for certain types of credit, whether there is any liability to pay interest such as under sight or usance drafts. When a credit is stated to expire at the counters of the issuing bank, documents must be received by the issuing bank on or before the date specified. If it expires in the country of the

beneficiary, conforming documents must be presented to the nominated bank on or before that date. If the date falls on a weekend or Bank holiday, UCP 500 allows presentation to be made on the next working day.

2. *Beneficiary details*. Provide the full name and postal address to ensure proper delivery to the beneficiary. Include a telephone, fax or e-mail details if requested to do so by the beneficiary.

3. *Credit to establish by tele-transmission/airmail/courier*. Issuing a documentary credit via tele-transmission is the quickest way to get a credit to an overseas beneficiary. Credits are usually sent via the inter-bank computer network (SWIFT) or fax. If the credit is to be sent by airmail or courier, brief details may be sent by SWIFT or fax in advance of the airmail credit which would be received a few days later.

4. *Partial shipments*. Under UCP 500 partial shipments of goods will be allowed unless the credit stipulates otherwise.

5. *Transhipment*. Transhipment occurs when the goods are off-loaded from one means of transport and loaded onto another. This does not usually pose any problems if the goods are containerized and the transport document covers the entire journey. A transfer from one vessel onto another also constitutes transhipment.

6. *Loading on board/despatch/taking in charge*. These terms relate to the type of transport document required. Bills of lading (see page 163) will provide evidence of loading on board whilst an air waybill (see page 160), truck waybill (CMR) (see page 170) and rail consignment (see page 170) show despatch from a particular location. A forwarders certificate of receipt (FCR) (see page 170) shows the taking in charge of the goods for future despatch or shipment. The point of departure and/or point of destination needs to be incorporated and should be consistent with the mode of transport.

7. *Latest shipment date*. This is the latest date on which the goods can be shipped and will be evidenced on the transport document. If a specific date is not provided, the latest shipment date will be the same as the expiry date.

8. *Draft (bills of exchange)* (see page 145). Drafts under documentary credits available for payment or acceptance in the country of the seller should be drawn on the bank nominated to pay or accept. In all other cases they should be drawn on the issuing bank.

9. *Goods description*. It is advisable to keep the description of the goods short and to the point. The proper place for fine detail, such as that provided in a proforma quotation, is in the contract. Excessive detail only adds to the complexity of the credit and cost of transmission.

10. *Trade terms* (Incoterms 2000). Use the trade term agreed in the contract (see page 287).

11. *Documents required*. The application form usually provides a list of the basic documents that are called for in a typical documentary credit transaction. These include bill of lading, air waybill, packing list, export licence, certificate of origin, weight list and so on (see chapter 9).

12. *Insurance*. If the goods are being purchased on a CIF or CIP basis the buyer requires an insurance document to be presented under the credit.
13. *Bank charges*. Unless the buyer specifies which party is to pay the bank charges relating to the transaction, the buyer may find that overseas bank charges are added to the bill when documents are presented. The usual course of action is that buyer and supplier pay the bank charges incurred in their respective countries.
14. *Transit/Usance interest*. If payment of interest under the credit has been agreed, the buyer must stipulate against whose account interest is to be applied.
15. *Confirmation*. Having the buyer's credit confirmed is designed to lessen the risk for the seller, but it is largely unnecessary for credits issued by most major banks. If the credit is not utilized, the cost of confirmation is borne by the buyer.
16. *Period of presentation*. If a period for presentation of documents is not stipulated, UCP 500 requires that documents must be presented within 21 days after the date of shipment, but in any event, before expiry of the credit. The buyer may select any period for which the documents are to be presented. However, if the buyer makes the period too long, the buyer may not receive the documents before the goods arrive. If the expiry date is different from the latest shipment date, the period for presentation should be the difference between the two dates.
17. *Special terms*. As far as possible, any special terms or conditions should be incorporated into the relevant document definition. Where this is not possible, the buyer must ensure that any terms or conditions to be imposed do not conflict with the terms or conditions expressed in the document definitions.

Finally, one must stress that the advising bank will check the credit is authentic and that all the documents called for are consistent with the terms of shipment. Readers are urged to study the documents flow chart shown in Figure 8.2.

Overall, according to UCP 500, article 10 documentary credits may be made available in one of four ways: by sight payment, deferred payment, acceptance and by negotiation. The supplier can incorporate the specific documentary credit in his or her proforma invoice or contract to provide the buyer with a proforma documentary credit. In essence, the type of credit is determined by two factors: (i) on whom the drafts (if any) are to be drawn and (ii) the method of reimbursement under the letter of credit. Each type of credit is distinguished by how the credit is available.

Sight payment

A credit which is available by sight payment usually allows the nominated bank to debit the account of the issuing bank on presentation of confirming documents. A draft payable at sight may be called for, drawn on the nominated bank. In the case of a confirmed credit, the nominated bank is nearly always the confirming bank.

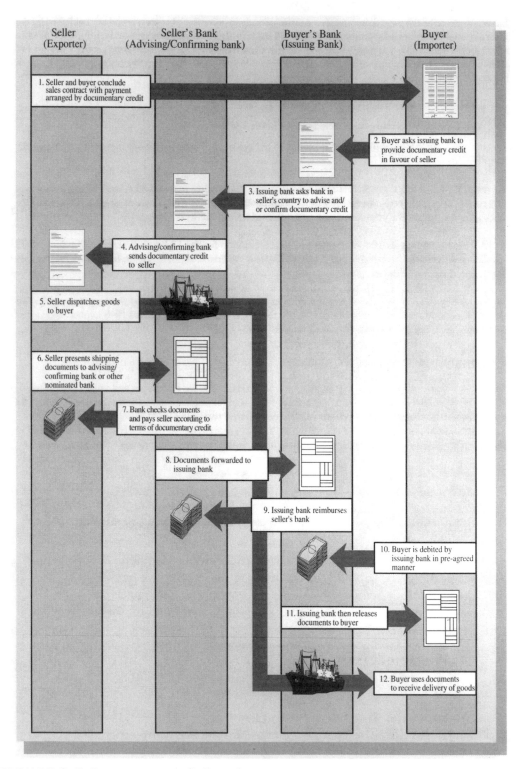

FIGURE 8.2 Documentary credit flow chart
Reproduced courtesy of HSBC Midland Bank PLC

If the credit is unconfirmed the supplier will receive payment only if the nominated bank is in a position to pay. This means that the nominated bank will take account of such factors as the standing of the issuing bank and country as well as the availability of sufficient funds before honouring a presentation under the credit. If the credit is confirmed the supplier will receive immediate payment as provided for in the credit terms.

Payment is made to the seller locally upon presentation of the confirming documents. A sight draft is usually called for, although payment can be made against documents alone. If payment to the seller is made before the buyer's account is debited, interest will be charged from the date that the paying bank is reimbursed. If the buyer wishes, can be authorized the paying bank to claim payment by tele-transmission and have the buyer's account debited upon receipt of the claim. In most cases this will be several days before the documents arrive.

Deferred payment

A deferred payment does not require the presentation of a draft; the nominated bank is authorized to debit the issuing bank's account at a future date against presentation of conforming documents. The date for payment is defined in the documentary credit, usually as a specific number of days after the date of despatch of the goods or after the date of presentation of the documents. If the credit is unconfirmed, the undertaking to effect payment on the due date is that of the issuing bank. Payment will only be effected on the due date by the nominated bank after taking account of the same factors as earlier described for sight payments. If the credit is confirmed, the undertaking to pay is made by the confirming bank. Payment will then be made on the due date by the nominated bank (if any) or by the confirming bank.

Acceptance

Credits which are available by acceptance require the supplier to draw usance drafts on a nominated accepting bank. These are accepted payable at a future date in accordance with the terms specified in the credit. If the credit is unconfirmed, neither the advising bank nor the nominated bank undertake to accept the drafts. These will be accepted only if the bank on which they are drawn is prepared to accept the payment risk of the issuing bank for the tenor of the drafts. This risk is assessed at the time of presentation of documents.

For a confirmed credit, the undertaking of the confirming bank provides for either (i) acceptance of drafts drawn on the confirming bank and their payment on the due date or (ii) the payment of drafts drawn on a nominated bank should that bank fail to honour the drafts on the due date.

Negotiation

The term negotiation is broadly defined as 'the giving of value' and can be applied to transactions of any tenor (sight or usance). The issuing bank must reimburse the bank which negotiates (give value for) drafts and/or documents drawn under its documentary credit. The credit may be made freely negotiable with any bank or negotiation may be restricted to a bank nominated by the issuing bank. If the credit is unconfirmed, the negotiating bank will only offer to give value if it is prepared to accept the payment risk of the issuing bank for the tenor of the drafts.

If it agrees to negotiate, it may do so 'with recourse', that is it may reserve the right to ask for its money back if payment is not received from the issuing bank as expected.

If the credit is confirmed, the confirming bank undertakes to negotiate confirming documents upon presentation and without recourse to the supplier or to bona fide holders (usually other negotiating banks). When the negotiating bank 'gives value', it does not receive immediate value itself. Consequently the negotiating bank deducts interest from its payment to cover the period between paying the importer and receiving payment from the issuing bank. Under this type of credit the seller is responsible for any negotiation interest unless the importer specifically authorizes the negotiating bank to charge interest to the supplier's account.

For usance transactions the period of interest will run from the date of negotiation until the due date. However, the due date will differ according to the way drafts are drawn. With those that have a determinable due date (e.g. 60 days after the date of bill of lading), the due date is known at the time the documents are presented. For those with an indeterminable due date (e.g. 60 days sight), the due date is calculated from the date of sighting by the issuing bank. In this case, the interest period is appreciably longer because, in addition to the usance period, the time the documents are in transit to the issuing bank must be taken into account and this can be anything up to 21 days.

For credits payable at sight, the period of interest should be quite small – essentially the time that the documents are in transit, time for document checking by the issuing bank and remittance of proceeds. If the credit allows the negotiating bank to debit the account of the issuing bank immediately (as with a sight payment credit) interest does not arise.

When considering the need for an amendment, study the whole credit thoroughly to ensure that all points have been covered. If amendments are received which were not requested by you, ensure that the amendment is not detrimental to the original terms. If the amendment is to a confirmed credit, check that the confirming bank has extended its confirmation to the amendment – it is not obliged to do so. This is particularly important if the amendments extend the expiry date of the credit. If the credit is being amended because of the fault of the buyer, the seller will endeavour to ensure that all costs related to the amendment are borne by the buyer. This includes the advising bank's charges.

Three other types of credit exist under documentary credits which we will now briefly examine. They are transferable credits, back to back credits and revolving credits.

Transferable credits

These are commonly used when one is acting as an agent between the buyer and seller. If a credit is designated as transferable, the agent or buyer is able to transfer some or all of the rights and obligations under the credit to a second beneficiary. Unless the credit states otherwise, it may be transferred only, once although if partial shipments are allowed, portions of the credit may be transferred to more than one second beneficiary.

The terms of the transferred credit must be the same as the original credit except for the following, all of which may be reduced or curtailed: amount; unit price; expiry date; latest presentation date and period of shipment. Furthermore, the percentage for which insurance cover must be effected may be increased in such a way as to provide the amount of cover stipulated in the original credit. You can substitute your own invoices and drafts for those of the second beneficiary as long as their value is not more than the amount stated in the original credit. It is often a requirement that the identities of the buyer and ultimate supplier are withheld from each other. This requires careful drafting of the original credit (and its subsequent transfer) to ensure that the documents do not disclose the names of the respective parties.

Back to back credits

In this type of arrangement, two credits are established completely independently of each other. The buyer establishes its credit in the exporter's favour. The buyer arranges for a second credit (usually based on the terms of the original credit) to be established in favour of the ultimate supplier of the goods or the supplier of raw materials. A back to back arrangement should only become necessary where the underlying contracts are on terms which do not match or where a transferable credit is unable to maintain secrecy on a particular aspect of the transaction such as value of the goods; true origin of the goods and the identities of the ultimate buyer and seller.

As with a transferable credit, some documents from the second credit will be substituted prior to presentation under the first credit. The second credit must be carefully drafted to maintain secrecy and ensure that the documents are still capable of compliance with the first credit.

Revolving credits

If the supplier makes regular shipments to a particular buyer, the supplier may wish for a series of shipments or even an entire contract to be secured by a single documentary credit. A credit which revolves automatically, either by amount or time would achieve this by allowing the value of the credit to be drawn each time a shipment of goods is undertaken. It is usually necessary for the creditor to specifically state that Article 41 of UCP 500 (relating to instalment shipments) does not apply.

URC 522 documentary collection

The procedures and responsibilities of the banks and other parties regarding the collection of payments based on documentary bills is found in the 'Uniform Rules for Collection' issued by the International Chamber of Commerce, publication No. 522, 1995 revision and introduced on 1 January 1996. It is subscribed to by the major banks throughout the world. The Uniform Rules for Collection are revised or updated regularly, according to market conditions. The rules as expressed in Article (a) are binding on all parties unless otherwise expressly agreed or contrary to the provision of a national state or local law. The documents for collection (handling by the bank) are found in sub-Article 2(b) and feature 'financial documents – bills of exchange, promissory notes, cheques or other similar instruments used for obtaining payment of money, commercial documents – invoices, transport documents, documents of title or other similar documents whatsoever, not being financial documents'.

A synopsis of the content/structure of URC 522 is given below:

A. General Provisions and Definitions
   Article 1 Application of URC 522
   Article 2 Definition of Collection
   Article 3 Parties to a Collection
B. Form and Structure of Collections
   Article 4 Collection instruction
C. Form of Presentation
   Articles Presentation
   Article 6 Sight/acceptance
   Article 7 Release of Commercial Documents
           Documents against acceptance (D/A) vs
           Documents against payment (D/P)
   Article 8 Creation of documents
D. Liabilities and Responsibilities
   Article 9 Good faith and reasonable care
   Article 10 Documents Goods/services/performances
   Article 11 Disclaimer for Acts of an Instructed Party
   Article 12 Disclaimer on Documents received
   Article 13 Disclaimer on Effectiveness of Documents
   Article 14 Disclaimer on Delays, Loss in Transit and Translation
   Article 15 Force Majeure
E. Payment
   Article 16 Payment without delay
   Article 17 Payment in local currency
   Article 18 Payment in foreign currency
   Article 19 Partial payments
F. Interest Charges and Expenses
   Article 20 Interest
   Article 21 Charges and Expenses

G. Other Provisions
    Article 22 Acceptance
    Article 23 Promissory Notes and other Instruments
    Article 24 Protest
    Article 25 Case-of-need
    Article 26 Advices

We will now examine documentary collections in greater detail.

Documentary collections are those which include shipping and commercial documents such as bills of exchange, bills of lading, invoices and insurance documents. These are submitted to the exporter's bank and then forwarded to the importer's bank for release to the importer against acceptance or payment in accordance with the terms set out in the remitting bank's collection order. In many areas of the world it is common practice to defer presentation, payment or acceptance until arrival of the carrying vessel. A documentary collection will take one of the following forms.

Documents against acceptance (D/A)

Documents are released to the importer against their acceptance of a term bill, payable at a fixed or determinable future date. The importer's acceptance, written on the face of the bill, signifies acceptance of the terms and an agreement to settle the bill on its maturity date. The importer's acceptance on the bill of exchange does not guarantee payment to the exporter; an accepted bill may still be dishonoured on the due date. However, an importer may be very reluctant to subsequently dishonour an acceptance as this may impact upon the importer's good name.

Documents against payment (D/P) or cash against documents (CAD)

In either case, the collection is payable upon presentation (at sight) and documents are released to the importer against payment of the amount due. CAD terms are used when a collection order does not contain a bill of exchange. Collections on D/P or CAD terms provide the exporter with more security than D/A bills or open account trade because title documents such as bills of lading (or in certain cases the goods themselves) are released to the importer only when payment has been made.

For the importer, there are few risks associated with bills for collection. However, unlike a documentary credit, shipment schedules and documentation cannot be controlled and, if payment has been made against a D/P or CAD collection, the importer runs the risk that the goods shipped may be of inferior quality. For the exporter, control of the goods is lost once a D/A bill has been accepted and the documents released to the importer. Where goods have been despatched to the importer by air, road or rail transport, documents of title are not issued and the goods are delivered directly to the consignee. In countries where foreign currency is limited, such as the LDC importer, delays in the receipt of proceeds may be experienced pending allocation of foreign exchange by the authorities. Usually this requires the exporter to issue a proforma invoice.

In the event of the buyer refusing to accept the goods, the exporter would have to consider storage of the goods, shipping them back to the exporter, finding an alternative buyer or even abandoning the consignment. The exporter can however request the collecting bank to protect their interests in case of default by the buyer, but this may not always prove practical and may be prohibitively expensive. The exporter's local agent is usually best placed to take action to protect the goods if problems are experienced.

Clean collections

A clean collection consists only of a bill of exchange. In most cases, the bill will have already been accepted by the importer and is being presented for payment on its maturity date. As with an open account trade the underlying shipping documents will usually have been sent direct to the importer.

Avalized bills

Avalization is the specific endorsement on a bill of exchange by a bank which guarantees payment should the drawee (the importer) default on payment of the bill at maturity. After acceptance of a term bill, the importer may request the bank to avalize the bill in accordance with the terms of a previously agreed banking facility for this purpose.

Avalization can help importers to establish new trading relationships with overseas suppliers or negotiate improved terms because, like a documentary credit, it provides an assurance of payment which the supplier can use to obtain non-recourse finance such as forfaiting (see page 150). However, settlement by documentary credit should be considered where the importer needs to exercise more control over the transaction through the DC terms and conditions and the stipulated documents.

Open account

The open account payment method is widely practised, especially in European and North American markets. It lowers costs and reduces procedural difficulties, but the risk to the supplier is much greater. Conversely, as displayed on the risk ladder analysis, it yields the highest degree of security for the buyer and eases cash flow problems.

Trading on open account terms implies that the exporter trusts the business integrity and ability to pay of an overseas buyer. This could arise by having established a long-term relationship with the buyer, through obtaining favourable status reports, or credit assessments on the buyer, or it may be that credit insurance provides the confidence to trade on these terms. Alternatively, market forces may simply dictate that open account terms are the only viable option with which to conduct business.

With open account trade, the goods and relevant documents are sent by the supplier directly to the overseas buyer who will have agreed to pay the exporter upon arrival of the documents or within a certain period after the invoice or shipment date. The exporter loses all control of the goods trusting that payment will be made by the buyer in accordance with the original sales contract. An open account arrangement is not entirely without risk to the buyer. For example, if the importer is committed to producing goods dependent upon receipt of imported materials, or has already 'on sold' the goods to a third party, losses could occur if the goods or materials fail to arrive on time or are faulty. This could be mitigated by using the pre-shipment inspection arrangement (see page 177).

A variation of the open account payment system is the consignment account. If an exporter is satisfied with the integrity of an importer or an appointed agent, arrangements might be made to forward goods on consignment. The exporter retains ownership of the goods until they are sold or for an agreed period, after which the buyer remits the agreed price to the supplier.

Advance payment

The advance method of payment is the least secure for the buyer who has to face several risks including: the goods never being shipped; the goods being shipped late; the wrong goods being shipped; problems with documentation and cash flow pressure. However, there is no risk for the exporter when payment is received in advance of the goods being despatched, but if payment is made by cheque, it should be remembered that this does not constitute payment until the cheque has been cleared through the banking system. This can be a significant period in some countries. Advance payment need not always be to the full value of the sales contract: it is quite common for a partial advance payment to be made, particularly for contracts involving capital goods.

Import loans

Buyers often seek loans from banks to fund their overseas purchases and ease their cash flow situation. Such loans provide the buyer with the flexibility to take a period of extended credit undisclosed to the seller, whilst allowing the buyer to offer optimum (usually sight) payment terms. As with a banker's acceptance, the buyer has time to sell the goods and realize the proceeds before having to repay the loan.

By offering immediate payment, the buyer may be able to negotiate better terms or prices with the supplier. Where a period of credit is still taken from the supplier, the facility can be used to meet the buyer's obligation on the maturity date of the draft and provide finance for a further period to match sales receipts.

Import loans usually cover individual shipments of goods. Where goods are consigned to the order of the bank, they can be warehoused in the bank's name for an agreed period and may be drawn from time to time (against each payment). If immediate possession of the goods is required, for example to fulfil orders already received, the goods may be released to the buyer 'in trust' for an agreed period, at the end of which payment would be required. In either case, the period of the loan is geared to the buyers' terms of trade and commences from the date of the bank's payment under the documentary credit.

Loans taken out in a foreign currency may reduce financing costs and if the buyer receipts in the same currency this can improve the buyer's currency exposure. Interest (fixed or variable) is linked to the base rate for the currency and is usually payable at maturity of the loan. Variable rate loans have the advantage of being able to be repaid early without penalty, for example, if the subsequent sale proceeds were received earlier than anticipated.

A recent innovation in trade finance is in the area of transaction based finance relative to the purchase and sale of goods. It is of special interest to companies experiencing difficulty financing imports through cash flow or to an importer with a profitable deal who may have been unable to obtain finance from a traditional bank route. The financial package involves the finance house acquiring the stock the importer is looking to buy and then sells the goods back to the buyer on a credit basis. The importer goes on to complete the transaction with his group of buyers.

There are basically three methods of settlement between parties involving advance payment and open account which we will now examine.

Priority payment

This is the quickest method of making an international payment with funds being remitted through the secure inter-bank computer network known as SWIFT (Society for Worldwide Inter-Bank Financial Telecommunication) or by fax. Payment instructions provided to the bank should include the beneficiary's full banking details as will ensure the earliest possible receipt of funds. Payment is usually effective for value within two business days although earlier value can sometimes be obtained when making payments in certain time zones in currencies such as the US dollar and the euro.

Mail payment

This is best used only for non-priority, low value transactions such as less than US$10 000 or currency equivalent. Mail payments are sent either by mail, SWIFT or courier, but there is no assurance of the value date on which funds will be paid.

International bankers draft

Basically, this is a cheque drawn by one bank upon another. This method of payment is particularly suitable for non-priority, low value payments or for those which are to be accompanied by documentation such as invoices. If the draft is in the local currency the beneficiary will usually present it through local cheque clearing and, in most cases, will receive the full amount without deduction of charges by the overseas bank.

Bill of exchange

In international trade, the bill of exchange is widely used to establish a written legal undertaking to pay a sum of money and provide a convenient mechanism for the giving or receiving of a period of credit. Bills of exchange are often referred to as drafts.

A bill payable 'on demand' or 'at sight' would be known as a sight bill or sight draft. If it is payable at a 'fixed or determinable future time', it is called a term or usance bill (draft), because the buyer (drawee) is receiving a period of credit which is equal to the term (usance) of the bill, that is the period between the bill's acceptance and payment. The drawee signifies an agreement to pay on the due date by writing an acceptance across the face of the bill. Hence the draft must be drawn on the party nominated in the credit as drawee (usually the issuing or confirming bank); the currency must be unambiguous (e.g. USD not $); it must be made out for the correct amount; words and figures must agree and the tenor must be as required in the credit. The credit terms may also stipulate that the draft bears reference to the credit, for example is marked 'Drawn under documentary credit number .... of (issuing) bank'. Provided that the credit does not stipulate that drafts are required in duplicate, a single draft (sale or sola of exchange) may be presented. Most bills of exchange are now generated by computer or printed on company stationery although they can still be purchased from commercial stationers. They vary in shape, size and layout.

Basically a bill of exchange has been defined as 'an unconditional order' in writing addressed by one person (the drawer) to another (the drawee) signed by the person giving it (the drawer) requiring the person to whom it is addressed to pay on demand, or at a fixed or determinable future time a sum certain in money to or to the order of a specified person or to the bearer (the payee).

If the bill is payable to the exporter, it must be endorsed on the reverse side before presentation to the bank. The endorsement can be 'in blank' or specifically to the order of the bank handling the documents on the buyer's behalf. When presenting documents under a documentary credit (DC), the bill of exchange must be drawn on the party nominated in the DC terms as drawee (usually the issuing or confirming bank). The DC terms may also stipulate that the bill of exchange bears reference to the DC e.g. is marked 'drawn under documentary credit .... of (issuing bank)'.

Promissory note

Although having similar characteristics to a bill of exchange, a promissory note does not always carry the same legal rights. In contrast to a bill of exchange, a promissory note is a promise to pay issued or drawn up by the buyer (the author of the document) in favour of the seller (payee or beneficiary). It differs from a bill of exchange in that it is written by the buyer to the seller, other than being drawn by the seller on the buyer. A promissory note provides a commitment to pay as does the acceptance of a bill of exchange.

A promissory note is usually defined as an unconditional promise in writing made by one person (the maker or buyer) to another, signed by the maker or buyer engaging to pay, on demand, or at a fixed or determinable future time a certain sum in money to, or to the order of, a specified person or to bearer (the payee or beneficiary).

Performance bonds

Finally, associated with trade finance we will briefly examine performance bonds. Overall, there are three parties involved in a performance bond: the supplier – an exporter or overseas contractor who supplies the goods or services and performs the prescribed terms of the contract of sale; the guarantor who issues the performance bond on behalf of the supplier, generally a bank, an insurance company, or a surety company; and finally the buyer to whom the performance bond is issued and who benefits from it.

A variety of bonds exist and these include bid/tender bonds: performance bonds; default performance bonds; retention bonds; advance payment or repayment bonds and conditional demand performance bonds. Readers are urged to study the ICC publication No. 458 'Uniform Rules for Demand Guarantees' which extols the preparation of performance bonds and guarantees.

Commercial and transport documents

As already stressed earlier, the payment of goods through the banking system or direct to the supplier does involve the collection and presentation of commercial and transport documentation. This is to comply with a combination of requirements, for example export customs clearance, prescribed terms under documentary credits (UCP 500) documentary collections (URC 522), Incoterms 2000 (ICC Publication No. 560), import customs clearance and the export sales contract.

We will now look briefly at most of the documents involved but they will be examined in greater depth in Chapters 9, 11, 12 and 13.

(a) Air waybill or air consignment note. Document involved in air freight distribution internationally acting as a receipt for goods despatched.
(b) Bill of lading. Document of title and cargo receipt for maritime distribution. It is negotiable and many types exist. Used extensively in deep sea container and bulk cargo shipments. The FIATA multi-modal transport bill of lading (MTBL) covers combined transport/multi-modalism, such as containers.

(c) Cargo insurance policy and certificate. Document confirming insurance of cargo in accordance with Incoterms 2000.

(d) Certificate of origin. Document usually issued by a chamber of commerce to specify the nature, quantity, value and country of origin of goods.

(e) Certificate of shipment. FIATA forwarders receipt document confirming receipt of goods.

(f) CIM. International consignment note relative to movement of goods by rail, primarily in Europe.

(g) CMR. International consignment note relative to carriage of goods by road.

(h) Courier receipt. A cargo receipt involving a small parcel or packet despatched by a courier service.

(i) Customs declaration. A wide variety of customs declarations exist. A common one is the Single Administrative Document Form C88 embracing export, movement and import customs clearance declarations.

(j) Exchange permit. Usually associated with the issue of an import licence in Middle East markets.

(k) Export invoice. An invoice from the seller to the buyer covering the goods and often constituting the export sales contract. Also termed commercial invoice.

(l) Export licence. Issued by a government authorizing the export of a specified consignment.

(m) Health certificate. Issued by a government to confirm that the agricultural and animal products which are being exported comply with the relevant legislation in the exporter's country.

(n) Letters of hypothecation. Banker's document outlining conditions under which an international transaction will be executed.

(o) Letters of indemnity. Authority to permit cargo to be released to a consignee without production of the original bill of lading.

(p) Mates receipt. Document issued in lieu of bill of lading.

(q) Packing list. Document giving details of the invoice, buyer, consignee, country of origin, vessel or flight details, port or airport of loading and discharge, place of delivery, shipping marks, container number, weight and/or volume (cubic) of merchandise and the fullest details of the goods including packaging data. Document widely used by customs and banks under documentary credit systems.

(r) Phytosanitary (plant health) certificate. Issued by a government agricultural department of the exporting country to confirm plant, material, forest trees and other trees and shrubs and certain raw fruit and vegetables are disease free.

(s) Pre-shipment certificate. Process whereby the buyer's agent, such as an SGS, examines goods during manufacture and on shipment and if all is in order issues a clean report of findings document. A mandatory document in up to 60 importing countries and required under documentary credit arrangements.

(t) Sea waybill. An increasingly popular maritime consignment note often used in open account transactions. It constitutes a cargo receipt.

(u) Quality certificate. Document issued by the exporter confirming the quality of the goods shipped in accordance with the export sales contract.

(v) Veterinary and health certificate. Document issued by a government department to verify the health of a shipment of livestock, domestic animals or agricultural products.

(w) Weight certificate. Confirms the weight specified in accordance with bill of lading, invoice, certificate of insurance or other specified document.

Counter trade

During the past ten years the volume of world trade conducted under counter trade terms has greatly increased. Today it features in the trading techniques of over 100 countries and represents up to 10 per cent of world trade. Basically, counter trade is an umbrella term for a whole range of commercial mechanisms for reciprocal trade.

These mechanisms include barter, counter purchase, offset, buyback, evidence accounts and switch trading. The common characteristic of counter trade arrangements is that export sales to a particular market are made conditional upon undertakings to accept imports from that market. For example, an exporter may sell machinery to country X on the condition that the exporter accepts agricultural products from country X in payment. Simple barter deals like this are unusual and most counter trade deals are much more involved.

Both importers and exporters are aware of the potential demands for and the complexities of counter trade, since it has, over recent years, become a common feature of trade with more than half the countries of the world. Counter trade can be a complex, expensive and uncertain mode of trading. It has the potential to distort and disrupt the growth of trade, inasmuch as it replaces the pressures of competition and market forces with reciprocity, protection and price setting. Moreover, it introduces an unfair bias against small and medium-sized firms who may be less able to handle the additional cost and staff effort entailed. It increases the risk that subsidised (often low grade) goods will be dumped in the home market (although most of these in practice go to third world markets).

Counter trade is an inherently ad hoc activity. The mechanics vary according to local regulations and requirements, the nature of the goods to be exported and the current priorities of the parties involved.

Importers and buyers should scan the press or internet for counter trade opportunities. Banks usually act as broker in formulating counter trade deals, which can be very complex. There are six main forms of counter trade which we will briefly examine.

1. *Barter.* The direct exchange of goods for goods. The principal exports are paid for with goods (or services) supplied from the importing market. A single contract covers both flows; in the simplest case no cash is involved.

2. *Buyback*. A form of barter in which suppliers of capital plant or equipment agree to repayment in the form of future output of the investment concerned. For example, exporters of equipment for a chemical works may be paid with part of the resulting output from that work.
3. *Offset*. A condition of buying some products, especially those embodying advanced technology to some markets, is that the exporter incorporates into his final products specified materials, components or sub assemblies, procured within the importing country. This has long been an established feature of trade in defence systems and aircraft.
4. *Counter purchase*. Concurrently with, and as a condition of, securing a sales order, the exporter undertakes to purchase goods and services from the country concerned. There are two parallel but separate contracts, one for the principal order which is paid for on normal cash or credit terms, and another for counter purchase. The value of the counter purchase undertaking may vary in value between 10 per cent and 100 per cent (or even more) of the original export order.
5. *Switch trading* (or swap deals). Imbalances in long-term bilateral agreements, usually between East European countries and developing nations, sometimes lead to the accumulation of uncleared credit surpluses in one or other country: for example Brazil at one time had a large credit surplus with Poland. Such surpluses can sometimes be topped by third parties, so that (for example) French exports to Brazil might be financed from the sale of Polish goods to France or elsewhere.
6. *Evidence accounts*. Companies or traders with a significant level of continuing business in certain markets may be required to arrange counter-purchased exports from those markets at least equivalent to their own imports with the country concerned. For example, a multinational firm with a local manufacturing subsidiary in a developing country may be required to ensure counter-purchased exports of equivalent value to their subsidiary's imports of materials and equipment.

An increasing number of buyers are now opting for counter trade business with beneficial results. To conclude we can summarize below the four main reasons driving counter trade.

(a) To finance trade which, due to a lack of commercial credit or convertible currency, would otherwise be precluded.
(b) To exploit a buyer's market to obtain better terms of trade or similar benefits.
(c) To protect or stimulate the output of domestic industries (including agriculture and minerals extraction).
(d) As a reflection of political and economic policies which seek to plan and balance overseas trade, as found in China and many South American and African countries.

Factoring

It was mentioned above that the supplier may experience cash flow problems in the trade cycle due to the lengthened payment period in international trade. This can be alleviated through factoring. Finance for export receivables can be provided by a factoring company who will purchase trade debts for cash providing the exporter with total credit protection for approved invoices. Up to 80 per cent of the invoice value is paid immediately upon presentation of invoices with the remainder becoming available as soon as payment is received from the buyer. If the buyer does not pay, the factor effects payment of the balance after a set period (typically 120 days) from the date payment fell due, which allows time for any problems to be resolved between the commercial parties.

Export factoring is most suited for short-term debts (typically up to 90 days) involving the sale of products or services which are complete at the point of invoicing and for trade with those parts of the world in which open account is the accepted method of transacting business. Most factors operate a 'two factor' system, whereby a correspondent factor in the buyer's country is used to assess the credit standing of the buyer. Factoring can also provide finance where credit protection is already available to an exporter through a credit insurance policy.

Forfaiting

A further method of alleviating the exporter's cash flow problem is found in forfaiting. The term 'forfaiting' is derived from the French *à forfait* which means to surrender or relinquish the rights to something. In return for a cash payment from a forfaiter, an exporter agrees to surrender or relinquish the rights to claims for payment on goods or services delivered to a buyer.

Most forfaiting transactions involve the forfaiter purchasing, at a discount, bills of exchange or promissory notes accepted or guaranteed by a bank. The guarantee can take the form of a separate document, but it is more usual for the buyer to obtain an aval for the bills or notes. An aval is a specific endorsement on the bills or notes by a bank, which guarantees payment should the drawee (the buyer) default on payment at maturity (see avalized bills, page 142). By this mechanism, the forfaiter provides non-recourse finance to the exporter – once the bills or notes have been sold, the exporter has no further involvement in the collection of the debt.

Forfaiting is popular with companies undertaking major export contracts where repayment is made via a series of bills over an extended term and for contracts involving goods or services with significant foreign content which may prevent the exporter from obtaining credit insurance. When tendering for new business, forfaiting can be used to fix the financing costs in advance and build them into the contract price.

International exchange rates

The subject of foreign exchange relates to the exchange of various currencies one for another. On the practical side it concerns the methods of settling foreign debts, the means of payment and the services of banks and brokers. Settlement of debts between parties in the same country is quite simply effected by the payment of money which the creditor is prepared to accept as it is the legal tender of the country. Likewise, benefits exist when the buyer and seller are situated in the euro zone where euro transactions prevail (see page 155). Where the buyer and supplier live in different countries and use different currencies, however, there arises the need for a system of conversion – fulfilled by the foreign exchange market. Unlike the markets in commodities or stocks and shares, the foreign exchange market has no centre but consists merely of telephone communications between dealers (at the banks) and brokers.

The price of one currency in terms of another is called the rate of exchange; it is the number of units of one currency that will be exchanged for a given number of units of another currency. Hence, rates against sterling or the euro are the number of foreign currency units to the pound or euro. It may be US dollars or Swiss francs. A glance at the financial press shows that two closing rates are quoted for each currency; the higher is the market's buying rate for that currency and the lower one is the market's selling rate. Transactions between dealers are conducted at approximately these rates. A banker who is asked to buy or sell foreign currency relies upon the market for cover and the prices at which he or she can obtain this cover are the market rates. Hence, in quoting to a customer the banker bases his or her rates on those ruling in the market; adjusted to make a provision for profit.

A willingness to do business in the currency preferred by your trading partners can provide significant competitive advantages, enabling the buyer to obtain products/services on a more competitiveness basis. A buyer trading in his or her domestic currency is assured of price currency stability with all the currency fluctuation risk being absorbed by the supplier. Conversely, the buyer accepts all the currency risk fluctuation when accepting the supplier's currency as the trading currency. It is important to bear in mind that most global business is transacted in the world's major currencies, whilst secondary currencies such as those in LDCs are not freely convertible and trade through a third currency such as the US dollar.

Hence, whenever buying or selling goods in currencies other than their own, importers and exporters become exposed to currency risk from the fluctuations in the exchange rate in the period between prices being agreed and payment being received. Management of this exposure is essential to minimize the potential risks and to maximize the profit from the underlying transactions. The technique of protecting against future exchange rate movements is usually referred to as 'hedging'.

The market rates quoted in the press are 'spot' rates, that is those applied to transactions for completion immediately or at the latest within two days from the date of the deal. If the exchange rate has moved in your favour between the signing of a contract and its settlement date, an exceptional benefit over and above that anticipated from the contract terms may be derived. Equally, the exchange rate may have moved in the opposite direction, adversely affecting the profitability of the underlying contract. As currency is a commodity like any other, its price will be governed by the interaction of demand and supply and hence short- and long-term factors influence buyers and sellers. The short-term factors fall into two categories: commercial and financial.

Commercial operations relate to trade in goods and services which make up the current account of the balance of payments and give rise to payments and receipts in various currencies thereby determining supply and demand in the foreign exchange.

Financial operations come under seven areas:

(a) Stock exchange operations – the purchase of securities on foreign stock exchanges (bourses) by private or corporate investors in order to yield a return, or in the expectation of a capital appreciation.
(b) Banking operations – the transfer of funds by bankers for investment or deposit in foreign centres.
(c) Speculation – transactions based on the expectation that the exchange rate of a particular currency will change in response to some political or natural event.
(d) Interest payments – interest on loans and dividends from investment.
(e) Loan repayments – the issue of a loan in one country on behalf of a borrower in another gives rise to a payment across the exchanges from the country of the lender to that of the borrower that will have an adverse impact on the exchange rate of the lending country's currency and cause that of the borrowing country to appreciate.
(f) Inter-governmental transfers – governments borrow from and lend to each other in the same way as private individuals and trading companies.
(g) Exchange stabilization – these are official operations in foreign exchange markets in order to control exchange rate movements by varying the relation between supply and demand.

Forward exchange

In view of the increasing amount of business conducted on credit terms, it is quite likely that a merchant will be liable to pay his or her supplier in the latter currency at a future date or to receive foreign currency at a future date from a buyer. With exchange rates floating at present, he or she is vulnerable to any changes in currency values that may occur in the interval between conclusion of the contract and the date on which payment is due. It is to provide cover against such exchange risks that the 'forward exchange' market came into existence. The merchant contracts with a bank to purchase or sell one currency in exchange for another at a predetermined rate on an agreed future date. Hence, he or she therefore knows how much he or she will eventually pay or receive in his or her own currency and any intervening fluctuations in the exchange rate will not affect him or her.

Forward contracts may be 'fixed' or 'option'. A fixed forward is a contract with a specific performance date. A forward option stipulates a period of time during which performance is to take place, the actual date being chosen by the customer. It should be clearly understood that the 'option' is not whether the customer deals or not – he or she is fully committed to the transaction – it relates only to the date on which he or she takes or delivers the currency concerned. Basically, the forward contract is one of the simplest hedging techniques, allowing the buyer or supplier to fix the exchange rate for the sale or purchase of a specific quantity of a currency for delivery at an agreed future date.

As a forward contract is a legally binding contract between the bank and the customer, a bank credit line is required to cover the amount and period of all forward contracts outstanding at any one time. The period of a forward contract can range from one day after spot value up to five years, depending on the currencies involved. Maturity of contract can be arranged either for settlement on a specific date (fixed contract) or on or between two dates (option dated contract) where the precise delivery date is not known.

The key benefit from a forward contract is that the buyer or supplier knows in advance the exact value of future transactions in domestic currency terms. As well as eliminating the exchange risk this can aid cash flow management and assist with budgeting, costing and pricing processes. However, one does not have the opportunity to gain from beneficial exchange rate movements during the life of the contract.

Forward rates

The forward exchange rate is linked to the prevailing spot rate and is derived from the interest rate differential between the two currencies over the term of the forward contract. It is not a view of the likely exchange rate movement during that term.

The ratio for forward exchange deals are quoted as a premium or discount on the spot rate, that is an amount above or below spot; sometimes they are at 'par' with spot. For example, if the dollar/sterling rate is quoted at a discount on the spot rate (measured in the conventional way as the number of dollars to a pound) then in terms of dollars, sterling is dearer forward than spot. Conversely, if the forward rate is at a premium, sterling is cheaper forward than spot. In calculating the rate for a forward deal, a premium is added to the spot rate, whereas a discount is deducted from it. Forward margins (discount or premium) are determined by interest rate differentials and by market expectations of future spot exchange rates. Currencies in which interest rates are relatively low tend to be dearer forward than spot in terms of currencies in which interest rates are relatively high. The press usually quotes forward margins for one, three and six months forward, but by arrangement with the bank it is possible to cover for longer periods depending on the currency concerned.

A buyer who has contracted to buy foreign currency but finds that he or she no longer requires it will still have to take delivery of the currency at the agreed forward rate; he or she can then sell it back to the bank at the ruling spot rate. Similarly, if the customer has not received the foreign currency he or she has contracted to sell, he or she will have to buy the amount required at the ruling spot rate for delivery to the bank. In practice, the bank may merely debit or credit the difference to the customer's account. Where circumstances cause a delay in fulfilment of a contract it may often be extended at an adjusted rate by arrangement with the bank.

A further way of mitigating currency fluctuation risk is the currency swap. These are transacted between multinationals and their banks, between banks on an international scale and between national state governments when it is advantageous to move out of one currency into another for a limited time without exposure to a foreign exchange risk. It is called spot against forward.

Currency options

A currency option overcomes the disadvantages of dealing in the spot market or of using forward contracts. A currency option provides the buyer with protection from adverse exchange rate movements (like a forward contract), yet allows the importer to benefit if the exchange rate moves favourably (as with a spot deal).

A currency option can be defined as providing the importer or exporter with the right, but not the obligation, to buy or sell a certain amount of currency at an agreed rate (called the 'strike price') on or between future date(s). The purchaser of the option pays a premium, in advance, for the benefit of being able to take advantage of any favourable movement in the exchange rate. In addition to the elimination of the exchange risk, the purchaser of the option also gains the flexibility of being able to decide: whether to exercise the option; how much of the option to exercise and, depending on the type of option bought, when to exercise the option.

Currency options are available in all currencies where a liquid forward market exists and, for major currencies, with maturities of up to five years. They can be used in conjunction with, or as an alternative to, spot dealings and forward contracts.

Average rate options

Where an exporter or importer has a series of regular payments or receipts and has budgeted for a particular exchange rate over the period, an average rate option (ARO) will provide the same protection as a currency option but, because of the averaging process, is achieved with lower premium cost. Although having the characteristics of a currency option, an ARO does not involve the physical buying and selling of currency; the underlying transactions are settled independently.

The company selects the rate it wishes to protect (the strike price) and agrees a mechanism by which the bank can calculate the 'average' rate. Average rate options are available in all major currencies for periods up to two years and the basis for deriving the average rate can be daily, weekly, monthly or any other period relevant to the underlying cash flows.

At the end of the agreed period the company is compensated by the bank if the average exchange rate is worse than the strike price. Compensation is not paid if the average rate is better than the strike price; the company will have benefited from the favourable rate movements when the underlying transactions were settled. Note that unless the company deals at the same time as the bank fixes its reference rates, there is likely to be a variation between the bank's average rate and the company's actual dealing average.

Foreign currency accounts

Any importer or exporter who regularly undertakes business in a foreign currency could benefit from a foreign currency account. This is especially true where a company is both paying and receiving funds in a currency as, by using a foreign currency account, the company can avoid the costs associated with converting the currency each time there is a transaction.

Borrowing in foreign currency, repayable from currency receipts, can eliminate exchange risk and may be less expensive than borrowing in sterling or the national currency of the buyer. This can reduce costs and provide the ability to tender and invoice in the buyer's currency, both of which can be critical success factors in obtaining new business. To the UK buyer trading in the EU euro zone, a euro-based account is advantageous both financially and competitively.

Euro currency

On 1 January 1999 a single European currency – the euro – was introduced in the twelve European Union countries who have formed an economic and monetary union. The twelve euro zone countries are Austria, Belgium, Finland, France, Germany, Greece, Ireland, Italy, Luxembourg, the Netherlands, Portugal and Spain. This move has resulted in a real change to the business environment throughout Europe. The twelve countries also share a single interest rate set by the European Central Bank, which is responsible for the monetary policy of the euro zone countries involving a total population of 280 million.

Overseas buyers are urged to set up a euro currency account and those electing to trade in the euro zone will experience intrinsic benefits. Overall, the euro has produced the following features and benefits.

(a) Cheaper transaction costs – countries in the euro zone do not have to change currencies when doing business.
(b) Stability of exchange rates resulting in countries in the euro zone no longer being affected by currency fluctuations when trading with each other.
(c) Transparent price differences – it has become more obvious when different euro zone countries charge different prices for the same goods and services.
(d) Companies operating in Europe have simplified their accounts and finances by trading in the euro, not only in the euro zone of twelve states, but also in other countries outside the euro zone embracing the three other states in the

European Union and also other European non-EU member countries. This embraces budgeting financial management.

(e) Companies situated outside the euro zone but which are in part of the EU, trade in the euro.

(f) Buyers and suppliers throughout Europe gain from using the euro, as bank charges have fallen and payments have been speeded up.

(g) Businesses have experienced fewer legal problems when using the euro in price agreements.

(h) Cross border competition has increased, placing companies outside the euro zone in a less favourable position against competitors within the zone.

(i) The euro has produced an impetus of cross border mergers.

(j) Distribution and procurement within the euro zone has become simpler and cheaper because companies do not undergo any exchange risk when trading.

(k) Raising finance has become easier and more attractive in the euro-bond and euro-equity share market.

(l) Companies have found it necessary to refocus their marketing and procurement strategies to combat opportunities and threats emerging from the transparency of euro-pricing with no exchange risk implication and greater price stability compared with the national currency.

(m) Companies worldwide who buy into the euro zone tend to trade in the euro. This enables the buyer to draw price comparisons from other sources both within the euro zone and outside it.

(n) The development of computerized technology will further stimulate the economic growth of the euro zone, particularly for organizations within the zone.

Factors influencing the level of exchange rates

The level of an exchange rate plays a crucial role in an exporter's strategy. It is a high risk area and buyers continuously study the exchange rate money markets to keep in touch with market trends and the best methods available to counter such variations. Moreover, one must bear in mind that a national currency devaluation cheapens procurement to that market.

A wide range of factors determine the level of individual country or zonal exchange rates. The major ones are detailed below, but it is stressed that the significance of each factor will be determined by local market conditions.

(a) The yield on the money markets reflected in the government central bank interest rate level. This is found in the forward exchange rate which is linked to the prevailing spot rate and is derived from the interest rate differential between the two currencies over the term of the forward contract.

(b) The actual central bank interest rate.

(c) The balance of trade and balance of payments performance and constituents. For example, a continuing trade deficit with no evidence of improvement will put pressure on the exchange rate level causing it to decline in value unless remedial measures are taken such as raising interest rates or curbing imports.

(d) The indebtedness of the country, such as IMF loans. This applies particularly to LDCs.

(e) A rise in the price of a barrel of crude oil on the world market will undermine the trade balance of some LDCs reliant on oil as an energy source and may account for more than 25 per cent of their import bill annually. Moreover, high oil prices are globally inflationary (see page 61).

(f) The long- and short-term market prospects in a country and particularly its composition of agricultural, industrial, commercial and service sectors.

(g) The economic forecast and range of economic indicators – inflation, interest rates, money supply, employment and production.

(h) The government's mandate to manage the economy and the government's competence to actually devise and carry out effective policies to sustain and develop its economy in a competitive global market.

(i) Whether the currency is traded on the open market or relies on a third currency such as the US dollar or the euro.

(j) The general market mood of the currency and its expectations as interpreted by economists, bankers and traders.

(k) Any unforeseen situation emerging such as hostilities, earthquakes or political developments.

(l) Policies adopted by international agencies – the IMF, OECD, World Bank, WTO and G8.

(m) Level of international reserves.

(n) The gross and net external debt expressed as a percentage of the gross domestic product.

(o) The country's net foreign debt and debt service.

(p) The country's net debt service as a percentage of exports of goods and services.

(q) A country joining a trading bloc such as the EU.

(r) Circumstances which create uncertainty.

(s) Any technological or infrastructure development providing improved prospects for a particular economy such as the provision of a hydro-electric dam, installation of a coal, gas or oil energy plant.

(t) The monetary policies adopted by a country.

(u) The financial market mechanism in a particular country.

(v) An analysis of the currency performance and factors determining its variation.

(w) Stock exchange operations, banking operations, interest payments, loan payments, inter-governmental transfers and exchange stabilization.

Recommended reading

- *Financial Times*.
- Uniform Rules for Collections, ICC Publication No. 522.
- Uniform Customs and Practice for Documentary Credits, ICC Publication No. 500.

9

Import documentation

An important part of international trade is to recognize at the outset that documentation provides tangible evidence that the goods ordered have been produced and despatched in accordance with the buyer's requirements. Hence, there is a need for the buyer to have a good understanding of the various documents involved in processing the import consignment together with the carrier's liability and CMI rules for electronic bills of lading. Moreover, it is also important to understand the role of such documents and their limitations, embracing their legal environment together with likely problems which they may encounter. The buyer's bank, freight forwarder, trade association or government department dealing with foreign trade can help with any queries. Consignment details need to be communicated accurately to various parties so both importers and exporters need to be familiar with the principal documents used. Documentation as discussed in Chapter 8 is used to comply with government regulations in both the buyer's and the seller's countries and has become an increasingly important factor in obtaining finance for international trade. It is the responsibility of the exporter to ensure that the documents for the transport of the goods are complete, accurate and properly and promptly processed in accordance with the contract of sale. Failure to do so can frequently result in costly consequences. Many software packages exist in the market to aid the buyer in the documentation processing. Information can be found on the Internet or further details will be available in the international trade press in the buyer's country. Electronic communication plays a major role today in the transmission of documents.

The importer, however, has a responsibility for accurately completing the necessary forms for the goods to be licensed for import and cleared through customs. As will be discussed in Chapter 13, the documents required for import customs clearance may include: certificate of origin, supplier's invoice, import licence, packing list, health certificate and a copy of the bill of lading, air waybill or sea waybill. Normally the supplier arranges to deliver the goods when and where the buyer requires, but much will depend on the buying terms: EXW, FCA, CPT, CIF, DDU or CFR (see pages 287–90). Incorrect documentation can cause delay in the clearance of goods at their destination. Goods can be impounded, warehoused or left on the quayside with the risk of damage, loss or consequent expense.

The avoidance of discrepant documentation is particularly important when the transaction is to be settled by documentary credit. Both the importer and exporter may suffer if discrepancies occur, as they can cause delay, lead to increased costs and lose the exporter the protection offered by the documentary credit.

The following measures ensure comprehensive and efficient processing of importation documents and therefore the smooth transit of consignments.

(a) Ensure a good liaison is maintained between the seller or buyer and their forwarding agents. On-line computer access facilitates transparency of the data in the supply chain.

(b) Check with customs which documents are required to process the imported consignment and ensure they are made available from the supplier.

(c) Ensure adequate funds are available to meet the import duty, VAT and other charges.

(d) Check that the goods received conform precisely to their description on the export invoice and carrier's documents. It is important that the information contained in the documents is consistent across all documents. The Master document is usually the export invoice.

(e) Make sure all the required documents are present in the specified numbers and that the original documents are signed (see ICC publication No. 560 Incoterms 2000) or endorsed where necessary. In addition, check whether any document has to be certified or legalized, for example by a chamber of commerce or local consulate.

(f) Ensure that the correct documents are used and that the maximum benefit will therefore be gained, for example by using the sea waybill (page 168) when appropriate in preference to the bill of lading (page 163). Also the correct and most advantageous commodity description must be featured on the specific documents to ensure that the minimum customs payment is made under the tariff (page 264).

(g) Ensure that the role and significance of original and copy documents are fully understood and that the relevant convention – the Warsaw Convention, CIM, CMR, Hague, Hague–Visby and Hamburg Rules – is being utilized. Also, decide at what stage under Incoterms 2000 that the title of the goods passes from the seller to the buyer (see page 287).

(h) Make sure that the carrier's documents such as the bill of lading, air waybill and sea waybill are likely to be completed by the buyer or the forwarding agent when the buyer takes charge of the transportation such as EXW, FCA, etc. (see pages 291–3, 298–9).

The above list should be read in consultation with Chapter 14, Processing the imported consignment. In processing an import consignment which involves extensive documentation, one must bear in mind that there are four contracts to execute: export sales contract; contract of carriage; financial contract and contract of cargo insurance. Failure to have the relevant documentation correctly completed will result in late delivery as customs will refuse to clear the goods. Documentation relating to finance; customs and cargo insurance is covered in Chapters 8, 13 and 12 respectively. The subject is very comprehensively dealt with in the companion volume 'Shipping and Air Freight Documentation for Importers and Exporters' (Branch, 2nd edn, 2000).

We will now look at the various consignment documents individually.

Air waybill

The air waybill is the consignment note used for the carriage of goods by air. It is often called an air consignment note and it is not a document of title or a transferable or negotiable instrument. The document travels with the cargo and it is not possible to use it as a negotiable instrument for letter of credit purposes, as the cargo would arrive at the destination airport days or sometimes weeks before the air waybill's arrival via the banking system, thereby allowing the consignee to take delivery of the goods. The air waybill is basically a receipt for the goods for despatch and is prima facie evidence of the conditions of carriage. Overall, there are usually twelve copies of each air waybill for the shipper, the sales agent, the issuing carrier (airline operator), the consignee, as a delivery receipt, for the airport of destination, the third carrier (if applicable), the second carrier (if applicable), the first carrier, as an extra copy for the carrier (when required), as an invoice and at the airport of departure. Copies 1, 2 and 3 are the originals. Not every copy is used for all consignments, but merely as circumstances demand. For example, the second carrier's copy would be used only if the consignment was conveyed on another airline to complete the transit – such as British Airways conveying it for the first leg of the journey and Air Canada for the remainder.

The standard IATA air waybill (AWB), used worldwide and mandatory, is the most important feature of the simplified system of documentation for air freight moving internationally. It is the basic airline document covering the movement of shipments on international air freight services. A single air waybill covers carriage over any distance, by as many airlines as may be required to complete the transportation. When goods carried by one airline for part of the journey are transferred to another airline, the original air waybill is sent forward with the consignment from point of original departure to the final destination. When issued by the airline, the air waybill features a unique reference number which commences with the carrier prefix (usually a bar code). The air waybill is the key to tracing the flight details of the consignment.

The air waybill is mandatory in use and must be completed in at least three parts: (i) the carrier (signed by the consignor), (ii) for the consignee (signed by the consignor and carrier) and (iii) for the consignor (signed by the carrier). The air waybill must contain the following data:

(a) The place and date of its execution.

(b) The name and address of the shipper.

(c) The names and addresses of the consignor and consignee.

(d) Customs data – the AWB is regarded as the skeleton pre-entry document, containing the following information: first carrier (airline); departure and destination airports and any special route to be followed; agents' IATA code (when the shipper is using an agent); value of goods and currency; full technical description of cargo dimensions; commodity code; rate class; chargeable weight and freight rate.

(e) Total freight amount prepaid and/or to pay at destination; precisely defined.

(f) Details of any ancillary charges payable.

(g) Signature of the shipper or agent.

(h) Signature of the issuing carrier (airline operator) or agent.

(i) Details of booked flight and actual flight.

Efficient service depends on the accuracy and completeness of the air waybill. Hence, the buyer, in consultation with the seller, must give clear and complete forwarding instructions to the airline or agent. To facilitate this procedure they may use the 'Shipper's Letter of Instruction', a standardized form which may be obtained from any airline, approved IATA Cargo Agent or forwarder. The main functions of the standard air waybill are as follows.

At departure airports it is a contract of carriage, a receipt for goods, provides a unique reference for handling inventory control and documentation reference, includes a description of goods and full rating information, includes special handling requirements, and provides basic details for the aircraft manifest. Post-flight information includes a document source for revenue collection, interlining accounting and proration and cargo statistics. At destination airports the air waybill provides a basic document for notification to the consignee, customs clearance and delivery to the consignee. Additionally, it is a source document for clearance and delivery charges accounting.

Where more than one package is involved, the carrier can require the consignor to make out separate air waybills. The air consignment note must be printed in one of the official languages of the country of departure, for example, French, German, etc. Erasures are not admissible, but alterations can be made provided they are authenticated by the consignor's signature or initials. If quantities, weights, or values are altered, they must appear in words as well as figures.

The air freight consolidation market continues to grow. This involves an IATA-accredited air freight agency providing a consolidation service and entering into an agency agreement with a forwarder in the country to be served. Usually it is the same company which has a global network. The agent markets the consolidation service and despatches the merchandise as one consignment with the airline. Consolidation usually takes place at the forwarders' premises which is normally located near or on the airport. Alternatively, it may be at the airline export shed where the consignment is placed on a pallet or ULD (unit load device). The documentation involved is the Master Air Waybill (MAWB), which is issued by the airline and identifies the forwarder as the shipper and the consignee as the forwarder in the destination country. Details of all the packages in the consolidation feature in the MAWB including weight, volume and cargo description. Such consignment details are often recorded on a cargo manifest which is attached to the MAWB. The IATA air freight agency issues to each shipper a House Air Waybill (HAWB) which provides a cargo description and records the MAWB number as a cross-reference. The HAWB should contain the information set out under documentary requirements when this need arises (see page 134 item 11).

Under a documentary letter of credit, certain specific information or instructions to be shown on the air waybill may be requested. This usually includes: names and addresses of the exporter, importer and the first carrier or airline; the names of the airports of departure and destination together with details of any special routes; the date of the flight; the declared value of the merchandise for customs purposes; the number of packages with marks, weights, quantity and dimensions; the freight charge per unit of weight or volume; the technical description of the goods and not the commercial description; whether the freight charge has been prepared or will be paid at the destination; the signature of the exporter (or his or her agent); the place and date of issue; and finally the signature of the issuing carrier (or his or her agent).

The international air carriage of goods is subject to either the Warsaw Convention 1929 or the amended Warsaw Convention 1955. Which of these Conventions applies depends on which Convention the countries of departure and arrival have ratified. For one of the Conventions to apply, both of the countries must have ratified the same Convention; if both have ratified the amended Warsaw Convention then, irrespective of whether they have both also ratified the earlier convention, the amended Warsaw Convention applies. The limit of liability is 250 Poincare (gold) francs or, if the Montreal Protocols 1–3 of 1975 have been ratified, 17 SDRs per kilo. Montreal Potocol No. 4 came into effect in June 1998. On 28 May 1999 in Montreal a new convention – the Montreal Convention of 1999 – was adopted. No countries have so far (2000) ratified or acceded it.

Today, world airlines and air freight consolidators have a fully computerized air freight documentation system permitting on-line access by major shippers, agents, customs and handling companies. This extends to the use of bar codes for automatic verifications, enabling cargo handling and sorting to be undertaken electronically. Hence, the seller and the buyer use electronic commerce to issue instructions, complete documents, track cargo and communicate.

ATA carnet

A carnet is a document that permits customs clearance of certain temporary imports and exports more easily, by replacing normal customs documents in the exporter's country and normal customs documentation and security in the country into which the goods are imported. ATA (admission temporaire/

temporary admission) is the main carnet used. It can be used for practically all kinds of goods and can provide for a simple entry to and exit from a single foreign country or for numerous multi-destination journeys during the validity of the carnet. Goods covered by ATA carnets are subject to the normal import/export prohibitions and restrictions and licensing rules. ATA carnets are issued by an accredited chamber of commerce and require security either in cash, by bank draft or counter guarantee.

The ATA carnet replaces the normal customs declaration and is not required for EU shipments of goods within the 15 states.

Bill of lading

We have already focused on the bill of lading in Chapter 8 in relation to its role in confirming shipment of goods under the documentary credit cycle. It is an important carrier's document and we will now examine the other aspects of particular interest to the buyer.

A bill of lading has been defined as a receipt for goods shipped on board a vessel, signed by the person (or his or her agent) who contracts to carry them and stating the conditions in which the goods were delivered to (and received by) the ship. Overall, it is used to control delivery of goods transported by sea and, in negotiable form, it is title to the goods which is realized by transfer and endorsement.

The salient points incorporated in a bill of lading can be conveniently listed as follows:

(a) Name of shipper (usually the exporter).
(b) Name of the carrying vessel.
(c) Full description of cargo (provided it is not bulk cargo) including any shipping marks, individual package numbers in the consignment, contents, cubic measurement, gross weight, etc.
(d) The marks and numbers identifying the goods.
(e) Port of shipment or dry port (CFS).
(f) Port of discharge or dry port (CFS).
(g) Full details of freight, including when and where it is to be paid – whether freight paid or payable at destination.
(h) Name of consignee or, if the shipper is anxious to withhold the consignee's name, the shipper's order.
(i) Terms of the contract of carriage.
(j) Date the goods were received for shipment and/or loaded on the vessel.
(k) Name and address of the notified party (the person to be notified on arrival of the shipment, usually the buyer).
(l) Number of bills of lading signed on behalf of the Master or his or her agent acknowledging receipt of the goods.
(m) Signature of the Ship's Master or his or her agent and the date.

The international rules reflected in international conventions regarding sea transport embracing the bill of lading document are as follows.

The Hague Rules were agreed at an international convention in Brussels in 1924 and govern liability for loss or damage to goods carried by sea under a bill of lading (see page 236). They are officially known as the 'International Convention for the Unification of Certain Rules relating to Bills of Lading' and are reflected in the UK by the Carriage of Goods by Sea Act 1924.

The Hague Rules were designed to apply to all exports from any nation which ratified the rules. Overall, they apply almost universally wherever they have not been superseded by the Hague–Visby Rules or Hamburg Rules, either by the application of law or by contractual incorporation into the terms and conditions of the relevant bill of lading. The main features of the Hague Rules are as follows:

(a) They provide minimum terms which a carrier may offer for the carriage of all goods other than live animals, non-commercial goods, experimental shipments and goods carried on deck where the bill of lading is claused to indicate such carriage.

(b) The carrier has to exercise due diligence to provide a seaworthy vessel at the commencement of the voyage and this duty cannot be delegated. The carrier is however protected in three cases: negligence in navigation; negligence in management of the vessel (as compared to care of cargo); and fire – unless by the actual fault or privity of the Carrier.

(c) Liability is limited to £100 per package in the UK – other nations have set alternative limits.

The Hague–Visby Rules were adopted in 1968 and are known as the Brussels Protocol (see page 237). These were enacted in the UK by the Carriage of Goods by Sea Act 1971. The 1968 convention recommended a range of amendments which is designed to apply to all bills of lading where (i) the port of shipment is in a ratifying nation; (ii) the place of issue of the bill of lading is in a ratifying nation and (iii) the bill of lading applies Hague–Visby Rules contractually.

The Hamburg Rules emerged in March 1978 in Hamburg, radically altering the liability which shipowners have to bear for loss or damage to goods in the courts of those nations where the Rules apply (see page 237). The main difference between the New Rules and the old Hague–Visby Rules are as follows:

(a) The carrier will be liable for loss, damage or delay to the goods occurring whilst in his or her charge unless he or she proves that 'he, his servants or agents took all measures that could reasonably be required to avoid the occurrence and its consequences'.

(b) The carrier is liable for delay in delivery under certain circumstances.

(c) The dual system for calculating the limit of liability either by reference to package or weight as set out in the Hague–Visby Rules has been readopted but the amounts have been increased by about 25 per cent to SDR 835 per package and SDR 2.5 per kilo.

(d) The Hamburg Rules cover all contracts for carriage by sea other than charter parties whereas the Hague and Hague–Visby Rules only apply mandatorily as an international convention where a bill of lading is issued. The Hamburg Rules are therefore applicable to waybills, consignment notes, etc.

(e) They cover shipment of live animals and deck cargo whereas the Hague and Hague–Visby Rules may not.

(f) They will apply to both imports and exports to and from signatory nations (i.e. all that nations trade) whereas the Hague and Hague–Visby apply to exports only.

The Hamburg Rules came into force in November 1992 but implementation has been delayed until April 2002.

There are a number of types and forms of bills of lading which are detailed below.

1. *Shipped bill of lading.* This confirms that the merchandise has been 'shipped in apparent good order and condition'. This is the most satisfactory type of cargo receipt and the supplier prefers such a bill as there is no doubt about the goods on board and, in consequence, no dispute on this point will arise with the bankers or consignee, thereby facilitating the earliest financial settlement of the export sale.

2. *Received for shipment bill of lading.* This is evidence of receipt of goods for shipment requiring a later dated clause or stamp 'shipped on board' to raise it to the status of a 'receipt for goods shipped'. The goods may originate from a dry port, CFS, ICD, etc.

3. *Through bills of lading.* This document covers two or more carriers getting the goods to their final destination. The onwards carriage may either be by a second vessel or by a different form of transport such as rail.

4. *Groupage and house bills of lading.* The shipping line issues a groupage bill of lading to embrace a collection of compatible consignments placed in one container and treated as a full load. A cargo manifest is issued supporting the bill of lading itemizing each cargo consignment in the container. The freight forwarder originating the consignment will issue a house bill of lading for each separate shipment and cross referring to the ocean bill of lading. It is important that the house bill of lading features the requisite information under a documentary credit.

5. *Transhipment bill of lading.* This type is issued by shipping companies when there is no direct service between two ports but when the shipowner is prepared to tranship the cargo at an intermediate port at his or her own expense.

6. *Clean bill of lading.* Each bill of lading states 'in apparent good order and condition', referring to the cargo. If this statement is not modified by the shipowner the bill is regarded as clean or unclaused. This type of bill of lading is acceptable to banks.

7. *Claused bill of lading.* If the cargo is damaged, inadequately packed, in second hand cases, if cartons are missing, wet or stained, the shipowner will endorse

the bill of lading accordingly. Hence, the bill of lading is regarded as claused, unclean or foul and is unacceptable to banks.

8. *Negotiable bill of lading.* If the words 'or his or their assigns' are contained in the bill of lading, it is negotiable. Bills of lading may be negotiable by endorsement or transfer.

9. *Non-negotiable bills of lading.* When the words 'his or their assigns' are deleted from the bills of lading, the bill is regarded as non-negotiable. Hence, the consignee or other named party cannot transfer the property or goods by transfer of the bills.

10. *Container bill of lading.* This type of bill of lading is identified with the carriage of container shipments. It covers the goods from port to port, or combined transport involving an inland point of departure to an inland point of destination under one document. This combined transport may be under FCA, EXW, CPT or DAF (see page 287) Incoterms 2000. Some years ago an attempt was made to draft a convention to cover loss or damage to goods carried under the Combined Transport Convention. This was known as the 'Tokyo–Rome Rules' or 'Tokyo Rules', but they proved unacceptable. However, there do exist the ICC Rules Combined Transport (ICC publication No. 298) which are widely used, especially by mega-maritime container operators.

11. *Straight bill of lading.* A non-negotiable bill of lading. In the USA the Promerene Act governs its operation.

12. *Negotiable FIATA combined transport bill.* This document is becoming increasingly used in the trade and is a FIATA bill of lading (FBL) employed as a combined transport document with negotiable status. It has been developed by the International Federation of Forwarding Agents Associations and is acceptable under the ICC Rules Uniform Customs and Practice for Documentary Credits (ICC publication No. 500) revision 1993. The FIATA bill of lading should be stipulated in letters of credit where the forwarder's container groupage service is to be utilized or a house bill of lading is to be issued (see page 165 item 4).

13. *FIATA multi-modal transport bill of lading* (MTBL). The FIATA multi-modal transport bill of lading is a negotiable document of title in line with the International Chamber of Commerce Uniform Rules for such documents. It is widely stipulated in letters of credit and shipping instructions and is recognized by the ICC Banking Commission Group as a carriers bill and by the British Bankers Association.

The methodology of the bill of lading is broadly as follows, and the procurement officer must be fully conversant with it. The supplier's agent or the buyer's agent under EXW, probably using electronic commerce – on-line computer – will ascertain the sailing schedule and effect the cargo reservation space on the vessel or container. It is important to note that the shipper always makes the offer by forwarding the consignment, whilst the shipowner either accepts or refuses it. It is the shipper's or agent's duty to supply details of the consignment, usually through electronic commerce, by completing the export cargo shipping instruction (ECSI) featuring shipping instructions from shipper to carrier. Ultimately, these data are featured on the bill of lading and the shipping company then signs the number of copies requested. The container may be accepted at the seaport or dry port ICD/CFS.

Suppliers and buyers and their agents need to give the shipowner accurate documentation data, issued promptly after receipt of the goods into the system. To facilitate fast processing of bills of lading, invoices and manifest, mega-container operators provide a sophisticated computerized system. This is why accurate data are required within an acceptable time scale. Not only does a computer enable large volumes of data to be processed in a fraction of the time of a manual operation, but it also guarantees consistency of information throughout the documentary chain. It further allows the production of the bill of lading and invoice immediately that goods have been packed into a container, provided the carrier has in its possession accurate and complete source documentation. Initially when a booking is made, whether FCL or LCL, the booking party is allocated a unique booking reference number. This must be quoted on all source documents to ensure immediate identification of the consignment in question.

To facilitate the data input of shipper's instructions to its computer and to ensure all relevant data are provided, mega-container operators prefer shipping instructions to be submitted in a standard format whether despatched by post, fax or e-mail. This is found in the export cargo shipping instructions (ECSI). In countries where the ECSI is not used, details and instructions should be conveyed in the customary form.

When the goods have been received on board ship, the bill of lading is dated and signed by or on behalf of the carrier, usually by the Master of the ship or agent and stamped 'freight paid' or 'freight payable at destination' as appropriate. If the cargo is in good condition and everything is in order, no endorsement will be made on the document and it can be termed a 'clean bill of lading'. Conversely, if the goods are damaged or a portion of the consignment is missing, the document will be suitably endorsed by the Master or agent and the bill of lading will be considered 'claused' or 'unclean'. The complete set of bills of lading is then returned to the exporter (seller) for prompt despatch to the importer (buyer). The buyer must have a negotiable bill of lading with which to clear the goods at the port of destination.

Bills of lading are made out in sets and the number varies according to the trade. Generally it is two or three, one of which will probably be forwarded immediately and another later. It is important that the buyer becomes familiar with the CMI rules for electronic bills of lading. Such rules must not conflict with the Uniform Rules of Conduct for Interchange of Trade Data by Teletransmission 1987 (NCID). Moreover, electronic data are equivalent to writing. Hence, the carrier and the shipper and all subsequent parties utilizing these procedures agree that any national or local law, custom or practice requiring the contract of carriage to be evidenced in writing and signed, is satisfied by the transmitted and confirmed electronic data residing on computer data storage media displayable in human language on a video screen or printed out by a computer. In agreeing to adopt these rules, the parties shall be taken to have agreed not to raise the defence that the contract is not in writing.

In the event of the bill of lading being lost or delayed in transit, the shipping company will allow delivery of the goods to the person claiming to be the consignee if he or she gives a letter of indemnity. This is usually countersigned by a bank and relieves the shipping company of any liability should another person eventually come along with the actual bill of lading.

Many bills of lading are consigned 'to order' and in such situations are endorsed, normally on the reverse, by the shipper. If the consignee is named, the goods will only be released to him or her, unless he or she transfers his or her rights by endorsement, subject to the bill of lading providing for this.

Associated with the bill of lading is the national standard shipping note (NSSN), the common short form and sea waybill.

The NSSN is a six-part set, copies of which are retained by those parties handling the goods until they are finally on board, from which a 'shipper' bill of lading is issued. The document is compiled by the supporter of the goods, or the shipper or freight forwarder, giving full details of the goods similar to those found on the bill of lading, against which it is matched before issue. The document is unacceptable for use with shipments of goods classified as dangerous.

The common short form bill of lading is fully negotiable and the normal bill of lading lodgement and presentation procedures remain unchanged. However, instead of the mass of small print on the reverse, there is an approved 'short form' clause on the face which embraces carriers' standard conditions with full legal effect. It conforms to the 'Uniform Customs and Practice for Documentary Credits', ICC publication No. 500.

The use of the negotiable bill of lading which has to be surrendered to the carrier at the destination in order to obtain delivery of the goods is traditional, but not without disadvantages. The document has to follow the goods and often, for commercial or financial reasons, passes through a variety of hands resulting in the goods being held up at their destination pending arrival of the document – and thus expenses and additional risks are incurred. Such situations have been reduced through electronic commerce but the benefit of the sea waybill in comparison with the bill of lading remains cogent and intrinsic.

The sea waybill is a non-negotiable document which evidences a contract of carriage of goods by sea and taking over or loading of the goods by the carrier and by which the carrier undertakes to deliver the goods to the consignee named in the document.

The commercial and financial feasibility of using the sea waybill clearly rests with the shipper and consignee and is dependent upon the type of trade transaction involved. The waybill is the natural choice for trading between multinational companies and associated companies, where no documentary transaction is involved and also for open account sales (see page 142). It can also be used for transactions between companies where a documentary credit transaction is not required. However, it can additionally be used in many cases involving banking transactions.

The point at which waybills are released will depend upon whether the document is 'received for shipment' or 'shipped on board'. In signing waybills the carrier or agent is required to insert the carrier's transmission address within the signature or date stamp.

If a received for shipment document were issued and the cargo was subsequently short-shipped, or a carrier's clause required (for example to indicate that damage was sustained whilst goods were on the quay), then a qualification report should be issued on the shipper, consignee and those concerned within the carrier's organization; information concerning such reports should also be made available to insurers on request. Use of the 'shipped' option would, however, obviate the need for a qualification report and in such circumstances the normal bill of lading procedures would apply.

If a 'shipped on board' document were issued, then the provision of the 'shipped' option should be in a manner which, if the document were to be presented under a documentary credit, it would satisfy 'Uniform Customs and Practice for Documentary Credits'. This refers to a procedure whereby waybills can be endorsed to specify that the goods mentioned have been loaded on board or shipped on a named vessel, the loading onboard date being specified.

Procurement executives should examine closely the use of the waybill with established suppliers and take full advantage of the electronic commerce which it offers. Finally, one must stress to the buyer that the legislation governing the bill of lading is not identical in every country regarding carriers liability, as has been demonstrated in the conventions examined in earlier pages.

Certificate of origin

This is a declaration which states the country (or countries) of origin of the goods and is common place in countries wishing to identify the origin of all imported goods (or their components) or where there are quotas or other import restrictions in force. It should be completed by the supplier and may have to be authenticated by a chamber of commerce or other authorized body in the exporter's country. In some instances, the certificate must also be legalized by the embassy or other representative of the country concerned. The certificate should include the name and address of the exporter, the manufacturer (if different), the importer, a description of the goods as prescribed on the commercial export invoice and, if required, the signatures and seals of the authorizing organization. It is not required for goods in 'free circulation' within the EU.

Generally, certification of origin for non-preferential purposes is a trade policy issue with wider connotations than preferential origin (see page 267). It may be required to identify favoured nation states' goods in order to reduce import duties or, from a negative perspective, to identify commodities originating from certain regions or countries the importation of which may be restricted or prohibited. The declaration may also be made on other commercial documents, such as the packing list or consignment note. The letter of credit may stipulate the provision of a certificate of origin as one of the documents required under the documentary credits and as prescribed by the buyer's bank (see page 134).

Certificate of shipment

The FIATA forwarders certificate of receipt (FCR) and forwarders certificate of transport (FCT) is a document widely used in the trade confirming receipt of the goods by the carrier. It is used under the FCA Incoterm 2000 involving a multi-modal transport operation. Also, under EXW when the goods are being despatched via a recognized forwarder groupage service and a recognized document confirming the goods are no longer in the control of the seller.

Charter party

A charter party is a contract whereby a shipowner agrees to place his or her ship or part of it at the disposal of a merchant or other person (known as the charterer) for the carriage of goods from one port to another port on being paid freight, or to let his or her ship for a specified period, his or her remuneration being known as hire money. The terms, conditions and exceptions under which the goods are carried are set out in the charter party.

CMR note

This transport document is used for international transport by road. It is not a document of title and is not transferable. It is more commonly known as a truck waybill or CMR consignment note.

The convention on the contract for the International Carriage of Goods by Road (CMR) was signed in Geneva in 1956 and enacted into the laws of the UK by the Carriage of Goods by Road Act 1965. The convention only appears to have been adopted by European nations and applies to contracts for the international carriage of goods by road in vehicles over the territories of two different countries of which at least one is a contracting party to CMR. Hence, it only applies to UK imports and exports by roll-on/roll-off ferry or the Channel Tunnel where goods remain on road vehicles throughout. If the same container on the same journey was lifted off the trailer at Dover onto a vessel and carried to the Continent and there lifted onto another trailer, there would have been no crossing of a frontier on a road vehicle and therefore the convention would not apply. Under this convention the carrier is liable for loss or damage from the time he or she takes over until the time he or she delivers the goods to the consignee, unless it can be proved that the loss or damage occurred because of one of the list of excepted perils. In short, these exceptions allow the carrier to escape liability if he or she has not been negligent. The carrier is entitled to limit his or her liability to

SDR 8.33 per kilo. The carrier is also liable for delay if the goods have not been delivered within the agreed time limit or, if there is no such agreement, within reasonable time.

The sender is responsible for the accuracy and adequacy of the documents and information which he or she must either attach to the consignment note or place at the carrier's disposal for the purposes of customs or other formalities which have to be completed before delivery of the goods. There is a duty on the sender:

(a) to ensure that the goods are properly packed;
(b) in the case of dangerous goods, to inform the carrier of the exact nature of the danger and indicate if necessary the precautions to be taken;
(c) to ensure the accuracy and adequacy of certain specified particulars which the consignment note must contain and of any other particulars or instructions given by him or her to the carrier.

The great majority of international road transport European (EU) consignments are conducted under open account payment terms. A bank will normally only make an advance against goods conveyed by CMR International Consignment Note if the goods are consigned to a bank in the buyer's country and are only to be released under payment by the buyer. The CMR consignment note must be carried on all hire and reward journeys involving an international transit.

Courier receipt

This document is used where the goods are despatched by courier service usually involving small parcels and packets. UCP 500 allows the presentation of a receipt issued by any courier company, unless one is specified in the credit.

Dangerous goods note

The carriage of dangerous classified cargo by sea or air or combined transport featuring international road transport requires special precautions, procedures or facilities concerning its shipment. A dangerous goods note, a multi-purpose document, is required for the whole journey using any combination of surface modes of transport. This is completed by the exporter.

When goods are being consigned by sea, the consignment must be accompanied by a document, the dangerous goods note, which contains information indicating the nature of the hazards of the goods. It combines the functions of application for stowage space on the transport unit(s), the dangerous goods declaration completed by the shipper, the special stowage order in the transport unit as allocated by the carrier; the container or vehicle packing certificate, the standard shipping note, and finally the 'back up' document for the forwarder or haulier. The sea transport regulations and nine dangerous goods classifications are laid down by the International Maritime Organisation (IMO) and are mandatory.

For shipments by air, a shipper's declaration for dangerous goods together with an air waybill is required. The nine dangerous goods classifications are laid down by the International Air Transport Association (IATA).

The dangerous goods declaration must be completed and signed by the shipper. Regulations are very stringent – especially by air – and overall cover labelling, stowage, packing, documentation and cargo acceptance and reservation acceptance procedures. Pre-booking involving stowage order number is compulsory.

Dock receipt

This may be issued by a Port Authority to confirm receipt of cargo on the quay or warehouse pending shipment. It has no legal role regarding processing financial settlement of international consignments. In the USA it is an acknowledgement of receipt of goods or container at a pier incorporating bill of lading terms from time of receipt.

Exchange permit

The exchange permit is found particularly in Middle Eastern trades and is usually associated with the issue of an import licence. They are usually issued by government departments, chambers of commerce or chambers of industry, thereby authorizing the import of a specific commodity. It is a means of regulating the flow of specific commodity imports and the funds associated with them.

Export invoice

The invoice for the goods bought represents the terms of the contract and is a major document in the financial payment, customs presentation, value and on carriage of the goods. The cargo description on the invoice must be identical on all other documents and determines the level of import duty. Export documents are never static and ideally the procurement executive must keep up-to-date in developments by contacting the supplier's embassy or consulate in the buyer's country, usually available over the Web. There is a continued stream of new overseas import regulations along with new developments and a constant issue of new forms, etc. Accordingly, the requisite invoice for a particular market should be checked to ensure that the correct one is used, otherwise serious delays will be encountered in processing the export order through customs. A further data source is the buyer's local customs office. Details of the various types of invoices are now examined.

Commercial invoice

This gives details of the goods and is issued by the seller (exporter). It forms the basis of the transaction between the seller and the buyer and is completed in accordance with the number of prescribed copies required. Usually it bears the exporter's own headed invoice form stationery and is printed on a computer. The invoice gives a description of the goods, stating prices and relevant Incoterms 2000 exactly as specified in the credit, as well as shipping. Overall, it contains the following information:

(a) name and address of buyer (importer) and seller (exporter);
(b) buyer's reference, that is, order number, indent number, etc.;
(c) number and types of packages;
(d) weights and measurements of the consignment;
(e) place and date of issue;
(f) details of actual cost freight and insurance – if so requested;
(g) total amount payable, embracing price of goods, freight, insurance and so on;
(h) export and/or import licence number;
(i) contents of individual packages;
(j) method of despatch;
(k) shipment terms;
(l) letter of credit number and details – if so requested;
(m) country of origin of goods;
(n) signature of exporter.

Basically the invoice is a document rendered by one person to another in regard of goods which have been sold. Its primary function is as a check for the purchaser against charges and delivery. With regard to insurance claims, and for packing purposes, it is useful evidence to verify the value and nature of the goods and in certain circumstances, it is evidence of the contract between the two parties; for example, packaging not being up to specification may give underwriters redress against the sellers. The invoice is not necessarily a contract of sale. It may form a contract of sale if it is in writing and contains all the material terms. On the other hand, it may not be a complete memorandum of the contract of sale and therefore evidence may be given to vary the contract which is inferred therefrom. In particular circumstances, the commercial invoice may be certified by a chamber of commerce and/or legalized by the consulate in the seller's country.

Consular invoice

Consular invoices are mandatory when shipping goods to certain parts of the world, particularly to those countries which enforce ad valorem duties. The invoices are specially printed documents which must be completed exactly in accordance with requirements and certified by the consul of the country to which the goods are consigned.

Customs invoice

This type of invoice may be required by the authorities of the importing country.

Proforma invoice

This type of invoice is prepared by the exporter and may be required in advance for a licence or for letter of credit purposes. The document includes the date, name of the consignee, quantity and description of the goods, marks and measurements of packages, cost of the goods, packaging, carriage freight, insurance premiums, terms of sale and terms of payment. The proforma invoice is despatched to the buyer to facilitate obtaining from the bank the requisite currency to buy the goods and subsequently issue a letter of credit. Additionally, it may be needed for an import licence. The buyer is usually situated in a country with exchange control regulations involving the central bank regulating on behalf of the government the volume of imports. In countries with serious hard debt problems delays can be experienced by the buyer when seeking the necessary funds, and exporters, when dealing with such territories, tend not to process the order until receipt of credit.

The following items must be borne in mind when the shipper, exporter or agent prepares the invoice and presents them to the bank under a documentary letter of credit.

(a) the invoice description of the goods agrees exactly with the documentary letter of credit;
(b) the invoice is addressed to the importer;
(c) the invoice includes exactly the licence and/or certificate numbers required by the credit;
(d) the invoice shows the terms of shipment mentioned in the credit.

Export licensing

Most countries exercise strategic export controls for a variety of reasons including security, foreign policy requirements, international treaty obligations and commitments, non-proliferation policy and concerns about terrorism or internal repression. Controlled goods include arms and military equipment; high technology industrial goods, for example, chemical and petroleum equipment; electrical and electronic equipment (including computers); scientific apparatus and instruments; atomic energy materials; antiques and scarce materials. The export licences are issued by the appropriate government department which scrutinizes each application submitted by the exporter.

Health certificate

Agricultural and animal products may require a certificate stating that they comply with the importing country's health regulations. It is issued at the importer's request to comply with the country's health regulations and confirms the product was in a good condition at the time of inspection prior to shipment and fit for human consumption. Overall, it confirms that the Food Hygiene Regulations have been complied with.

Import licensing

Import controls are imposed for a variety of reasons embracing foreign policy requirements, international treaty obligations and commitments; concerns about terrorism or internal repression, protection of home industry against imports and the wide range of measures emerging to preserve hard currency and lessen the risk of an excessive balance of trade deficit contributed to by the importation of non-essential goods. The latter situation emerges in less developed countries.

The appropriate government department in the buyer's country controls the issue of licences as required by customs on importation.

International convention concerning the carriage of goods by rail (COTIF/CIM)

The COTIF Convention concerning International Carriage by Rail was signed in Berne in May 1980. It was given legal effect in the UK by Section 1 of the International Transport Conventions Act 1983. COTIF abrogated the existing CIM convention which did not have force of law in the UK and an amended draft of CIM was attached to COTIF as Appendix B to govern the carriage of goods. CIM applies if either the place of loading or the destination of the goods is a COTIF member state.

Like CMR, the COTIF/CIM applies only to international carriage. The opening of the Channel Tunnel extended the application of COTIF/CIM recourse. As a private company the Channel Tunnel operates an independent contract not subject to any mandatory law in which liability for delays is excluded and a limitation of SDR is applied. The terms and conditions of COTIF/CIM are similar to CMR but limitation is subsequently higher at SDR 17 per kilo.

The COTIF/CIM document is a consignment note (not negotiable) under a common code of conditions applicable to countries mainly in Europe and the Mediterranean countries. The consignment note is completed by the shipper, agent or originating carrier and involves a container or cargo wagon. It provides a common code of conditions, simplified documentation, flexibility of freight payment, no intermediate handling (usually) nor customs examination in transit countries, through transits and minimum customs documentation.

Letters of hypothecation

This is a banker's document outlining conditions under which the international transaction will be executed on the exporter's behalf, the latter of whom will have given certain pledges to his or her banker. It may be by direct loan acceptance or negotiations of draft thereto.

Letters of indemnity

The role of the letter of indemnity is to permit cargo to be released to a consignee without production of the original endorsed bill of lading, or to permit the issue of a duplicate set of documents when the original bills of lading have been lost or mislaid in transit. It is a document of legal and commercial convenience and should be used with care and caution.

Mates receipt

A mates receipt is sometimes issued in lieu of a bill of lading. It has no legal authority regarding the processing of the financial settlement of international consignments but merely confirms cargo is placed on board a ship pending issue of a bill of lading.

Packing list

Today, in many countries, the provision of a packing list document is mandatory for customs and banks under documentary credits. It is very much in evidence in containerized shipments.

The document – often called a packing note – is provided and completed by the shipper at the time the goods are despatched and accompanies the goods and the carrier's documents throughout the transit. The packing list gives details of the invoice, buyer, consignee, country of origin, vessel or flight date and number, port or airport of loading, port or airport of discharge, place of delivery, shipping marks, container number, weight and/or volume (cubic) of the merchandise and the fullest details of the goods including packaging information.

Parcel post receipt

The parcel post receipt is issued by the Post Office for goods sent by post. It is both a receipt and evidence of despatch. It is not a document of title and goods should be consigned to the party specified in the credit. Goods sent by post should be consigned to the party specified in the documentary credit.

Phytosanitary (plant health) certificate

Buyers sourcing plant material, forest trees and other trees and shrubs from overseas, together with certain raw fruit and vegetables must be accompanied on importation with a phytosanitary certificate. In some countries the importation of certain species of plants from certain areas of the world is prohibited. Application for such plant health certificates should be made to the agricultural department of the exporting country.

Pre-shipment inspection certificate

Today an increasing number of buyers are using the pre-shipment inspection certificate mechanism. This embraces an audit of the quality of the goods, the quantity being exported and the price(s) proposed and market price(s) comparison at the time of shipment. An organization which undertakes such work – which can extend to transhipment en route – is the Société Générale de Surveillance (SGS) or ship classification societies such as Bureau Véritas. The SGS representative will examine the goods at the place of manufacture or assembly prior to despatch. This is to ensure they comply with the description found in the export sales contract, bill of lading or export invoice. Subsequently the goods will be examined and checked as they are loaded into the container or onto the ship. In situations where sellers are at variance with SGS opinion, they may present their position to the SGS principals, either directly or through the importer or buyer.

If everything is in order, a clean report of findings (CRF) will be issued by SGS to their principals. This is required together with other commercial documents such as the bill of lading, the letter of credit, the invoice in order to obtain payment via the commercial bank and/or customs clearance import. If a non-negotiable report of findings (NNRF) is issued by SGS, the seller (exporter) may opt to discuss the matter with the principal involved, who remains the final arbiter. Such a situation arises where goods are shipped before SGS inspection has taken place. In due course, SGS will issue the pre-shipment inspection certificate to confirm the goods have been supplied in accordance with the contract.

The SGS do not have the right to approve or prevent shipment of the goods. The opinion expressed by SGS is given after all the factors are provided to SGS by the seller. It is made in good faith but without any liability to the seller for any loss, damage or expense arising from the issuance of the report of findings. Currently, some 35 countries require that both the letter of credit contracts relevant to the import of goods contain a condition that a clean report of findings covering quality, quantity and price must be presented together with other documents required to negotiate payment.

The International Federation of Inspection Agencies (IFIA), on behalf of the members administering government-mandated pre-shipment inspection programmes, is promoting the following Code of Practice to be observed by those members.

1. Activities of pre-shipment inspection companies (hereinafter 'PIC') in the country of export may be undertaken on behalf of a foreign government, government agency, central bank or other appropriate governmental authority and may include:
   (a) physical inspection for quantity and quality of goods;
   (b) verification of export prices, including financial terms of the export transaction and currency exchange rates where appropriate;
   (c) support services to the customs authorities of the country of importation.
2. The general procedures for physical inspection of goods and the examination of the price of exports out of any particular country will be the same in all exporting countries and the specific requirements established by the importing country will be administered by the PIC in a consistent and objective manner.
3. The PIC will provide assistance to exporters by furnishing the information and guidelines necessary to enable exporters to comply with the pre-shipment inspection regulations of the importing country. This assistance on the part of the PIC is not intended to relieve exporters from the responsibility of compliance with the import regulations of the importing country.
4. Quantity and quality inspections will be performed in accordance with accepted national and international standards.
5. The conduct of pre-shipment activities should facilitate legitimate foreign trade and assist bona fide exporters by providing independent evidence of compliance with the laws and regulations of the importing country.
6. Pre-shipment activities will be conducted and the clean report of findings, or notice of non-issuance thereof, will be sent to the exporter in a timely and convenient manner.
7. Confidential business information will not be shared by the PICs with any third party other than the appropriate government authority for which the inspection in question is being performed.
8. Adequate procedures to safeguard all information submitted by exporters will be maintained by the PIC, together with proper security for any information provided in confidence to them.
9. The PIC will not request from exporters information regarding manufacturing data related to patents (issued or pending) or licensing agreements. Nor will the PIC attempt to identify the cost of manufacture, level of profit or, except in the case of exports made through a buying agent or a confirming house, the terms of contracts between exporters and their suppliers.
10. The PIC will avoid conflicts of interest between the PIC, any related entities of the PIC or entities in which the PIC has a financial interest and companies whose shipments the PIC is inspecting.
11. The PIC state in writing the reason for any decision declining issuance of a clean report of findings.
12. If a rejection occurs at the stage of physical inspection, the PIC will, if requested by the exporter, arrange the earliest date for reinspection.

13. Whenever so requested by the exporter and provided no contrary instruction has been issued by the government authority, the PIC will undertake a preliminary price verification prior to receipt of the import licence on the basis of the binding contractual documents, proforma invoice and application for import approval. An invoice price and/or currency exchange rate that has been accepted by the PIC on the basis of such preliminary price verification will not be withdrawn, provided the goods and the previously submitted documentation conform with the information contained in the import licence. The CRF, however, will not be issued until appropriate final documents have been received by the PIC.

14. Price verification will be undertaken on the basis of the terms of the sales contract and it will take into consideration any generally applicable and allowable adjusting factors pertaining to the transaction.

15. Commissions due to an agent in the country of destination will be treated in confidence by the PIC and will be reported to the appropriate government authority only when so requested.

16. Exporters or importers who are unable to resolve differences with the PIC may appeal in writing, stating the facts of the specific transaction and the nature of the complaint, to a designated appeals official of the PIC. Exporters wishing to appeal the results of a pre-shipment inspection may also seek review of the decision of the PIC in the importing country.

In cases where a PIC is considered not to have observed any article of this Code of Practice, this may be reported to the Director-General of IFIA.

The World Trade Organisation's Uruguay round of talks in 1994 established an independent review procedure administered jointly by an organization representing PIC agencies and an organization representing exporters – to resolve disputes between an exporter and a PIC Agency. The obligations placed on PIC user governments include non-discrimination, transparency, protection of confidential business information, avoidance of unreasonable delay, the use of specific guidelines for conducting price verification and the avoidance of conflicts of interest by the PIC agencies.

The Pre-Shipment Inspection System (PIS) has been introduced for the following reasons:

(a) To minimize the loss of foreign exchange through over-invoicing; concealed commission payments and illegal money transfers.

(b) To minimize losses of revenue and duty payments through under-invoicing.

(c) To reduce evasion of import controls and help combat smuggling.

(d) To help control landed prices and therefore control local inflation.

(e) To avoid dumping of cargo through the incidence of shipping merchandise of substandard goods.

(f) To avoid the incidence of loss through shipment of underweight cargo or short shipments.

Buyers are urged to become familiar with the Pre-Shipment Inspection System and use it when market conditions justify it.

Quality certificate

A quality certificate is issued by the exporter and confirms for the buyer that the quality and specification of a particular consignment of goods is in accordance with the supplier's sales contract at the time of shipment. This may involve taking samples for testing purposes. It may be a complete shipment involving a chartered vessel. The quality certificate is usually required under the letter of credit terms.

Ship's delivery order

A delivery order is written authority to deliver goods, etc. to a named party in exchange for the bill of lading, usually at the port of destination. It is issued at the port of destination and is subject to all the terms and conditions of the carrier's bill of lading. It must not contain any reservations or clauses other than those appearing in the bill of lading except where increased obligations or extra cost may be incurred in giving delivery beyond the bill of lading. The document is issued at the port of destination in exchange for an original bill of lading and is legally recognized as a token of an authority to receive possession.

The delivery order should be addressed to the ship's Master and the need for it arises when the buyer may not wish to know the identity of the supplier abroad for trade reasons. It is important that the document is endorsed by the party to whom it is made out. However, if it is issued in one port for delivery in another and the freight is payable at destination, the order would then be consigned to the carrier's agent to ensure that it would have to be presented and released before collection of the goods is authorized.

Veterinary and health certificate

A veterinary or health certificate may be required when livestock, domestic animals or agricultural products are being exported. It should be signed by the appropriate health authority in the exporter's country. It could feature on the letter of credit.

Weight certificate

A weight certificate confirms that the goods accord with the weight specified on the bill of lading, invoice, certificate of insurance or other specified document. In so doing, it confirms to the buyer, seller, insurance company or other specified party that the goods were at a specified weight at the time of shipment. It is requested by the buyer to confirm the weight of the goods in accordance with the export sales contract at the time of shipment. It is usually required under a letter of credit involving a bulk cargo shipment under chartered tonnage.

Recommended reading

- *SITPRO News* quarterly.
- WTO *Focus*.
- Branch, A.E. (2000) *Shipping and Air Freight Documentation for Importers and Exporters and Associated Terms*, 2nd edn, Witherby & Co Ltd.
- *The Merchants Guide*, P&O Nedlloyd.
- Uniform Customs and Practice for Documentary Credits, ICC Publication No 500.

10

International physical distribution strategy and management I

Introduction

Procurement is all about professionalism, logistics and profit motivation and closely involves distribution strategy and management. This embraces the decision-making process of evolving the most suitable and acceptable method of transporting the goods from the seller's supply point to the buyer's premises. It is a very important cost element in buying goods overseas – a point which cannot be overstressed – and the buyer must make the decision about which distribution mode to accept – sea, air, road, multi-modal – and whether he or she wishes to take responsibility for arranging the transportation under EXW, FCA or FOB, or whether to entrust this task to the seller under CIF, CPT, CIP or DDU.

The international distribution network is customer, market and logistically driven. Shippers require quicker services, lower rates, a wider multi-modal network system and more frequent services. Examples arise in the growth of the hub and spoke global container network, the expansion of airports and seaports and a much improved overland infrastructure serving strategically located airports and seaports. Trade is all about bringing the buyer and seller closer together through the efficiency of the transport system and enabling the buyer to purchase goods in all types of countries: fully developed and industrialized, newly industrialized, developing countries and less developed countries. Countries for example which do not have access to the global container network are seriously disadvantaged in their trade development. Hence, distribution is a fast moving area subject to continuous change and is market led. The buyer needs to monitor continuously such changes and review his or her sourcing strategy as access to the market changes through improved international physical distribution networks.

Distribution is also an area which is attracting senior management attention in the buyer's company on an increasing scale as world markets become more competitive and increasing emphasis is being placed on the 'total product concept', the value added benefit the buyer obtains from the purchase of the goods from a particular country or region. This benefit embraces not only the product and the related benefits associated with the supplier in terms of price, quality, technology, design, accessibility or flexibility, product range and non-price areas – after sales, brand image, position in the marketplace – but also the method of distribution adopted to enable the goods to reach the buyer. Factors which feature prominently in the choices mode include efficiency and quality of service together with total cost. The buyer and supplier must remain in close contact to facilitate the development of the buyer's needs through empathy. An increasing number of carriers are obtaining BS 5750 and ISO 9000 quality standard registration to enhance their market profile (see page 19).

Today the buyer must be computer and logistically focused. Full use must be made of electronic commerce and all the ingredients of the logistics elements including supply chain management, computerized warehouse operation and management, customer asset management, barcode systems for inventory control and just-in-time technology. Planning, tracking and adequate control systems with the ability to be flexible to meet changing markets needs are essential in the logistic environment.

International physical distribution – strategy

Before we examine the ingredients of the physical distribution environment, it is important that the procurement manager takes a strategic focus on the elements of the situation as discussed below.

1. *Company objectives*. This is found in the business plan spanning three to five years. It will be driven primarily by profitability. It is quite possible that the company may have switched from domestic component sourcing to overseas sourcing during the past five years. This means a refocus will be required on the most acceptable distribution arrangements compatible with the channels of distribution already in place. A strategic view must be devised.

2. *Company resources*. Large companies have substantial cash flow and human resources to develop specalisms within the company including logistics. High volume import flows yield lower unit costs per shipment. Discounted rates can be negotiated with carriers on volume guaranteed contracts. Moreover, larger companies rely less on intermediaries in the management and execution of the distribution network, thereby realizing significant cost savings and exercising closer and more direct control over the total logistics operation. Also large companies tend to have experienced and high calibre personnel. Hence, major cost benefits potentially exist for the high volume importer to buy under EXW or FAS terms thereby taking charge of the overall distribution and logistics network. Also, such a strategy will support a specialist team to undertake the negotiation and control mechanism logistically driven with the production and assembly, retailing and marketing divisions. Many companies place such overseas sourcing in the hands of the logistics division of Maersk, Sealand, Hapag-Lloyd or P&O Nedlloyd (see page 194) – full details can be found on the relevant company website.

The smaller company has limited resources in finance, production assembly and labour. Such companies rely on consolidated distribution networks with their lower unit cost – whether by sea (container/truck) or air – rather than full load volume movements.

The extent to which both large and small companies have specialist staff engaged in shipping and warehouse distribution activities depends on the markets, products and the international distribution networks on which they depend, the complexity of the operation and the volume of business. The development of the global logistic operator is taking over much of the work hitherto undertaken in the traditional shipping and warehouse departments.

3. *Legal and political constraints.* Buyers located in some countries are subject to mandatory exchange control regulations which compel them to use their national shipping and airlines. This limits their flexibility of choice. Usually they buy under EXW or FCA terms relying on a local forwarding agent to organize the international distribution.

4. *The company position in the marketplace.* The higher the company profile, the more likely it is that the company will be a market leader and will play an influential role in the distribution arrangements. Smaller companies work through intermediaries.

5. *The sales forecast and market stability.* The level of import business will determine the company's organizational structure – a small volume may place complete reliance on the freight forwarder to handle all the importation arrangements including customs clearance and related documentation.

6. *Level and nature of competition.* Buyers situated in competitive developed countries will be well placed to provide a sophisticated logistics network. As trade grows the infrastructure improves with a special focus on service quality and high technology. Transit times are reduced and the range of options increased. Overall, the value added benefit is more closely analysed by the buyer when selecting the sourcing country.

7. *Costs.* There are over 30 cost elements in an international distribution network. These include handling, freight, packing, customs clearance insurance, import duty, bank charges, exchange rates, agents' commission, interest on capital in transit, warehouse, trucking and documentation. Hence, there is an intrinsic incentive for the buyer to take control of the distribution arrangements and constantly monitor the costs. A strategic focus is required, based on cost efficiency and accessibility.

8. *Value added benefit.* The procurement manager's choice of distribution network should be based on the perceived value or benefits it yields to the buyer and the resulting benefits. It may be that the buyer is located in a distripark in the Port of Rotterdam (see page 187). This permits, for example, a range of spices to be imported in bulk in containers, warehoused and subsequently mixed, processed and packaged with differing languages and distributed to wholesalers, retailers or customers. Such distribution would be in response to an on-line computer or e-mail request direct to the distripark.

Another example is the development and expansion of the hub and spoke container network. This reduces transit times and offers significant benefits to the buyer.

An increasing number of buyers conduct a matrix audit of available distribution systems using a benchmark rating of 1–5. This would embrace freight rate, service frequency, transit time, TQM, reliability, customer relations, brand image, technology, flexibility and electronic commerce. The audit is subject to continuous updating.

Value added benefit is an important element in developing a successful strategic focus in physical distribution.

9. *Flexibility of service.* The discerning procurement strategist will opt for the flexible distribution network able to respond efficiently to varying levels of import business. Flexibility arises in the range of facilities offered by the carrier and the route options. The larger the carrier the greater the options.

10. *Frequency of service, transit time and service reliability* are all major factors. Low frequency services involve a longer lead time to delivery of goods and generates high stock piling, which does not favour a just-in-time strategy. Low cost services port to port often result in sluggish transits and transhipments. Moreover, the cargo receives a low priority in the handling process. Basically, competitive transit times and frequent reliable services at a competitive rate are the best ingredients to facilitate overseas market development and enable the buyer to maximize his or her profits from the imported products. In such situations stock can remain at an optimum low level and can be replenished as it is consumed.

11. *Total quality management* (TQM). Most buyers adopt a strategy of employing a carrier with total quality management accreditation ISO 9001 or BS 5750. This benchmark does generate complete confidence in the structure and management of the services with continuous focus on the shipper. This extends to the professional competence of the managers who will be adequately qualified and undergo continuous training.

12. *Logistics.* As stressed earlier the company must be computer and logistics literate. This requires substantial investment in resources including a trained workforce committed to this ideology.

13. *Location.* Finally, one must consider the strategic geographical location of the departure and arrival airports or seaports especially the hinterland each serves, its infrastructure and general accessibility. Ports like Rotterdam, Dubai, Zeebrugge and many others around the world have become trading distribution centres. The procurement manager must use the Internet to evaluate the options available and especially the value added benefit each offers, together with their accessibility. The total overall cost of the transit method chosen and the benefit it yields to the importer are important.

To conclude our analysis it is important that the buyer has synergy with the distribution channel and continuous dialogue prevails to ensure that the most acceptable service is provided. Complete transparency with all parties in the supply chain are paramount. One must remember that we operate in a fast moving market and that the strategic tactics employed must be subject to continuous review. Market research techniques must be used.

The procurement officer today has a global outlook. He or she constantly seeks new supply sources and provided the product and price are acceptable, will target those markets given that the physical distribution is adequate. Many manufacturers and suppliers are choosing to manufacture in low labour cost markets with technical skills responsive to adequate technical training and with sustainable neighbouring markets to buy their products. This involves transfer pricing and technology; inwards and indigenous capital investment; an indigenous labour force and transfer of management skills. Other developments include joint ventures and operating alliances.

We will now examine the international distribution strategy options available to the buyer and other techniques of importation but would stress that the buyer would use a mixture of these options depending on company resources, infrastructure, cost efficiency factors and profile of the supply source.

1. Near and distant markets. Near markets are easier to visit for the buyer than distant markets. In European countries the buyer can use his or her own transport to convey the goods on trans-European contracts. Moreover, the freight cost is lower and the transit time is quicker. Additionally, the buyer is likely to have a better knowledge and understanding of the near market in terms of its infrastructure, culture, risk and 'ongoing' developments. Many small companies tend to buy in near markets as access is easier and it absorbs less of their resources, especially in terms of manpower. Conversely, the distant market, with longer transit times and higher freight costs and import duties, may offer lower EXW prices and a wider product range. The procurement officer may entrust all the distribution arrangements to a global logistics operator, for example Hapag Lloyd or P&O Nedlloyd, which will overcome many of the previous problems mentioned earlier in this paragraph.

2. The routing of the imported consignment needs to be continuously evaluated and must be decided on a value added basis. This includes transit time, freight rate and the geographical location of the sea or airport. The shortest route may not be the most advantageous in terms of service frequency, transport mode or degree of reliable high tech infrastructure.

3. The development of the sea–land bridge and the sea–air bridge concepts continue on a global basis. Sea–air development examples can be found in Dubai and Singapore. Dubai is strategically placed at the cross roads of Asia, Europe and Africa. Singapore is regarded as the trading hub of the Far East market. Manufacturing and trading companies around the world increasingly recognize that efficient production and marketing must be matched by an equally efficient system of shipping goods to the buyer. Goods are shipped from Singapore and neighbouring feeder ports and on arrival at Dubai are

transhipped via air freight services to Frankfurt or New York. This system is ideal for fast moving imported products.

4. The distriparks found in the major ports of the world such as Rotterdam, Zeebrugge and Singapore provide a new dimension to international physical distribution. The importer leases a warehouse in the port environs, assembles, processes and labels his or her products with substantial cost savings. Subsequently, the goods are sold on to a customer, the buyer being situated in the same country or outside of it. The componentized items involved can be sourced from the cheapest markets and only attract import duty when they enter their market of sale. This is a growth market and is an ideal way for the procurement manager to access goods.

5. Free trade zones are similar to distriparks. They enable the user to lease land and accommodation from the port authority and undertake the manufacture or a componentized assembly process. Favourable cost savings are realized, including local taxes and rates in the earlier years. Many are called 'industrial zones' and operate in countries which are keen to develop an industrial base. Importers set up these zones and develop an industrial transplant or assembly plant to vitiate the high freight cost, obtain more favourable import tariffs through componentized assembly, take advantage of more favourable labour rates and enter markets which are restrictive by using local labour in the manufacturing and assembly process. The distriparks and FTZs are favourable techniques for an importer setting up a business in an overseas territory.

6. Inwards investment. In recent years the growth of inwards investment – that is foreign investment – has been phenomenal and it is yet to reach its peak. Companies target markets in which to set up a manufacturing or assembly base – usually with a limited volume of indigenous manufacture or production, but the bulk of the business relies on imported raw materials and components for assembly. The location is strategically chosen for its access to nearby volume markets with the bulk of the production serving the indigenous population.

7. The benefit of serving a single market is found in the EU (see page 42). Importers conducting pan-European trade benefit from a good infrastructure and the free circulation of goods, capital, services and labour.

8. Similarly importers situated in economic blocs or customs unions should strive to do business within those countries and take full advantage of the liberalization of trade within those blocs and unions.

9. Customs planning. This involves a wide range of customs activities (see chapter 13) including tariffs, duty preference, VAT, inward processing relief, customs warehousing, free zones, carnets, import licensing, import valuation and local import control. Study Figure 13.1 on page 272 on computerized customs clearance system.

10. Consolidation. The consolidation of cargo is a growth market by air, truck and container. It is economical and a network of services exist worldwide.

Importers shipping small consignments should utilize consolidation, usually through an agent.

11. Packaging. Basically, packing is a form of protection and an aid to handling, identity and stowage. Excessive packing increases the volumetric size of the goods and can thereby increase freight costs on high volume products. The buyer and supplier must work closely together to produce the most acceptable packing specification.

12. Loadability and stowage. Aligned to packing is the general loadability and stowage of the cargo. The buyer and supplier should work together to devise a stowage plan to make the best use of the cubic and weight capacity of the truck or container. The buyer is really the lead player as he or she determines the product specification and a variation in the composition of the product or components may yield reduced volumetric space thereby improving the quantity of items shipped. Professional help should be enlisted from the road haulier or container operator. A 10 per cent improvement in loadability will lower the distribution cost of the imported product. This tends to be a neglected area of distribution by the buyer using the full load or FCL container. Good loadability is realized through the correct mode of transport and type of transport unit used. A wide range of container types exist (see page 205) and buyers should take full advantage of the situation to remain competitive.

13. Distribution centres. Associated with distriparks, districentres and free trade zones, are distribution centres. Under this concept the exporter will centralize all of his or her products on one distribution centre which will feed into the neighbouring market. Overall, it can be described as a cluster market distribution centre concept. It improves the service to the buyer who usually has on-line computer ordering access. It is widely practised in the EU where one distribution centre may serve several countries.

14. Third countries. An increasing volume of buyers' business is now conducted on a third country basis. For example, an order placed with a Japanese company can be supplied to the EU from a manufacturing plant in Taiwan.

15. The currency used in the freight rate does require careful evaluation (see page 226).

16. The most advantageous Incoterms 2000 must be used suitable for the buyer's needs (see page 287).

17. The freight forwarder or carrier must be thoroughly audited, particularly in terms of value added benefit and TQM (ISO 9001 and BS 5750). The audit matrix is given in Table 10.1.

    The matrix shown in Table 10.1 must not be regarded as exhaustive; it requires adaptation in the light of the buyer's circumstances. The buyer will determine the weighting criteria.

18. Transport distribution analysis techniques should be employed to devise the most suitable method of distribution (see page 223).

19. Full use should be made of EDI.

TABLE 10.1 Audit matrix of international physical distribution

	Very poor 1	Poor 2	Medium 3	Good 4	Very good 5	% weight	Result grade × weight
Supplier's country infrastructure							
Route option							
Packaging							
Carrier modes –							
Sea							
Combined transport							
Air							
Truck							
Transit time by mode							
Freight rate							
Import Tariff							
Seaport infrastructure							
Airport infrastructure							
Service frequency							
Service reliability							
Quality service							
Freight forwarder							
TQM							
Logistics focus							
TOTAL						100%	

20. The growing development of Local Import Control should be evaluated by the buyer (see page 270).
21. Integrators such as DHL and TNT are becoming very popular with the buyer who requires small packages urgently under a guaranteed schedule.

The foregoing list of strategic options is not exhaustive but requires careful evaluation. The distribution process has become very sophisticated in the past decade and involves many elements, each with cost and efficiency factors.

Decision-making process

The process of making the decision about the most acceptable channel of distribution will vary by circumstances. Each procurement executive will have different priorities. Product sourcing is a complex business the first stage is to decide on the most acceptable product and supplier; the second is to evolve the most efficient distribution channel consistent with the buyer's objective. Buyers frequently alter their product sourcing and this requires continuous logistics planning to coordinate resources to continue to achieve the company's objectives.

The following checklists have been compiled as a guide to the relevant evaluation criteria. We will begin by looking at the evaluation of the international physical distribution of a buyer's market.

(a) Buyer's market stability.

(b) Short- and long-term profitability from the supplier's contract of sale.

(c) Near or distant market.

(d) Infrastructure in the supply chain – existing and planned.

(e) Routing options and cost/value added benefit from the supplier's premises to airport or seaport and distribution to the buyer's premises.

(f) Import regulations – documentation, licensing, tariffs and duty.

(g) Airlines, shipping companies, serving the buyer and any flag discrimination such as routing on the supplier's national airline or shipping company. Evaluation should include schedules, rates, frequency, transit times, reliability and overall quality of service, including TQM.

(h) Availability of buyer's resources and experience in terms of personnel and overall logistics identifying cost factors both short- and medium-term. Buyers today rely on logistics and EDI to develop efficient supply chains. Many rely on the logistical resources of a mega container operator.

(i) A transport distribution analysis (see page 223) relating to the capital cost which will be tied up in transit rates, transit time, packaging, interest on capital, insurance, import duty and handling charges.

(j) Availability or development of information technology, especially in the areas of management information control. For example, in 2000 P&O Nedlloyd introduced a 'Track and Trace' facility for customers on its website. This enables the shipper (buyer or supplier) to track the current status of his or her shipment using the P&O Nedlloyd booking reference number, bill of lading reference or container number. The system is continuously updated from the P&O Nedlloyd in-house systems and does not display any commercially sensitive information so access does not require prior registration.

(k) Any customs benefit such as a preferential customs tariff may be in place between the two trading nations – the supplier and the buyer – thereby offering favourable import duty levels not available in other import sourcing markets.

(l) The risk areas in the suppliers market. This embraces exchange and political risk including security risk.

(m) A profile of the supplier and airlines and shipping companies serving the country both directly and through transhipment hub routes and connecting overland routes including transit countries and any attendant security risk. The latter applies to buyers in land locked countries who, where economical, may prefer to air freight goods directly to the buyer's main international airport thereby avoiding overland transit and handling costs at the seaport.

The buyer should produce a grid or comprehensive tabulation of the foregoing points as a first stage in the evaluation. This exercise can either be done on a consignment basis or over a period of time as consignments are predicted or forecast.

The next stage is to summarize the data in the tabulation with a view to reconciling them with the buying company's international physical distribution strategy. In so doing, potential difficulties with some carriers will be identified or discussions can be initiated between the procurement international logistics manager and acceptable carrier(s).

At this point, the international logistics manager or import manager will probably have up to three options in response to earlier enquiries. A major factor is the total product cost of each option and the value added benefit each brings, to both the importer and the supplier. Many shippers use transport distribution analysis (see page 223) to aid their decision making. It is possible that buyers will tend to patronize carriers with whom they have contracts on other routes or where there has been favourable earlier experience, but when entering new contracts with previously unused suppliers a fresh approach is required to retain competitiveness. Creative thinking is required, involving all members of the buyer's team but especially the logistics division but also including the production and assembly divisions.

The third stage is to carry out some test transits. Each stage of the transit should be monitored in order to identify any problem areas. Full liaison must be maintained with all parties involved in the transit. A significant factor in the distribution network adopted is the loadability of the transport unit. This is determined by the configuration of the packing and its stowage effectiveness, with broken stowage being kept to a minimum. This involves close liaison between the import, procurement or logistics manager and the carrier to make sure that the most suitable truck or container is provided. Loadability can be improved by breaking down the consignment into smaller units.

The next stage is to evaluate the test transit(s) and, following consultation with all interested parties but with the buyer taking the lead, decide on the most appropriate distribution network and firm up the total cost of the product.

The final stage is to devise an action plan to execute the decision. This must be controlled by the buyer or international logistics manager and be monitored through the budgetary control methods. Good planning is an essential ingredient to an efficient international distribution network, plus a total commitment from all the parties in a transparent logistic supply chain.

Problem areas and possible solutions

The international physical distribution network is high tech and has become very competitive. Innovation and the need for greater efficiency are becoming very much in evidence as we move through the millennium. Distribution is becoming more logistically and EDI driven. The shipper – buyer or supplier – is demanding quicker transits and more logistically driven networks. This requires heavy investment. Hence, the carrier market is seeing the development of operating alliances, mergers and acquisitions in an attempt to widen their customer base, lower unit cost, raise capital and avoid duplication of resources such as agents, berths and information systems. The carrier is encouraging synergy with the shipper. Seaports and airports are playing an increasingly decisive role in the development of trade. Both the seaport and the airport – particularly the latter – are becoming trade centres.

The discerning buyer must keep up-to-date with new developments, both those planned and under construction and those recently completed such as road/rail bridge linking Denmark and Norway which has opened up new buying opportunities. However, one must acknowledge that problem areas do arise in the distribution network which the buyer must resolve. Given below are a number of problems together with possible solutions.

1. Industrial disputes, or a build up of traffic at a seaport, can seriously disrupt a service and result in the goods arriving late and beyond the expiry date of the import licence and letter of credit. Alternative routes should be explored at the earliest possible time, including the possibilities of transferring to air freight. Such situations build up over a period of a few days and a contingency plan should be devised at an early stage and put in place.

2. The range of truck and container types tends to increase, but it does generate an imbalance of their use. This is especially true of the container business. An example can also be seen in a market where liquid imports predominate and perishable foodstuffs and machinery are exported thereby requiring two different types of containers. It is primarily a carrier's problem but the buyer may be able to negotiate a discounted rate on the return truck or container which otherwise would be empty.

3. Many countries cannot accept the 40ft container on their road network due to weight and length restrictions. Hence, the 20ft container is employed to give a door to door multi-modal transport service. However, where such restrictions exist and, subject to port equipment and a nearby container base being suitably equipped, the buyer can opt for a 40ft container on a long haul with its much larger capacity and lower cost per tonne. The goods can be transferred at the port or container base to a lorry, railway wagon, inland waterway or 20ft container for onward transit.

4. Dangerous goods and indivisible loads such as transformers or engineering plant can weigh up to 250 tonnes and require special arrangements. Dangerous goods (see page 230) require pre-shipment booking at an early stage. As for indivisible loads, these products require special arrangements and a freight forwarder or haulier specializing in this work will have a project forwarding department to handle such transits. The procurement manager is well advised to entrust such shipments to an accredited freight forwarder specializing in this work. The following points are relevant to shipments requiring special handling.

(a) The port of departure, and any destination areas need to be checked out to ensure they can handle such a shipment, checking especially for the availability of heavy lifting equipment. It is important to check the infrastructure serving the port.

(b) The shipowner will have a plan and specification of the shipment to evaluate the stowage and handling arrangements; and also to identify the weight distribution. The procurement or logistics manager should be closely involved as parts of the indivisible load may be able to be broken down to aid stowage and handling with resultant freight cost savings.

(c) The transportation of an indivisible load to and from the ports requires pre-planning particularly regarding the route and time scale.

(d) The rates are usually assessed on a cost plus profit basis.

Advantages of the indivisible load shipment to the buyer are numerous. They include: lower transportation cost, quicker transit, much reduced site assembly cost, less risk of damage in transit, lower insurance premium, less technical aid and staff resources required by the buyer as there is no extensive site assembly, equipment can be tested and fully operational in the factory before despatch, less risk of malfunctioning equipment. The results are earlier commissioning of the equipment which in turn brings it into quicker productive use with profitable benefits to the buyer.

5. A large volume of trade is shipped in small packages. The buyer has the option of despatching it as a package attracting published rates, or under consolidated arrangements. The latter usually involves an agent for an air freight or sea transport LCL container movement. Buyers are urged to use consolidated shipments whenever possible.

6. Buyers are urged to monitor closely all transits and any irregularities, initiating early remedial measures with the parties concerned. If it is difficult to establish the cause of the problems such as late arrival, damaged cargo, missing merchandise, etc. Test transits should be undertaken. On-line computer access to the carrier with a tracking system such as P&O Nedlloyd facilitates this problem solving.

7. International physical distribution tends, in some companies, to be given a low profile in the management structure, especially at the more senior level. This is now changing as companies become more globally focused in sourcing their products and acknowledging that to remain competitive they must have a professionally qualified team managing their international physical distribution. Moreover, it is a high cost area and efficiency can be improved through the employment of professionally qualified and experienced personnel.

8. Exchange risk still remains evident in many markets but a range of measures can be taken to minimize it.

9. Cargo insurance features in Incoterms 2000. Buyers should check that the goods have been insured and take contingency measures when in doubt.

10. Documentary credits should be checked to ensure they comply with the buyer's wishes.

11. Faulty documents cause late delivery of the goods (see page 158). The buyer must employ professionally qualified personnel to handle such documents and ensure that the most advantageous arrangements are in place.
12. Full use should be made of electronic commerce.
13. A logistics distribution plan should be devised.

Logistics strategy

Buyers today are increasingly looking at the total production and value added chain. Import managers are looking more closely at the logistics part of their business. Basically, the science of logistics is the ability to get the right product to the right place at the right time. As a result, the buyer is no longer interested in the point to point operator such as airport to airport, or seaport to seaport, but the total distribution service in terms of the value added chain. This approach is linked to the just-in-time concept in management techniques. In consequence it has stimulated the expansion of express air services and integrated operators such as UPS.

Integrated operators offer a complete package for the air cargo shipper embracing not only collection and airport to airport flight, but delivery to the importer's address with a guaranteed arrival time. The integrator undertakes all the customs documentation and clearance. Products ideally suited to this market are, for example high tech items and pharmaceuticals but it is a less appropriate method for the traditional engineering and manufacturing sectors where consolidation shipments are more appropriate. Most integrators have logistics departments whose task is to identify customer needs, tailor solutions to their specific problems and provide them with a value added service. Other areas covered by the integrators include the provision of waybills, invoices, management reports, availability of a bonded warehouse, stock control and so on. Overall, the aim is to combine production warehousing distribution and transport for shippers on a global basis.

Undoubtedly the mega container operators such as P&O Nedlloyd, Maersk and Hapag Lloyd are driving global logistic expansion. Many mega container operators have their own logistics divisions thereby encouraging buyers to place their international distribution sourcing arrangements with the shipowners. Their service embraces all elements of the distribution network including warehousing, supplier selection, packaging, customs clearance and associated documentation.

With an increasingly competitive market, logistics operations are under close scrutiny to minimize costs whilst maximizing customer service. This involves supply chain modelling, warehouse and plant location, warehouse and transport operational modelling, stock optimization, warehouse design and equipment, systems and operations specification, and the implementation of change. Logistics strategies are particularly relevant in trading blocs and also to fast moving products where competition is fierce and service paramount to the customer. Cost must be kept to a minimum if the integrator is to remain competitive.

Overall, an effective logistics strategy focuses on efficient international supply chain management. Importers are constantly searching for ways to improve their efficiency not only by streamlining procedures, but also by identifying and exploiting any available cost saving opportunities.

Effective international supply chain management requires taking a holistic view of the entire process from the product design through the sourcing of materials and manufacture to delivery to the final consumer. Understanding the dynamics of the business to derive an appropriate logistic strategy is not in itself sufficient. In an international environment where components are purchased and products sold in multiple destinations with different tax and tariff jurisdictions, understanding the customs, VAT and direct tax implications of that strategy is essential. Often this means a careful balancing act weighing potential VAT savings against an increased corporation tax liability, or opportunities for customs reliefs against logistical preferences. We will now consider this point by means of a hypothetical case study.

A UK based wholesale and retail Fashion House engaged in fashion design features ten areas of potential cost saving as illustrated in Figure 10.1. The principles demonstrated apply equally to business across a range of industries.

Each new season's collection is designed in the UK from where appropriate materials are sourced. Fabric is purchased from Japan, buttons, etc. from Taiwan and tags and labels from the UK. Production is outsourced to a third party 'cut, make and trim' (CMT) contractor in Thailand, identified by the Fashion House's international purchasing office (IPO) in Singapore. The CMT manufacturer is responsible for purchasing the packaging materials locally. Samples are collected and stored by the IPO prior to being delivered to a third party quality assurance laboratory.

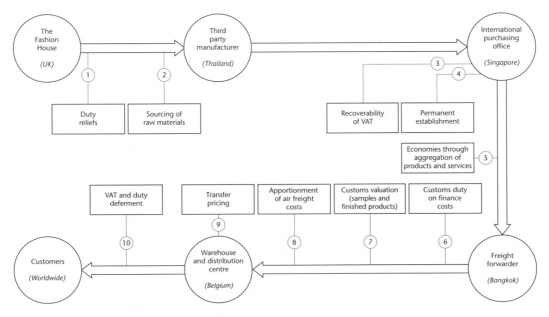

FIGURE 10.1 Ten issues to consider

The collection is sent via a freight forwarder in Bangkok to a distribution centre in Belgium operated by the Fashion House's Belgian subsidiary. Payment to the manufacturer is made in USD letters of credit against forwarder's receipts. The collection is despatched from Belgium to wholesale customers across Europe and the company's own retail outlets. A small number of orders are also obtained via the company's Internet website. The Belgian subsidiary recharges the UK parent for its services. Any unsold stock is shipped to an independent factory outlet in Poland for sale. Overall, as illustrated in Figure 10.1 it identifies ten cost savings areas: duty reliefs; sourcing of raw materials; recoverability of VAT; permanent establishment; economies through aggregation of products and services; customs duty on finance costs); customs valuation (samples and finished products); apportionment of air freight costs; transfer pricing; and VAT and duty deferment.

To conclude our brief analysis, it is likely that global logistics strategy will feature more in the buyer's sourcing strategy and carriers will respond more to the challenge of change and opportunity as we move on through the millennium. Again the buyer's planning must feature strongly in the formulation and execution of this strategy.

Customs planning

For many years a large number of companies engaged in international trade regarded payment of customs duties and the cost of compliance with customs law and regulations as unavoidable expenses with little or no scope for planning.

The buyer or procurement management is well advised to speak to a management consultancy company specializing in customs law and regulations. This is an area where enormous savings can be realized by tackling one of the many areas which offer such opportunities. If a company buys overseas, savings can be realized by the judicious use of reliefs. Most manufacturer's products contain items 'bought in'. Hence, many customs planning considerations apply to the sale and export of finished and semi-finished products.

Customs planning involves arranging a company's affairs to ensure that it suffers minimum possible exposure to taxation within the law. The taxes involved are import duties, Common Agriculture Policy levies, excise duties and VAT. Savings can be realized in the cost of complying with customs requirements. HM Customs and Excise offer a variety of simplified procedures to ease both their own administrative burden and traders' costs of compliance. Effective customs planning offers the following benefits to the procurement officer:

(a) minimizes the trader's exposure to customs duties;
(b) maximizes the trader's use of facilities and reliefs;
(c) minimizes the trader's cost of compliance;
(d) improves the trader's profitability and cash flow;
(e) avoids the risk of seizure and penalties.

Given below are the main areas of customs planning for the buyer to consider.

1. The tariff is the centre of customs planning. It determines the rate of duty on imported goods according to their description and specification listed against a numerical commodity code. Situations can arise when the goods are wrongly described and attract a higher rate of duty than necessary. Hence, the buyer and seller must confer to ensure the correct tariff is applied. It may be advantageous to import the goods in a componentized form rather than as a finished product – the former overall attract a lower tariff band. It will, however, involve the buyer in assembly costs following arrival of the componentized units.

   Customs planning is desirable at the design stage of a new product, whether it is to be imported as a finished product for onward sale or to be used by the importer in a further manufacturing process. Furthermore, if imported items are to be used in the manufacturing process, one must evaluate the financial merits of importing components rather than sub-assembly from individual components. For the buyer sourcing in more than one country there is a further aspect to be considered. Over 50 countries now use the Harmonised System of Tariff Classification and Commodity Coding (HS). Hence, from the buyer's standpoint the same tariff classification will be appropriate to the same commodity code in each of the sourcing countries although of course there are likely to be considerable differences in rates of duty. Ideally, it is worthwhile agreeing the appropriate commodity codes with suppliers when importing.

2. The customs value of the vast majority of the consignments is based on the price actually paid or payable for the goods by the importer. Adjustments upwards or downwards frequently need to be made to invoiced prices. These include commission, discounts, transport, insurance and price review clauses – it also embraces the strategy of transfer pricing (see page 60). These aspects are of particular concern when applied to transactions between related parties such as trading between companies in a multinational group.

3. Customs warehousing is amongst the most useful of the various reliefs available. It permits goods liable to import duty to be stored in an HM Customs and Excise warehouse without duty or VAT being accounted for until the goods are removed from the warehouse. A limited range of minor handling operations may be carried out on the goods whilst they are in the warehouse, where they remain for up to five years. When needing to be moved they must be entered for export or removed to another similar warehouse or transferred to another regime as inwards processing relief.

4. The origin of the imported goods and the route they follow to the EU has considerable influence on their liability to duty. If they are imported from a country with a preference agreement with the EU, then the rate is reduced or even zero. The question often arises as to whether the supply source can be changed or whether the specification can be varied or componentized to include less offshore elements of value.

The buyer should ascertain whether suspension of the full rate of duty may be available from specified countries at certain times in particular goods. Similarly, a quota may be in force which allows predetermined quantities of goods meeting certain tariff descriptions to be imported at a lower than full rate of duty. Such benefits extend to buyers of UK goods provided that they are imported into a country that has entered into a trading agreement with the EU. Hence, the supplier who plans to ensure that his or her goods originate in the EU can provide a certificate of origin (see page 169) to permit more competitive prices to overseas customers.

5. Outward processing relief arises when the goods are exported for a manufacturing process and then returned to the EU. Prior authorization by customs is required before the relief is allowed. The duty payable on the goods returned is reduced by the nominal duty that would have been charged on the exported elements.

6. Buyers should check whether the seller requires an export licence. These are issued in the supplier's country by the appropriate government department. Careful planning and continued monitoring are essential by the buyer.

7. Inward processing relief is available to traders who are buying goods from countries that are not members of the EU. The imported goods may be used for virtually any manufacturing process and are relieved from import duty. The buyer has to seek prior authorization from customs to suspend the import duty (the suspension method) or to recover it once the products have been imported (draw back method).

The buyer must not regard the foregoing points as an exhaustive list. Other items include free trade zones, processing for free circulation and anti-dumping duties. The range differs in each country around the world, reflecting government strategies and bi- and multilateral trading agreements. Customs planning forms an important element in the physical distribution strategy and alas is too often an area neglected by the buyer. It requires continuous monitoring of the customs duties and regulations. Arthur Andersen and Coopers and Lybrand are market leaders in this field.

Multi-modalism

As stressed earlier the importer must ideally buy under FCA or delivered terms DDU or DDP and CIP or CPT terms (see Incoterms 2000 pages 287–302) and move away from airport-to-airport or seaport-to-seaport transit. This involves a strategy of buying goods under a multi-modal environment or what many users call combined transport. It offers the total product cost embracing a door to door service under DDU/DDP terms.

Overall, multi-modalism can be defined as the process of providing a door to door or warehouse to warehouse service to the shipper which embraces two or more forms of transport. This involves the merchandise being conveyed in a unitized form in the same unit throughout the transit. It embraces a scheduled and/or dedicated service.

Forms of multi-modalism are:

(a) containerization – FCL/LCL/road/sea/rail;
(b) land bridge – trailer/truck–road/sea/road;
(c) land bridge – pallet/IATA container–road/sea/air/road;
(d) trailer/truck – road/sea/road;
(e) swap body – road/rail/sea/road.

A development which has emerged in recent years from combined transport operations, multi-modalism is the term used for non-vessel operating carrier (NVOC) operations or non-vessel operating common carrier (NVOCC) operations. Multi-modalism may arise in a container (FCL or LCL) movement or trailer transit. In such a situation, carriers issue bills of lading for the carriage of goods on ships which they neither own nor operate. A freight forwarder will usually issue the FIATA multi-modal transport bill of lading (see page 166).

All forms of multi-modalism involve a dedicated service usually under NVOCC or NVOC.

The features of multi-modalism may be summarized as follows:

1. It provides a dedicated service with each operator or carrier committed to the schedule.
2. It operates under NVOCC or NVOC arrangements.
3. A strong feature is its provision of a regular, reliable, competitively priced quality door to door service with acceptable transit times. Hence, the value added benefit is considerable to the multi-modalism users; and it is usually fully computerized involving EDI, thereby enabling the operator to monitor the package throughout its transit. Overall, it places the multi-modal user in a strong competitive situation.
4. It develops and coordinates the best features of the transport modes to the advantage of the shipper.
5. It is an ideal environment for EDI and undoubtedly as EDI expands on a global basis, the multi-modal network will move with it.
6. The multi-modal network is very extensive and fast growing. The wide range of services it can offer stimulates the development of markets worldwide.
7. It is consumer led and market driven in its development in a logistic environment. Overall, it is bringing markets and the buyer and seller closer together and especially so in the high tech and fast moving consumer markets including foodstuffs.
8. An increasingly large number of operators are providing logistics departments to customize services to their client's needs.
9. Good asset utilization of multi-modal infrastructure permits competitive door to door or warehouse to warehouse through rates to be offered. Thus it exploits economies of scale and yields a favourable return on transport investment. Basically it is a high tech operation.

10. Under the auspices of the ICC and other international bodies a common code of liability and processing documents is now permitted. This has created confidence in the market and the handling of all multi-modal documents by banks, carriers, agents, buyers, sellers and port authorities. It also permits a through door to door or warehouse to warehouse rate to be quoted.

11. Operators are strongly committed to multi-modalism and as time moves on its extension will gather momentum and the existing networks will be further improved and diversified. It will be market and technologically driven aided by an increasingly discerning shipper.

12. Multi-modalism is giving a new impetus to the role of seaports and airports especially the former port authorities worldwide who are developing not only the port enclaves through districentres and free trade zones, but who are also initiating and encouraging the infrastructure operators on which they rely to develop and improve existing multi-modal networks. Examples include the port of Singapore, Dubai, Klang, Zeebrugge and Rotterdam. Overall, port authorities are tending to coordinate their activities and develop their strategy on an unprecedented scale. Many are striving to become trading centres following the examples of Zeebrugge and Rotterdam. Many are being privatized and have an enhanced role through the development of the containerized hub and spoke system. The port authority today is only part of the total product network.

13. Associated with item (12), the changing pattern of international distribution is resulting in less port to port cargo and the accelerated growth of multi-modalism. This relieves port congestion and develops ICDs, dry ports, free trade zones and the use of local import and export control customs arrangements. It encourages the development of a new vision and enthusiasm at all levels of the supply chain to improve the value added benefits which accrue to the exporter and importer in using the network system.

14. As indicated earlier, many multi-modal operators have a logistics department to counsel and develop shippers' needs. This is encouraging closer harmony between the shipper and the operator and ensures an ongoing market led commitment from both the user and provider of the multi-modal network.

15. Buyers should undertake market research to monitor the multi-modal network and its development. It will serve to identify new sourcing opportunities (see item 13).

16. Multi-modalism develops new market sourcing, improves commodity quality, raises loadability, lowers transit times, reduces packing and aids the development of consumer, high tech, fast moving markets. It brings different cultures and the international business world closer together in both their objectives and ideology.

17. The system favours both large and small shippers by accommodating full load or consolidated consignments.

To conclude our analysis, the buyer must be conscious that multi-modalism will contribute significantly to a changing international trade pattern. It will open up countries with low labour cost skills to the westernized markets of Europe and North America which have greater buying power. Such industrialized, high labour cost countries are increasingly reliant on the development of their global manufacturing business by producing within the low cost markets and relying on multi-modalism to distribute goods in a cost effective manner to buyers located in high GDP markets.

Multi-modalism strategy

The strategy of adapting to multi-modalism is essentially market and technology led. It is an ongoing strategy, with market growth providing the cash flow necessary to fund continuing investment. Moreover, as the system develops the economies of scale with lower development costs, as has been experienced in computerization, has made it an exciting time and one full of opportunity, but it is a strategy which requires professionalism and high quality training at all levels. We will briefly consider the aspects which require special attention by the buyer.

(a) The buyer must continuously study trading patterns and trends to identify and develop new opportunities for multi-modalism. Existing systems must be continuously evaluated and improvements identified.

(b) Trading blocs such ASEAN, NAFTA, the EU and MERCOSUR continuously review both their internal market and external market multi-modal systems structure. Plans are continuously being produced and feature new developments and improvements to the infrastructure. Visit the EU Internet website on planned infrastructure improvements within a five year period.

(c) The Pacific Rim is a popular region for product sourcing and one where the infrastructure is fast growing, especially in the area of multi-modalism featuring maritime containers. Again buyers are urged to visit the ASEAN and APEC Internet websites.

(d) Multi-modalism strongly favours a 'just-in-time' strategy.

Buyers are reminded that the multi-modal network adds value to their business opportunities. Hence, the need to take a strategic view and study the global opportunities. Continuing port investment and development of the hub and spoke system, coupled with the annual growth of containerization in a logistic driven environment will all play major roles. Hence, the need for the buyer to focus on the multi-modal network availability when determining sourcing markets.

Recommended reading

- HM Customs Notices.
- Coopers and Lybrand publications on Customs planning.
- Arthur Andersen publications on Customs planning.

11

International physical distribution strategy and management II

Containerization

Containerization is a growth market and the discerning buyer must focus more attention on the benefits and application of containerization in the international physical distribution planning process. Each year the range and technology of the container and its infrastructure continues to improve to the benefit of the importer.

Containerization is a method of distributing merchandise in a unitized form thereby permitting an intermodal transport system to be evolved providing a possible combination of rail, road, canal and maritime transport. Today we have the sixth generation of container ships of 8000 TEUs in service. By the year 2005 containerized cargo will account for some 60 per cent of all cargo moved by sea. In 1990 it was 40 per cent. The growth is emerging for two reasons: (i) transfers from the bulk cargo division, particularly the reefer and fruit carriers and (ii) organically as the benefits of containerization through multi-modalism and logistic focus accelerate trade development.

The growth in containerization is being driven by two areas: hub and spoke systems and multi-modalism embracing air freight or rail land-bridge.

An example of the hub and spoke system is found in hub ports such as Singapore, Hong Kong and Rotterdam which all rely on smaller ports to feed containers into the mega container service.

An example of a land-bridge is the North American double stack container trains between the west- and east-coast ports. Dubai and Singapore offer an example of an air freight bridge to Europe involving cargoes from the Far East. Numerous other examples of both air and land-bridges exist and can be found on the websites of mega container and major freight airlines.

The buyer may use a complete ISO (International Standards Organisation) container, full container load (FCL), or despatch his merchandise to a container base or an inland clearance depot (ICD) for it to be consolidated with other compatible cargo en route to a similar destination country, area or region for despatch as a less than container load (LCL).

The features of containerization can be conveniently summarized as follows:

1. It permits a door to door service which may be from the supplier's factory site to the retail distributors store – an overall distance of some 6000 km. Overall, it may be an FCL or LCL movement.
2. No intermediate handling at terminal transhipment points, that is rail and road terminals or seaports can speed up transits.
3. Less packing required for containerized shipments. In some situations, particularly with specialized ISO containers such as refrigerated ones or tanks for liquid or powder, no packing is required. This produces substantial cost savings and raises service quality.
4. The absence en route of intermediate handling plus quicker sea transits compared with break bulk cargo shipments lowers the risk of damage and pilferage.
5. This reduced risk of cargo damage and pilferage allows low insurance premiums.
6. Elimination of intermediate handling coupled with the other inherent advantages of containerized shipments results in the cargo arriving in a better condition, thereby enhancing the quality of service.
7. Emerging from the inherent advantages of containerization, rates are likely to remain more competitive.
8. Maritime container shipments are much quicker compared with break bulk cargo. Shipowners and Port Authorities continue to invest heavily in port equipment and its infrastructure to speed up transhipment arrangements, quicken port turn-round time and improve transit time. Port operations today are very high tech and logistically focused.
9. Overseas trade generally is being encouraged by the faster transits times and other inherent advantages of containerization.
10. Quicker transits and more reliable maritime schedules and in many cases increased service frequency are tending to encourage many importers to hold reduced stocks and spares. This produces savings in warehouse costs, lessens the risk of obsolescent stock and reduces importer's working capital. It exploits the benefits of the just-in-time concept and improves inventory control and warehouse management results.
11. Containerization encourages the rationalization of ports of call.
12. Documentation is simplified by the use of through documentation or combined transport bill of lading, involving a common code of liability for the through transit.
13. Similarly to item (12) a through rate can be quoted. For example, this can include both the maritime and surface transport cost of the ISO container. Hence, it is an ideal mode for delivered quotation under CIP, DDU and DDP.
14. Overall, transits are more reliable, particularly disciplined controlled transit arrangements in maritime schedules. Most major container ship operators have computer equipment to facilitate the booking, stowage and control of containers throughout the transit. For example, P&O Nedlloyd have a track

and trace facility for customers on its Website. This enables the shipper, buyer or seller to track the current status of his or her shipment using the P&O Nedlloyd booking reference number, bill of lading reference or container number. The system is continuously updated from the P&O Nedlloyd in-house systems and does not display any commercially sensitive information so access does not require prior registration.

15. Containerization is allowing the emergence of new markets which were previously difficult to access.

16. Not all merchandise can be conveniently containerized. However, the percentage of such traffic falls annually as new types of maritime containers are introduced. GE Sea Co Service Ltd is a market leader and innovator in container development (see below). Buyers are urged to visit their website: www.geseaco.com

17. Maritime containerization has greatly facilitated the development of consolidated or break bulk consignments. This favours especially the SME buyer or importer unable to originate a full container load which is consolidated through a container base.

18. Containerization facilitates the maximum use of computerization in many areas, especially container control, customer billing, container stowage in the vessel, container tracking, document processing, cargo reservation and so on.

19. The international maritime container network expands annually as ports and berths are modernized together with their infrastructure. This has seen the development of the dry port such as Ipoh, Malaysia; the development of new container berths, the relocation of container berths to accommodate larger vessels, such as in the ports of Klang and Bangkok; the development of air freight and land-bridges; the development of feeder services to serve major ports; the new generation of high capacity containers; the provision of new container types especially palletized and high cube (9ft 6in high) (see page 206) and the provision of distriparks, free trade zones and trading centres, as found in the ports of Rotterdam and Zeebrugge.

An increasing number of buyers are now arranging their own international transport arrangements featuring the container on an intermodal basis. Buyers are particularly urged to make the best use of the available weight/volumetric limitations of the container type chosen and design the packaging arrangements accordingly, with broken stowage being kept to a minimum. Hence, product design and packaging profile are key elements in the container stowage plan. This requires continuous liaison with the supplier.

The following container specifications have been kindly provided by GE Sea Co Services Ltd (Tables 11.1, 11.2, 11.3) and should prove an excellent aide memoire for the shipper aiming to choose the ideal container to match the commodity being shipped and its packaging in an economical manner. The tables feature only dry box and dry freight special maritime containers; wet cargoes are transported in tank containers.

TABLE 11.1 Maritime container types and swapbodies and their cargoes

Type of container/equipment	Possible cargoes
High cube containers	Carpets, freezers, white goods, ovens, low value tobacco, toys, balloon cargo, scrap paper.
20 ft Bulk container	Malt, beans, grain, granules, gravel, sand, nuts and bolts, printers ink, screws, sugar, dry chemicals, ores.
20 ft Half height (open top)	Drums, pipes, rails, rods, steel beams and ingots, marble slabs, copper blisters/anodes, heavy ores, castings, grinding media.
20 ft & 40 ft Open tops	Agricultural and construction machinery, boats, flitches, glass, ingots, logs, scrap, salt hides (with added protection), rolls of plastic sheet, some bulk cargoes, project cargo.
20 ft Produce carrier/Open side	Produce, livestock, side load items.
20 ft Ventilated Containers	General cargo, cargo affected by heat or which requires ventilation, cocoa beans, coffee beans, beans, onions, potatoes, produce, seeds, spices, tobacco, pulses, garlic, metal goods liable to rust, damage, storage of electronic goods.
20 ft & 40 ft Flatracks and platforms flats	Agriculture machinery, air conditioners, boats, boilers, coils, construction machinery, electric generators, electrodes, large irregular shaped items, logs, machinery, newsprint or paper rolls, pipes, rods, steel beams, tanks, tinplate, transformers, trucks, motor vehicles, overheight/overlength items, plywood sheets, project cargo.
SeaCell and 2 palletwide containers	Two palletwide requirements, plus other general applications.
Swapbodies	Two palletwide requirements, Intermodal operations, general cargoes.

Dry box and dry freight special maritime containers and swapbodies: outline descriptions

8 ft wide ISO units

20 ft Dry freight container (BX2)

For general cargo this is the most widely used container. Early units can carry a payload of approximately 22 tons, since 1994 approximately 27.7 tons, with cubic capacity of 33 m^3 (1150 ft^3). Laden fork lift pockets are fitted.

40 ft Dry freight container (BX4)

Again used for general cargo, can carry a payload of at least 26.6 tons with a cubic capacity of 67 m^3 (2238 ft^3). Fitted with Gooseneck tunnel.

40 ft High-cube container (9'6") (BW4)

High-cube 40 ft containers are restricted to certain trades and are designed for 'balloon' cargoes that are light, bulky and which 'cube out' before they 'weigh out'. The high-cube container allows shippers to reduce transportation costs by virtue of the 12 per cent greater volume. Fitted with Gooseneck tunnel.

45 ft High-cube container (9'6") (BW5)

High-cube 45 ft ISO container restricted to North American Intermodal and certain trades. Designed for similar cargoes as BW4, but for even greater cargo volume. Unit has 25 per cent more volume than a BX4. Units are designed with MGW of 30 480 kg so a payload of 25 680 kg is possible, cubic capacity 86 m^3. Units built with corner castings at 40 ft and 45 ft positions, reduced stacking at 40 ft position. Fitted with Gooseneck tunnel.

20 ft Bulk container (BK2)

Bulk containers are designed for the carriage of dry, homogeneous, free-flowing cargo. These units eliminate the need for expensive bagging and offer maximum utilization of cargo space, though some particular cargoes require propriety polythene liners. The loading and discharge can be performed at production plants; loading is through roof hatches and discharge is through either end wall, letter box style or door discharge hatches.

Bulk units have similar specifications as standard dry freight containers and as such they can be used on return trips for general cargo eliminating the problem of 'one-way' leasing, inherent in special cargo trades. Some units are plywood lined.

20 ft Product carrier (OP2)

The produce carrier is designed to carry commodities that require side loading and unloading and full ventilation which is fitted with full height, removable side grills for sidewall cargo retention and pull down tarpaulins to protect the cargo from the elements. These units can be used for dry freight cargo as well as cargoes that require ventilation, which gives them a much broader range of application.

20 ft Open side container (OS2)

The open side container is an earlier design of the produce carrier with similar applications. The unit has a greater number of loose components and is fitted with cargo retention slats and swing down low flaps at floor level on each side plus pull down tarpaulins to protect the cargo from the elements. Both the produce carrier and open side container can be easily adapted for carrying livestock.

20 ft Half height open top container (OH2)

Half height containers are designed to carry low volume dense cargoes that would otherwise result in wasted space if loaded into an 8'6" container. Two of these units stow in the same space as a standard 20 ft container and will allow approximately twice the weight of cargo to be carried in one TEU slot, thus saving space on both the full and empty move. The rear door in the majority of units is flap down and can be used as a ramp to aid entry of FL trucks into the container. The balance have opening side gates, or opening end gates.

20 ft and 40 ft Open top container (OT2 & OT4)

Open top containers are designed for loading through both the top and rear doors (which are fitted with swinging headers). They are suitable for the carriage of awkward, indivisible or over-height cargoes. With the tarpaulin covering in place the cargo is protected from the elements. Roof bows serve not only to stop water pooling on the tarpaulin, but also as structural members to reinforce the top side rails. 40 ft unit fitted with Gooseneck tunnel.

20 ft Ventilated container (VB2 & BV2)

Ventilated containers 'SeaVents', are designed to transport general cargo and hydroscopic cargoes such as coffee and cocoa needing ventilation plus cargo susceptible to rust damage. Ventilation is natural with the vent chambers creating a Venturi which draws in cool air through the bottom row of ventilators and expels moisture laden warm air through the top row of ventilators. The units are built to the same interior specification as standard 20 ft dry freight units and can therefore be used for ventilated cargo in one direction and dry freight cargo in the other.

Most insurance underwriters are recommending the use of ventilated containers rather than dry freight containers for hydroscopic cargoes or tinned goods, because of the large number of claims that result from damage to cargo due to container sweat, which results from condensation trapped in sealed containers. Ventilation is the only sure and fool-proof way of removing condensation from the inside of the container, and so protecting valuable cargo from damage.

20 ft and 40 ft Flatrack and platform flats

Flatracks are designed to containerize or unitize cargoes that would otherwise be carried breakbulk. They are ideal for oversized and awkward cargoes and are instrumental in reducing loading and discharge time. Flatracks and platform flats enable operators of cellular ships to carry cargoes that might otherwise have to be refused. There are five basic designs: fixed end, collapsible, spring assisted collapsible end, SeaDeck or Domino combined units and platform flats.

20 ft and 40 ft Fixed end flatracks (FR2 & FR4)

This is the basic unit with a solid bulkhead and is relatively inexpensive to lease. It is primarily suited to a balanced trade when cargo is available in both directions. When positioning empty, the units take a full container slot.

20ft Collapsible flatrack (FC2)

This is the basic version of a collapsible unit and is consequently the least expensive to lease. Collapsing is not spring assisted and, although simple, two men are required. The bulkhead is not solid but has a triangular end frame linking the corner posts so overlength cargoes can protrude in the clear areas. When empty, units can be interlocked together, four into 7'7" (2.37 m) or five into 9'6" (2.90 m). FC2 and FS2 have identical interlocking systems so mixed stacking is possible.

20 ft and 40 ft Spring assisted collapsible flatrack (FS2 & FS4)

Spring assisted with a solid bulkhead these are easier and quicker to collapse and erect. When empty, units of identical lengths can be interlocked together. Five FS2 or three FS4 fit into 8'6" (2.6 m). FC2 and FS2 can be interlocked together. FS4 can be interlocked with FB4 and FX4.

20 ft and 40 ft Seadeck combined collapsible flatrack and platform (FB2 & FB4)

The ultimate combined unit which greatly improves flexibility as it can be used both as flatrack and a platform flat; when collapsed the end walls fold flush into the floor. Wheeled and crawler equipment can be driven over the end to simplify loading. Ideal for intermodal services that require a forward bulkhead (headache board), as one end can be up and the other down. Seven FB2 or four FB4 fit into 8'6". Early FB4 interlocked with FS4 and FX4, but since April 1990 have been fitted with fliplock so can be interlocked with any 40 ft module. FB2 fitted with fliplock so can interlock with any 20 ft module.

20 ft and 40 ft Platform flats (FX2 & FX4)

A simple platform designed for carrying overlength, overwidth, awkward and problem stow cargoes. Particularly suitable for the creation of temporary 'tween decks in container ships for non-containerizable cargo and for use in ro-ro operations. When empty, units of identical length can be interlocked together and top lifted, seven FX2 into 7'9" (2.36 m) or eight into 8'11" (2.72 m) and four FX4 into 8'6". FX4 can be interlocked with FB4.

Worldwide two palletwide units

SeaCell two palletwide dry freight containers

SeaCell is the revolutionary new container design which offers two pallet internal width and can be stowed in deep-sea ships both in cellguides and on close deck

TABLE 11.2 Two Palletwide Units – Number of Pallets (one tier)

	20 ft Sea cell or box	7.15 m Swap	7.45 m Swap	30 ft Bulk	40 ft Sea cell or box	13.6 m Swap
Euro 800 × 1200 mm	14	17	18	22	30	33
Metric 1000 × 1200 mm	10	14	14	16	24	26
Gitter 835 × 1240 mm	11	12	16	17	23	26
Aussi 1167 × 1167 mm	10	–	–	14	20	–

fittings. SeaCell is a truly intermodal, two palletwide container that can be operated worldwide.

SeaCell has a standard ISO frame, so the corner castings are at normal positions. However, unlike conventional dry freight boxes, the side walls have corrugations which extend beyond the frame width. This unique corrugation design allows SeaCell units to stow next to each other, with the corrugations fitting together. When SeaCell is stowed next to a standard box, the corrugations fit into the dead space between them. This design allows SeaCell to be used on ships with narrow container cells or close deck fittings for ISO containers.

SeaCell is covered by worldwide patents and patent applications.

20 ft (2.48 m wide) Dry freight SeaCell (SC2)

Palletwide units suitable for up to 1200 mm wide pallets stowed side by side. Suitable for deep-sea use as built to full ISO strength standards. Additional cube also makes them suitable for shippers of non-palletized cargo.

20 ft (2.48 m wide) High cube SeaCell (SW2)

These high cube containers have some 12 per cent increased cubic capacity over the 8′6″ units. The majority are in use in Australia.

40 ft (2.48 m wide) Dry freight SeaCell (SC4)

Units have slim profile front wall and door to enable unit to have 12.1 m internal length, which is required for pallet compatibility. Suitable for deep-sea use as built to full ISO capability. Approximately 3 m^3 additional capacity over a 40 ft 8′6″ unit.

40 ft (2.48 m wide) High cube SeaCell (SW4)

These high cube containers have some 12 per cent increased cubic capacity over the 8′6″ unit.

20 ft (2.48 m wide) High cube bulk SeaCell (SK2)

Three loading hatches in roof and discharge hatches in door end. All in use in Australia.

Regional two palletwide units

20 ft (2.5 m wide) Intermodal container (LB2 & LW2)

Palletwide units, height available 9′6″ (LW2). Corner castings inset to ISO positions. Units have reduced stacking ability, so restricted to intermodal domestic or short sea routes. LB2 all in service in Australia. The majority of LW2 are in Australia, some are in Europe. Fitted with laden fork pockets.

20 ft (2.48 m wide) SeaCell intermodal container (CW2)

These high cube 9′6″ containers have asymmetric corrugations and consequently are cellguide friendly. Ideal for both intermodal domestic operations as they permit six high laden stacking. Fitted with laden pockets. All units in service in Australasia.

20 ft (2.5 m wide) Intermodal open top (LT2)

Palletwide 9′ high open top with conventional container door one end and letterbox discharge hatch at the other end. All units in service in Australia.

20 ft (2.5 m wide) Intermodal flatrack (LY2)

Palletwide 8′6″ high spring assisted flatrack. Laden fork pockets, side-gates can be fitted if required. All units in service in Australia.

40 ft (2.5 m wide) Intermodal container (LE4, LN4 & LW4)

Unit can accept two Euro pallets 1.2 m wide side by side. Heights available: 8′6″ (LE4), 9′ (LN4) and 9′6″ (LW4). Corner castings are inset to ISO dimensions and units are fitted with grapple lift points. Units have reduced stacking ability. Side door 8′6″ version available, one pair of slim doors each side. Some units do not have gooseneck tunnels. LE, LN & LW4 in service in Europe; LW4 in service in Australia. Australian LW4 fitted with empty lift fork pockets.

7.15 m Class 'C' Swapbody (KA2, KB2, KC2, KE2, KF2, KG2 & KH2)

Use currently restricted to Europe, but would consider other regional domestic markets.

2.5 m wide units

KA2 units are 7.15 m long, 2.5 m wide and 2.6 m high and fitted with a pair of bi-fold doors each side and a pair of end doors. Units not fitted with demountable legs but these could be retro-fitted as all the mounting points are installed. Empty top lift and empty stacking only, payload 21 000 kg.

brieflyKB2 units are 7.15 m long, 2.5 m wide and 2.7 m high and fitted with end doors one end. Fitted with demountable legs. Laden top lift and laden stacking 3 high, payload approximately 13 000 kg. Some are fitted with a keyhole lashing system.

KC2 units are as KB2, but are fitted with a roller shutter end door at one end. All are fitted with a keyhole lashing system.

2.55 m wide units

KE2 is as the KB2, but is 2.55 m wide. Payload 15 245 kg. All are fitted with a keyhole lashing system.

KF2 is as the KC2, but is 2.55 m wide. Payload 15 225 kg. All are fitted with a keyhole lashing system.

KG2 units are 7.45 m long and 2.55 m wide with curtainsides both sides. Payload 14 600 kg.

KH2 units are 7.45 m long and 2.44 m wide with a roller shutter door. Fitted with a keyhole system. Payload 15 100 kg.

13.6 m (2.5 m wide) Class 'A' swapbody (KD5)

This unit was specifically designed for intermodal road/rail operations within Europe. Two high laden stacking, top lift at 40 ft positions or grapple lift. Payload 29 800 kg.

Air freight

We have comprehensively examined the features of containerization and it would seem appropriate to consider air freight briefly as it is the other major means of distribution for commodities. Basically, air freight is ideal for cargoes with a high value to low weight ratio and those which are urgent.

The main features of air freight are briefly listed below.

(a) High speed, quick transits.
(b) Low risk of damage or pilferage, with consequent competitive insurance premiums.
(c) Simplified documentation – one document, an air waybill is used throughout the air freight transit and is interchangeable between IATA accredited airlines.
(d) Common code of liability conditions to all IATA accredited airlines.

TABLE 11.3 Maritime container and swapbodies descriptions

Container type	Internal (mm)	Door opening (mm)	MGW (kg)	Tare (kg)	Payload (kg)	Capacity (cbm)
8ft ISO Dry Freight						
20ft Box	L 5900	W 2340	24 000	2400	21 760	33
20ft × 8ft × 8ft 6in	W 2352	H 2280				
UT Code (BX2)	H 2386					
40ft Box	L 12033	W 2340	30 480	3730	26 750	67.6
40ft × 8ft × 8ft 6in	W 2352	H 2275				
UT Code (BX4)	H 2389					
40ft High Code	L 12033	W 2340	30 480	3920	26 560	76.3
40ft × 8ft × 9ft 6in	W 2352	H 2580				
UT Code (BW4)	H 2694					
45ft High Cube	L 13558	W 2340	30 480	4800	25 680	86
45ft × 8ft × 9ft 6in	W 2354	H 2586				
UT Code (BW5)	H 2696					
Special Boxes						
20ft Bulk	L 5892	W 2302	24 000	2450	22 550	31.8
20ft × 8ft × 8ft 6in	W 2326	H 2235				
UT Code (BK2)	H 2324					
20ft Open Side	L 5903	End door	25 400	2931	22 469	30.8
20ft × 8ft × 8ft 6in	W 2309	W 2235				
UT Code (OS2)	H 2258	H 2150				
		Side opening				
		W 5641				
		H 2003				
20ft Produce Carrier	L 5896	End door	25 400	3150	22 250	30.8
20ft × 8ft × 8ft 6in	W 2310	W 2290				
UT Code (OP2)	H 2260	H 2155				
		Side opening				
		W 5689				
		H 2098				
20ft Ventilated Box	L 5900	W 2340	24 000	2350	21 650	33
20ft × 8ft × 8ft 6in	W 2346	H 2276				
UT Code VB/BV2	H 2389					
Open Tops						
20ft Half Height	L 5912	W 2284	24 000	2135	21 865	14
20ft × 8ft × 4ft 3in	W 2227					
UT Code (OH2)	H 1060					

Container type	Internal (mm)	Door opening (mm)	MGW (kg)	Tare (kg)	Payload (kg)	Capacity (cbm)
20ft Open Top 20ft × 8ft × 8ft 6in UT Code (OT2)	L 5889 W 2335 H 2312	W 2340 H 2225	24 000	2020	21 980	31.8
40ft Open Top 40ft × 8ft × 8ft 6in UT Code (OT4)	L 12044 W 2350 H 2374	W 2336 H 2287	30 480	3980	26 500	66.3
Flatracks		Interlocking into				
20ft Fixed End 20ft × 8ft × 8ft 6in UT Code (FR2)	L 5946 W 2286 H 2327	8ft 6	23 220	2900	20 320	
20ft Collapsible 20ft × 8ft × 8ft 6in UT Code (FC2)	L 5860 W 2407 H 2292	4	25 000	2900	22 100	
20ft Spring Assisted 20ft × 8ft × 8ft 6in UT Code (FS2)	L 5949 W 2197 H 2271	5	30 000	2600	27 400	
20ft SeaDeck 20ft × 8ft × 8ft 6in UT Code (FB2)	L 5950 W 2224 H 2226	7	35 560	2820	32 740	
40ft Fixed End 40ft × 8ft × 8ft 6in UT Code (FR4)	L 11551 W 2110 H 1968		30 480	5300	25 180	
40ft Spring Assisted 40ft × 8ft × 8ft 6in UT Code (FS4)	L 12005 W 2438 H 1949	3	35 562	4995	30 567	
40ft SeaDeck 40ft × 8ft × 8ft 6in UT Code (FB4)	L 12078 W 2438 H 1947	4	45 000	5300	39 700	
Platform Flats 20ft Flat 20ft × 8ft × 1ft 2in	L 6058 W 2438	7	26 900	1500	25 400	
UT Code (FX2) 40ft Flat 40ft × 8ft × 2ft 1in UT Code (FX4)	L 12189 W 2438	4	40 000	4220	35 780	

Container type	Internal (mm)	Door opening (mm)	MGW (kg)	Tare (kg)	Payload (kg)	Capacity (cbm)
SeaCell Two Palletwide Dry Freight Containers						
20ft Dry Freight 20ft × 2.48m × 8ft 6in UT Code (SC2)	L 5897 W 2426 H 2390	W 2374 H 2280	30 480	2340	28 140	34.2
20ft High Cube 20ft × 2.48m × 9ft 6in UT Code (SW2)	L 5898 W 2426 H 2698	W 2358 H 2585	30 480	2780	30 480	38.5
40ft Dry Freight 40ft × 2.48m × 8ft 6in UT Code (SC4)	L 12100 W 2426 H 2389	W 2356 H 2379	34 000	4060	29 940	70.1
40ft High Cube 40ft × 2.48m × 9ft 6in UT Code (SW4)	L 12089 W 2426 H 2683	W 2358 H 2586	34 000	4250	29 750	79
20ft Bulk 20ft × 2.48m × 9ft 6in UT Code (SK2)	L 5889 W 2420 H2665	W 2358 H 2585	30 480	3030	27 450	38
Regional 2 Palletwide Dry Freight Containers						
20ft Intermodal 20ft × 2.5m × 9ft UT Code (LB2)	L 5921 W 2414 H 2529	W 2400 H 2426	30 000	2650	27 350	36.2
20ft SeaCell Intermodal 20ft × 2.48m × 9ft 6in Australian Spec UT Code (CW2)	L 5902 W 2420 H 2695	W 2358 H 2586	30 000	2620	27 380	38.5
20ft High Cube 20ft × 2.5m × 9ft 6in UT Code (LW2)	L 5910 W 2424 H 2715	W 2400 H 2608	30 000	2600	27 400	38.9
40ft Intermodal 40ft × 2.5m × 8ft 6in UT Code (LE4)	L 12095 W 2440 H 2376	W 2440 H 2231	32 000	3860	28 140	70.1
40ft Sidedoor 40ft × 2.5m × 2.6m UT Code (LE4)	L 12095 W 2440 H 2400	End door W 2440 H 2256 Sidedoor each side W 2500 H 2281	32 000	4100	28 050	70.8

Container type	Internal (mm)	Door opening (mm)	MGW (kg)	Tare (kg)	Payload (kg)	Capacity (cbm)
40ft × 9ft Intermodal 40ft × 2.5m × 9ft UT Code (LN4)	L 12095 W 2440 H 2528	W 2440 H 2383	32 000	3950	28 000	74.6
40ft High Cube Intermodal 40ft × 2.5m × 9ft 6in UT Code (LW4)	L 12095 W 2440 H 2680	W 2440 H 2535	32 000	4000	28 000	79.1
Regional Open Top 20ft Bulk Open Top 20ft × 2.5m × 9ft UT Code (LT2)	L 5928 W 2426 WH 2566	End door W 2348 H 2453 Hatch W 2118	30 000 H 400	2700	27 300	36.9
Flatrack 20ft Intermodal Flatrack 20ft × 2.5m × 8ft 6in UT Code (LY2)	L 5906 W 2398 H 2296	Into 8ft 6in 5	26 000	3085 With gates	22 915	
Swapbodies 7.15m Sidedoor C15 7.15 × 2.5 × 2.6m UT Code (KA2)	L 7010 W 2440 H 2296	End door W 2430 H 2210 Sidedoor each side 6400	24 000 H 2202	3500	20 500	39.3
7.15m Box C22 7.15 × 2.5 × 2.7m UT Code (KB2)	L 7040 W 2440 H 2445	W 2440 H 2361	16 000	2400	13 600	42
7.15m Roller Shutter C22 7.15 × 2.5 × 2.7m UT Code (KC2)	L 6982 W 2440 H 2445	W 2334 H 2237	16 000	2625	13 375	40.9
13.6m Class 'A' C22 13.6 × 2.5 × 2.67m UT Code (KD5)	L 13455 W 2440 H 2500	W 2440 H 2468	34 000	4200	29 800	82.5
7.15m Box C343 7.15 × 2.55 × 2.7m UT Code (KE2)	L 7040 W 2490 H 2445	W 2440 H 2361	18 000	2775	15 225	42.8

Container type	Internal (mm)	Door opening (mm)	MGW (kg)	Tare (kg)	Payload (kg)	Capacity (cbm)
7.15m Roller Shutter C343 7.15 × 2.55 × 2.7m UT Code (KF2)	L 6989 W 2490 H 2445	W 2334 H 2237	18 000	2775	15 225	42.2
7.45m Curtainside C343 7.45 × 2.55 × 2.7m UT Code (KG2)	L 7300 W 2528 H 2417	W 2470 H 2312 Side opening W 7070	18 000 H 2340	3400	14 600	44.6
7.45m Roller Shutter C343 7.45 × 2.55 × 2.7m UT Code (KH2)	L 7289 W 2490 H 2445	W 2334 H 2237	18 000	2900	15 100	44.4

Measurements and other details are averaged

(e) Virtually eliminates packing cost. This is an important cost saving attributed to air freight and the buyer may find it worthwhile to engage professional packaging services to ensure the merchandise has the correct packing specification for this mode of transport.

(f) Ideal for palletized consignments. A substantial volume of merchandise is now moving on pallets which aids handling, reduces packing needs, facilitates stowage and lessens the risk of damage or pilferage.

(g) Quick transits reduce the amount of capital tied up in transit.

(h) Quick reliable transit eliminates the need for extensive warehouse storage accommodation provided by the importer, reduces the risk of stock piling and therefore obsolescence, deterioration and cuts the levels of capital tied up in warehousing and stock provision. Moreover, it enables the buyer to replenish his or her stock quickly, for example when stocks of a commodity has been exhausted more quickly than forecast.

(i) Ideal for a wide variety of consumer type cargoes particularly consignments up to 1500–2000 kg. Ideal cargoes include perishable products, computer hardware and software, fashionable goods, urgent documents, newspapers, electrical goods, spares, high tech goods, flowers, foodstuffs, brochures, photographic material and so on.

(j) The existing very extensive international air freight network continues to expand which aids its development and increases its share of the international trade market. This in turn encourages new markets to the air freight sector thereby aiding international trade development.

(k) Parity obtains on rates on IATA scheduled international services and competition exists only on service quality. Consolidation rates are decided individually by accredited IATA agent consolidators.

(l) Services are reliable and to a high quality.

(m) Major airports worldwide – compared to seaports – tend to be situated in the centre of commercial/industrial areas. In consequence, the airport is in many situations, more closely situated to the industrial and commercial market, giving it a competitive advantage in terms of lower collection and distribution cost.

(n) Air freight facilitates the just-in-time concept with the air freight distributor forming a link between the central warehouse or manufacturing plant and the 'point of sale'. Goods are simply replenished as they are sold at the importer's premises. Examples are fashionable and perishable goods.

(o) The air freight network worldwide is more extensive and offers more frequent flights than the maritime network. Hence the lead time is much reduced.

(p) The 'value added benefit' found in fast transits and service frequency is profound. The spares replacement market serving factory plant or the computer software and hardware markets are good examples.

(q) Services are being improved all the time and new ones are being developed through the concept of combined transport operations.

(r) Air freight capacity is increasing as the latest generation of aircraft emerge.

(s) New airports continue to be introduced globally or existing ones modernized – Hong Kong, Malaysia, Kuala Lumpur and Japan are examples. All are hub airports which offer feeder air freight services within the region.

(t) Buyers must be aware that air freighters do have limited capacity together with constraints on dimensions and weight restrictions.

(u) Some buyers may choose to charter an air freighter in exceptional circumstances when the cargo volume and circumstances justify such a course of action. This may be required for project cargo (see page 221 item 9, 230).

(v) The air freight market is very high tech with bar codes on the consignments and on-line computer access to IATA agents and airlines. This enables data on pre-booking, schedules and accounts to be accessed and also allows cargo tracking.

Finally, a further development in the past decade has been the international air express market. This involves FEDEX, TNT, UPS and DHL. Currently such courier services, called integrators, operate in over 150 countries and offer guaranteed transit times. The service operates from airport of departure to the consignee's premises. The rates are inclusive of export processing, international carriage, import processing, international processing, customs clearance and delivery to city centres.

Packages up to 50 kg may be consigned on the express service. Products include documents, computer diskettes, computer print outs, brochures, tapes, books, annual reports and so on. The express market is high tech with on-line computer access and tracking.

International road transport

The road vehicle is a low capacity but very versatile unit of transport which is most flexible in its operation.

Today international road hauliers operate in three main markets.

1. Collection and delivery of the buyer's goods. This includes collection of cargo from the supplier's premises and delivery to the carrier's depot, which may be an ICD, seaport or airport. Likewise at the destination, following customs clearance, the goods will be delivered to the buyer's premises.
2. Providing overland international road haulage services such as from Frankfurt to Istanbul.
3. Operating road-sea-road services involving ro-ro (roll-on/roll-off) ferry services. This might be an international road haulage service between Greece and Italy involving a road-sea-road service, or UK to Spain featuring a road-sea-road service using the seaports of Poole and Cherbourg. The ro-ro market is a growing market.

We will now examine the salient features of the international road haulage market.

(a) It has a high distributive ability and offers a door to door service without intermediate handling.
(b) No customs examination arises in transit countries provided the haulier is affiliated to TIR, as the cargo passes under customs bond when the unit is passing through one of their transit countries. Insofar as transit countries within the EU are concerned, no customs examination arises.
(c) It is a very flexible operation which is particularly useful when circumstances demand a change in routing through road works, a blockage or disrupted shipping services.
(d) It is very competitive within certain distance bands compared to air freight, both in terms of transit times and rates.
(e) Documentation is simple as, under CMR, a through consignment note is in operation within a common code of liability conditions (see page 170).
(f) The service tends to be reliable and to a high standard. Delays usually only occur when bad weather prevails or due to some other exceptional circumstances.
(g) The TIR vehicle may be 12.20 m (trailer) or 15.50 m (articulated vehicle) with an overall gross weight capacity of 42 tonnes (44 tonnes in Continental Europe).
(h) It is ideal for general merchandise and selective bulk cargo in small quantities conveyed on a specialized road vehicle. The service is renowned for its groupage service under freight forwarder sponsorship in Europe and the Middle East. Some shippers are now using their own vehicles to distribute their own goods.
(i) Packing costs are less when compared with conventional shipping (break bulk cargo) services.
(j) The driver accompanies the vehicle throughout the road transit thereby exercising personal supervision and reducing the risk of damage and pilferage.

(k) The trailer service is very flexible and helps to develop the business.

Buyers are urged to examine the international road haulage transit in preference to air freight for distances up to 600 km with no topographical constraints. Rates are likely to be cheaper and the overall journey time door to door may be only marginally longer. It is a question of evaluating distribution costs against transit times door to door.

International rail transport

Rail transport falls into the following categories with respect to international trade.

(a) A feeder service to and from a seaport. It may involve a dry port such as Ipoh to Port Klang in Malaysia conveying containers.
(b) A land-bridge concept whereby double stack container trains operate between the east- and west-coast ports of North America such as Halifax to Seattle. These form part of a dedicated service integrated with deep-sea mega container ships from Europe to North America and North America to the Far East. Hence, the shipper can feature in a sea–rail–sea service conveying goods from Rotterdam to Seoul.
(c) The movement of bulk cargo dry or wet to and from an industrial plant in a complete train load to a seaport. This may be crude oil, phosphate, coal, timber or iron ore.
(d) The train load movement or wagon load operation overland as used in the pan-European market. This mode is used for the movement of general merchandise, cars, liquid cargoes in tank wagons, containers and swapbodies.

Basically, rail movement is most economical in complete train load operations and in circuit working. It is very much a growth sector with containerization especially in North America and Europe. Buyers are urged to use combined transport featuring the container for the longer transit and ideally with the overland dedicated rail transport to and from the container maritime terminal. This provides a door to door service.

Transport distribution analysis

The procurement officer is becoming increasingly conscious of the transport costs inherent in the final delivered price of the product bought. Hence, the tendency for many importers across the world is to have their own shipping and logistics departments. This will enable the buyer to build up an expertise of international distribution techniques designed to secure the best method of distribution for their company products. They study the market closely and monitor the changing infrastructure especially with a view to identifying areas where added value emerges through faster transits, development of the hub and spoke system and the sea-air-land bridge. Moreover, in the final analysis of the country product sourcing, the transportation cost will feature in the criteria. Nearer markets are likely to be but are not always cheaper in terms of international distribution costs.

There are three stages in the transport distribution analysis which we will now examine.

Evaluating the suitability of transport modes

This is the process of determining the ideal mode(s) of transport and route for a particular consignment. Some services vary considerably from summer to winter due to market demands and climatic conditions. Moreover, air freight may be ideal for the despatch of a small quantity, urgently required but for a larger consignment needed less urgently a deep-sea container LCL schedule under consolidation arrangements may be more suitable.

With the WTO strenuously developing the concept of free trade with no impediments to trade, buyers are looking closely at the implication of tariff and non-tariff barriers when sourcing from a particular country. Country 'A' may have a favourable trading relationship with the buyer's country with no import duty whereas country 'B' may attract a 50 per cent import duty. Hence, although the freight costs from country 'B' may be lower than country 'A', this cost advantage may be outweighed by the higher import duty emerging from country 'B' products.

Hence, the buyer must continuously review his or her distribution strategy in the light of changing trading conditions. We will now examine the salient aspects in the evaluation of transport mode and routing, suitability, etc.

1. The buyer's choice is the prime consideration and this is found in the export sales contract. It is interrelated with the delivery trade terms.
2. The nature of the commodity, its dimensions, weight and whether any special facilities are required for it during the transit. For example, livestock require special facilities and meat requires refrigerated accommodation. This is a major consideration and one must establish through research and enquiry whether the actual dimensions are ideal to allow maximization of the container capacity and lessen the risk of broken stowage. The enterprising buyer will constantly review the configuration of the consignment – perhaps it could be componentized, if this will allow a better loadability in the container with reduced freight costs.
3. The degree of packing and cost thereof. Packing costs can form a very significant proportion of the overall distribution expense. The buyer must ensure the packing needs are adequate and not over-generous thereby incurring higher packing costs without justification and increased volumetric freight rates (see page 228).
4. The degree to which the consignment as presented aids handling. For example, palletized cargo facilitates handling by fork lift truck whilst cartons

are ideal for containers. Conversely, the awkwardly shaped cargo may require special facilities and handling arrangements and may therefore be subject to a freight surcharge. A point to bear in mind is the growing tendency to stack cargo to make the best use of warehouse cubic space and accordingly the consignment needs to be adequately robust to survive this sort of handling.

5. Any statutory obligations imposed relative to the transit. This is applicable to dangerous cargo and refrigerated foodstuffs. Certain products need special facilities both in the transport mode and at the terminal. This in itself restricts the choice of route, service and transport mode. For example, the movement of meat, offal, etc. requires special facilities both by the operator who ships it and in terms of inspection facilities at the import terminal. Additionally, most countries have weight and length restrictions on road vehicles.

6. Dangerous cargo. Stringent regulations exist regarding packaging, labelling, stowage and mixture of dangerous cargo with other cargoes during transit. This can restrict service routing and schedules. Pre-booking arrangements are very stringent. Mandatory regulations are laid down by IMO, IATA, ADR and RID (see page 230).

7. Suitability and availability of transport services. This embraces a raft of factors including transport unit limitations in terms of capacity, weight, allowances, dimensions, departure and destination locations and convenience to the consignor and consignee, terminals, specification of transport unit, transit time, frequency, degree of technology, on-line booking and tracking, documentation, customs clearance facilities, adequacy of logistics and TQM.

8. Transit time and related urgency of consignment. To determine the transit time overall one must take into consideration the periods of collection and delivery, the customs examination at exportation and custom clearance at importation, as well as the voyage, flight, etc. transit time. The transit time is the total period from the time of collection to the goods being received at the buyer's premises. Often the dedicated multi-modal service offering combined transport can prove to have the quickest transit time.

9. Quantity of cargo and period over which the shipment is to be made. In broad terms the greater the quantity available for shipment, the lower the overall distribution cost per tonne or kilogram. For example, if the buyer can originate a full container, trailer, or cargo wagon load, the overall freight charge will be much lower than despatching the cargo under consolidation arrangements. Furthermore, a substantial quantity of cargo conveyed over a period of time could attract a concessionary tariff. Project forwarding involves contractors importing a vast quantity of goods over maybe two years – for example when building a subway, telecommunications network, hospital or power station. Such situations require the appointment of a major freight forwarder who can negotiate special contracts with particular carriers on a discounted rate basis against a cargo volume guarantee.

10. Insurance of cargo (see page 243). Container and air freight shipments are the most competitive in terms of insurance. Break bulk cargo is exposed to more handling and transhipment which attracts usually less favourable insurance premiums.

11. Incoterms 2000. This requires particular consideration to ensure that the most suitable term is chosen (see pages 287–302).

12. Freight and documentation. The actual cost of sea freight tends to be much lower than air freight, but it is not practicable to consider this cost in isolation: the total overall distribution cost including all its elements must be calculated. Air freight tariffs compared with road and rail tend to be higher, but the margin lessens significantly the longer the transit. Documentation costs between various transport modes do not vary a great deal, but with the development of the combined transport concept in recent years involving multi-modalism, it has been simplified with the advent of through rates and consignment notes with no intermediate customs examination in transit countries. The development of LEC and LIC yields the maximum benefits of localised customs control to the buyer and seller.

13. Overall distribution costs. From the previous points, the reader will realize how important it is for the buyer to produce an overall distribution cost and evaluation of the realistic alternatives to arrive at a firm conclusion. The four most decisive factors are terms of export sales contract, commodity specification, freight and overall transit time including service quality – in short the overall value added benefit obtained by using the transport mode selected. Other factors embrace the cost of packing, convenience and reliability of the service, insurance premium, documentation and ware-housing. For example, to the buyer a frequent service requires less storage in the warehouse, a reduced risk of product obsolescence, less working capital and the facilitation of a smoother production flow.

14. Express service. These are found in the integrator's network of packages and documents offering guaranteed schedules as offered by TNT, DHL and FEDEX (see page 217).

15. Logistics. The buyer's distribution plan should be logistically driven (see page 194).

The five elements of transport services

There are five factors which influence the choice of transport service: speed, frequency, reliability, service quality and cost. These factors were considered within a strategic focus in chapter 10. However, there are a number of other factors on which the buyer must focus.

1. Speed is expensive for the carrier and has become a major factor in the global logistics market. A quick transit enables the buyer to respond more quickly to market opportunities and demand and reduces warehouse needs through

reduced stocks. Speed is particularly important with high value cargoes but less so with low value commodities.

2. The frequency of service is critical to the buyer who requires a short lead time and quick service. Air freight is frequent and quick and is therefore suitable for cargoes such as fashionable garments or urgent spares.

3. Services which are unreliable are unacceptable to a buyer who purchases goods against a programmed production unit, such as car components serving a car assembly. Carriers today place a high priority on operating reliable services in a global competitive market.

4. Costing of individual transport services is an important facet of evaluating tenders based on a delivered price DDP, DDU or when entrusting the distribution arrangements to a forwarding agent under EXW or FCA. Total distribution costs were discussed above under item (13). When performing any costing exercise the buyer must have a sound understanding of freight rate calculation (see pages 226–9).

5. Finally a total quality management evaluation is important and accreditation under BS 5750 or ISO 9001 should be sought. At the very least, the Directors of the transit companies chosen should be professionally qualified and the company should be free of any litigation cases. It should be high tech and have a continuous investment programme. Overall, the carrier should extol 'best practice'.

Transport distribution analysis

Transport distribution analysis is the third and final element to examine. It is a technique by which alternative methods of distribution are analysed and the optimum pattern of transportation selected. It is often called physical distribution management. Today the buyer is looking for a one-stop operator who will take care of all the arrangements from the time the goods leave the supplier's premises until the goods reach their destination, as prescribed by the importer.

To illustrate the analysis process, we will consider a case study. Table 11.4 contains data on a consignment of electrical appliances from Seoul, Korea to London. It is stressed that the figures are not intended to be current but merely serve to illustrate the factors involved in the analysis. We will briefly examine the factors involved.

1. Quantity, type of packages and their configuration. This must specify the quantity of cargo available for despatch and method of packing.

2. Total weight of consignment. This should be quoted on a net or gross weight basis usually in kilograms.

3. Total volume of shipment. This should be given on a m^3 or ft^3 basis. Usually for certain high value commodities there is an advantage in despatching by air, whereas for sea transport weight and measurement rates (whichever produces the greater revenue) will apply (see page 228).

TABLE 11.4 Distribution analysis: electrical appliances from Seoul, Korea to London (gross weight for surface transportation: 173 kg (21.89 ft³))

	Air transportation cost (£)	Surface transportation cost (£)
Value ex works	2600	2600
Transportation cost Packing	19	53
Transportation to air/seaport of departure, handling	5	20
Air/sea freight	117	12
Transportation from air/seaport of destination, handling	13	43
Import duties	130	134
Insurance	6	7
Cost price	£2890	£2869
Cost of capital tied up in transit	4	4
Unpacking/refurbishing/storage	not evaluated	not evaluated
Total cost	£2894	£2903
Cost difference	+ 0.3%	
Time advantage	41 days	

Cost determinants
  (a) Value per kg ex works UK £15.00
  (b) Freight proportion air:sea 9.9:1
  (c) Density 219 in³/kg

4. Value of goods ex works. This is the value of the goods at the factory awaiting collection and will feature on the export invoice (see page 172).
5. Packing cost. Packing cost can represent a formidable percentage of the total distribution cost by sea transport – especially in the case of break bulk but less for containerized shipments – whereas for air freight packing costs are greatly reduced.
6. Inland charges at point of origin. This embraces all the costs incurred to transport the goods from the factory to the nominated carrier's terminal airport, seaport, inland clearance depot or dry port for despatch overseas.
7. Freight. This includes air and sea freight comparisons. Usually air freight is more expensive. It may feature a comparison between multi-modal distribution embracing either air or sea transit (see Table 14.1).
8. Inland charges at destination. This includes cartage, handling charges, customs clearance, agency expenses and demurrage. It includes the transportation cost from airport or seaport to ultimate destination.
9. Duty and taxes. This includes VAT or its equivalent. Also it features import duties – where applicable – based on the cargo description customs classification.
10. Insurance. This represents insurance of the goods.

11. Cost of capital tied up with transit. During the period of transportation from door to door the buyer has invested money into the merchandise without receiving an equivalent interest or deriving a profit from it. The longer the transit and the higher the merchandisable value, the greater the capital investment involved. This factor may be of minor importance for a single shipment, but carries greater significance for all consignments during a specified period.

12. Unpacking and refurbishing. The inherent advantages of air freight tends to favour such a shipper insofar as unpacking and refurbishing are concerned when compared with maritime transport. Reduced packing tends to make unpacking less expensive. Moreover, any special refurbishing process for the goods before use is not necessary, such as degreasing of machinery and apparatus, ironing of textiles, etc.

13. Inventory and storage costs. The cost of keeping stocks at the place of production and consumption involves four basic elements as follows:
    (a) cost of capital tied up in inventories;
    (b) obsolescence, deterioration, insurance, taxes, etc.;
    (c) administration and handling;
    (d) warehousing and administration.

    The cost percentage on the average stock value may be as high as 25 per cent per year, but much depends on warehouse location and size, plus the type of commodity. The specific advantages of air freight speed, reliability and frequency – may result in a reduced lead time for the buyer and enable him or her to increase the shipping frequency for the fast moving items. Instead of shipping quantities covering the demand for several months, it might be favourable to air freight more frequently, covering only several weeks' demand. This produces a lower working stock, less warehouse accommodation and reduced risk of stock deterioration or obsolescence; it is also in line with the concept of just-in-time (see page 75). The consignment itself should be of optimum size to contain transportation costs (see pages 223–4 and Table 11.4).

    Both the high quality of air freight and the shorter lead time considerably lowers the risk of stock piling, commodity deterioration or obsolescence to the buyer thereby reducing financial risk. A reduction of working capital and service stocks, results in a reduced average stock level for the importer so that the turnover rate is increased and the inventory and storage costs are decreased.

14. Marketing. Many buyers rely on a high percentage of the componentized products being bought overseas. Hence, when the goods have been assembled they are despatched overseas and the buyer claims inwards processing relief (see page 265). A key problem experienced by such companies is the realization of the marketing objectives in terms of overseas sales performance. These companies are logistically driven and the problem arises when insufficient attention is given to distribution. Logistical planning is essential at all times and especially when demand for the company product surges and the buyer has to quickly activate overseas sourcing to enable the goods to be

assembled, customized, appreciate added value and re-exported. The speed with which the buyer can obtain the overseas sourcing and subsequent assembly for despatch to the overseas customer augurs well for repeat purchase. Such clarity is found in air freight distribution.

15. Speed. A high speed transport mode reduces stock levels – both static and in transit – and the financial implications are therefore apparent. In effect the average lead time between manufacture and sale is shortened and this results in a saving in financial resources. In reality it improves company cash flow or liquidity.

16. Other costs and revenue factors. In addition to the transport and distribution costs already examined, the specific performance criteria of a transport mode has an influence on other costs and revenue factors in ordering, production and administration. These hidden advantages are often difficult to evaluate but they require consideration by the buyer to find the most profitable method of distribution. In revenue marketing terms the buyer who opts for a logistically focused strategy develops the company brand image thus helping to increase sales.

Freight rates

It is important that the buyer has a broad appreciation of the basis on which the freight rate is based. This will help the cost analysis formation regarding sourcing goods overseas. It will also facilitate a strategic focus, that is whether to use air freight or sea transport. Moreover, it must be remembered that the freight cost is only one of the elements to consider in selecting the transport mode.

Rate making has changed significantly in recent years as a result of the development of multi-modalism (see page 198). No longer is the rate based on one carrier on a port to port (CIF) or airport to airport basis, it also involves two or three carriers providing a dedicated door to door service featuring one composite utilizing rate, for example the sea–land-bridge from the Far East to North America using the gateway ports of Vancouver, Los Angeles, Seattle and double stack container trains. For example, a consignment from Malaysia to Industrial Europe via Dubai would involve three major legs: (i) a rail journey from the dry port of Ipoh to Port Klang; (ii) a sea leg between the ports of Klang and Dubai; and (iii) a flight from Dubai to Frankfurt. Additionally, there would be collection and delivery charges for, say, a 40 mile road journey to Ipoh and a 70 mile rail journey to the consignee warehouse in Frankfurt. Furthermore, the transhipment and handling charges at the ports of Klang and Dubai and at Dubai airport will be included. Overall, the rate would feature the following:

(a) consignor premises and collection to Ipoh based on a zonal road rate charge;
(b) processing of cargo handling, packaging and documentation at Ipoh;
(c) agents' charges including customs formalities;

(d) rail journey from Ipoh to Port Klang;

(e) handling charges at Port Klang raised by the Port Authority to cover transhipment cost;

(f) shipowner freight cost Port Klang to Port Dubai;

(g) handling and transhipment charges at Port Dubai to convey goods from port to airport, these are raised by the airport authority and agent;

(h) handling charges at Dubai Airport including documentation, these are raised by the airport authority and agent;

(i) air freight charges from Dubai to Frankfurt raised by the airline;

(j) handling, documentation and customs import duty at Frankfurt Airport, these are raised by the airport authority and the agent;

(k) delivery by rail or road to the consignee's warehouse; rail charges made by the German railways and road charges raised by road hauliers.

This list demonstrates the coordination and facilitation required by international trade distribution and which are undertaken by a mega container logistics carrier or a freight forwarder. The rate from Ipoh to Frankfurt will not feature any import duty as this is a local charge for the importer in Frankfurt. Overall, the list also demonstrates the complexity and range of parties involved in developing a multi-modal rate. Note that it excludes cargo insurance.

Basically the tariff raised for a consignment includes: the tariff cargo rate – published by an airline, shipowner or freight forwarder; customs clearance charges at an airport, seaport, inland clearance depot or dry port; freight forwarder's commission; import customs duty based on commodity specification; disbursements and miscellaneous charges; cargo insurance premium; delivery/collection charge; transhipment tariff; documentation charge; demurrage; handling cost; wharfage cost; cargo dues; rebate; bunker or fuel surcharge; currency surcharge and any surcharge raised for heavy lifts or the excessive height or length of consignments.

To illustrate the calculation of the freight rate applicable to all transport modes we will now look at an example.

Consider the despatch of the following luxury food items from Lisbon to Aberdeen – all items packed in tri-wall cartons.

6 cartons 120 × 80 × 80cm; weight of each carton 50 kg
Freight rates are
Air €4.50 per chargeable kg
Sea €300 per tonne W/M
Road €400 per chargeable kg

Chargeable weight/volume ratios for each mode should be assumed to be (CBM = Cubic Metre)

Air 6 CBM = 1000 kg
Sea 1 CBM = 1000 kg
Road 3 CBM = 1000 kg

Air – volumetric

$$1 \text{ carton} = \frac{12 \times 80 \times 80}{6000} \text{ kg}$$

$$6 \text{ cartons} = \frac{6 \times 12 \times 80 \times 80}{6000} \text{ kg} = 768 \text{ kg}$$

Air freight €4.50 per kilogram
Total air freight volumetric 768 kg × €4.50 = €3456

Weight:
1 carton 50 kg
6 cartons 6 × 50 kg = 300 kg
Air freight rate €4.50 per kilogram
Total air freight weight = 300 kg × €4.50 = €1350
Sea rate = €300 per tonne W/M (1000 kg)
Rate per kilogram = €0.33

Sea – volumetric

$$1 \text{ carton} = \frac{12 \times 80 \times 80}{6000} \text{ kg}$$

$$6 \text{ cartons} = \frac{6 \times 12 \times 80 \times 80}{6000} \text{ kg} = 4608 \text{ kg}$$

Sea freight rate = €0.33 per kilogram
Total sea freight rate volumetric 4608 kg × €0.33 = €1520.64

Weight:
1 carton = 50 kg
6 cartons = 6 × 50 kg = 300 kg
Sea freight rate = €0.33 per kilogram
Total sea freight rate = 300 kg × €0.33 = €99

In some trades the rate would be based on the nearest tonne, in which case the volumetric rate would rise from 4608 kg to 5000 kg and yield €1650 and the weight from 300 kg to 1000 kg to produce €330.

Road – volumetric

Rate €400 per chargeable 1000 kg
Road rate per kilogram €400 ÷ 1000 = €0.4

$$1 \text{ carton} = \frac{120 \times 80 \times 80}{3000} \text{ kg}$$

$$6 \text{ cartons} = \frac{6 \times 120 \times 80 \times 80}{3000} \text{ kg} = 1536 \text{ kg}$$

Road freight rate €0.4 per kilogram
Total road freight 1536 kg × €0.4 = €614.4

Most carriers would calculate the road freight rate when mention is made of 'per 1000 kg' chargeable on the basis of rounding to the nearest 1000 kg. Hence, the volumetric rate would rise from 1536 kg to 2000 kg yielding €800 and the weight from 300 kg to 1000 kg producing €400.

The carrier would charge the volumetric or weight rate (W/M) whichever will yield the highest income. Hence, in the example the answer would be as follows:

Air (volumetric) €3456
Sea (volumetric) €1520.64 (€1650 nearest tonne)
Road (volumetric) €614.4 (€800 nearest tonne)

Buyers are reminded that air freight consolidation by air, road–sea–road and ISO container are ideal for the smaller consignment. Also, judicious use of packaging can reduce the volumetric weight and improve stowage and loadability.

Given below is an alphabetical list of the salient freight rates available.

Ad valorem.	This is based on the declared value of the cargo. Hence €2000 with a 2.5 per cent ad valorem rate would be charged €50.
Antiques.	Antiques including art treasures require special packaging by an accredited company and special freight rates apply.
Bloodstock.	This involves the movement of race horses.
Box.	A container rate.
Commodity.	Rates associated with special commodities, particularly air freight.
Commodity box.	A container rate.
Consolidated.	The rate for consolidated consignments is usually based on the weight/measurement (W/M) option. Also termed the groupage rate.
Dangerous cargo.	Conveyed under ADR, RID, IMO and IATA regulations involving a rate about 50 per cent above the general cargo rate (see page 230).
Express air freight service.	For packages documents usually involving couriers/integrators.
FAK (Freight All Kinds).	This rate applies to all cargo irrespective of commodity type.
Fixture.	Chartering a vessel.
Groupage.	See consolidated entry.
Household effects.	Removal of household furniture. Special packaging and rates apply.

Indivisible loads.	Such consignments are of excessive weight or dimensions and require special handling equipment and arrangements.
Livestock.	Special rates and arrangements apply.
Lump sum freight.	This is an amount payable for the use of the whole portion of a ship.
Pallets.	Rates applicable to palletized cargo.
Postal.	There is a wide variety of postal services ideal for documents, small packages and samples.
Project forwarding.	This involves the coordination through a freight forwarder of all the international transportation arrangements of all products relative to a major capital project such as a new airport terminal or power station, etc.
Rebate.	A discount on a published rate attained through negotiation on a guaranteed volume over a specified period.
ro-ro rates.	Applicable to road haulage movement (see page 217).
Trade vehicles.	Rates involving the movement of cars, lorries, buses, etc.
W/M option.	option weight/measurement – ship option based on weight or measurement evaluation.

Dangerous cargo

Dangerous goods have been defined as those substances so classified in any Acts, rules, bye-laws or having any similar properties or hazards. It is an area in international distribution which is very complex and a number of criteria apply, as discussed below.

1. The international regulations which prescribes the dangerous goods rules are defined by the following organizations by transport mode:
   (a) *International Maritime Organisation* (IMO). The Dangerous Goods Note documentary requirements are found in the *Merchant Shipping (Dangerous Goods and Marine Pollutants) Regulations 1990*. This features the IMDG International Maritime Dangerous Goods code and features nine classes of dangerous goods as found in Figure 11.1.
   (b) *International Air Transport Association* (IATA). IATA rules apply to all IATA air freight services and IATA Agents. Again it features nine classes of dangerous goods as found in Figure 11.2. There is no parity between the IMO and IATA classifications.
   (c) ADR – This features the European Agreement concerning the international carriage of dangerous goods by road 1999 edition and the *Carriage*

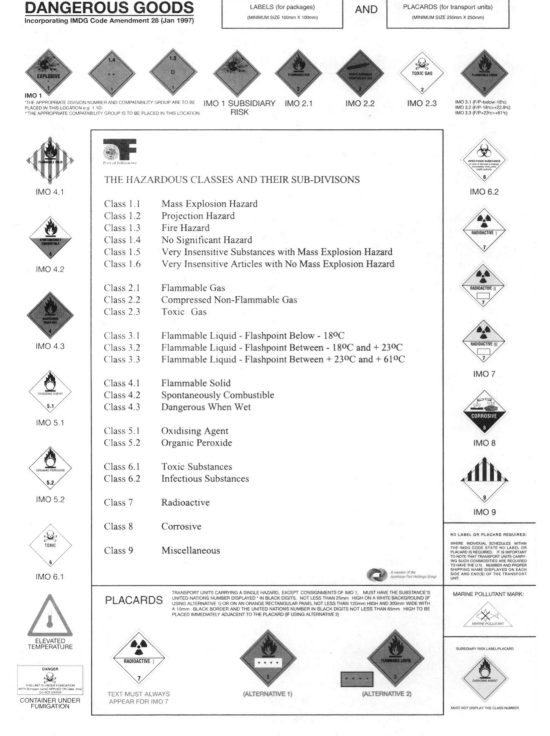

FIGURE 11.1 IMO dangerous goods labels and associated dangerous goods classifications
Reproduced courtesy IMO

Class 1	Explosives	This class is comprised of the divisions; 1.1, 1.2, 1.3, 1.4 and 1.5. Explosives also have a compatibility group letter. **Usually, only explosives of Class 1, Division 4, compatibility Group S are acceptable for carriage on passenger aircraft.**	
Class 2	Gases	This class comprises three divisions: 2.1 Flammable gases, 2.2 Non flammable, Non toxic gases and 2.3 Toxic gases.	
Class 3	Flammable liquids	Remember that the *flash point* of a Flammable Liquid is the temperature at which a vapour from the liquid could be ignited by a flame or spark. *It is not* the temperature at which it would ignite spontaneously.	
Class 4	Flammable solids Spontaneously combustible substances Water reactive	This class comprises three divisions: **4.1** Flammable solids, **4.2** Substances liable to spontaneous combustion, and **4.3** Water reactive substances which in contact with water, either emit flammable gases or become spontaneously combustible. (Also known as 'Dangerous When Wet').	
Class 5	Oxidising substances; Organic peroxides	This class comprises two divisions: **5.1** 'Oxidising Substances and **5.2** Organic Peroxides.'*	
Class 6	Poisonous (toxic) and Infectious substances	This class comprises two divisions: **6.1** Poisonous substances, and **6.2** Infectious substances.	
Class 7	Radioactive materials	This class has no divisions, but there are three categories for non-fissile materials which are determined by the radiation level of the complete package. **Fissile materials are not usually acceptable for air carriage without special arrangements.**	
Class 8	Corrosives	Substances in this class cause damage to the skin and/or metal.	
Class 9	Miscellaneous dangerous goods (including magnetized materials)	This class comprises substances whose properties do not match those of any of the other eight classes, but would pose a risk to safety if not properly prepared for carriage.	
NOTE:	Subsidiary Risk	Some Dangerous Goods have properties which meet the definition of more than one hazard class or division. The less serious hazard of such substances is described as a subsidiary risk.	

FIGURE 11.2 IATA dangerous goods labels and the associated dangerous goods classifications
Reproduced courtesy British Airways

of Danerous Goods by Road regulations 1996 (S.I. 1996 No. 2095) (1968) and subsequent amendments. This applies primarily to European countries. The dangerous goods classifications under the ADR transport regulations are the same as those outlined in the IMDG code for sea transport see Figure 11.1. The packaging, labelling, vehicle, tank vehicle and tank container requirements are thus dependent on the class, item number and properties of the goods to be carried.

(d) RID – the international regulations concerning the carriage of dangerous goods by rail (1978) and subsequent amendments. The RID transport regulations, again, are the same as for sea transport, shown in the IMDG code (Figure 11.1).

2. The pre-booking arrangements are very stringent for both air and sea

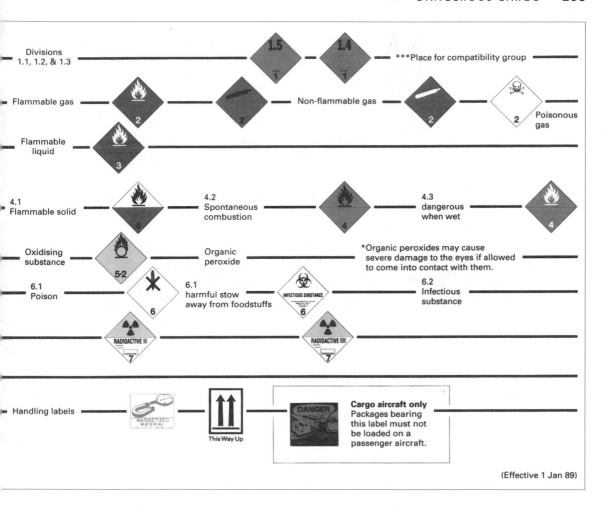

Divisions 1.1, 1.2, & 1.3
***Place for compatibility group
Flammable gas
Non-flammable gas
Poisonous gas
Flammable liquid
4.1 Flammable solid
4.2 Spontaneous combustion
4.3 dangerous when wet
Oxidising substance
Organic peroxide
*Organic peroxides may cause severe damage to the eyes if allowed to come into contact with them.
6.1 Poison
6.1 harmful stow away from foodstuffs
6.2 Infectious substance
Handling labels
MAGNETIZED MATERIAL
This Way Up
DANGER
Cargo aircraft only Packages bearing this label must not be loaded on a passenger aircraft.

(Effective 1 Jan 89)

transport. A stowage order number is issued for the flight and voyage. Moreover, the airline Pilot or ship's Master may refuse to take the consignment if circumstances do not favour such shipment.

3. Stringent packaging – both inner and outer packaging must be clearly labelled and show correct documentation and shippers' declaration. This applies to all transport modes. Also, limits are imposed on the size and quantity of packaging, especially for air transport. Generally speaking, cargo classifications cannot be mixed.

4. A technical specification of the consignment is required – not a commercial one. The carrier may decide to examine or sample the goods before acceptance and allocation of the cargo classification.

5. The importer is urged to liaise closely with the carrier in the movement of the dangerous goods and conduct a pre-shipment dialogue to ensure all the appropriate regulations are adopted.

6. Containerized dangerous cargo shipments are a growth market. Sea Co are market leaders and frequently introduce new high tech container tank designs for the movement of high density liquids and gases. Importers who are involved in such shipments may wish to take advantage of Sea

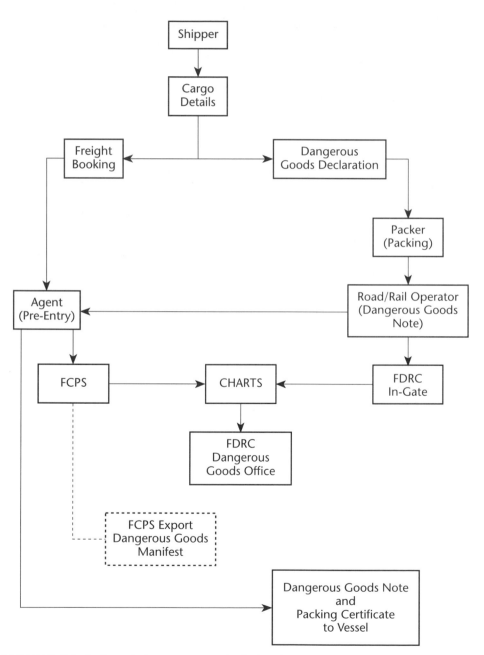

FIGURE 11.3 Export dangerous goods declarations
Reproduced courtesy Felixstowe Dock and Railway Company

Co's expertise and contact one of their global offices or visit their website. A flowchart illustrating the documentary procedure is shown in Figure 11.3.

Finally, one must stress that dangerous goods regulations are subject to continuous change and importers fresh to the business are urged to contact an accredited carrier to determine the dangerous goods shipment criteria.

International Transport Conventions

It is important the buyer is broadly familiar with the International Transport Conventions which are complex and subject to review from time to time. Moreover, the buyer must be aware of the carrier's liability especially within the context of any claims.

Basically, the international convention sets out the minimum terms and conditions for the international carriage of goods which carriers cannot contract to the detriment of merchants. Carriers can, of course, offer more favourable terms to merchants. Generally speaking international conventions aim to regulate international carriage and in most cases national carriage is allowed freedom of contract, although in most countries, there are standard trading conditions which are usually applied.

In the area of maritime transport there are three parties who have traditionally provided the fora for the discussion and drafting of international conventions involving CMI, UNCITRAL and IMO.

1. CMI. An international committee of maritime lawyers. All major trading nations have a national association of maritime lawyers which is responsible for monitoring developments in maritime law in its country and making appropriate recommendations to its government on matters relating to maritime law. These national maritime law associations subscribe to an international forum known as the Comité Maritime International (CMI) domiciled in Belgium whose prime aim is the promotion of international uniformity in the law governing maritime matters. National delegates meet in Conference approximately every four years to discuss maritime legal developments and approve draft rules – like the Uniform Rules for Sea Waybills and potential conventions like the Hague and Hague–Visby Rules.
2. UNCITRAL. The Geneva based United Nations Commission on International Trade and Law (UNCITRAL) is the UN equivalent of the CMI. The major difference is that whereas the CMI consists of commercial lawyers and practitioners, UNCITRAL is a forum of politicians and academic lawyers. Hence, the CMI deliberations evidence commercial practicability, those of UNCITRAL reflect a pre-eminence of political expediency.
3. IMO The International Maritime Organisation is based in London and is a specialized agency of the United Nations, primarily concerned with maritime

safety and the prevention of marine pollution. It is closely involved in the preparation of international conventions and codes which also embraces dangerous goods.

A brief review of the international transport conventions now follows.

International conventions relevant to sea carriage

This is a very complex area and several conventions exist which we will now examine. Buyers are urged to check with their carrier when any doubt arises regarding the applicable convention.

Hague Rules

These rules were agreed at an international convention at Brussels in 1924 and govern liability for loss or damage to goods carried by sea under a bill of lading. They are officially known as the International Convention for the Unification of certain rules relating to Bills of Lading which were signed in Brussels on 25 August 1924 and were given effect in the United Kingdom by the Carriage of Goods by Sea Act 1924.

The Rules were designed to apply primarily to all exports from any nation which ratified the Rules. Much case law exists on the Rules. They apply almost universally wherever they have not been superseded by the Hague–Visby rules or the Hamburg rules either by the application of law or by contractual incorporation into the terms and conditions of the relevant bill of lading.

The main features of the Hague Rules are discussed below.

1. They provide the minimum terms which a carrier may offer for the carriage of all goods other than live animals, non-commercial goods (such as personal and household effects), experimental shipments and goods carried on deck where the bill of lading is claused to permit such carriage.
2. The carrier has to exercise due diligence to provide a seaworthy vessel at the commencement of the voyage and this duty cannot be delegated. The carrier also has to care for the goods properly during the transit. Provided the carrier has complied with these requirements, if loss or damage still occurs, the carrier can rely on a number of stated defences. The majority of these merely elaborate on the general principle that the carrier is only liable for loss or damage caused by his own negligence, or that of his servants, agents or subcontractors. However, the carrier is still protected in three areas where the loss or damage has been caused by negligence: negligence in navigation; negligence in the management of the vessel (as opposed to care of the cargo); and fire unless by the actual fault or privity of the carrier (i.e. the person in the company with the guiding hand). A recent change is the introduction of the ISM (International Safety Management) which states that this would probably be the designated person.

3. Liability was limited to £100 per package in the UK (before the Hague–Visby Rules superseded the Hague Rules). Other nations, in enacting the Hague Rules, have set alternative limits expressed in their domestic currency, whilst carriers contractually incorporating the rules usually make separate provision for the limit – usually £100 or USD 500 per package.

Hague–Visby Rules

In 1968 a further international conference adopted some revisions to the Hague Rules, principally affecting limitation. The amended Rules are officially known as the 'Brussel Protocol' signed on 23 February 1968, but are more popularly known as the Hague–Visby Rules and were given effect in the United Kingdom by the Carriage of Goods by Sea Act 1971.

Limitation was amended to provide a weight/package alternative and originally set in Poincare Francs. This proved inconvenient as the Poincare Franc is a fictitious currency in constant need of redefinition in terms of currencies. With no readily available source of such information, frequent revaluations in national currency of the Poincare Franc limits were necessary. Accordingly, the 1979 Special Drawing Rights (SDR) Protocol came into effect in February 1984 in those states which had contracted thereto. The states in which SDR limits are operative in October 1999 number 31. Limitation in terms of SDRs is now the greater of SDR 666.67 per package or unit or SDR 2 per kilo.

The 1968 convention provided that the Visby amendments would come into effect after the convention had been ratified by ten nations, five of whom had to have a minimum gross registered tonnage of one million tons. These requirements were satisfied in June 1977. By October 1999 the Rules applied to over 40 states.

The Visby amendment is designed to apply to all bills of lading where the port of shipment is in a ratifying nation; the place of issue of the bill of lading is in a ratifying nation; and the bill of lading applies Hague–Visby Rules contractually.

It seems unlikely that any changes will be made in the near future until the matter has been exhaustively debated but the outcome is likely to be some sort of compromise to placate the Hague–Visby and Hamburg camps.

Hamburg Rules

In March 1978 an international conference adopted a new set of rules – the Hamburg Rules – which radically altered the liability which shipowners have to bear for loss or damage to goods in the courts of those nations where the Rules apply. The salient difference between the new rules and the old Hague–Visby Rules are as follows.

1. The carrier will be liable for loss, damage or delay to the goods occurring whilst in his charge unless he proves that 'he, his servants, or agents took all

measures that could reasonably be required to avoid the occurrence and its consequences.'

3. The carrier is liable for delay in delivery if 'the goods have not been delivered at the port of discharge provided for under the contract of carriage within the time expressly agreed upon or, in the absence of such agreement, within the time which it could be reasonable to require of a diligent Carrier having regard to the circumstances of the case.'

3. The dual system for calculating the limit of liability, either by reference to package or weight as set out in the Hague–Visby Rules, has been readopted but the amounts have been increased by about 25 per cent to SDR 835 per package and SDR 2.5 per kilo.

   The liability for delay is limited to equivalent to two and half times the freight payable for the goods delayed, but not exceeding the total freight payable for the whole contract under which the goods were shipped. In no case shall the aggregate liability for both loss or damage and delay exceed the limit for loss or damage.

4. The Hamburg Rules cover all contracts for carriage by sea other than charter parties, whereas the Hague and Hague–Visby Rules only apply mandatorily as an international convention where a bill of lading is issued. Hence, the Hamburg Rules are therefore applicable to waybills, consignment notes, etc.

5. The Hamburg Rules cover shipment of live animals and deck cargo whereas the Hague and Hague–Visby Rules may not.

6. The Hamburg Rules will apply to both imports and exports to and from a signatory nation (i.e. all that nation's trade) whereas the Hague and Hague–Visby Rules apply to exports only.

The Hamburg Rules became operative at an international convention one year after ratification or accession by 20 nations with no minimum tonnage qualification. The requisite 20 nations were obtained in November 1991 and the Hamburg Rules came into force in November 1992. Overall, 28 countries have adopted the rules – many of them less developed or developing countries.

Combined transport

A number of attempts have been made to produce an acceptable draft convention to cover loss or damage to goods carried under a Combined Transport Document. This embraced the Tokyo Rome Rules, the Tokyo Rules and the TCM convention. All failed to gain adequate support but ultimately the ICC took the opportunity to make several amendments to earlier drafts and published the ICC Rules for a Combined Transport Document (ICC Brochure No 298). This has become widely accepted by many mega container operators today.

The debate and dialogue continue towards a more widely acceptable set of multi-modal rules with a common liability approach throughout the different modes of transport. At the beginning of 1999, following the lack of success of the UNCTAD, MMO and UNCTAD/ICC Rules, the ICC launched a discussion paper to revive interest in a multi-modal convention but this was rejected by the Shipping Industry. However, the 'assessment' is ongoing in an effort to promote the UNCTAD/ICC Rules.

International Air Carriage Convention

Warsaw Convention

The international air carriage of goods is subject to either the Warsaw Convention 1929 or the amended Warsaw Convention 1955. Which of these conventions applies depends on which convention the countries of departure and arrival have ratified. For one of the conventions to apply both of the countries must have ratified the same convention; if both have ratified the amended Warsaw Convention then, irrespective of whether they have both also ratified the earlier convention, the Amended Warsaw Convention applies. Contractual carriers (such as freight forwarders acting as principals) are subject to the conventions. Unlike other transport conventions, both Warsaw Conventions require that certain information is stated on the air waybill, the absence of which will prevent the carrier from relying on both the exclusions and limitations of liability in the convention and, in the case of the Amended Warsaw Convention, will not entitle the carrier to rely on the limitations of liability. The limit of liability is 250 Poincare (gold) franc or, if Montreal Protocols 1–3 of 1975 have been ratified, 17 SDRs per kilo.

Montreal Protocol No. 4 came into effect in June 1998. The scope of application of this Protocol is currently (2000) unclear (other than that it will not apply to carriage by air to the USA) but where it is applied there will be some important changes.

(a) It will no longer be necessary for an air waybill to be issued in order for the convention to be applicable. This is clearly designed to remove the need for tangible documentation to facilitate electronic 'documentation'.
(b) The 'all necessary measure' Hamburg Rules-style defence is replaced by a menu of specific defences (like the Hague Rules).
(c) The possibility of breaching the limitation in Article 22 is removed and this limit is now unbreakable.

On 28 May 1999 in Montreal, a new convention, the Montreal Convention of 1999, was signed and adopted by 53 nations. No countries have, so far (2000), ratified or acceded to it.

International Road Transport Convention

The convention governing the International Carriage of Goods by Road is the CMR (Europe) Convention relative au contrat de transport international des Marchandises par Route. It was signed in Geneva in 1956 and enacted into the laws of the United Kingdom by the Carriage of Goods by Road Act 1965. The convention has only been adopted by 26 countries who are primarily European. It applies to contracts for the international carriage of goods in vehicles by road over the territories of two different countries of which at least one is a contracting party to CMR. It therefore only applies to UK imports/exports by roll-on/roll-off ferry or the Channel Tunnel where goods remain on the road vehicles throughout. If the same container on the same journey was lifted off the trailer at the port of Dover onto a vessel and carried to the continent and there lifted onto another trailer, there would have been no crossing of a frontier on a road vehicle and therefore the convention would not apply.

Under this convention, the Carrier is liable for loss or damage from the time he takes over until the time he delivers the goods to the Consignee, unless he can prove that the loss or damage occurred because of one of the list of excepted perils. Hence, these exceptions allow the carrier to escape liability if he has not been negligent. He is entitled to limit his liability to SDR 8.33 per kilo. The carrier is also liable for delay if the goods have not been delivered within the agreed time limit, or if there is no such agreement, within a reasonable time.

International Rail Transport Convention – Carriage of Goods

The COTIF Convention Concerning International Carriage by Rail was signed in Berne in May 1980. It was given legal effect in the UK by section 1 of the International Transport Conventions Act 1983 with effect from May 1985. COTIF abrogated the existing CIM (Europe) Convention Internationale concernant le transport des Marchandises par chemin de Fer – International Convention on Carriage of Goods by Rail which did not have the force of law in the UK and an amended draft of CIM was attached to COTIF as Appendix B to govern the carriage of goods. Overall, COTIF has a wider application and covers passengers as well as goods. CIM applies if either the place of loading or the destination of the goods is a COTIF member state.

In common with CMR, COTIF/CIM applies only to international carriage and is not applicable to domestic traffic. The opening of the Channel Tunnel extended the application of the COTIF/CIM recourse. As a private company, the Channel Tunnel operates an independent contract not subject to any mandatory law in which liability for delays is excluded and a limitation of SDR 8.33 (the same as CMR) is applied.

The terms and conditions of COTIF/CIM are similar to CMR but limitation is substantially higher at SDR 17 per kilo.

Freight forwarders – role and selection

Basically a freight forwarder is a person or company which is involved in the processing and/or movement of goods across international boundaries on behalf of another company or person. The freight forwarder provides services in two main fields: the movement of goods out of a country on behalf of importers/exporters or shippers – in which case the forwarder would be termed an export freight agent; and bringing goods into the country on behalf of importers – in which case the forwarder is called an import freight agent, customs clearance agent or customs broker.

The freight forwarder has four prime activities:

(a) to provide a range of independent services such as packing, warehousing, port agency and customs clearance;
(b) to provide a range of advice on all the areas relative to the international consignment distribution as found in transport distribution analysis (see page 223);
(c) to act as shipper agent processing transport and/or shipping space on behalf of his/her principal or shipper and executing his or her instructions;
(d) as a principal, usually as a multi-modal transport operator conveying the goods from A to B, crossing international frontiers and usually involving several carriers, often as an NVOCC.

Basically, the freight forwarder provides a range of services depending on the trade and company resources. Most freight forwarders are SMEs and operate in niche markets. Very few have a global presence but they do link up with other freight forwarders in the markets they serve and have some form of operating alliance. We will now examine briefly their activity in the two main areas of export and import.

Export: transport distribution analysis

Freight forwarders will make transport arrangements. This is a major function involving the booking and despatch of the goods between the consignor and consignee premises or other specified points.

The following elements are involved.

(a) Documentation – all prescribed documentation for the goods having regard to all the statutory requirements and terms of export sales contract.
(b) Customs – all the customs arrangements including documentation and entry requirements at time of exportation and importation.
(c) Payment of freight and other charges – payment of freight to the prescribed carrier including any handling charges raised by airport, seaport or elsewhere during the transit.
(d) Packing and warehousing – packing of goods for transit and warehousing provision.
(e) Cargo insurance.
(f) Consolidation, groupage and special services – this may be by air, road/truck or container.

Import

The freight forwarder's role in imports includes the following activities:

(a) Notification of arrival – the process of informing the importer of the date and location of the goods' arrival and requisite documents for customs clearance.
(b) Customs clearance – presentation and clearance of the cargo through customs. This needs to focus on all the requisite documents.
(c) Payment of VAT duty, freight and other charges. The agent will coordinate and effect payment of all such charges on behalf of his or her principal at the time of importation.
(d) Delivery to the importer – the process of delivering the goods to the importer's premises following customs clearance.
(e) Breaking bulk and distribution – process of distributing the goods on arrival in the destination country.

Buyers of importers wishing to use a freight forwarder should consider the following elements in their selection criteria.

(a) Membership of the relevant trading association. In the UK, this will be BIFA, the British International Freight Association. Also look for accreditation to BS 5750 – the British Standards in Quality systems.
(b) Profile of the freight forwarder and the nature of his or her business.
(c) Value added benefit emerging from employing the freight forwarder.
(d) The alternative cost of the buyer or importer doing the work and the requisite organization structure.
(e) Volume of business and any seasonal variation.
(f) Terms of export sales contract.

An increasing number of importers entrust their business to freight forwarders, buying an EXW or FAS and entrusting all the distribution arrangements to the freight forwarder.

Recommended reading

- *The Merchants Guide*, P&O Nedlloyd publication.
- ICC Rules for Combined Transport Document, ICC Brochure No. 298.
- British Airways Dangerous Goods brochure.
- Felixstowe Deck and Railway Company Customer Guide to procedures for handling dangerous goods, 1999.
- International Maritime Dangerous Goods Code published by the International Maritime Organisation.
- Dangerous Goods Note: SITPRO completion guide, www.sitpro.org.uk

12

Cargo insurance

Marine cargo insurance covers physical loss or damage to goods whilst in transit by land, sea and air and offers considerable opportunities and cost advantages if managed correctly. It is defined in the Marine Insurance Act 1906 as a contract of marine insurance and is a contract whereby the insurer undertakes to indemnify the assured in a manner and to the extent thereby agreed against marine losses, that is to say, the losses incidental to marine 'adventure'. This includes cargo insurance involving the maritime conveyance of merchandise from one country to another.

Overseas buyer's strategy

The benefits to the buyer of undertaking the cargo insurance arrangements are outstanding and the following points are relevant.

1. *Cost.* Many importers erroneously believe that the supplier includes the cargo insurance for free when, in fact, this cost is included in the purchase price. Moreover, it can often be difficult to obtain information from suppliers as to what these costs embrace or whether the costs are being loaded.
2. *Profit.* The seller is likely to obtain some commission from the insurance arrangements. This represents part of the profit element of the total price of the product as embraced in the Incoterm and contract of sale. This profit element could feature with the buyer if the importer opted to do all the cargo insurance arrangements.
3. *Cover.* An important issue is the type of cover being provided. Is it comprehensive 'all risks' or just 'total loss'? Is it on a warehouse to warehouse basis or just warehouse to destination port with no overland cover to the buyer's nominated address? Without this information an importer may not be aware that he or she is paying too much for insurance which does not meet his or her needs and which may leave the buyer with uninsured exposure.

4. *Market security.* Another consideration is who is actually insuring the goods. The security of some overseas insurers may not compare favourably with the security of insurers in the highly regulated UK market. In the event of goods arriving damaged in the UK, the importer will have to deal with the UK agent of the overseas insurance company – an agent who will be working for the insurer or seller and not the importer. This can lead to delays in processing and settling claims (see page 151). Moreover, it does not engender good relations between the buyer and the seller.

5. *Carriers.* Importers often rely on making recoveries from hauliers or shipping companies who deliver the goods. This can be problematic if the exact time and place of loss cannot be established. Some carriers pay small claims in order to maintain a business relationship or avoid costly exchanges of further correspondence. In the event of large losses, however, they will almost certainly invoke the limits of liability under their conditions of carriage, as they are entitled to do. Obtaining full settlement may be a protracted and difficult process.

Following a strategic evaluation of the major disadvantages of entrusting the suppliers to arrange marine cargo insurance, what incentives exist for the importer to take control of the cargo insurance. These may be summarized as set out below.

1. By using a specialist marine cargo insurance broker, the importer will be able to obtain 'open cover' (see page 249) which is reviewed annually with rates determined by the buyer's own loss record. For as long as the importer relies on the supplier's insurance, he or she will be tied to the insurance cost dictated by the supplier's loss record – which may embrace sales to other customers in areas or countries of high risk.

2. Insurance cover arranged in the UK is generally more comprehensive and price competitive than that from overseas markets.

3. The buyer knows exactly what cover he or she is getting and exactly what it is costing in his or her national currency.

4. In the event of a loss, the importer's specialist marine cargo insurance broker will take on the claims administration work and will also be technically competent to negotiate with insurers in the event of a contentious claim.

5. The insurance broker, following the investigation of a claim, can suggest ways and means to minimize future losses such as better packing, re-routing cargo, etc. (see page 255).

6. Risk management measures and controls can be initiated at corporate level.

Finally, one must remember that the supplier has his or her own view and strategy regarding the exporter insuring the goods. Areas of concern include the following.

1. When the exporter is totally reliant on the buyer arranging adequate insurance on goods which probably have not been paid for, in the event of

the goods arriving damaged or if the buyer's insurance does not cover the loss, can the exporter be certain of payment?

2. If the goods or shipping documents are rejected on arrival at destination, this can often result in the insurance risk reverting to the exporter – who may not have arranged any insurance.

3. When a foreign insurer has settled a claim the exporter's branded goods could be sold as salvage ('seconds').

4. In the event of the buyer insuring the goods, the seller relinquishes control of the insurance cover and any profit benefit emerging from the commission earned.

Buyers today are focusing more on taking charge and control of the distribution arrangements focusing on using Incoterms, EXW, FCA, FAS, FOB, CPT, DAF, DES, DEQ, DDU, DDP which places an option on either the buyer or the seller to contract for the insurance (see Incoterms 2000, ICC booklet No. 560).

Cargo insurance market

There are no fixed rates in marine insurance and the actual premium for a particular cargo is assessed on the incidence of losses in that trade and the risk inherent in the cargo conveyance. This process of assessing the premium is known as underwriting and the cargo insurance contract is embodied in a document called a policy cargo insurance, underwritten by Lloyd's underwriters and insurance companies. In accordance with the provision of the Lloyd's Act of 1982 – which repealed many of the provisions of earlier Acts – Lloyd's is now controlled by the Council of Lloyd's.

A considerable proportion of the business transacted in the London market is placed with insurance companies. Apart from the many British companies operating in the market there are also a large number of overseas companies. The basic difference between the Lloyd's underwriter and his or her company counterpart is that the liability of the former is 'served and unlimited', whereas the latter is a salaried employee of a limited liability company and has no personal liability in respect of the risks which he or she underwrites on behalf of his or her employer. Apart from this, the insurance companies transact business in a similar manner to that followed by the Lloyd's Underwriters. Hence, there is no difference as far as the underwriting of a risk is concerned and it is quite usual for both Lloyd's and insurance company underwriters to participate in the same risk.

The great majority of the business transacted in the London market is handled through the intermediary of an insurance broker. The broker is the agent of the assured, or his or her principal and as such is subject to the common law of agency insofar as, if his or her principal is prejudiced as a result of negligence, then the principal may sue for damages. Effectively, brokers' services are provided without cost to the assured whose remuneration brokerage is paid by the underwriters with whom the principal's business has been placed.

The role of the broker is, first, to advise clients as to their insurance needs and secondly, to comply with clients' subsequent instructions and obtain the cover required at the best possible rate of premium. The booking company may be a small organization of less than a dozen people and the large Lloyd's brokers of today are international organizations employing several thousand people worldwide.

Fundamental principles of cargo insurance

The basic principles of cargo insurance embrace four principles which we will now briefly examine: insurable interest, utmost good faith, indemnity and subrogation.

Insurable interest

Insurable interest arises when a person ships goods or other movables (exposed to maritime perils) where he or she stands in any legal or equitable relationships to the adventure or insurable property at risk therein in consequence of which he or she may:

(a) benefit by the safety or due arrival of the insurable property, or
(b) be prejudiced by its loss, or by damage thereto or by the attention thereof, or
(c) incur liability in respect thereof.

It is important to understand the difference between the subject matter insured and insurable interest. Insurable interest is the financial interest of a person in the subject matter insured. Thus the insurable interest of the cargo owner is not the goods – the subject matter insured – but his or her financial interest in such goods and accordingly the buyer should insure to the extent of that interest.

The most common forms of insurable interest in cargo insurance are the following.

(a) Ownership of the goods. The cargo owner has an insurable interest in the goods since he or she will benefit by their safe arrival or be prejudiced by loss or damage thereto.
(b) Charges of insurance (premium). The assured has an insurable interest in the premium paid in respect of any insurance he or she may effect.
(c) Freight. This is the cost of transporting the goods.
(d) Defeasible interest. An interest which may cease for reasons other than the operation of maritime perils – for example the insurable interest of the seller of goods ends when the title of the goods passes to the buyer.
(e) Contingent interest. This arises when the interest of the seller ceases and the interest of the buyer commences.
(f) Commission. The Agent may act for a cargo owner on a commission basis.
(g) Forwarding expenses. The contract of affreightment will probably include a clause allowing the carrier to discharge the goods at a port other than the one

designated where, for some reason, they cannot be delivered or discharged at the destination port.

Utmost good faith (uberrimae fidei)

This requires that if the utmost good faith be not observed by either party to the cargo insurance contract, the other party may avoid the contract.

This involves a material circumstance which would influence a prudent underwriter as to the desirability of the risk, where there is a non-disclosure of a material circumstance, the underwriter may avoid the contract. The underwriter may also avoid the contract if the broker is guilty of misrepresenting the risk during the placing negotiations.

Indemnity

The purpose of insurance is to protect the insurable interest of the assured whereby, in the event of loss or damage to the subject matter insured resulting from an insured peril, he or she is placed in the same position that he or she enjoyed immediately before the loss was incurred. This is an indemnity and provides as a basic principle that after indemnity the assured may not be in a better or worse position prior to the loss. Hence, one cannot make a 'profit' from a loss.

Subrogation

Subrogation allows the underwriter to inherit the rights and liabilities of the assured following payment of a claim to recover the payment from a third party responsible for the loss. It is limited to the amount paid on the policy.

Methodology affecting cargo insurance – problem areas and possible solutions

Under the terms of the export sales contract and reflecting earlier negotiations, the contract will identify which party will be responsible for arranging the insurance for the goods in accordance with the Incoterm used. Irrespective of the transit being undertaken, it is important that the insurance cover is in force for the entire transit including any loading, unloading and temporary storage.

Hence, the insurance cover for the goods should embrace the following:

(a) transportation of merchandise to the seaport, airport or ICD/dry port of departure;

(b) period during which the goods are stored awaiting shipment or loading;

(c) the time whilst on board the ship, aircraft or other transport mode such as truck/canal;

(d) the 'off loading' and storage on arrival at destination seaport, airport, ICD/dry port, or other specified place;

(e) transportation to the nominated buyer's address.

Where the supplier elects to be responsible for arranging the insurance, the insurance policy and certificate will be sent with the shipping documentation as evidence of cover. Insurance cover arranged by the supplier may end when the goods are landed at the seaport or airport of arrival which can lead to problems, as given below.

(a) Cover needing to be arranged for the transit of goods from the port of arrival to the buyer's premises or those of the ultimate purchaser.

(b) Goods arriving damaged or incomplete at the port of arrival may lead to disputes between seller and buyer. Unless the goods are inspected immediately upon arrival, it will be difficult to prove where the loss or damage occurred. Many shippers take a photograph of damaged goods on arrival as it proves good evidence when processing the claim.

(c) The buyer may experience delay in claiming settlement if insurance is arranged by an overseas insurer.

The foregoing problems can be circumvented by several mechanisms, as follows.

(a) Extension of the seller's cargo insurance cover to the ultimate destination with the buyer assuming responsibility for the insurance premium relating to the period after arrival at the port of entry.

(b) Separate insurance cover being arranged by the buyer covering the final stages of the transit although this may not resolve demarcation disputes.

(c) The buyer taking responsibility for insurance from the supplier's premises to the ultimate destination.

Cargo insurance policy

On 1 January 1982 a new Marine Policy form and New Institute Cargo Clauses were introduced in the London marine insurance market, displacing the SG (Ship Goods) Form of policy adopted by Lloyd's on 1 January 1779.

We will now briefly examine a Companies Marine Policy subscribed to by the Insurance Companies which are members of the Institute of London Underwriters. It will be recalled that the cargo insurance market is underwritten by Lloyd's underwriters and insurance companies.

The Companies Marine Policy serves as a contract of cargo insurance and as detailed below there are three main types of policy: single shipment, annual and open.

(a) Single shipment or facultative shipment.
    (i)   Optional type of policy having agreed to cover specific shipments.
    (ii)   Used mainly by importers/exporters with occasional shipments.
(b) Annual shipments.
    (i)   Issued for a twelve month period subject to payment at inception of a minimum deposit premium.
    (ii)   Adjustable at the end of the period on the total value of sendings.
    (iii) Suitable for risks where sendings are regular and comprised of low value goods.
(c) Open policy.
    (i)   Once issued this policy remains in force until no longer required – can be cancelled by assured or insurer.
    (ii)   Reviewed annually to ensure assured requirements continue to be met.
    (iii) Premium payable in arrears being calculated according to value of shipments each month.

The buyer will determine his or her policy choice according to three factors: frequency of shipments; annual value of shipments and ease of operation.
    The method of declaration falls into five divisions.

(a) Assured letter, e-mail or on-line computer declaration – used where an annual value of sendings or turnover is required for adjustment purposes; no documentation is usually issued by the assured and it is usually utilized for small annual policies.
(b) Small declaration – issued by assured companies to brokers, agents and assureds and used for declaring individual shipments on an import cover.
(c) Large declaration – issued by assured companies to brokers, agents and assureds; used when regular multiple shipments are involved, usually on import cover and normally submitted on a monthly basis.
(d) Certificate of insurance – issued by assured companies to brokers, agents and assureds; usually issued on export covers for individual shipments and normally submitted in monthly batches.
(e) Evidence of insurance contract – freely assignable document; reflects cover of master policy and gives details of the claims settling agent to be used.

Marine insurers use standard wording known as Institute Clauses and the clauses used depend on the nature of the goods shipped. The Institute Cargo Clauses fall into three categories 'A', 'B' or 'C' plus additional clauses such as Institute War and Strike Clauses. The buyers insurance broker will provide advice on which clauses will be used for maritime shipments.
    Proof that the goods are insured for risk of loss or damage during transit is often asked for in the documentary credit. This can be evidenced by either an insurance policy or a certificate. However, where the credit specifically requires presentation of a policy, an insurance certificate is not acceptable. Established importers or exporters will usually cover all their exports under an open policy (see above). In this case, individual pre-signed insurance certificates are issued for

each shipment – either by the insurer or by the importer or exporter. This avoids the need to take out a fresh policy with each shipment.

Insurance documents must be issued and signed by insurance companies or underwriters or their agents. Cover must be for at least the full CIF or CIP invoice value plus 10 per cent unless the credit stipulates otherwise and the risks to be covered must appear on the face of the insurance document. It must also be issued in the currency of the documentary credit and be dated on or prior to the date of shipment unless it is clear that cover is effective from such a date.

Where the documentary credit requires cover against 'all risks' without specifying the particular risks to be covered, an insurance document containing an 'all risks' clause or notation is acceptable. However, it is advisable to obtain cover as per Institute Cargo Clauses 'A' risks as a minimum; there are fewer exclusions from the 'A' risks than for other classifications (see page 249).

The insurance document is usually required to be issued 'in negotiable form' which means that the party in whose favour the document has been issued (usually the seller but may be the seller's agent) must endorse it 'in blank'. Some documentary credits require the endorsement to be made to the order of a named party (typically the buyer or the issuing bank). Claims under the policy can only be submitted by a party in whose favour the document has been issued or endorsed.

The requirements for completion of an insurance certificate are as follows: the name of the party in whose favour the document has been issued; name of vessel or flight details; place from where insurance is to commence – typically the seller's warehouse or the port of loading (depending upon any documentary credit requirements) – and the place where insurance ceases – usually the buyer's warehouse or the port of destination; insurance value to be that specified in any credit – usually CIF or CIP value plus 10 per cent. If the credit does not state the insured amount, a minimum of 10 per cent over full invoice value is required; marks and numbers to agree with those on other documents; the goods description, which must be consistent with that in the credit and on the invoice; name and address of claims settling agent together with the place where claims are payable (if required in the credit); countersigned by importer or exporter, where necessary; the date of issue must be no later than the date of the transport document unless cover is shown to be effective prior to that date.

Given below is a checklist of discrepancies and likely errors and their consequences relative to the insurance document, which the buyer must study closely.

(a) It has been issued and/or signed by an insurance company or underwriter or an agent on their behalf.
(b) It is not a broker's certificate or cover note unless the presentation of such has been specifically authorized.
(c) If the insurance document indicates it is issued in more than one original, all originals are presented unless authorized in the credit.
(d) It is not dated later than date of shipment, despatch or taking charge.

(e) It is issued in the currency of the creditor. If cover in a different currency is required, that it is presented in that currency.

(f) It provides adequate cover and contains the same details in respect of special risk as stated in the credit terms. Unless otherwise stipulated, cover must be 10 per cent above the CIF or CIP value. If the CIF/CIP term is not used, a minimum of the full invoice value plus 10 per cent is required.

(g) It has been endorsed to the order of a specified party issued in a transferable form, or endorsed by the insured if issued in the latter's name.

(h) It shows marks, numbers, weights, qualities and a description of the goods that match the bill of lading and other documents.

(i) It does not show unauthenticated alterations.

(j) It shows the method of carriage of the goods, the point of loading on board, despatch or taking in charge, the name of the carrying vessel, if appropriate, and the port of discharge or place of delivery.

(k) It specifically covers transhipment when the transport document shows this will take place.

(l) It states a named place where claims are payable when required.

(m) It covers 'Loaded on Deck' when this is permitted within the credit term or when despatch is effected in containers which may be loaded on deck – check the appropriate jettison clauses.

One must stress that the buyer's team responsible for the transportation arrangements must check out – perhaps using the Internet – all available cargo insurance brokers and ensure that adequate insurance cover is secured. Ensure good professional advice is sought.

Cargo insurance claims

Most insurance company policies require that immediate notice is given to the nearest branch or agency in the event of damage giving rise to a claim under a policy on goods. When notified of damage, the company's agent or Lloyd's agent proceeds to appoint a suitable surveyor to inspect the goods and to report on the nature and extent of the damage. A common practice is for a report or certificate of loss, incorporating the surveyor's findings, to be issued to the consignees, the latter paying the fee. This is the usual procedure for Lloyd's agents. This certificate of loss is included with the claim papers and if the loss is recoverable under the insurance cover, the fee is refunded to the claimants.

In some circumstances, the claim papers are returned to the place where the insurance was effected and subsequently presented to the underwriters. However, where goods are sold on CIF terms and the policy is assigned to the consignees, arrangements are made for any claims to be paid at destination. In such cases the consignees approach the agents named in the policy for payment of their claims. The Lloyd's agent undertakes this service. The policy must be produced by the claimant when a marine claim is put forward because of the freedom with which the marine policy may be assigned. In circumstances where the policy or certificate of insurance has been lost or destroyed, underwriters are generally willing to settle the claim, provided the claimant completes a letter of indemnity.

The presentation of claims is by negotiation on documents supporting the assured case. It is very difficult to state with any degree of legal precision exactly on whom the onus of proof falls in every case, but generally speaking the assured must be able to prove a loss by a peril against which he or she was insured. Once the assured has presented a prima facie case of loss by a peril insured against, the onus is on the insurers to disprove liability.

The buyer must produce the following documents when making an insurance claim.

(a) The export invoice issued to the buyer together with shipping specification and/or weight notices.
(b) The original bill of lading, charter party, air waybill, CMR or CIM consignment note.
(c) Original policy or certificate of insurance.
(d) Survey report or other documentary evidence detailing the loss or damage occurred.
(e) Extended protest or extract from the ship's log for salvage loss, particular average in goods or total loss of goods for maritime consignments.
(f) Letters of subrogation for total loss or particular average on goods.
(g) Any exchange of correspondence with the carriers and other parties regarding their liability for the loss or damage.
(h) Any landing account or weight notes at final destination.
(i) Account sale (salvage) or invoice for reconditioning charges.

Having established the documents required to deal with the claim, it is important that a code of procedure is devised to process the claim. Figure 12.1 features a cargo claim and its main elements. Figure 12.2 shows the development of the cargo claim and its constituents from the factory to the buyer (consignee).

Given below are brief details of the claims procedure which involves a bulk shipment.

(a) Receiver notifies his or her agent of damage or loss and allows the ship's agent three days to examine the cargo.
(b) When the extent of damage is ascertained by the receiver or shipowner's agent, the shipowner and P&I Club must be told.
(c) A large claim may require a P&I Club surveyor or consultant to examine the cargo. Ideally it should be a joint survey embracing the P&I Club, and the insurer and consignee agreements to avoid any subsequent disagreement over the findings. An early examination is essential and the agent must establish from the ship's Master and confirm with the shipowner or P&I Club the actual name of the P&I Club involved.
(d) When the cargo claim facts are established, correspondence starts as detailed in Figures 12.1 and 12.2 involving interested parties, shipowners, receivers

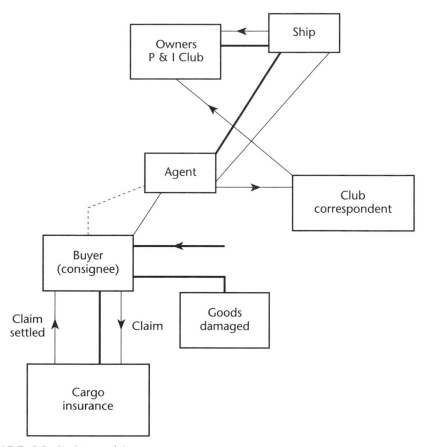

FIGURE 12.1 Cargo claim

agents, P&I Club, cargo receiver, shipowner's agent, cargo insurance company or Lloyd's, lawyers, etc.

(e) The receiver's agent role is decisive in all stages to ensure prompt settlement is obtained and quick action is essential in the early stages.

It will be appreciated that circumstances will vary. The claim could emerge at the factory or warehouse of the buyer, rather than at the destination port as has been discussed above.

It is important that clean receipts for imported cargo acceptance should never be given when the goods are in a doubtful condition but the receipt should be suitably endorsed and witnessed if possible, for example if one package is missing. Furthermore, if the loss or damage incurred was not readily apparent at the time of taking delivery, written notice must be given to the carriers or other bailees within three days of delivery acceptance. It is desirable that the claim be processed as quickly as possible.

Smaller consignments by containers, FCL or LCL, truck movements, multimodal, air freight are dealt with in original documents, duly authenticated and working closely with the insurance broker. Buyers should be aware of the carrier's

(e) failure of goods to arrive on a specified date resulting in a compensation claim;
(f) poor or inadequate packing;
(g) inadequate or poor stowage;
(h) poor handling or stacking of cargo resulting in damage, crushing, etc.

To minimize the level of cargo claims, it is desirable that the importer initiates adequate measures. The following list should not be regarded as exhaustive, but should identify key areas for evaluation and the measures to be taken.

(a) Undertake a transit test to determine where the delays, damage or pilferage occurs and take remedial measures.
(b) Documentation content and layout should be continuously improved to specify the circumstances and reasons for a claim.
(c) Full use should be made of the carrier's on-line computer tracking system for individual consignments. Most major airlines and mega container operators have such a system.
(d) Quality control of product, transport service and packaging should be improved.
(e) Packaging should be analysed for its adequacy, handling and stowage acceptability together with compatibility with atmospheric conditions and weather exposure.
(f) Pilferage – aim to improve security and properly evaluate alternatives for routing, packaging, cargo packing, marking identity, etc.
(g) Breakage – aim to improve packaging and better handling and stowage techniques.
(h) An evaluation of the cost of alternative means and remedies should be made and their likelihood of success evaluated.
(i) Improve staff training on claims prevention.
(j) Devise a code or procedure for reporting missing and damaged cargo.
(k) Carriers should be encouraged to have an adequate number of claims prevention staff.
(l) All available technology should be used to lessen such claims.
(m) Produce a brochure on claims prevention.
(n) Initiate early discussions with carrier(s) and other parties in the supply chain to devise remedial measures to resolve difficulties and monitor transit performance.

It is most important that claims be kept to a minimum and thereby ensure that cargo insurance premiums remain at a competitively low level. Damaged cargo severely disrupts the buyer's supply chain, assembly, production and distribution programmes. The need to deal with claims promptly cannot be overstressed.

Recommended reading

- The Merchants Guide, P&O Nedlloyd.

13

Import customs practice

Customs practice – a strategic focus

This chapter examines the customs procedures adopted in the United Kingdom which are laid down by HM Government. The UK is a member of the European Union (EU) and accordingly goods are in free circulation for those commodities which originate and are manufactured in any of the 15 states forming the single market. Goods which are imported from a third country which is outside the single market such as the USA, the Far East, Switzerland, etc. are subject to rigorous customs procedures.

The EU and UK have numerous bi-lateral and multi-lateral trade and customs agreements both with individual countries and economic trading blocs across the world. This enables preferential import tariffs to be adopted and the buyer should check out the situation with the local customs office to establish the tariff levels and whether any preferential tariffs (see page 267) exist having regard to the goods to be imported and the country of importation. Such tariffs change almost without notice reflecting the political and economic climate.

It is appropriate at the commencement of this chapter that we focus on customs policy in the next millennium covering the international movement of goods, excluding intra-EU trade. This involves the evaluation of the following major international incentives and developments in the business world which are driving further changes in the business and customs environment. The buyer or strategist formulating short- and long-term business plans should especially note such changes which are being driven by the World Customs Organisation (WCO) in their efforts to accelerate trade development in a fast changing international environment and with a rising global population. They are as follows.

(a) The growth and globalization of international trade involving the global village and product outsourcing on a logistic basis.
(b) The exploitation of new markets through new technology and continuing improved international distribution network due to multi-modalism (see page 198).

Overall, the G7 initiative will have a profound favourable effect in the initiative to facilitate trade and its development through standardized and simplified customs procedures globally in a electronic commerce environment.

Customs and international supply chain management

We have, in Chapter 5, examined logistics and it is appropriate to return to the subject within the context of customs and its alignment to the international supply chain management. Supply chain management is focused on efficiency and coordinating the efforts of procurement, manufacture, marketing and distribution. Each of these four elements may be located in a different country. As materials and goods are moved from one country to another borders are crossed and any goods or materials shipped become subject to customs authorities control.

Political initiatives in liberalizing trade and finance, coupled with technological innovations in information, communications and transport technology have stimulated the ongoing process of globalization. However, national borders are not perfectly transparent as they remain instruments of national government policy. Many national governments, within the limits of economic and political realities, have the power to define and set trade regulating tariffs. Customs authorities, by administering and supervising the movement of goods and materials across national frontiers, play a key role. Costs for business can be identified in three areas as follows.

1. Direct costs associated with paying duties embracing: customs duty, excise duty, anti-dumping duty, countervailing duties, CAP levies, import VAT and compensatory interest.
2. Costs for business associated with the compliance of import restrictions and in meeting obligatory customs requirements such as prescribed accounting procedures and information requirements – including statistics – and compulsory document requirements.
3. Costs which may include opportunity costs by failing to take advantage of any customs regime or trade concessions. Likewise, the inappropriate use of any customs regime, or procedures, may give rise to future liabilities.

As goods and materials move across national frontiers managing the customs function is a key factor to success within the efforts of supply chain management. Within each of the supply chain functions, which include procurement, manufacture, marketing and distribution, customs considerations can have a significant impact.

In procurement it is prudent to consider preferential tariffs that may exist if goods and materials are sourced from countries for which preferential tariffs exist. For example, the duty rate in the EU on a television tube sourced in Malaysia is 14 per cent while for a television tube obtained in Thailand it is 9.8 per cent, in South Africa 7.3 per cent and in Poland 0 per cent subject to meeting certain conditions. In manufacturing it is prudent to consider any customs regimes that give duty rate advantages. They may suspend, reduce or defer the duty burden. Customs regimes available in the UK and the EU include customs warehousing, inward processing relief, outward processing, returned goods relief and processing under customs control.

When the buyer becomes involved in market sourcing selection, it is important to bear in mind changes in duty rates which may give greater or reduced scope in terms of the market size. For example, as China enters the WTO it can be assumed that Chinese tariff barriers will be significantly reduced, thus creating market opportunities as goods exported to China become more competitive. Similarly, opportunities may arise for buying sourcing (importing) as trade agreements such as Mercosur (Southern Common Market – of Latin America), North American Free Trade Area (NAFTA) or ASEAN Free Trade Area (AFTA) further develop, expand and consolidate.

The buyer's team must be very alert to new trading opportunities: for example the recent reciprocal Trade Agreement between Mexico and the European Union operative from 1 July 2000 (see page 316).

In distribution, as products are exported compliance with export and import formalities have to be considered. These include filing export and import declarations as well as paying the appropriate amount of duty. Awareness and application of customs policy and procedures is crucial to the efficient movement of goods across national frontiers.

Outline of available customs regimes

When supply chains take on an international dimension it is essential to take account of customs requirements and procedures. Failure to take account of customs law can, in extreme cases, lead to the commitment of a criminal offence. Inefficient management of customs control can lead to increased inventory costs, delays at frontiers and loss in supply chain responsiveness.

There are a number of customs regimes available to traders in the UK that could enhance a firm's competitiveness in terms of cash flow, duty liability and customs clearance time. Trade off considerations that need to be made are the advantages that an available regime may bring, against any compliance, accounting or reporting costs, operating costs and any commercial restrictions imposed by the regime.

Customs facilities available to the importer include the following.

(a) Import into free circulation – customs duty and import VAT is paid and goods are removed from customs control; some goods may be subject to import licences.
(b) Customs warehousing – enables goods to be stored without payment of import duty or VAT until released for free circulation or placed under another customs regime (see page 272).
(c) Free zones – enables goods to be stored and processed without payment of import duty or VAT (see page 269).

(d) Inward processing relief (IPR) suspension and drawback – allows conditional relief from duty on imported materials and components for use in the manufacture of products for export; under IPR suspension duty is suspended while under IPR drawback duty is paid and later reclaimed (see page 265).

(e) Processing under customs control – allows specific dutiable components and materials to be imported without payment of duty, processed into finished products and released for free circulation at the duty rate of the finished goods – the rate may be lower than the rate of the components and materials used in the production process.

(f) Temporary importation – gives relief from duty for goods imported for a given period of time – maximum 24 hours – and re-exported in the same state.

(g) Returned goods relief – allows relief on re-importation of goods previously exported.

(h) End use – reduced or zero duty rates for goods intended for a specified end use.

(i) Other – goods are re-exported, destroyed or otherwise disposed of without payment of duty.

Customs facilities available to exporters include the following.

(a) Export – goods leaving the EU may be subject to licensing requirements, export duties and commercial policy measures.

(b) Outward processing relief – allows relief from duty on EU goods re-imported after repair or process abroad.

(c) Community Transit – an EC customs procedure which controls and facilitates the movement of certain goods from one part of the EC to another, delaying duty and VAT payment.

(d) ATA carnet – may be used to simplify customs clearance of temporarily exported goods; the carnet replaces normal customs documents both at export and re-import (see page 162).

(e) TIR carnet – subject to certain conditions, this allows goods to travel across national frontiers with the minimum of customs formalities, duty and VAT free.

Outside the EU, other customs regimes may exist that could give an international supply chain similar competitive advantages. These embrace free trade zones, distriparks, export processing zones or tariff suspension for industries identified as being essential in developing the governing economy. Any one of these regimes could give the overseas buyer considerable advantage – for example third country assembly, processing or distribution – in managing cost and duty liabilities and should be considered when planning and managing an international supply chain.

To develop further customs issues, it is essential for the supply chain professional to take into account considerations that go beyond the actual physical handling of goods. There are many customs considerations worthy of attention that could add value to the supply chain. In many instances, customs issues can be deal breakers or makers, depending on trade policies, duty, rates and feasible customs regimes.

Customs law is not static. Rules and regulations are constantly reviewed and businesses need to be aware of developments and changes and their interpretation. Opportunities may exist or evolve that could give a business a competitive advantage and reduce the impact on the supply chain of crossing international borders.

For example, electronic commerce is becoming more widespread globally with traders reporting to customs electronically (see page 273). Usually as a prerequisite, some form of paper trial is required. Electronic reporting and electronic declarations (see page 271) can simplify complying with customs requirements. Electronic reporting is usually subject to customs authorization. The G7 initiative will accelerate this development (see pages 258–60).

Another example is customs warehousing which in principle allows the storage of goods free of duty and import VAT. Rather than use third party public customs warehouses or private customs warehouses that need to comply with rigid specification, an alternative may be to operate 'e' customs warehouses. This type of warehouse is truly virtual; the company's inventory system is used to track and control inventory for customs warehousing purposes rather than a specific physical location.

Supply chain operators reaching across the European Union may consider Single European Authorisation. This allows a company to report all its import and export activities across the EU and account for duty and VAT in one place.

Less technically complex, supply chain operators may be wise to check whether any tariff suspensions – where duty is never paid – are available for the goods they move. Subject to specific criteria and approval, duty suspension and quotas may be granted for goods which are not produced in the EU or are insufficiently available within the EU.

The procurement director team must be aware that customs considerations form an integral facet in the management of any international supply chain. Customs law is complex but the correct application of rules and regulations may produce intrinsic advantages. Moreover, the international trading environment is constantly evolving with a direct impact on customs control in the movement of goods. Customs law is constantly evolving and the supply chain professional needs to be aware of any changes.

We will now examine in broad detail the customs and VAT systems operative in the UK. It is stressed that the UK is a member of the EU which allows free circulation of intra-community goods with no trade or customs barriers. Hence, goods bought within the EU have a different system than those bought outside, both in terms of customs and VAT.

It is stressed that the customs system in the UK for non-community sourced goods are likewise found in many overseas territories albeit subject to variation in accordance with local government regulations. Readers overseas are urged to contact their local customs office to determine local customs arrangements.

Finally, it must also be stressed that customs procedures and data capture are now computer driven.

We will first examine the Customs Regime to be followed by VAT.

Customs tariffs

All products imported into the UK from outside the EU are identified by numerical codes as listed in the customs tariff. For statistical purposes and in compliance with EU regulations there must be a formal declaration – of all imports originating from outside the EU – to the customs authorities showing the tariff code of the product concerned. Each item has only one correct classification under the harmonized tariff system which has been adopted by 85 per cent of the world's trading nations. It follows that the code used by the supplier – at either four- or six-digit level – should be the same as that used by the buyer on importation. If the supplier uses an incorrect code, it will mislead the buyer or importer who may pay more or less duty than is legally due. The goods description which must be of a technical specification and not commercial as recorded on the export invoice provided or compiled by the supplier, will be the key factor to determine the product customs classification, its code number and ultimately the rate of duty payable at the time of importation by the consignee on the export invoice or his or her forwarding agent on his or her behalf. A wide variety of duty exemptions exists. Effective customs planning may lessen the import duty level or eliminate it provided certain conditions are complied with and adequate customs pre-planning is adopted as mentioned earlier (see page 197–8 items 1–7).

The foregoing data are found in the Customs Tariff published in three volumes annually and updated monthly: Volume I contains general information about import and export matters; Volume II features the schedule of duty and trade statistical description, codes and rates; Volume III contains information about customs freight procedures including directions for completing the customs declaration found in the Single Administrative Document. The Customs Tariff includes 15 000 headings, set out in 97 chapters, broken down into sections, headings and sub-headings. The tariff is not used for intra-EC trade. The integrated tariff of the United Kingdom is based on the Combined Nomenclature (CN) of the European Community. The CN is in turn based on the Harmonised Commodity Description and Coding System used worldwide. Importers are urged to become familiar with the Tariff to ensure the most appropriate tariff code is adopted and in so doing liaise with the supplier.

Customs reliefs

A wide range of Customs duty reliefs exists which we will now examine briefly and the buyer is urged to become familiar with them. Further details are available from the local customs office together with other reliefs.

Inward processing relief (IPR)

A range of duty reliefs are available for goods imported into the UK and their applicability is dependent on the goods re-exported under the control of the customs authorities. An example is found in the inward processing relief whereby the goods may be processed or assembled on a componentized basis and subsequently re-exported. The customs regulations and procedures are stringent and subject to continuous review. Adequate documentation must be provided to substantiate the imported merchandise. Moreover, adequate pre-planning must be undertaken involving the buyer, supplier and customs. An increasing number of goods are now being treated in this way as global manufacturing strategies and companies switch from a domestic supplier to an overseas source and subsequently export the componentized, assembled finished product. Overall, there are four types of authorization: simplified authorization (form C101); simplified authorization (form C&E810); specific authorization; and community authorization. The simplified authorization (form C101) is granted at the time of import. Traders must hold the other authorizations before the goods may be imported under IPR – they cannot be issued retrospectively.

The trader must decide whether to use the suspension or drawback method of obtaining duty relief. With suspension the trader does not pay duty or import VAT as long as the shipper exports the goods or the products made from them or the goods are sold to another IPR trader or disposed of using one of the methods specified by HM Customs and Excise. In regard to drawback the shipper pays the duty and VAT at import. The trader claims the duty back only if the shipper exports the goods or products and sells them to an IPR suspension trader or disposes of them using one of the methods specified by HM Customs and Excise. Further details are given in HM Customs Notice No. 221 and amendments.

Customs warehousing

An increasing number of buyers and importers are using the concessionary facilities provided under customs warehousing and free zones (see page 269). A customs warehouse is a system or place authorized by the customs authority for the storage of non-Community goods under duty suspension. It permits traders to delay duty and/or VAT payments on imported goods; to delay having a customs treatment applied to imported goods; to permit shippers to re-export non-Community goods (in which case import duty and/or VAT may not be payable at all), or to help traders who have difficulty at the time of import in meeting particular conditions such as certain import licensing requirements. It also caters for the storage and warehousing of goods originally imported into another customs regime, for example IPR or PCC (processing under customs control). Overall, the customs warehouse can either be a place or inventory system authorized by customs for storing non-Community goods which are chargeable with import duty and/or VAT, or which are otherwise not in free circulation.

Depending on the circumstances and type applied for, that is premises based or system based, a customs warehouse may, for example, be the whole of a building, a small compartment in a building, an open site, a silo, a storage tank or an inventory system. A person who is authorized to operate a customs warehouse must take responsibility for the security and proper control of the warehouse goods. Customs carry out audit based checks on their activities to ensure the correct procedures are being carried out and that all duties are paid on the due date.

There are six types of customs warehouse allowed under EC regulations and at present (2000) the UK operates only types A, C, D and E as defined below.

1. Type A is a public warehouse authorized for use by warehouse keepers whose main business is the storage of goods by other traders. The warehouse keeper is responsible for the security of the warehouse goods and undertakes to see that all customs obligations are met. In addition, the warehouse keeper is responsible for accounting for any shortage of warehoused goods. The warehouse keeper may also act as an agent and complete some or all of the official documentation as required.

2. Type C is a private warehouse for use by individual traders for the storage of goods. The warehouse keeper need not necessarily own the goods but must be the depositor, that is the person bound by the declaration placing the goods under the customs warehousing procedure or to whom the rights and obligations of such a person have been transferred. The warehouse keeper must complete all official documentation relating to the warehousing activities.

3. Type D is also a private warehouse as defined for type C. However, the rules of assessment applicable to the warehoused goods are applied when the goods are entered to the warehousing procedure. The rules of assessment cover the nature, value and quantity of the goods.

    The premises of a warehouse authorized under types A, C or D may be either at one location or more than one location. The warehouse address will be the location where the warehouse records are kept. No combination of types A, C or D warehouses is permitted in the same premises or location. However, goods within a type E warehousing system can be stored on the premises of a type A, C or D warehouse.

4. Type E is a form of private warehousing in which a company and its commercial accounting and stock controls and systems are authorized. The goods may be stored at any notified storage site belonging to the authorized trader or in transit between such locations, with movements between one such site and another permitted without any official documentation. The authorization will be granted only to a private warehouse keeper who must be the depositor but not necessarily the owner of the goods. The authorized trader must complete all official documentation.

Goods which can be warehoused are:

(a) non-Community goods liable to customs duties and/or VAT (whether or not eligible for preference if put into free circulation);

(b) non-Community goods for which necessary supporting documents, e.g. DOTI licences are not available at the time of import;

(c) non-Community goods imported to another suspensive regime, e.g. IPR, temporary importations, etc. warehoused for export from the Community;

(d) non-Community goods processed for free circulation (PFC);

(e) non-Community goods not subject to a full rate of customs duty in the tariff but liable only to import VAT;

(f) Community goods or non-Community goods in free circulation eligible for CAP refunds on export and warehoused in a specially approved warehouse under CAP pre-financing arrangements.

Goods which cannot be warehoused are: carcasses and animal products unless the required import licence and/or health certificate is presented at the time of import; goods liable to excise duties unless excise duty is paid before the entry is made for customs warehousing. See HM Customs and Excise Notice No. 232.

A valuation declaration is an official form on which the importer provides information about the valuation of imported goods in a single consignment for Customs duty and VAT purposes. It is required when the goods are liable to ad valorem duty imported into the EC and the import declaration is found on the SAD form. A range of exceptions exists regarding goods liable to customs duty including consignments below a certain value (£4000 in 2000), goods of no commercial value such as personal belongings; customs value based on Simplified Procedures Values, fresh fruit and vegetables and importers who have registered a general valuation statement. Two kinds of value declaration exist: form C105A is used if a consignment includes goods from more than one seller with all of whom the buyer has identical terms of trading. In such a situation the consignee must attach a list of sellers to whom the declaration applies. The second method features form C105B and covers a range of diverse situations as found in HM Customs Notice No. 251. The valuation must be signed by an authorized employee such as a director, manager, sole proprietor or the principal authorized agent.

Associated with the customs valuation declaration is a general valuation statement (GVS). This is a numbered document (a season ticket) which may be quoted on entry documents and used instead of individual valuation declarations when the buyer regularly imports goods from named suppliers under the same terms of trading from non-EC sources. The GVS is valid for 3 years – applications must be completed by the importer and the appropriate form C109A or C109B used to apply for the GVS number at time of importation.

Tariff preferences – imports

The Generalised System of Preferences (GSP) is widely used and enables importers to benefit from the preferential tariff treatment. Overall, the consignee pays a lower rate of import customs duty or levy charge, or none at all, on the goods imported provided specific conditions are complied with and the appropriate documentation is supplied at the time of importation.

A wide range of countries feature in the scheme and details are found in Volume I Part 7 of the Tariff which is issued annually and the preference customs duty rates in Volume II Part 2 of the tariff. Changes to preferential arrangements take place from time to time – sometimes at very short notice – and these are found on the Customs and Excise website http://www.hmce.gov.uk. Overall, the GSP represents trade agreements on a bi-lateral or multi-lateral basis whereby reciprocal import customs duty rates are reduced to stimulate trade. The WTO are very keen to facilitate such government strategies existing both between individual trading nations and between economic trading blocs.

Some of the GSP schemes operate under a ceiling or tariff quota thereby limiting the quantity of certain goods which can be imported under the preference. The 'origin rules' – the place or country from which the goods are exported or sourced – will vary. Some countries require the product to be wholly produced in the preference country, whilst others specify that it has been manufactured there in accordance with the rules which govern the use of imported materials. Buyers are urged to check with their suppliers that the origin rules are being complied with and obtain written confirmation that they have been met in order to satisfy customs at the time of importation. If a claim for GSP is invalid full duty payment applies. Customs officials will examine the goods to check authenticity with the documents and certificates at the time of importation.

Three types of preference documents cover the majority of commercial importation: form EUR 1; an invoice declaration; or form A. Some preference receiving countries also use form EUR 2 for goods sent by post. Form A is used for imports from GSP countries. All other preference countries use the form EUR 1. The invoice declaration is a simplified form of preference document that may be used in some countries in place of the EUR 1. Form A is a certificate of origin used by exporters in GSP countries. It must be stamped and signed by a particular government authority. Form A must normally cover only one consignment.

The European Community GSP scheme is one of the most widely used import preference regimes. The GSP origin rules are, with a small number of exceptions, identical to those in preferential trade agreements described earlier which the European Community has concluded with the EEA, Switzerland, the Baltic States, and the central and eastern European countries. The GSP beneficiary countries have been formed into groups for origin purposes: ASEAN, CACM and ANDEAN. In short this means that materials or parts originating in one country in the group, in accordance with GSP rules of origin, may be regarded as originating in another country in the group to which they are sent for further processing or for inclusion in a finished product. This arrangement, which is commonly known as 'cumulation of origin' helps the finished product to meet the appropriate rules for export to the EC under preference.

The foregoing system is described in greater detail in HM Customs Notice No. 826 and buyers are urged to study countries featuring in the GSP system and source such markets if the products are acceptable to their criteria.

End-use relief

This applies to a range of imported goods which will qualify for a reduced or zero rate of duty using end-use relief, provided the goods are identified with a prescribed use under customs control and within a specified period. Overall, end-use relief can assist certain industries and trades within the EC by providing favourable rates of duty on certain goods imported from outside the EC, provided those goods are put to a prescribed use. To obtain relief an authorization is required to import the goods to end-use relief. The goods must then be put to a prescribed use within a certain period and records kept about the goods and their treatment. If the goods are not put to the prescribed use, duty will be due.

End-use relief from duty and VAT (where applicable) applies to goods of any description being imported for construction, maintenance, conversion, fitting out or equipping of certain boats or other vessels, including drilling and production platforms as described in Part I of the Customs tariff (Part 9 Section). Goods imported under IPR drawback may also be transferred to end-use relief (see page 265).·

The range of circumstances in which the end-use relief applies is diverse. In the UK the end-use relief is explained in HM Customs Notice No. 770.

Free zones

A free zone is an enclosed area in which non-Community goods are treated for the purpose of import duties as being outside the customs territory of the Community. Customs duty, import VAT or other import charges are not due provided the goods are not released for free circulation. Hence, payment of import duties (including agricultural charges) and import VAT is suspended when goods are placed in a free zone. The free zone regime can include goods originally imported into another system such as IPR. Goods enter the free zone by direct importation by sea or air; from the seaport or airport next to the free zone; from a port, airport or ICD which is some distance from the free zone; from another free zone; from a customs warehouse; from an excise warehouse in the UK; from IPR for further processing or export or from elsewhere in the UK. Goods can be moved from the free zone to customs warehouse using form C88 (SAD).

The operations permitted in a free zone include storage, usual forms of handling, processing and destruction. When goods subject to VAT are imported into a free zone, the VAT charge at importation is suspended. Import VAT becomes payable by the owner when the goods are removed from the free zone to the UK market, or used or consumed within the free zone whether for business or non-business purposes. The acquisition of Community and non-Community goods from a trader registered for VAT in another EC Member State should be treated in the same way as the acquisition of goods in the rest of the UK. The tax must be accounted for on the acquirer's VAT return for the period covering the time of acquisition. The value for VAT must include any duty paid. Free zones are fully explained in HM Customs and Excise Notice No. 334.

Local Import Control (LIC)

Local Import Control is a scheme which gives the buyer the opportunity to have customs clearance procedures carried out on goods – not in free circulation – but imported in containers or vehicles at the consignee's premises instead of at the place of importation such as at the seaport or airport. To be able to take advantage of the LIC in the UK, the trader must be able to send information to Customs by computer media. LIC gives the buyer more control over imports and also reduces delivery time by minimizing the risk of delays at the place of importation. From time to time HM Customs will carry out anti-smuggling checks on the goods and container or vehicles when they arrive at the consignee's premises.

To qualify for the scheme an importer must:

(a) be a regular importer of goods in containers or vehicles that are capable of being made secure;
(b) be able to provide for the local Excise and Inland Customs Advice Centre (EIC) audit staff the records relating to the transaction, that is bills of lading, despatch notes, import entry forms, sales invoices, air waybills, freight documentation etc.;
(c) employ a consignee who uses a computerized periodic entry system to provide data on imports to Customs.

The trader is obliged to tell EIC on each occasion when goods are expected to arrive and delivered to the consignee's premises. When the goods arrive at the place of importation, the trader arranges to present the appropriate transit documents to Customs – probably forms C88 (SAD) and C21 for inventory system items. If the transit documents are correct and the vehicle secure, the goods can be moved without delay to the buyer's premises. On arrival of the goods at the trader's premises, the vehicle must be examined and seals checked to ensure the goods are intact.

An initial entry containing a unique consignment reference number and date must be inputted to the consignee's computer record immediately on arrival of the goods at the trader's premises. The date of this computer input is treated as the date of acceptance of the entry. Alternatively, the trader may present a simplified initial entry on SAD Copy 6. Additionally, supporting documents must also be presented such as an import licence or preference document.

Goods imported under the LIC procedure are cleared and can be discharged immediately on arrival at the approved premises provided the buyer has given the agreed notice of the intended arrival of the goods and an initial entry has been made on the computer or SAD copy has been accepted by EIC staff. The only exception to this rule is when the local customs staff wish to examine the goods.

The LIC is very popular and traders are urged to use this facility. It speeds up transit and eliminates any customs clearance delays at airports or seaports. Local customs clearance ensures that the goods can be cleared quickly and absorbed into the trader's production, assembly or distribution system promptly. Any customs queries can be dealt with locally and not at a distant seaport or airport with the increased cost of engaging a customs clearance agent. The foregoing analysis obtains in the UK HM Customs Notice No. 470. Similar arrangements apply globally.

Customs Freight Simplified Procedures (CFSP)

In 2000 the Customs Freight Simplified Procedures (CFSP) were introduced replacing scheduling and period entry. Overall, it enhances and simplifies Customs procedures for clearing UK imported goods, either at the frontier or by removal from a warehouse. Under CFSP, formalities at the frontier are kept to a minimum with the bulk of fiscal and statistical data being supplied to Customs at a later date. This strategy accords with the WCO objective (see page 257) of reducing the burdens on business, promoting trade and moving from transaction checking at the frontier to a systems based audit inland using traders' commercial records with an electronic commerce focus.

Three procedures exist under CFSP: a simplified declaration procedure, a local clearance procedure and Customs warehousing.

Simplified declaration procedure

The simplified declaration procedure is used to release goods to free circulation IPR, PCC and TI; or to Customs warehousing at the frontier. To enter goods to free circulation, IPR, PCC and TI using this procedure, a simplified frontier declaration containing a minimum amount of information is required at the frontier. The acceptance of the simplified frontier declaration establishes the tax point and base date for the submission of the supplementary declaration.

A supplementary declaration is subsequently required for all goods declared using the simplified declaration procedure. This is an electronic message sent to CHIEF (see page 278) which contains fiscal and statistical information and allows Customs to calculate the tax and duties due. Data are despatched monthly. A flowchart to illustrate this process is shown in Figure 13.1.

Local Customs clearance procedure

The local Customs clearance procedure is used to release goods to a Customs procedure from the designated premises. Each consignment must be allocated a unique consignment reference. The goods may be moved from the frontier to the specified trader's premises under Community transit or UK transit procedures. A simplified declaration procedure, usually in electronic form, is required unless the goods arrive via another Member State. In these circumstances the existing Community transit movement can continue from the frontier to the stated destination.

When the goods have been removed from temporary storage and have entered a customs procedure, an electronic supplementary declaration is

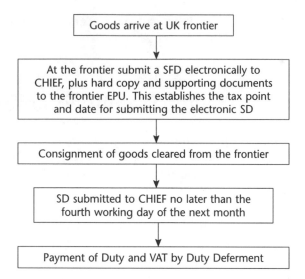

FIGURE 13.1 Outline diagram of goods entered to free circulation using the simplified declaration procedure

Reproduced courtesy H.M. Customs and Excise

submitted based on the date shown in the traders records. Study the flowchart in Figure 13.2 showing goods entered to free circulation using the local clearance procedure.

Customs warehousing

Under the Customs warehousing option it is essential that other Customs warehousing requirements are fulfilled, in which case the trader may remove goods from the warehouse by recording details in the trader's records. Supporting documents will need to be retained and produced to Customs on request. The recorded date of removal of the goods will determine the tax point and the date for the submission of the electronic supplementary declaration. The flowchart in Figure 13.3 illustrates the Customs warehouse procedures.

There are four principles of the Customs Freight Simplified Procedures. These are detailed below.

(a) *Authorization.* The importer must be authorized by Customs to operate simplified procedures and hold specific/general authority for associated procedures e.g. Customs Warehousing, IPR/OPR.
(b) *Accelerated removal/release.* The importer may remove goods from the frontier under transit to the buyer's premises for clearance or release to free circulation or warehousing ex frontier by making a simplified frontier declaration containing the minimum of details.

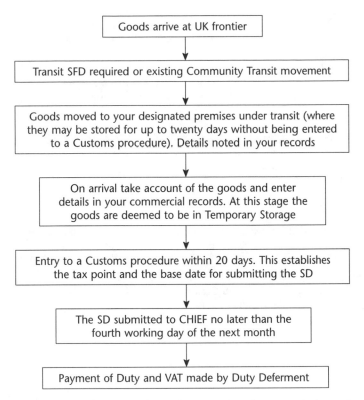

FIGURE 13.2 Outline diagram of goods entered to free circulation using the local clearance declaration procedure

Reproduced courtesy H.M. Customs and Excise

(c) *Electronic reporting.* The importer must submit statistical and fiscal details of the goods to CHIEF electronically using a supplementary declaration within a defined time scale.

(d) *Audit.* Customs may undertake a post clearance audit of the trader's commercial systems and records to provide assurance that the procedures are operating satisfactorily.

The advantages of the Customs Freight Simplified Procedures are as outlined below.

(a) Gain accelerated release of the goods by Customs at the airport or at an inland depot, subject to anti-smuggling checks.

(b) Use one or more of the simplified procedures in combination with normal entry and warehouse procedures to suit the needs of the buyer's business.

(c) Achieve cash flow benefits. For example local clearance allows the importer to store goods for up to 20 days before release to a Customs procedure or use. This means that within this time the buyer can choose the release date (and therefore tax point) at the most convenient time for the importer's business.

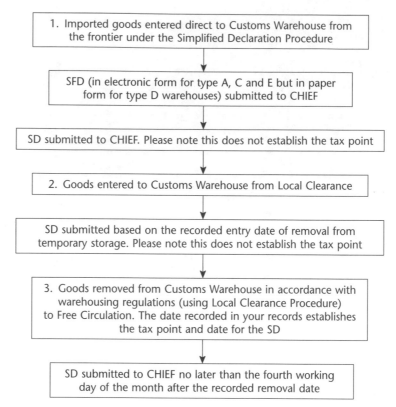

FIGURE 13.3 Outline diagram of CFSP customs warehousing procedures
Reproduced courtesy H.M. Customs and Excise

(d) Carry out UK transit movements under the local clearance procedure under a (limitless) guarantee waiver, avoiding the need to finance a comprehensive guarantee (except for a few specified CAP goods).

(e) Submit most frontier declarations (including UK transit) and all supplementary declarations by electronic means resulting in paperless trading and reduced documentation.

(f) Build a partnership with Customs so that assurance visits are cost effective, selected on the basis of risk and test the completeness of the importer's internal controls.

(g) Use third party service providers to submit electronic declarations.

(h) Avoid demurrage cost.

(i) Avoid period-end panics.

(j) Avoid temporary warehousing cost.

(k) Plan reliable frontier clearance times.

(l) Improve clearance times.

(m) Reduce the buyer's administration burden.

(n) Permits customs to calculate the import duty.

UK Buyers are urged where convenient to adopt CFSP with all its inherent advantages. Further details can be found in HM Customs and Excise Notice Nos. 759, 760.

Value Added Tax

From 1 January 1993, following the completion of the Single Market, there were important changes in the way that VAT is charged and accounted for on goods moving between Member States of the European Community (EC). For VAT purposes, the terms 'imports' and 'exports' for intra-EC movements of goods disappeared. They were replaced by new arrangements for zero-rating intra-EC supplies of goods and by 'acquisition'. VAT on goods traded between EC Member States is not collected at the frontier on 'importation'. Instead, goods supplied between VAT registered traders are zero-rated on despatch, and any VAT due is payable on acquisition of the goods by the customer. The customer accounts for any VAT due on their normal VAT return at the rate in force in the country of destination of the goods. When VAT registered traders despatch goods to unregistered traders or private individuals in another EC country, the supplier must usually charge VAT at the rate in force in the country of despatch.

There are also special rules for freight transport and associated services.

In addition, special arrangements apply to certain supplies to non-registered persons, including sales of new means of transport (boats, aircraft and motor vehicles) to private individuals, distance sales and purchases by exempt bodies and non-taxable organizations. There were also requirements for providing details of trade statistics.

A transaction involving the movement of goods between EC Member States is treated for VAT purposes as a supply of goods in the Member State from which the goods are despatched. For most of these supplies between VAT registered traders in different Member States, VAT need not be charged on despatch. It is, however, due from the customer on acquisition of the goods concerned in the Member State to which they are delivered. For supplies of goods to customers in other EC Member States who are not registered for VAT, tax is normally charged and accounted for by the VAT registered supplier in the Member State from which the goods are despatched. The exceptions to these general rules are in respect of the following:

(a) goods to be installed or assembled at a customer's premises and distance sales above a certain level where tax should be charged and accounted for by the supplier in the Member State to which the goods are delivered;
(b) supplies of new means of transport and goods subject to excise duty purchased for non-private purposes where VAT must normally be paid by the customer in the Member State of destination;
(c) supplies to diplomats, international organizations, NATO forces and other entitled persons and bodies in other Member States which may in certain circumstances be relieved from VAT.

If the buyer is registered for VAT in the UK and receives goods from another EC Member State supplied by a business registered for VAT in that country, the buyer must account for VAT in the UK on acquisition of the goods. The rate of tax due is the one applicable to the supply of identical goods in the UK. No tax will therefore be due on the acquisition of goods which are currently zero-rated in the UK.

The rules for determining the time of acquisition (tax point) are related to the ones for time of acquisition of intra-EC supply. Acquisition is treated as taking place at the same time as the corresponding supply of the goods in the Member State of despatch. The tax point for acquisitions is therefore either:

(a) the fifteenth day of the month following the one in which the goods were despatched to the UK buyer; or

(b) the date the supplier issued an invoice to the UK buyer (including an invoice issued before the goods are sent to the buyer), whichever is the earlier.

Unlike the rules for supplies of goods in the UK, part or full payment for the goods does not create a tax point for acquisitions. The buyer needs to account for acquisition tax when he or she makes a part or full payment to the EC supplier. However, if the EC supplier sends the buyer a tax invoice for the amount paid, the buyer should account for acquisition tax in respect of that amount, provided the date of issue of the invoice is earlier than the fifteenth day of the month following the one in which the goods were despatched by the supplier.

Where goods are invoiced to the UK buyer more than a month before delivery, the reference date of the Intrastat Supplementary Declarations becomes the date the goods are received.

The buyer must account for any VAT due on the VAT return for the period in which the tax point occurs and, subject to the normal rules, may treat this tax as input tax on the same VAT return.

VAT on acquisitions will, in most cases, be due in the country where the goods are received. However, to ensure that acquisition tax is accounted for on goods moving between EC countries, Member States have agreed to a 'fall-back' provision. This provides that acquisition tax is due in the Member State where the acquirer is registered for VAT, if it is not accounted for in the Member State to which the goods have been sent.

If the buyer gives a UK VAT-registered number to the EC supplier to enable the supply of goods to be zero-rated, the buyer will be liable to account for acquisition tax in the UK unless he or she can demonstrate that tax has already been paid in the Member State to which the goods were sent. If the buyer is a member of a group registration and/or a self-accounting branch of a VAT registration, the buyer's UK VAT registration number should include a three digit identifier which the buyer should agree in advance with the local office.

If the buyer has accounted for acquisition tax in the UK and the buyer is later required to account for acquisition tax in the country to which the goods were sent, the buyer may obtain a refund of the tax paid in the UK. The buyer should only need to claim a refund if, and to the extent that he or she has not claimed full input tax credit in respect of that acquisition. The buyer does not need to account for acquisition tax in the UK if he or she can demonstrate that he or she has accounted for acquisition tax in the country to which the goods were sent, or the buyer's customer has accounted for the tax.

Current VAT in the single market arrangements are detailed in HM Customs and Excise Notice No. 725.

For VAT purposes, goods imported from outside the EC are treated as imported into the UK where:

(a) they arrive in the UK directly from outside the EU and the trader enters them for home use in the UK or customs duty otherwise becomes payable on them; or
(b) they have been placed in another EU country or in the UK under a duty suspension arrangement involving one of the following situations and the trader enters them for removal to home use in the UK, or otherwise customs duty becomes payable on them:
   (i)   temporary storage,
   (ii)   free zones,
   (iii)   customs warehousing,
   (iv)   inwards processing relief (duty suspension system),
   (v)   temporary importation (including means of transport) with total relief from customs duties,
   (vi)   external Community transit (TI) arrangements,
   (vii)   goods admitted into territorial waters,
   (viii) excise, warehousing.

The value for VAT-imported goods will be their customs value, plus the ancillary charges for freight etc. The Customs' computerized system for handling import entries (CHIEF) will allow VAT paid on the trader's imports under the government contractor, registered consignee and bulked entry procedures to be included in VAT certificates. Basically, when customs duty is due on goods, it coincides with VAT importation payment. Current import VAT arrangements are described in HM Customs Notice No. 700.

VAT distance selling arrangements to the UK

Distance selling occurs when a taxable person in one EC Member State supplies and delivers goods to a non-taxable person in another Member State. The non-taxable customer may include private individuals, public bodies, charities and businesses which are not VAT registered because their turnover is below the registration threshold or whose activities are entirely exempt.

If the buyer's supplier from another EC Member State who is not already required to register for VAT in the UK, and the value of the distance sales to the UK exceeds the annual UK threshold for distance selling (in 2000 £70 000), the buyer will be liable to register for VAT in the UK. The threshold does not apply to sales of goods subject to excise duty. Further details can be found in HM Customs and Excise Notice No. 725.

Valuation of imported goods for VAT purposes

The value for VAT of imported goods is their customs value (see page 197) plus – if not already included in the price – the following:

(a) all incidental expenses such as commission, packing, transport and insurance costs incurred up to the goods' first destination in the UK;

(b) all such incidental expenses where they result from transport to a further place of destination in the EC if that place is known at the time of importation;

(c) any customs duty or levy payable on importation into the UK;

(d) any excise duty or other charges payable on importation into the UK (except the VAT itself).

The term 'incidental expenses' also covers such items as transport, customs clearance charges, quay rent, entry fees, demurrage, handling, loading and storage costs. Generally, where supplies of services qualify for zero-rating because they are supplied in connection with an importation of goods, the cost of those services should be included in the value for import VAT.

Certain costs, for example, royalties and licence fees, should not be included in the value for import VAT as they are taxable under the reverse charge and international service arrangements.

The Customs Handling of Import and Export Freight (CHIEF) computer calculates the value for VAT by adding any duties, levies and additional costs to be included in the VAT value to the value declared in Box 22 of the import declaration (the SAD form C88). Where any of these additional costs, which need to be added to arrive at the VAT value, are not included in the total invoice value (Box 22) or the other value build-up boxes (63–67), the buyer must declare them in the adjustment for VAT value box (Box 68).

If the value for VAT is less than that which CHIEF would normally calculate for customs duty purposes, or the declaration is made at a manual location, the buyer must calculate the amount of VAT payable manually. Except at manual locations, the buyer must enter the code 'VAT' in the Rate column of Box 47. The buyer must enter the calculated payment in the amount column.

If goods are liable to ad valorem customs duty (that is, a duty chargeable on the basis of value), a declaration on Form C105 (Valuation Declaration) or Form C109 (General Valuation Statement), made for duty purposes, will also generally be acceptable for VAT. However, the declaration will only provide information which helps determine the customs value of the goods, and it should not be regarded as establishing their full value for VAT purposes.

Where goods are not liable to ad valorem duty but are liable to VAT at the standard rate, a valuation declaration for VAT is needed only if the value exceeds £4000 and the importer is not registered for VAT; or if the importer is registered for VAT and the goods are not for the purposes of the business; or deduction of input tax would not be allowed; or the value of the goods is not being determined under customs valuation method 1 (see Notice 252, Section 1).

There are no arrangements for registering a General Valuation Statement for VAT only entries. Individual valuation declarations must be made where necessary. Whether or not a valuation declaration is required for the goods, evidence of value must be produced. Acceptable evidence is a copy of the seller's invoice or other document against which payment will be made. This will include fax or similar messages used instead of invoices. Further details are contained in Customs and Excise Notice No. 702.

VAT warehoused and free zone goods

With respect to community goods received from other EU countries, only a limited range of goods placed in a warehouse will be subject to excise duty. Putting the buyer's goods under a warehousing regime has the following implications:

(a) VAT on imports of non-Community goods is payable when such goods leave the warehousing regime for home use in the UK;

(b) for UK-produced goods in the warehouse, VAT is payable only if the goods have been supplied while warehoused in the UK;

(c) VAT is not due on most supplies of goods which takes place within warehouses (but VAT is due on the last (or only) supply within the warehouse of goods on which import VAT is not due);

(d) VAT invoices are not issued for goods supplied in the warehouse.

The major difference is that when goods are received from other EC Member States they are not treated as imports requiring import entry but are usually dealt with under acquisition arrangements. Treatment depends on whether the goods are Community goods (that is, goods produced in the EC or goods introduced from outside the EC which have been put into free circulation in the EC) or non-Community goods. Further details are given in Customs and Excise Notice No. 702.

The acquisition of Community and non-Community goods from a trader registered for VAT in another EC Member State, and placed in a UK free zone, should be treated in the same way as the acquisition of goods in the rest of the UK, and tax must be accounted for on the acquirer's VAT return for the period covering the time of acquisition. The value for VAT must include any duty paid.

When the buyer removes from a free zone into home use in the UK or uses or consumes, in the zone, goods which have arrived in the free zone as non-Community goods not yet put into free circulation in the EC, the buyer has to pay any import VAT either in cash or under the duty deferment arrangements.

Supplies of free zone goods are treated for VAT in the same way as supplies of similar goods elsewhere in the UK. However, the pre-1993 arrangement remains for the supplier to zero rate a supply of free zone goods where the customer has agreed to clear them from the zone on payment of any VAT due on importation.

VAT fiscal warehousing

On 1 June 1996 fiscal warehousing became available in the United Kingdom. It is a new warehousing regime which enables a specified range of EC commodities to be traded in a VAT-suspension regime, subject to certain conditions, and avoids many of the administrative burdens of VAT. Supplies of goods and associated services which take place within the regime are relieved from VAT, as are supplies and acquisitions of goods intended to be placed in the regime. Liability to VAT may arise when the goods are removed from the arrangements. Fiscal warehousing offers a trading environment for eligible EC goods compatible with the VAT-free trading facilities available in excise warehouses and customs warehouses.

Any of the goods contained in an agreed EC-wide list are eligible to be placed in a UK fiscal warehouse for trading within the transfer between EC fiscal warehousing regimes. All goods entered to fiscal warehousing must be in free circulation. In fiscal warehousing eligible goods placed in a notified warehouse, under the control of an authorized fiscal warehouse keeper, may be traded by dealers who will not be required to be VAT registered if that is their only business activity. Supplies of such goods, and of certain services, within a fiscal warehousing regime are relieved from VAT until the goods are removed, as are supplies of such goods which are to be placed in the regime.

VAT may become due when the goods finally leave the fiscal warehousing regime and will correspond to the amount of tax which would otherwise have been due on the final supply of goods in the warehouse, plus the amount of tax which would have been applied to any of the relieved supplies of services relating to those goods effected after the final supply of goods. The person liable to pay any VAT due on removal is the person who causes the goods to cease to be covered by the regime. More information about fiscal warehousing is contained in Customs Notice No. 702/9, Warehouses and free zones.

VAT – Freight transport and associated services

The cost of transport and insurance forms part of the value of goods for customs purposes. VAT will therefore be due on the receipt or acquisition of the goods by the customer. Hence VAT will be accounted for in the same EU country as the one in which the customer has the right to recover the tax. The transport of goods between EU Member States is taxed either in the Member State where the customer is registered for VAT or, if the customer is not a VAT registered person, which includes a private person, in the Member State from which the goods are removed, that is the place of departure.

Supplies of ancillary services and the services of intermediaries connected with the movement of goods between Member States are taxed according to the same rules as apply to intra-community transport services. However, when supplied to a customer who is not registered for VAT, ancillary services are taxed in the Member State in which they are physically performed and intermediary services are taxed in the Member State where the service which is being arranged is taxed.

Rejected imports – repayment or remission of duty and VAT

Situations do arise when imported goods are rejected for a range of reasons. This embraces failure to comply with the terms of the export sales contract, goods are defective, or merchandise has been damaged whilst being cleared by Customs. The importer can claim repayment or remission of import duty and VAT on goods imported subject to the following:

(a) the goods were rejected because at the time of declaring them to a Customs procedure involving payment of charges (e.g. for free circulation), they were defective, did not comply with the terms of the contract under which they were imported, or were damaged before being cleared by Customs;

(b) the goods are those declared to Customs;

(c) the goods have not been used more than was necessary to establish that they were defective or did not comply with the contract;

(d) the goods have not been sold after they were found to be defective or not to comply with the contract.

Additionally, there exists a range of special situations where repayment or remission of import duty and VAT may be claimed as detailed below. Such a list must not be regarded as exhaustive.

1. Stolen after entry to a system of duty relief, provided the goods are recovered promptly and returned to the same duty relief system in the state they were in when stolen.

2. Inadvertently withdrawn from a system of duty relief, provided that as soon as the error is found, they are returned to the same duty relief system in the state they were in when withdrawn.

3. In a means of transport which it is impossible to open on arrival at its destination after the goods have been released for free circulation, provided they are immediately re-exported.

4. After release for free circulation, returned to the non-EC supplier under outward processing arrangements to eliminate faults to bring them into line with contract, which the supplier then decides to keep because the defects cannot be remedied or because it is uneconomical to do so.

5. Now liable to charges but originally allowed duty relief and re-exported without customs supervision, provided repayment would have been allowed at the time of export if the charges had been collected at import.

6. Forbidden to be marketed by a judicial body, and are re-exported from the EC or destroyed under customs supervision, provided they have not been used in the EC.

7. Entered by a declarant empowered to do so on their own initiative and which, through no fault of this declarant, cannot be delivered to the consignee.

8. Addressed to the consignee in error, for example wrongly labelled, not ordered by the consignee, or received in excess of the quantity ordered, provided the consignee refused the goods immediately the excess was discovered (no claim may be made if the consignee accepts excess goods, as such action is considered to amend the original contract, even if the goods are subsequently rejected), provided the goods are re-exported to the original supplier or to an address specified by them.

9. Found to be unsuitable because of an obvious factual error in the consignee's order, for example wrong goods received due to quoting an incorrect reference number.

10. Found not to have complied, at the time of entry to free circulation, with the rules in force concerning their use or marketing and cannot therefore be used as the consignee intended.

11. Unable to be used because of official measures taken after the date of entry for free circulation, for example new safety or hygiene laws prevent the goods from being used for their intended purpose.

12. Entered to a system of duty relief which is refused through no fault of the consignee, for example where relief under a tariff quota is claimed but refused because the quota has been exhausted.

13. Delivered to the consignee after a fixed delivery date, for example because of shipping delays.

14. Found to be unsaleable in the EC and are to be donated to charities. The goods must be either exported and given free of charge to a charity operating outside the EC (provided that the charity is also represented in the EC); or delivered free of charge to a charity operating within the EC (provided that the charity is eligible to import similar goods free of import duty under Customs Notice No. 317, Imports by Charities, or Customs Notice No. 371, Goods for Disabled People).

15. Liable to customs charges for reasons other than entry to free circulation, for example failure to meet post-import conditions, but where Community transit or other documentation can be produced to prove entitlement to zero or reduced rates of charge.

Further details can be found in HM Customs and Excise Notice No. 266.

Temporary importations into the European Union

Duty relief applies to certain goods temporarily imported into the European Union. This extends to certain goods permanently imported for consumption or for use at exhibitions or similar events. If the relevant conditions are not met, duty may have to be paid on the goods and in addition the goods are liable to forfeiture. Also, future authorizations of relief may be withheld from anyone who makes improper use of the temporary importation arrangements.

An import declaration form C88 is required for all goods imported to any of the reliefs. A wide range of goods are eligible for relief from duty featuring items for exhibitions, animals for training, scientific equipment, film commercial samples, medical instruments, works of art, teaching aids, etc. In place of an import declaration, an ATA carnet (see page 162) may be used for commercial samples, professional equipment and goods for exhibitions. Further details of temporary importations can be found in HM Customs Excise Notice No. 200.

Recommended reading

- *SITPRO News*, July 2000 issue.
- *Logistics and Focus*, Vol. 2 No. 9, November 2000.
- Institute of Logistics and Transport publications.
- HM Customs & Excise notices, as specified.

14

Processing the imported consignment

An important activity of buying overseas is the processing of the import consignment through all its numerous procedures. It is an area which must be fully understood by the importer. However, before examining the procedures involved, we must first consider the contract of affreightment embraced in the terms of delivery.

Contract of affreightment and terms of delivery

The basis of a price quotation depends on the correct interpretation of the delivery trade terms. The supplier will, through experience, accumulate information which will enable him or her to quote accurately. It is important to bear in mind that each delivery trade term quoted embraces three basic elements: the stage at which title to the merchandise passes from the exporter (seller) to the importer (buyer); a clear definition of the charges and expenses to be borne by the supplier and the buyer; and finally the stage and location where the goods are to be passed over to the buyer.

The international consignment delivery terms embrace many factors, in particular: insurance, air or sea freight plus surface transport costs, customs duty, port disbursements, product cost, packing cost, etc. Moreover, the importance of executing the cargo delivery in accordance with the prescribed terms cannot be overstressed and this involves a disciplined processing the export sales contract order dealt with elsewhere in this chapter. In the ideal situation, the sales export contract, including the delivery terms should be undertaken on a critical path analysis programme devised by the buyer in consultation with departmental colleagues within the company and relevant outside bodies, that is booking cargo space, processing financial aspects, obtaining a certificate of origin, etc. Such a strategy is based on the buyer controlling the transit in consultation, when appropriate, with the supplier under EXW FCA. In the event of the goods being sold on a delivered basis – group D page 289 – the critical path analysis programme would be initiated by the supplier and departmental colleague in consultation with the buyer. Overall, such planning will be computer driven.

There must be no ambiguity in the interpretation by either party of the delivery terms quoted, particularly in the area of cost and liabilities. If such problems arise much goodwill is lost. Moreover, costly litigation could arise. It is essential therefore that the buyer (importer) takes the lead and agrees with the seller the terms of delivery, their interpretation and that this is reflected fully in the export sales contract price and recorded explicitly in the export invoice. Such a situation could be overcome by quoting the provision of Incoterms 2000. It must be stressed that special provisions in individual export sales contracts will override anything provided in Incoterms 2000. Also, any breaches of the contract and their consequences together with the ownership of the goods are outside the influence of Incoterms 2000.

The need for every buyer to have a thorough knowledge of Incoterms 2000 cannot be overstressed. This extends especially to the buyer's logistic import team responsible for processing the imported product and the interpretation of the Incoterm 2000. The booklet, Incoterms 2000 No. 560 is available from local chambers of commerce together with Incoterms 2000 – Transport obligations cost and risks diagram, ICC 1999 publication No. 614.

An international trade deal can involve up to four contracts and the buyer or importer must have a broad understanding of each of them. The four contracts are:

(a) the contract of carriage – bill of lading, air waybill, etc.;
(b) the insurance contract (see Chapter 12);
(c) the contract of finance (ICC booklet No. 500 on Uniform Customs and Practice for Documentary Credit 1993);
(d) the export sales contract (usually involving Incoterms 2000).

There are three main areas of uncertainty in international trade contracts and their interpretation: (i) the uncertainty as to which country's law will be applicable to their contracts; (ii) the difficulty emerging from inadequate and unreliable information; (iii) the serious problem of the diversity of interpretation of the various trade terms. The latter point can involve costly litigation and the loss of much goodwill. Therefore there must be a practical relationship between the various contracts required to perform the international sales transaction. This usually embraces the four contracts mentioned earlier. However, it is stressed that Incoterms relate to only one of these contracts; namely the contract of sale. Furthermore, buyers using Incoterms 2000 should clearly specify that their contract is governed by 'Incoterms 2000'. It is important that the year 2000 features on the trade document, otherwise the possibility arises of interpretating an earlier edition (1990).

The role of Incoterms 2000 is adopted in 96 countries and provides the buyer and the seller with a set of international rules for the interpretation of 13 Incoterms. Such a range of terms enables the business person to decide which is the most suitable for his or her needs, knowing that interpretation of such terms will be the same in any individual country affiliated to the terms.

It must be recognized, however, that it is not always possible to give a precise interpretation. In such situations, one must rely on the customs of the trade at the airport, seaport or ICD. Buyers are urged to use terms which are subject to varying interpretation as little as possible and to rely on the well-established internationally accepted terms. The buyer must decide whether he or she wishes to control all the transportation arrangements and accept all the associated costs as under Groups E and F (see Figure 14.1) or whether to entrust all the arrangements and much of the cost associated with Group C and D. Today more buyers are opting to take charge of the transportation and obtain the benefit of lower cost, especially when a high volume of business is involved. Alternatively, buyers keen to have competitive quotations on a delivered basis with much of the cost being borne by the seller and reflected in the price opt for Group D. Today, there is movement away from the port to port terms FOB, CIF, CFR and more towards multi-modalism – combined transport embracing the sea and/or air leg plus the overland connections. The previous two revisions of Incoterms 1990 and 2000 reflects this trend as globalization develops and the role of EDI becomes more prominent. Logistics and their buyers' teams are driving this trend together with the continuing expansion and development of the international infra-structure, especially containerization. The buyer accordingly is urged to take full advantage of the resources available and thereby develop a more competitive business by using the most advantageous Incoterm option.

The buyer is warned against varying the Incoterm 2000 used, for example EXW loaded, FOB stowed, DDP (delivered duty paid). The addition of a word or letter could change the contract and its interpretation. It is essential that any such variation be explicitly stated in the contract to ensure that each party to the contract is aware of its obligations and acts accordingly. Basically, whenever possible, the same expressions as found in the 1980 UN Convention on Contracts for the International Sale of Goods (CISG) has been used in the Incoterms 2000.

Four further points need to be considered. The role of the bill of lading is fully explained on pages 163–9. Incoterm 2000 recognizes that paper documents may be replaced by electronic messages, provided the parties have agreed to communicate electronically. Such messages could be transmitted directly to the party concerned or through a third party. One such service that can be usefully provided by a third party is the registration of successive holders of a bill of lading. Systems providing such services – for example the Bolero service – may require further support by appropriate legal norms and principles as found in the CMI 1990 rules for Electronic Bills of Lading and articles 16–17 of the 1996 UNCITRAL Model Law on Electronics Commerce.

The second point is that the buyer and the seller must remember that Incoterms 2000 only define their relationship in contract terms and has no bearing directly or indirectly on the carrier's obligations to them as found in the contract of carriage. The law of carriage will determine how the seller under the Group F terms should fulfil his or her obligation. In practice the Incoterm 2000 F Group requires the seller to deliver the goods for carriage as instructed by the buyer.

A further point is the increasingly common practice for the buyer to arrange pre-shipment of the goods at the place of shipment. It is desirable that this location is specified at the time when the contract of sale is entered into.

The final point for both the buyer and the seller to bear in mind is that the seller is under no obligation to procure an insurance policy for the buyer's benefit under any of the 13 terms except CIF and CIP. However, in practice, many contracts request the buyer or seller to arrange insurance from point of departure in the country of departure to the point of final destination chosen by the buyer.

Incoterms 2000

A summary of the 13 terms are given in Table 14.1 (see also Figure 14.1 page 288 Incoterm 2000 group analysis).

An area of importance relative to Incoterms 2000 is the risk of loss or damage to the goods and the obligation to bear the cost relating to the goods passing from the seller to the buyer when the seller has fulfilled his or her obligations. In reality, this happens when the title or ownership of the goods passes from the seller to the buyer. A summary of when this transfer occurs is given below.

Group E

EXW – When the goods have been delivered by the seller at the named place at the seller's premises or another named place, for example a warehouse not cleared

TABLE 14.1 Incoterms 2000 –

Group	Description	Abbreviation	Meaning
Group E	Departure from factory – all carriage paid by the buyer.	EXW	Ex works
Group F	Main carriage unpaid by seller	FCA FAS FOB	Free carrier Free alongside ship Free on board
Group C	Main carriage paid by seller	CPT CIP CFR CIF	Carriage paid to Carriage and insurance paid to Cost and freight Cost insurance and freight
Group D	Arrival – carriage to delivered paid by the seller	DAF DES DEQ DDU DDP	Delivered at frontier Delivered ex-ship Delivered ex-quay Delivered duty unpaid Delivered duty paid

DAF – Delivery at terminal
DAP – Delivery at place

Incoterms 2000 – Group Analysis

Group E

> EXW – Ex Works (. . . named place) – suitable for all modes of transport – buyer collects and responsible for all carriage

Group F

> FCA Free Carrier (. . . named place) – suitable for all modes of transport – main carriage unpaid
>
> FAS Free Alongside Ship (. . . named port of shipment) – suitable for maritime and inland waterway transport only – main carriage unpaid
>
> FOB Free On Board (. . . named port of shipment) – suitable for maritime and inland waterway transport only – main carriage unpaid

Group C

> CPT Carriage Paid to (. . . named place of destination) – suitable for all modes of transport – main carriage paid
>
> CIP Carriage and Insurance Paid to (. . . named place of destination) – suitable for all modes of transport – main carriage paid
>
> CFR Cost and Freight (. . . named port of destination) – suitable for maritime and inland waterway transport only – main carriage paid
>
> CIF Cost Insurance and Freight (. . . named port of destination) – suitable for maritime and inland waterway transport only – main carriage paid

Group D

> DAF Delivered at Frontier (. . . named place) – suitable for all modes of transport – delivered at frontier point
>
> DDU Delivered Duty Unpaid (. . . named place of destination) – suitable for all modes of transport – delivered at named place of destination
>
> DDP Delivered Duty Paid (. . . named place of destination) – suitable for all modes of transport – delivered at named place of destination
>
> DES Delivered Ex Ship (. . . named port of destination) – suitable for maritime and inland waterway transport only – delivered on board the vessel at the named port of destination
>
> DEQ Delivered Ex Quay (. . . named port of destination) – suitable for maritime and inland waterway transport only – delivered on board the named quay (wharf) at the specified port of destination

E Term – is the term in which the buyer's obligation is at its maximum.

F Term – requires the seller to deliver the goods for carriage as instructed by the buyer.

C Term – requires the seller to contract for carriage on usual terms at his own expense.

D Term – requires the seller to be responsible for the arrival of the goods at the agreed place or point of destination at the border and within the country of import. The seller must bear all the risk ad cost in bringing the goods thereto.

[handwritten margin note: More sufficient for buyer]

FIGURE 14.1 Incoterm 2000 analysis

for export and not loaded on any collecting vehicle and prior to export customs clearance.

Group F

FCA – When the goods have been delivered to the carrier by the seller at the named place after export customs clearance.

FAS – When the goods have been placed alongside the ship by the seller at the named port of shipment after export customs clearance.

FOB – When the goods pass the ship's rail at the named port of shipment by the seller after export customs clearance.

Group C

CFR – When the goods pass the ship's rail at the named port of shipment by the seller after export customs clearance.

CIF – When the goods pass the ship's rail at the named port of shipment by the seller after export customs clearance.

CPT – When the goods have been delivered by the seller to the nominated first carrier after export customs clearance.

CIP – When the goods have been delivered by the seller to the nominated first carrier after export customs clearance.

Group D

DAF – When the goods have been delivered by the seller at the named frontier place before import customs clearance.

DES – When the goods have been delivered by the seller on board the ship at the named port of destination prior to import customs clearance.

DEQ – When the goods have been delivered by the seller on the quay or wharf at the named port of destination prior to import customs clearance.

DDU – When the goods have been delivered by the carrier or seller at the named place of destination prior to unloading and import customs clearance.

DDP – When the goods have been delivered by the seller cleared for import customs clearance but not unloaded.

Incoterms 2000 can be divided into recommended usages by modes of transport as follows: all modes (i.e. combined transport) EXW, FCA, CPT, CIP, DAF, DDU; and conventional port to port or sea transport only FAS, FOB, CFR, CIF, DES, DEQ. The buyer must ensure the correct terms are used. Consider a containerized contract applying FOB or CFR where the risk transfers from seller to buyer on loading on board ship. On delivery damage is discovered. It is impossible to show where the damage arose, and whether it was before or after shipment. Under FOB/CFR a dispute would ensue; under FCA/CPT it would be clear that the risk would be with the buyer once the goods are in the hands of the combined transport operator for carriage. Incoterms 2000 reflect the changes and development of combined transport and associated documentation together with electronic data interchange. In analysing each term the buyer and seller should identify a number of aspects. For the seller the following aspects are relevant:

(a) supplying (goods) in conformity with the contract;
(b) licences and authorizations;
(c) place of delivery (not delivery of goods);
(d) carriage of goods contract and insurance;
(e) documentation and notice to buyer;
(f) transfer of risks;
(g) transfer and division of costs;
(h) checking, packages marking;
(i) other obligations.

For the buyer, the relevant aspects to consider are:

(a) licences and authorizations;
(b) notices, receipt of documents;
(c) taking delivery;
(d) transfer of risks;
(e) transfer and division of costs;
(f) other obligations.

As we progress through the next decade the transmission of documents and trade information by electronic commerce will become increasingly common (see page 312). Moreover, the buyer will require a delivered price (group D) to enable him or her to compare quotations on a like for like basis from different originating countries. This will obviate the buyer having to calculate the distribution cost as an add-on to the Incoterm 2000.

Factors determining the choice of Incoterms 2000

Personnel involved in buying goods overseas have a wide choice in selecting the cargo delivery term most acceptable to the sale. The strategy boils down to two options for many buyers. First, to take control of the goods transportation arrangements and accept the related cost as found under EXW or FCA. This will probably involve appointing a forwarding agent in the seller's country to coordinate all the resources, which is likely to involve a combined transport shipment. The other option is to accept quotations on a delivered price basis under a combined transport arrangement embracing CIP, CPT, DDU, DDP and DAF – especially the latter three.

The following factors are relevant in the evaluation of the choice of cargo delivery term.

(a) Basically the buyer is the stronger party in the negotiations.
(b) The buyer has the opportunity of controlling the transit arrangements together with the cost when concluding contracts under EXW and FCA and funds them directly with the carrier. The importer of volume shipments from such a supplier may be able to get a discount through the quantity of business generated to the trade or route.
(c) An increasing number of less developed countries follow a policy of encouraging buyers to ship their goods on their national airlines or shipping lines.
(d) The seller can maximize his or her income when selling under CIP/CIF terms.

Overall, the most decisive factors in determining the ideal Incoterm 2000 are experience of the trading market and development of a good business relationship between buyer and seller. Every effort should be made to buy under combined transport terms (Figure 14.2).

Description of Incoterms 2000

EXW (ex works) named place

This term commits the buyer to the maximum arrangements for the conveyance of the consignment to the specified destination. The supplier merely ensures that the goods are available at an agreed date at his or her premises, factory or warehouse. The seller minimizes his or her obligations whilst the buyer obtains the goods at the lowest possible price by contracting with the carrier to the destination specified and securing insurance cover for the transit throughout. The seller's obligations cease when the buyer accepts the goods at his or her premises, factory or warehouse. It is usual for the buyer to appoint an agent in the seller's country to look after all the collection, transportation, insurance and documentation arrangements in consultation with a shipping line or airline and involving a container, truck or palletized shipment. If the parties agree, the seller can be responsible for the loading of goods on departure and bear all the risk and cost.

The principal obligations of the seller include the following.

(a) Supplying the goods in accordance with the contract of sale.
(b) Making the goods available to the buyer at the customary delivery point or as specified in the contract of sale to enable the goods to be conveyed on the transport unit arranged by the buyer.
(c) Providing, at his or her expense, the necessary packing (if any) to enable the buyer to convey the goods on the specified transport.
(d) Giving the buyer prompt notice when the goods will be available for collection.

Salient Features Emerging From Incoterms 2000

(a) the Incoterms have tended to focus on the tangibles in the contract of sale and not intangibles as found in computer software;

(b) Incoterms embraces the contract of sale and relations between the buyer and seller. It only has an interface with the contracts of insurance, transport and finance and no *prima facie* legal specifications regarding the duties the parties may wish to include in the contract of sale;

(c) Incoterms remain primarily intended for use where goods are sold for delivery across national boundaries;

(d) revision needed to adapt to the terms of contemporary commercial practice;

(e) substantive changes have been made in two areas: customs clearance and payment of duty obligations under FAS and DEQ (see p. 297) and loading and unloading obligations under FCA (see p. 298);

(f) the terms are, wherever possible, the same expressions as those in the 1980 UN Convention on the Contracts for the International Sales of Goods;

(g) the opportunity has been taken in the 'introduction' of ICC booklet No 560 to clarify a number of terms featured in the 13 Incoterms. These include shipper, delivery, usual, charges, ports, places, points, premises, ship, vessel, checking, inspection, no obligation, customs clearance, and packaging;

(h) a feature of the 1990 revision of Incoterms identified the clauses dealing with the seller's obligation to provide proof of delivery permitting a replacement of paper documentation by EDI messages provided the parties had agreed to communicate electronically. The 2000 revision has endeavoured to improve upon the drafting and presentation of the Incoterms in order to facilitate their practical implementation.

FIGURE 14.2 Incoterms 2000 – salient features

(e) Bearing all risks and expenses of the goods until they have been placed at the disposal of the buyer as specified in the contract of sale.

(f) Rendering the buyer on request every assistance to provide in the country of delivery or of cargo origin, all the relevant documentation required in the process of exportation.

Obviously the buyer's responsibilities are more extensive, as shown below.

(a) Taking delivery of the cargo and paying for the goods in accordance with the contract of sale terms.

(b) Funding any pre-shipment expense.

(c) Bearing all the cost and risk of the goods from the time they have been placed at his or her disposal by the seller in accordance with the sales contract terms.

(d) Funding any customs duties and taxes arising through exportation.

(e) Bearing additional costs incurred and any related risk inherent through the buyer to give instructions about the place of delivery within the prescribed period.

(f) Funding all costs in obtaining the documents required for the purpose of exportation and importation and for passing through transit countries.

The EXW should not be used where the buyer cannot obtain an export licence. In such a situation the FCA term should be used.

FOB (free on board) – named port of shipment – sea transport

This is a long established term and much case law exists in this area. Under this term the goods are placed on the ship by the seller at the specified departure port detailed in the sales contract. The risk of loss of, or damage to, the goods is transferred from the seller to the buyer when the goods pass over the ship's rail. Under such terms the seller bears all the cost and risk of conveyance up to the ship's rail and the buyer accepts the residue of the transit cost including sea freight and insurance. This term is used frequently and is to the advantage of the buyer because the cargo can be conveyed on the shipping line of his or her choice. Insurance is arranged by the buyer. Overall, the prime advantage to the buyer is that he or she takes charge of goods and transit from the time the goods pass over the ship's rail at the port of departure. The seller, however, is responsible for the export customs clearance. Given below are the seller's responsibilities.

(a) Supplying the goods in accordance with the contract of sale.

(b) Delivering the cargo on to the named vessel at the specified port of shipment within the agreed period or on the agreed date and in so doing promptly informing the buyer.

(c) Providing all the documentation and bearing all the costs to process the goods through export customs clearance.

(d) Bearing all the costs and risks of the goods until such time as the goods have effectively passed over the ship's rail at the departure port.

(e) Providing the customary packing of the goods unless it is the custom of the trade to ship the cargo unpacked.

(f) Paying the cost of any cargo scrutiny prior to delivery of the cargo.

(g) Providing the buyer on request and at the buyer's expense the certificate of origin.

(h) Supplying the buyer on request and at the buyer's expense every assistance to obtain a bill of lading, sea waybill and other documentation issued in the country of shipment or origin necessary for the importation process both in transit countries and the destination country.

The buyer's responsibilities are featured below.

(a) Arranging at his or her expense and risk the pre-shipment cargo inspection.

(b) Bearing all the costs and risks of the cargo from the time it has passed the ship's rail at the port of shipment and paying the price as specified in the contract of sale.

(c) Paying all costs to the seller to obtain bills of lading, certificate of origin, consular documents and any other documentation including electronic messages as proof of delivery required to process the cargo through importation both in transit countries and the country of destination.

The term is used only for sea transport – port to port. When the ship's rail serves no practical purpose, such as ro-ro or container traffic, the FCA term should be used.

CFR (cost and freight) – named port of destination

Under this term the seller must pay the costs necessary to bring the goods to the named port of shipment, the risk of loss or damage to the goods as well as of any additional expenses is transferred when the goods pass the ship's rail. This is identical to CIF except that the buyer is responsible for funding and arranging the cargo insurance.

The seller's obligations in CFR include the following.

(a) Supplying the goods in accordance with the contract terms.

(b) Arranging and paying for the conveyance of the goods to the specified port of destination by the customary route.

(c) Providing and paying for any export licence or other governmental authorization necessary to export the cargo.

(d) Funding all the export customs clearance arrangements at the port of departure.

(e) Bearing all the cargo risk until such time as it passes over the ship's rail at the port of departure.

(f) Supplying promptly and paying for the usual transport documents such as the clean shipped negotiable bill of lading for the agreed destination port, together with any invoice of the goods shipped.

(g) Providing and paying for the customary packing of the goods unless it is the custom of the trade to ship the cargo unpacked.

(h) Funding any cargo scrutiny prior to the loading of the cargo.

(i) Paying any cost of dues and taxes incurred relative to the process of exportation in respect of the cargo prior to shipment.

(j) Providing the buyer on request and at the buyer's expense a certificate of origin and consular invoice.

(k) Rendering the buyer on request and at the buyer's expense and risk every assistance to obtain any documents required in the country of shipment and transit countries necessary for the conveyance of the cargo to its destination. This features electronic messages as agreed between the seller and the buyer.

The buyer must ensure that the seller provides a full set of clean on board or shipped bills of lading. If the bill of lading contains a reference to the charter party, the seller must also provide a copy of the latter. The buyer must ensure these provisions are complied with by the seller. The factors relevant to the buyer include the following.

(a) Acceptance of the documents as tendered by the seller (subject to their conformity with the terms of the contract) and payment of the goods, etc. as specified in the contract of sale.

(b) Receiving the goods at the port of destination and with the exception of the sea freight, all the costs and charges incurred during the voyages.

(c) Funding all the unloading expenses at the destination port including lighterage, wharfage, etc. unless such costs have been included in the freight or collected by the shipowner at the time freight was paid.

(d) Funding any pre-shipment cargo inspection arrangements.

(e) Undertaking all the risk when the cargo has passed the ship's rail at the departure port, in the event of the buyer failing to give instructions (by the specified date or within the agreed period) relative to the destination port, all additional costs and risks will be borne by the buyer subject to the goods being duly appropriated to the contract.

(f) Paying all the costs to obtain the certificate of origin and consular documents.

(g) Meeting all charges to provide any other documentation specified relative to processing the consignment in the country or transit countries.

(h) Paying all customs duties and other taxes raised at the time of importation.

(i) Obtaining and paying for any import licence or related documentation required at the time of importation. Also electronic messages as agreed with the buyer or seller.

(j) The cost of transporting goods to the buyer's premises beyond the destination seaport is for the buyer's account and likewise the risk emerging therefrom.

The CFR permits the buyer to arrange and fund the cargo insurance. The CFR term should be used only for sea and inland water transport. When the ship's rail serves no practical purpose, as in the case of ro-ro or container traffic, the CPT term should be used.

CIF (cost, insurance and freight) – named port destination

This is a long-established and popular cargo delivery term. It is identical to CFR except that the seller arranges and funds the cargo insurance and not the buyer. A point to bear in mind concerning insurance cover is that the seller has to procure marine insurance against the buyer's risk of loss or damage against minimum coverage and duration to the goods during the carriage. In the event of the buyer wishing to have the protection of greater cover, the buyer would either need to agree as much expressly with the seller, or to make his or her own extra insurance arrangements.

Overall, the seller delivers the goods when they pass the ship's rail at the departure port. The seller must pay the costs and freight necessary to bring the goods to the named port of destination but the risk of loss of or damage to the goods, as well as any additional costs due to events occurring after the time of delivery are transferred from the seller to the buyer. The seller is required to clear the goods for export.

DES (delivered ex ship) – named port of destination

This cargo delivery term is not used extensively. It requires the seller to make the goods available to the buyer on board the vessel at the destination seaport specified in the contract. The seller has to bear the full cost and risk of the goods to bring them to the destination port. The cost and arrangements to unload the cargo at the destination seaport and process the goods through importation are borne by the buyer.

The seller's main obligations embrace the following.

(a) Supplying the goods in accordance with the contract of sale terms.
(b) Making the goods available to the buyer on board the vessel at the agreed destination point to enable the cargo to be conveniently discharged.
(c) Bearing all risk and expense of the cargo conveyance to the destination port until promptly collected by the buyer.
(d) Providing and paying for the customary packing of the goods unless it is the custom of the trade to ship the goods unpacked.
(e) Paying the cost of any cargo scrutiny prior to collection of the cargo by the buyer.
(f) Promptly informing the buyer of the expected date of arrival of the vessel and providing the buyer with a bill of lading and any other documents to enable the buyer to take delivery of the consignment. This may be an electronic message as agreed with the seller and the buyer.
(g) Providing the buyer on request and at his or her expense the certificate of origin and/or consular invoice.
(h) Rendering the buyer on request and at the buyer's expense every assistance to provide the requisite documentation issued in the country of shipment and/or origin required for importation in the destination country or transit countries.

The obligations of the buyer include the following.

(a) Bearing all the risks and expenses from the time the cargo has been placed at the disposal of the buyer on board the vessel awaiting discharge at the destination port.
(b) Bearing all the cost associated with the provision of documentation obtained by the seller necessary for the importation of the goods in both destination and transit countries.
(c) Obtaining, at the buyer's expense, all licences or similar documents necessary for the importing process.
(d) Bearing all customs charges and other duties and taxes incurred at the time of importation.

The term can be used only when the goods are to be delivered by sea or inland waterway or multi-modal transport on a vessel in the port of destination. If the parties wish the seller to bear the costs and risks of discharging the goods, then the DEQ term should be used.

DEQ (delivered ex-quay) – named port of destination

Under this term the seller delivers the goods when they are placed on the quay or wharf and made available to the buyer who is responsible for import clearance. The seller has to bear the full cost and risk involved in bringing the goods to the quay. The buyer has to clear the goods for import and to pay all formalities duties, taxes and other charges upon import. If the parties wish to include in the seller's obligations all or part of the cost payable upon import of the goods, this should be made clear by adding explicit wording to this effect in the contract of sale.

The seller's obligations feature the following.

(a) Supplying the goods in accordance with the contract of sale terms.
(b) Making the goods available to the buyer at the specified quay or wharf within the period given in the sales contract and bearing all the associated risks and costs; the buyer being responsible for clearing the goods for import and paying for all the formalities.
(c) Providing and paying for the customary packing of the goods unless it is the custom of the trade to ship the cargo unpacked.

The buyer's main tasks are as follows.

(a) Paying the price as prescribed in the sales contract.
(b) Taking delivery of the goods as specified in the contract.
(c) Bearing all the expenses and risks of the goods from the time the cargo has been effectively placed at the disposal of the buyer.
(d) Bearing all the costs of importing the cargo.

The costs of pre-shipment are borne by the buyer.

The term can be used only when the goods are to be delivered by sea or inland waterway or multi-modal transport on discharging from a vessel on the quay in the port of destination. However, if the parties wish to include in the seller's obligations the risks and costs of the handling of the goods from the quay to another place (warehouse, terminal, etc.) in or outside the port, the DDU or DDP terms should be used.

FAS (free alongside ship) – named port of shipment

The obligations of the seller are realized when the goods have been placed alongside the quay or on lighterage at a specified port of shipment and export customs clearance has been completed. Hence, the buyer has to bear all the costs and risks of loss or damage to the goods from this point onwards. If, however, the parties wish the buyer to clear the goods for export, this must be stated explicitly in the contract of sale. Overall, it is an ideal term for the buyer who wishes to take charge of the transit following export customs clearance.

Given below are the salient features found in the FAS term relative to the seller.

(a) Supplying the goods in accordance with the contract of sale terms.
(b) Arranging delivery of the cargo by the date or within the agreed period alongside the specified vessel at the loading berth and port as named by the buyer.
(c) Obtaining, at the seller's expense, any export licence and other official authorization and carrying out all customs formalities necessary for the export of the goods.
(d) Bearing all costs and risks of the goods until they have been effectively delivered alongside the vessel and cleared through customs.
(e) Providing and paying for the customary packing of the goods unless it is the custom of the trade to ship the cargo unpacked.
(f) Rendering to the buyer on request and at the buyer's expense the certificate of origin.
(g) Assisting the buyer on request and at the buyer's expense to obtain any documents issued in the country of origin or shipment including bills of lading and/or consular documents required for importation of the goods into the destination country and their passage through transit countries. This will include cases where the seller and the buyer agree to use electronic messages.

The buyers responsibilities include the following.

(a) Giving the seller prompt notice of the name of the vessel, loading berth and delivery dates.
(b) Bearing all the expense and risk of the goods from when they have been effectively delivered alongside the vessel as specified which includes the export clearance undertaken by the seller.
(c) Funding any additional cost and accepting the risk in the event of the vessel not arriving on time or the shipowner being unable to accept the cargo.
(d) In the event of the buyer failing to notify the seller of the name of the vessel, and port of shipment within the prescribed period, the buyer would bear all consequential costs and risks from the expiry date of the notification period, subject to the goods being duly appropriated by the seller to the contract.
(e) Meeting all costs of obtaining any documents necessary for importation of the goods including the bill of lading and consular documents.

FCA (free carrier) – named place

This term is primarily used for the combined transport operation such as a container or ro-ro operation involving a road trailer and sea ferry. The term is ideal for the buyer who wishes to take charge of the transportation following export customs clearance undertaken by the seller at the carrier's premises nominated by the buyer. The chosen place of delivery has an impact on the obligation of loading and unloading the goods at that place. If delivery occurs at the seller's premises the seller is responsible for loading. If the delivery occurs at any other place the seller is not responsible for unloading. This term is also used by freight forwarders engaged in the international road haulage business transporting goods under the buyer's instructions. The risk of loss of or damage to the goods is transferred from the seller to the buyer at the time the nominated carrier accepts them at the prescribed place. When the seller has to render to the buyer, or other person prescribed, the bill of lading, waybill or carriers receipt as evidence of the delivery acceptance of the goods, the seller's contractual obligations are fulfilled. Such documentation may be communicated electronically in accordance with the agreement between the buyer and seller.

The FCA may be used for any mode of transport including multi-modal transport. The buyer must contract at his or her own expense for the carriage of goods from the named place, except when the contract of carriage is made by the seller at the buyer's request, risk and expense. Usually, the buyer entrusts all the transportation arrangements to an accredited forwarding agent located in the vicinity of the seller's premises. This term is increasingly preferred by the buyer.

CPT (carriage paid to) – named place of destination

Under this term, which is growing in popularity with the buyer, the seller not only delivers the goods to the carrier nominated by him or her, but must also pay the cost of carriage necessary to bring the goods to the named destination. This may involve several carriers under multi-modalism. The buyer's risk commences when the goods have been delivered into the custody of the first carrier.

The buyer is responsible for the import customs clearance and all the associated costs and documentation including transport documents. Such transport documents may be communicated electronically if the buyer and seller agree. The buyer must fund any pre-shipment inspection cost and cargo insurance. If the buyer and seller agree to the seller undertaking the insurance, the CIP term (see below) must be used. CPT may be used irrespective of the mode of transport including multi-modal transport which includes ro-ro and container movements.

CIP (carriage and insurance paid to) – named place of destination

This term is identical to CPT except the seller contracts to arrange and fund the cargo insurance against the buyer's risk of loss of or damage to the goods during the carriage. This is on a minimum cover basis to the contracted carriage of destination. If the buyer wishes to have greater cover, he or she would either agree as much expressly with the seller or to make his or her own extra insurance arrangements. The seller is responsible for export customs clearance, whilst the buyer is responsible for import customs clearance and associated costs including transport documents. The transport documents may be communicated electronically if the seller and buyer agree. The term is suitable for any transport mode and is ideal for the buyer who wishes the seller to quote a price inclusive of all carriage and insurance charges to a named destination beyond the airport and seaport usually involving an overland or waterway transit.

DAF (delivered at frontier) – named place

A major difference between DAF, DES, DEQ, DDU, DDP Group D and CFR, CIF, CPT, CIP Group C is that under the former the seller's cost and risk is maximized because he or she must make the goods available upon arrival at the agreed destination, whilst with the latter the seller arranges and pays for the main carriage but without assuming the risk of the main carriage. Hence, this is a further reason why buyers are preferring to opt for the Group D delivered Incoterm category.

Under the delivered at frontier term (DAF) the seller's obligations are concluded when the goods arrive at the named frontier point or place at the frontier but before the customs border of the adjoining country. A key factor in this term is to name the frontier and place. The seller is not responsible for unloading the cargo and associated risk unless the buyer and seller agree for the seller to undertake this task – unloading and risk – and be responsible for the cost. The buyer is responsible for the import customs clearance and transport documents. The transport documents may be communicated electronically provided the seller and the buyer agree. The cargo insurance provision and cost must be agreed between the seller and the buyer. Usually the buyer opts for the insurance cover funding. The pre-shipment inspection arrangements are arranged and funded by the buyer in consultation with the seller.

This term may be used irrespective of the transport mode when goods are to be delivered at a land frontier. When delivery is to take place in the port of destination, on board a vessel or on the quay (wharf), the DES or DEQ term should be used.

DDP (delivered duty paid) – named place of destination

This term is the ultimate term sought by the buyer who wishes to receive the goods at an inclusive delivered price to the consignee's premises named by the importer. The price of the goods will feature all the elements embracing the product, packaging, export and import customs clearance, carriage, import duty, taxes and other charges including loading and unloading. Insurance provision and funding arrangements are optional and the buyer and the seller must agree whichever party elects to undertake the responsibility. The buyer must arrange and fund any pre-shipment inspection arrangements. Proof of delivery involving the carrier's documents can be communicated by an electronic message if the buyer and seller agree. The seller may use his or her own transport throughout the conveyance. The buyer's role is to accept the goods at the named place of destination and the buyer is responsible for all subsequent movement and costs of the goods, including handling. Any form of transport may be used.

In a situation whereby the buyer or seller wishes to exclude the seller's obligations featuring some of the costs payable upon import of the goods, such as VAT, this must be made very explicit in the contract of sale and export invoice.

The DDP term should not be used if the seller is unable to obtain, directly or indirectly, an import licence. If the buyer wishes to bear all the risks and costs of the import, the term DDU (see below) should be used. When delivery is to take place in the port of destination on board the vessel or on the quay (wharf), the DES or DEQ terms should be used. This term may be used for any mode of transport.

Finally, the buyer should bear in mind that the DDP term represents the maximum obligation of the seller whereas the EXW term represents the minimum.

DDU (delivered duty unpaid) – named place of destination

This term is identical to DDP except the buyer is responsible for the import customs clearance embracing customs formalities and payment of formalities, customs duties, taxes and other charges. This term is popular amongst buyers. Hence, the seller fulfils his or her obligations when the goods have arrived at the named point or place of destination in the country of importation. The seller has to bear the full cost and risk involved in bringing the goods thereto, excluding import customs clearance and associated costs. If the parties wish to include in the seller's obligation the costs and risks of the import customs formalities, this must be made clear in explicit wording in the export sales contract. Hence, the buyer is responsible for import customs clearance and associated costs and documentation. If the buyer and seller agree the transport documents may be communicated electronically. Insurance provision is optional and the buyer and seller must agree whichever party elects to undertake the responsibility. The term may be used irrespective of transport mode. When, however, delivery is to take place in the port of destination on board the vessel or on the quay (wharf), the DES or DEQ terms should be used.

Summary

To conclude our comprehensive analysis of Incoterms 2000 focused particularly on the buyer's needs, the following checklist may prove helpful.

(a) Endeavour to do as much planning as possible for each imported consignment. Close liaison with the seller and the buyer's forwarding agent is essential.
(b) Ensure buying personnel are fully conversant with Incoterms 2000 especially delivered – Group D and EXW and FCA – whereby the buyer can take charge of the transit.
(c) All personnel involved in the documentation processing of the import consignment must be fully trained and professionally qualified involving, for

example, Chartered Institute of Purchasing and Supply, or Institute of Export qualifications.

(d) Take great care in selecting a suitable forwarding agent both in the seller's and buyer's countries.

(e) Monitor closely each stage of the transit – use a carrier with an on-line tracking system such as P&O Nedlloyd.

(f) Formulate a logistic supply chain plan.

(g) Regularly review the logistic supply chain arrangements. Keep up-to-date with changes and opportunities arising in the infrastructure.

(h) Adopt a financial focus on the delivery term used especially whether it is a delivered term or one where the buyer takes full control. Evaluate the value added benefit emerging and how it fits in with the logistics plan.

(i) Study closely the Uniform Customs and Practice for Documentary Credits 1993 ICC brochure No. 500.

Overseas trade contract

The formulation of the contract represents the conclusion of what may have been difficult and prolonged negotiations. The skills required and constituents of the contract were dealt with in Chapters 6 and 7. Emerging from the contract is the export sales contract, ultimately expressed in the export invoice. This represents a major document in the processing of the imported consignment and all other documents must be aligned with it. This document will feature the Incoterm chosen and will have an interface with the cargo insurance and finance arrangements. Given below are the main features contained in the export sales contract.

(a) The seller's registered name and address.

(b) The buyer's registered name and address.

(c) A short title of each party quoted in items (a) and (b).

(d) The purpose of the contract.

(e) Number and quantity of goods, precisely and fully described using a technical not a commercial description. The buyer must ensure that the good's description reconciles with the buyer's specification and customs tariff details (see page 264).

(f) The price. This may be in sterling, USD or euros. Goods sold in the buyer's currency ensures there is no currency exchange risk to the buyer, but products quoted in the seller's currency transfers all the risk to the buyer. The seller and buyer may opt to use a third currency, such as USD. Those buyers and sellers who are both located in the euro zone will use the euro, thereby obviating any currency risk between the two parties.

(g) Terms of delivery. The buyer opting to manage and control the multi-modal transit will opt for EXW, FCA, or FAS whilst those requiring a delivered price will choose CPT, CIP, DAF, DDU or DDP.

(h) Terms of payment – open account, letter of credit, etc. require careful evaluation.

(i) Method of shipment – ideally multi-modal if the product and infrastructure makes this feasible (see page 198).

(j) Cargo insurance (see page 243).

(k) Import and/or export licence details and other instructions.

(l) Shipping, freight and documentary requirements and/or instructions. This includes marking of cargo.

(m) Contract conditions, for example sale, cargo delivery, Incoterms 2000, performance (quality) of goods, arbitration, etc.

(n) Signature of both parties by responsible party director/manager.

The above checklist must not be regarded as an exhaustive model as each contract will reflect many varying conditions. Remember that negotiation is often done by electronic commerce as we enter the twenty-first century.

Management of the export order

A sound logistically focused strategy is required in the management and processing of the imported consignment. It must be fully integrated with the production, assembly, processing and distribution arrangements. The system must be fully computerized. Readers are urged to study the Purchasing and Supply Module flowchart shown in Figures 14.3 and 14.4.

Overall, there are six areas which require the attention of the procurement officer: cash flow, administration, payment, insurance, risk areas and total cost.

The time scale for payment can impose a severe strain on the smaller company with limited resources. The payment cycle is longer than in the domestic market. Moreover, if the product is under a staged payment system such as a ship, the shipowner may have to wait two or three years before the vessel is launched and operational and ultimately generates revenue. The payment cycle embraces not only the product price but also freight, insurance, customs tariff and VAT. Options do exist where the latter can be temporarily alleviated through good customs planning. Overall, payment for the goods requires an effective and professional system with continuous monitoring. The administration must be logistically driven and feature continuous product monitoring in the supply chain.

The payment must be budgetary controlled and this must be driven by the buyer's treasury department. It is closely related to the penultimate paragraph analysis of the time scale. Overall, it must ensure adequate funds are available to meet the payment terms. This may mean negotiating a loan with a bank.

Most buyers today opt to arrange their own insurance arrangements for the reasons outlined in Chapter 12. The insurance portfolio results must be monitored to ensure claims are kept to a minimum and likewise premiums.

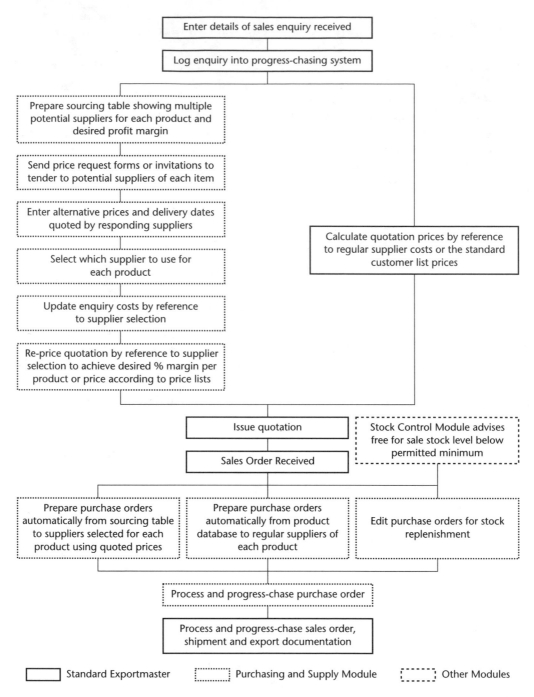

The flow chart above illustrates the usual way in which the Exportmaster Purchase and Supply System is used in an export department or trading office.

The program is very adaptable and configurable so many different combinations of procedures and documentation can be achieved. The full capabilities and possibilities of the system are best appreciated through a demonstration of the module in conjunction with the standard Exportmaster package. Please call us for details of scheduled demonstration dates.

FIGURE 14.3 Exportmaster Computerized Export Management System Purchasing and Supply Module

Sourcing products from multiple potential suppliers	Purchase order entry and editing
Price requests and invitations to tender	Purchase order documentation
Assembly of potential supplier pricing and delivery	Purchase order progress chasing
Pricing of sales quotations by reference to supplier offers	Status and action reporting
Automatic purchase order creation against sales orders	Database of supplier information

For export traders or manufacturers who buy in products for export, this module provides the means of creating supplier orders either for stock purchases or for back-to-back purchases against sales orders. It also offers powerful facilities for the sourcing and pricing of enquiries.

The purchase price and currency for a product may be held on the Exportmaster product database together with a supplier code. This code references supplier details, such as name, address, payment terms, etc., on a separate database with full maintenance facilities.

The sourcing section enables the user to enter multiple suppliers for each product in an enquiry, to add prices and delivery dates when quoted by each supplier and finally to select which supplier to use for each item. Quotations can be priced or re-priced and purchase orders prepared using this information automatically. Price request forms and various printed sourcing reports are available.

The editing section allows the user to prepare a purchase order in much the same way as an Exportmaster sales order. Standard data from the supplier database may be edited and merged with user inputs. Product line items together with their purchase prices may then be added by the user from the product database. In addition to allowing the preparation of completely new orders, this section permits editing of existing purchase orders and copying of master or previous orders.

The automatic section enables the user to prepare a purchase order or purchase orders from a selected sales order with a minimum of user input. The program scans each line item in the sales order, looks up the supplier code and price information in the product database or in a sourcing document, sorts out the line items into batches for each different supplier found, assembles a purchase order for each of the relevant suppliers and saves each order on file. Automatically prepared purchase orders may be amended by the user via the purchase order edit section.

The processing section permits documentation, status reporting and progress chasing, allows for the set-up of different purchase procedures and is fully user-configurable.

The module has full multi-currency capabilities. Purchase orders can be prepared in currencies different from those on sales orders or from the system's base currency. Different currencies can even be used for different products ordered from the same supplier.

The Purchasing and Supply System is an optional module designed for use with the Exportmaster export management package.

Exportmaster Limited, 33 St. Peter's Street, South Croydon, CR2 7DG
Tel: 020 8681 221 Fax: 020 8667 1816

FIGURE 14.4 Exportmaster Computerized Export Management System Purchasing and Supply Module

The risk areas are numerous. These embrace currency, liquidation of supplier, hostilities, loss of goods in transit, etc. The criteria of supplier and country sourcing selection need careful analysis.

The total cost requires continuous evaluation relative to all the elements. This embraces alternative suppliers, components and complete products; purchasing goods within the euro zone (see page 155) on a trans-EU basis rather than outside it; taking full advantage of customs planning (see page 196) and transport distribution analysis (see page 219) embracing quicker transits, different routes and modes and less capital tied up in transit.

The international trade market is one of continuous change and the buyer must be alert to this and the opportunities and risk it brings.

Processing the consignment through customs according to transport mode

Deep-sea containerization

The following discussion assumes the cargo originates outside the EU and is not in full circulation.

Most mega container operators import customs facilities are computer driven to assist importers to conduct an early release of the cargo by customs at the ports of arrival and inland clearance depots. Prior to the arrival of the vessel, the shipowner will despatch a 'notice of arrival' to the 'Notify Party' and 'Consignee' named on the bill of lading or waybill. This document provides details of the imported goods, expected vessel arrival date and the shipowner's local office dealing with the consignment. Any amendments to the delivery requirements or a transfer of interest in the goods must be notified to the shipowner.

If the sea freight and/or other charges are payable at the destination an invoice detailing these charges will be despatched to the nominated payer. In such instances it is important for the importer to arrange payment of these charges at the earliest opportunity. Such charges were due at the time of issue of the bill of lading and delivery of the goods cannot be effected until payment has been made.

Normally there are three restraints which have to be dealt with before the goods can be released to customers:

(a) clearance by customs or any other relevant authority, e.g. veterinary and forestry authorities;
(b) surrender of an original bill of lading or waybill correctly endorsed;
(c) payment of all outstanding charges.

In countries and ports where the consignment is delivered into and shipped out of a 'free port' the foregoing requirements may not be applicable.

In regard to customs clearance, the consignee must forward the requisite documentation to the import customs clearance agent or the local shipowner's office. Normally customs entries can be lodged prior to the arrival of the vessel and usually the time scale is four days prior to the vessel's arrival to gain a speedy customs clearance.

The documents required are detailed below:

(a) completed valuation form for Customs DVI/C 105 or general valuation statement if goods are dutiable and exceed £4000 CIF value (2000);
(b) certificate of origin;
(c) supplier's invoices;
(d) import licence;
(e) packing list;
(f) health certificate as appropriate;
(g) preference certificates e.g. GSP, EUR 1.

Most customs entries which are despatched from the shipowner's or agent's office use the direct trader input (DTI) system for customs entry clearance. Additionally, many such offices can lodge entries in the entry processing unit (EPU) associated with the inland clearance depot (ICD) or port. Such entries must be submitted four working days prior to the vessel's arrival. Delay in submitting the customs entry can delay import clearance with the prospect of incurring storage costs in the warehouse. Customs have the right to examine the goods presented for import customs clearance. This is called 'turn out' and the cost is borne by the consignee: the container is opened up, its contents examined and the customs entry validity and associated documentation checked. Ultimately, if the Customs are satisfied with the customs entry, they will issue a release document. At this stage import duty and VAT charges (see page 275) will be raised and must be paid before release of the goods unless deferred payments exist. The next phase is the release of the goods by the shipowner or agent on presentation of an original bill of lading correctly endorsed or the waybill. Payment of any freight charges must be made prior to the release of the goods.

Buyers resident in the USA importing containerized shipments must follow a slightly different import customs clearance procedure. Custom House Brokers have facilities at US arrival ports and inland regional depots to clear goods. A computerized system is linked to the US Customs Service. Approximately seven days' customs clearance notice is required prior to the arrival of the vessel at a US port. Shipowners must respond accordingly and despatch on 'arrival notice' to the notify party and consignee named in the bill of lading or waybill. Customs entries can be lodged three days prior to arrival of the vessel. The documents required include: certificate of origin; supplier's invoice; import licence; packing list; health certificate; etc. and a copy of the bill of lading. If ocean freight is to be paid at destination, a freight invoice detailing the freight and charges due will be raised. Normally there are three prerequisites to the carrier releasing the goods to a customer.

(a) Clearance by customs or any other relevant governmental agency, e.g. US Department Agriculture, or the Food and Drug Administration.

(b) Surrender of the original bill of lading correctly endorsed through to the party claiming delivery or proof of identity if the contract of carriage is a negotiable bill of lading.

(c) Payment of outstanding freight and charges. Before goods covered by a negotiable bill of lading can be released it must be correctly endorsed and surrendered to the shipowner or agent. Goods which are not cleared and removed from the ocean terminal within eight days may be taken into General Order Status, although actual practice may vary from one Customs District to another. General Order involves seizure by customs. If such goods are subsequently not released they may be sold on without prior notice to the importer and expenses incurred deducted before remitting any balance to the importer. Payment of freight and charges must be made prior to the release of the goods.

Bulk cargo shipment

A significant volume of cargo is moved in bulk shipments. These embrace raw materials, foodstuffs and manufactured goods such as cars. The vessel may be under charter to the supplier (manufacturer) or buyer. The ship will be under a charter party contract and the merchandise carried will feature on the bill of lading or sea waybill. These are subservient to the charter party. The customs clearance procedure will be broadly the same as for a containerized movement subject to any variation applicable to the commodity shipped. Customs are particularly interested in the relevant health certificates associated with the product and its quality and weight or quantity. This may embrace a weight certificate (see page 180).

Trailer cargo

A large volume of trailer movements move in 'free circulation' trans-EU business. Such movements cross national boundaries by road or by ferry. The cargo movement is subject to VAT compliance as explained on pages 275–83.

For goods originating outside the EU, such as Switzerland, the customs procedure explained for containerized business will apply. The carrier's document is the CMR consignment (see page 170). Cargo may be cleared within 4–6 hours following arrival at the ferry port.

Air freight

A large volume of goods is imported by air freight, much of it under consolidated movement involving the IATA Agent. The documentation and procedure are similar to goods originating in maritime containers outside the EU. However, the exceptions are that the carrier's document is the air waybill, house air waybill, and the customs entry can be presented some four days prior to the arrival of the aircraft. Stringent security checks are in operation in processing the cargo when presented to the airline by the shipper or airline.

Dangerous cargo

Dangerous classified cargo is subject to stringent regulations both by air and sea regarding documentation, stowage, packaging, handling, quantities labelling, etc.

The goods are subject to stringent examination at the time of shipment, whether by container, trailer or air. The carrier's document, embracing the dangerous goods note, will feature the commodity classification and technical cargo description signed by an executive of the shipper. Imports for goods not in 'free circulation' are similar to the containerized cargo but usually more rigorous. Customs clearance is usually accorded a priority and adequate planning and preparation by the buyer and clearance agent is paramount to ensure prompt customs clearance.

Recommended reading

- Incoterms 2000, ICC publication No. 560.
- HM Customs & Excise notices, as prescribed.

15

International purchasing facilitation

We have now reached the final chapter and it is appropriate that we examine a range of import facilitation organizations and major trading blocs which the buyer can target.

Import trade facilitation organizations

British Importers Association

The British Importers Association aims to look after the interest of importers concerned with importing into the UK. It is the flag ship of the importing business and grows in influence annually. Membership is comprised of individual businesses and import trade associations. There are three types of membership:

(a) *Ordinary membership*. Open to companies, firms, partnerships or sole traders in the United Kingdom principally concerned with importing or providing import services.
(b) *Association membership*. Open to trade associations and similar organizations in the United Kingdom whose members are concerned with importing.
(c) *International membership*. Open to foreign organizations engaged in trade or promotion of trade with the United Kingdom.

The Association works closely with HM Customs and Excise, and the Department of Trade and Industry when new import policies and tariffs are being negotiated. It produces a bi-monthly magazine *Importing Today* and runs seminars.

Readers are urged to visit their website. E-mail import@hemming-group.co.uk. Similar organizations exist in countries overseas.

Chambers of Commerce

Most countries of the world have in their major commercial/industrial cities a Chamber of Commerce. This organization is often affiliated to the Central Chamber of Commerce in their capital city and usually bears the name of the International Chamber of Commerce. The National Chamber of Commerce is likewise responsible to the International Chamber of Commerce whose headquarters are in Paris.

Overall, the local Chamber of Commerce is an excellent data source of import information. Many have an on-line database available to their members.

Additionally, many developed and developing countries have their own National Chamber of Commerce based in major countries of the world. For example, in London you will find the Arab–British Chamber of Commerce, the Brazilian Chamber of Commerce, the Belgian Chamber of Commerce, the Japanese Chamber of Commerce, the Netherlands–British Chamber of Commerce, the New Zealand UK Chamber of Commerce and the American Chamber of Commerce. This list is not exhaustive. These bodies can provides a wealth of data promoting their countries' goods and services. All are available on the Internet. Major trading countries have similar National Chambers of Commerce in their capitals.

Trade associations

Trade associations represent their members and promote their products. A large number exist in the United Kingdom and many are import focused. These include the Oriental Carpet Traders of London, the Association of Canned and Preserved Food Importers and Distributors, the British Jewellery and Giftware Association, the British Photographic Importers Association, the Fruit Importers Association, the Toy and Giftware Importers Association and the Watch and Clock Importers Association. All are available on the Internet. Similar organizations, often of wider diversity, exist in countries worldwide. They are particularly useful as a data source for information on import regulations and reliable importers.

Organisation for Economic Co-operation and Development (OECD)

The Organisation for Economic Co-operation and Development (OECD) is based in Paris, France. It has 25 member countries plus 33 countries classified as partners in a transition programme – a forum permitting the governments of the industrialized democracies to study and formulate the best possible policies in all economic and social spheres.

Issues, examined in recent years by the OECD include the creation of employment; economic growth and rising living standards through fiscal, monetary and structural economic policies; managing competition among nations in an era which is seeing the globalization of production and the continuing opening of borders to trade and investment; trade facilitation such as through certification of agricultural seeds; consolidating and advancing reform in agricultural policies and improving the efficiency of governments and the quality of public sector spending and taxation.

Overseas buyers are urged to visit the OECD website for product sourcing opportunities and market trends and to study or evaluate the OECD's country reports and opportunities.

The Baltic and International Maritime Conference (BIMCO)

The Baltic and International Maritime Conference (BIMCO) is based in Bagsvaerdvej, Denmark and serves as a forum in which shipowners and other persons and organizations concerned with the shipping industry can consider action on all matters affecting their industry and can establish contacts with charterers, shippers, merchants, receivers or other interested parties. BIMCO has acted as a hub for the exchange of information for nine decades and has an extensive database on world ports facilities and charges; trades; freight taxes; bill of lading and charter party documents; and shipping software data in 70 countries. It also produces BIMCO bulletins and market reports on a wide range of products. International Purchasing personnel are urged to visit the BIMCO website http://www.bimco.dk

Barclays Bank PLC

Barclays Bank PLC is one of a number of banks which provide regular data on a range of products for the international trade entrepreneur. These include individual country reports totalling over 50 countries, plus the *West European Economic Survey, Commodities Survey, Euro Zone* and *Quarterly Economic* reviews.

Overseas buyers are encouraged to contact Barclays and benefit from their global markets data. E-mail: information centre@barclays.co.uk

Electronic commerce

We have already discussed in many parts of this book electronic commerce and we have mentioned the Bolero system. The author makes no apology for featuring it again, particularly with reference to an address given by Jim Poon OOCL's Managing Director for Asia Pacific at the Singapore 2000 Conference in March 2000. Poon stressed that IT – in particular e-commerce – will have as huge an impact on the shipping industry as containerization first had 35 years ago, revolutionizing the way in which traders and merchants communicate and do business with customers. E-commerce epitomizes the future. Moreover, it is just another tool of business – albeit a tool which is changing the way in which operators serve their customers (importers and exporters).

Until recently e-commerce concentrated on business to business. This is beginning to change, with a greater emphasis on diversifying and involving all sectors of the international trade business. It is forecast that it will grow from US$50 billion in 1998, to one trillion by 2001 and seven trillion by 2004, representing 7 per cent of the world trade.

The impact of this development will be very profound on the container industry in the area of supply chain management. It will bring about a de-layering effect enabling businesses to eliminate inefficient components, to downsize organizations, to improve business processes and to customize solutions for the smallest customer segment. In effect the entire supply chain management in logistics can now become a virtual enterprise with all participants – from shippers, shipping companies, logistic providers and eventually retailers and consumers joining together to form a strategic alliance.

New technology has given shippers unprecedented control by making bookings on the Web directly – and in so doing by-passing customer services. This is in addition to tracking and tracing cargo movements throughout their transit.

The OOCL was one of the first container carriers to launch the internet bill of lading. This facility is linked to the 'Bolero' which seeks to eliminate paper documents and replace documents of title with secure electronic messages. The idea is to use electronic waybills as contracts of carriage or receipts and for the central data registry to perform the document of title control function, thereby retaining the document of title approach, to which commerce appears to be inextricably attached as the only way to operate a secure international transaction.

To date Bolero has proceeded as a project assisted by funds from the EU and BIMCO, without succeeding in producing a viable system. Currently a Bolero Association has been formed as a 'Club' of interested parties, including exporters, importers, freight forwarders, carriers, banks and insurers to develop the idea to fruition. The Association is funded by membership subscriptions and sponsorship by SWIFT who act as the central registry and the TT Club (a special mutual insurer of carriers and allied contractors).

One of the problems and restrictions of the 'Bolero' system is that it can only operate between users who are members of the Association and have signed an undertaking to abide by a detailed set of rules to create contractual rights, duties and obligations between users to replicate the effect of existing trade laws and practices (e.g. Documents of Title) in order to facilitate the financing of letter of credit transactions using the concept of holdership (the right to obtain delivery of the goods) which is transferable. To transfer the title to non-members requires reversion to a paper document. In short, future technology is restrained to meet the constraints of present day operations.

In September 1999 the Bolero Association commenced operations offering a service to a restricted number of members. This was accomplished after a series of delays to overcome problems, not least of which was how to overcome the potential exposure if Bolero ordered delivery of a valuable cargo to the wrong party. However, a contractual limit has been evolved of US$100 000 per incident which is rather inadequate for high value commodity contracts.

The cost of the service is still far from clear but its complexity must prevent it from being cheap. Bolero claim, however, that compared to the alleged cost of inefficient paper based systems, cost will be outweighed by savings and will be further enhanced by the increased efficiencies it will bring to its users. The Association sees 'Bolero' operating for waybills as well as a central clearing house for all international trade documents including bill of lading. It is to be noted that the Incoterm 2000 acknowledges in each of the 13 terms that electronic commerce may be used for the carrier's documents subject to the agreement of the buyer and seller.

The buyer is urged to keep up-to-date on the development of electronic commerce on a global basis.

Economic blocs and customs unions

Economic blocs and customs unions are ideal markets to target for product sourcing. Moreover, their market share of world trade continues to grow and most have bi-lateral or multi-lateral trade agreements with other countries and/or economic blocs or customs unions, offering very favourable trading conditions especially in the areas of preferential tariffs and quota systems.

Over 100 economic blocs and customs unions are in existence and many of them are being enlarged through increased membership, such as the EU, whilst new ones are being formed and developed.

Features of economic blocs and customs unions of special interest to the procurement officer include the following:

(a) lower tariffs;
(b) more competitive in price terms and product specification/design;
(c) higher political profile;
(d) lower risk;
(e) more political and exchange risk stability;
(f) increased volume of inwards investment;
(g) encourages infrastructure development and higher standards through inwards investment and more MNIs raising management standards and efficiency and lower unit costs;
(h) much improved channels of distribution and stimulation of logistical focus;
(i) develops fully the economic blocs and customs union resources and extols the best practice concept;
(j) opens up new markets and a fresh generation of management culture and technical skills;
(k) attracts expatriates who bring new skills and raise expectations within the region.

The international purchaser is urged to visit the websites of the following selection of economic blocs and focus particularly on their commodities currently available and future investment plans and trends. A visit to the region is urged in the longer term relative to any product sought.

European Union (EU) – Economic and Monetary Union

Some fifteen Member States – Austria, Belgium, Denmark, Finland, France, Germany, Greece, Ireland, Italy, Luxembourg, Portugal, Spain, Sweden, the Netherlands and the United Kingdom. Twelve of the countries operate within the euro zone (see page 155) the exceptions being the United Kingdom, Denmark and Portugal.

European Free Trade Agreement (EFTA)

The European Free Trade Agreement (EFTA) is a trading and economic bloc involving seven countries – Austria, Finland, Iceland, Liechtenstein, Norway, Sweden and Switzerland.

North American Free Trade Agreement (NAFTA)

The three countries Mexico, Canada and the USA, constitute one of the world's largest and richest trading blocs. By 2007 it is planned to abolish almost all tariffs and trade barriers. Mexico signed a trade liberalization agreement with the EU operative in 2001 (see page 316).

Association of South East Asian Nations (ASEAN)

ASEAN was formed in 1967 and today has ten members including Brunei, Cambodia, Indonesia, Lao PDR, Malaysia, Myanmar, the Philippines, Singapore, Thailand and Vietnam. It is a trading group which has certain economic and free trading links designed to develop the resources in the region and free trading links.

MERCOSUR

Mercosur was formed in 1985 and today embraces Argentina, Brazil and Uruguay with Chile and Bolivia as associate members. A customs union was formed in 1995 and, in the same year, trade liberalization with the EU.

Asia Pacific Economic Co-operation (APEC)

The Asia Pacific Economic Co-operation forum objective is to create a goal of free trade in the Pacific by 2020. No trade agreement exists at the moment. It has a membership of 12 countries including the USA, Japan, Malaysia, Australia, Thailand, etc.

CARICOM

The Caribbean Community and Common Market is the Caribbean trade bloc and a regional community whose principal objective is economic integration. It has 14 members.

Commonwealth of Independent States (CIS)

Formed in 1991 as a successor to the Soviet Union, the Commonwealth of Independent States embraces Armenia, Turkmenistan, Tajikistan, Kyrgystan, Georgia, the Russian Federation, Uzbekistan, Azerbaijan, Ukraine, Belarus, Moldova and Kazakhstan.

Central American Common Market (CACM)

Members – Costa Rica, Guatemala, El Salvador, Honduras and Nicaragua.

Latin American Integration Association (LAIA)

Members include Argentina, Bolivia, Brazil, Chile, Colombia, Ecuador, Mexico, Paraguay, Peru, Uruguay and Venezuela.

The Commonwealth

A long-established group of countries with strong economic and political ties of which the United Kingdom is the mother country with the monarch as the head of the Commonwealth. Leading countries include Australia, New Zealand, the United Kingdom, India, Pakistan, Canada, Singapore, Malaysia, Bahamas and South Africa. Preferential tariff agreements exist between the United Kingdom and Commonwealth countries.

Economic Community of West African States (ECOWAS)

Members include Benin, Burkina Faso, Cape Verde, Gambia, Ghana, Guinea, Guinea-Bissau, Côte d'Ivoire, Liberia, Mali, Mauritania, Niger, Nigeria, Senegal, Sierra Leone and Togo.

Communauté Francaise Africaine (CFA)

The Franc Zone members Benin, Burkina Faso, Cameroon, Central African Republic, Chad, Comoro Islands, Congo, Côte d'Ivoire, Equatorial Guinea, Gabon, Mali, Niger, Togo and Senegal.

Co-operation Council for the Arab States of the Gulf

Members: Bahrain, Kuwait, Oman, Qatar, Saudi Arabia and the United Arab Emirates.

Mexico and European Union Trade Agreement

An example of a reciprocal trade agreement was introduced on 1 July 2000 between Mexico and the European Union. It provides overseas buyers with an insight into a trade agreement.

The agreement brings Mexico into the family of countries whose exports benefit from access to the EU market at a reduced or zero rate of duty. Equally, EU goods exported to Mexico will benefit from a preferential tariff treatment. The agreement does not affect Mexico's status as a Beneficiary Country under the Generalised System of Preference (GSP) or its membership of NAFTA. It is important for overseas buyers to remember this fact when looking at the scope and coverage of the EU/Mexico Trade Agreement and understanding its application.

Like all trade agreements there are exceptions to the range of goods covered to meet the needs and concerns of certain industrial sectors. The EU/Mexico agreement reflects this situation for both Mexican exports to the European Union and Community goods exported to Mexico.

Probably the most complex and sensitive area of international trade is agriculture, covered by Chapters 1 to 24 of HM Customs and Excise Tariff. The effect of the trade agreement on the export of Mexican agricultural goods is as follows:

(a) some agricultural products do not qualify at all, although their exclusion will be reviewed in three years' time;

(b) other agricultural exports will not immediately benefit but will come on stream after three years on a sliding scale of annual reductions from the basic rate of duty;

(c) certain agricultural goods will receive a reduced, preferential rate of duty from 1 July 2000 subject to annual tariff quotas; and

(d) the remaining agricultural products receive either a nil rate of duty from the start of the agreement, or to varying sliding scales of annual reductions over 3, 8 or 9 year periods.

Companies importing Mexican agricultural produce should check carefully to see into which group their imports fall.

For the first two categories, EU importers can continue to claim the GSP rate of duty, (see page 267) where available and where the Mexican goods qualify under the GSP preferential rules of origin and are accompanied by a valid Certificate Form A.

The provisions for Mexican exports of industrial goods follow the same format but are considerably simpler because the range of products affected by any exclusions, delays in the implementation date or sliding scale annual reductions are smaller. Again companies should check to see whether their imports from Mexico are affected by any of the restrictions.

Broadly similar provisions apply to EU originating goods in both the agricultural and industrial sectors exported to Mexico. There are special conditions for the importation into Mexico of certain fishery products, some processed agricultural produce and vehicles, including motor vehicles. Again, companies should carefully check the rules for their products when evaluating Mexico as a new marketing opportunity and building an export strategy.

As with all trade arrangements there are strict rules of origin that goods must meet in order to qualify for preferential tariff treatment. Many of the origin rules and conditions for goods imported from, or exported to Mexico are identical to those for other bi-lateral trade agreements. However, there are some significant differences that can affect whether goods are considered as originating either in Mexico or the EU. New and unique origin rules cover a wide range of products especially within the textile and footwear sectors.

There is, however, no substitute for companies thoroughly researching the rules of origin to ensure their products qualify for preferential tariff treatment. A common mistake is to assume that goods which satisfy the rules of origin for one particular trade agreement, say Norway, must also qualify for exports to other countries benefiting from preferential trade arrangements.

The effects of the new trade agreements on documentation are: qualifying EU goods must be accompanied by an EUR 1, or an invoice declaration; and similarly qualifying Mexican exports must be accompanied by the EUR1 which will be issued by the Ministry of Trade and Industrial Development (SECOFI – Secretaria de Commercio y Fomento Industrial) or an invoice declaration.

The declaration is for consignments valued at less than 6000 euros and can be made on the invoice, delivery note or other commercial document.

In a departure from normal preferential trade agreements, EU and Mexican exporters must enter the first four digits of the tariff heading of the goods in Box 8 (description) of the EUR I. Failure to comply with this rule could result in the certificate being rejected and preferential tariff treatment being denied.

Documentation for goods not originating in Mexico or the EU (for example Canadian, Swiss or Japanese) will continue to be covered by certificates of origin where these are a requirement of the trade transaction.

The future

As we progress through the early stages of the twenty-first century, the pace of change in the conduct and execution of international trade will accelerate. Such change will focus on four areas relative to international purchasing: electronic commerce, logistics, globalization and the rising product standards accreditation development.

Overseas buyers will increasingly rely on e-commerce for product and market research, including product standard accreditation and development, business to business negotiation and the execution of the export sales contract delivery arrangements in a logistic environment. Companies will develop regional brands such as the euro brand and set up assembly and distribution centre(s) relying on product outsourcing within the region and outside it. Such development will be driven by intense competition and high tech developments in a global environment. This will place more stress on companies' procurement teams to seek out quality competitively priced products with the latest technology and accreditation across the world with reliable logistically driven supply chain routes which offer a delivered price to the buyer, or provide the option of the buyer to put in place the delivery arrangement through his or her forwarding agent. Hence, pricing will focus on a total product delivered price. The price of the product plus the delivery arrangement to the consignee's address which feature not only the carriage charges but also import duty, VAT, etc. Planning and research will feature more in this strategy than hitherto.

The role of international agencies and continuing enlargement of economic blocs and customs unions will play a major part in the procurement team strategy and focus. An emphasis will be placed on trade facilitation. This will drive trade expansion stimulated by inwards investment. Company mergers and acquisitions will continue as organizations endeavour to become more competitive in price, design and market penetration. Overall, it will provide new opportunities for product sourcing.

From the above it will be realized that the international purchasing process will continue to demand higher standards of the personnel involved. Buying products overseas in a successful manner is a complex business and one which involves many elements, each of which is subject to continuous change in a global environment where e-commerce, logistics, technology and politics are all influential. It is a challenging task but one of great opportunity and risk. Complete professionalism is essential in all its areas. It is hoped that this book will help the students, undergraduates and international entrepreneurs in their endeavours to develop and execute a successful international purchasing strategy.

Appendix A

International purchasing/ trade organizations

Association of British Chambers of Commerce
9 Tufton Street
London SW1P 3QB

Association of International Courier and Express Services (AICES)
Unit 1B, Gallymead Road
Colnbrook
Berkshire SL3 0EN

Baltic and International Maritime Council
161 Bagsvaerdvej
2880 Bagsvaerd
Denmark

British Importers Association
Suite 8, Castle House
25, Castlereagh Street
London W1H 5YR

British International Freight Association
Redfern House
Browells Lane
Feltham
Middx DW13 7EP

British Standards Institution
389 Chiswick High Road
London W4 4AL

Chartered Institute of Purchasing and Supply
Easton House
Easton on the Hill
Stamford
Lincolnshire PE9 3NZ

Confederation of British Industries
Centre Point
103 New Oxford Street
London WC1A 1DU

Cotecna International Ltd
Hounslow House
730 London Road
Hounslow
Middx

Dun and Bradstreet Ltd
Holmers Farm Way
High Wycombe
Bucks HP12 4UL

Electronic Data Interchange Association
148 Buckingham Palace Road
London SW1 9TR

European Union (EU)
European Parliament
97–113 Rue Belliard
1047 Brussels
Belgium

Export Master Systems Ltd
33 St Peter's Street
South Croydon
CR2 7DG

Freight Transport Association
Hernes House
St Johns Road
Tunbridge Wells
Kent TN4 9UZ

Fruit Importers Association (FIA)
D114–115 Fruit and Vegetable Market
New Covent Garden
London

G.E. SeaCo Services Ltd
Sea Container House
20 Upper Ground
London SE1 9PF

HM Customs and Excise
C E Heath House
61 Victoria Avenue
Southend on Sea
Essex SS2 6EX

Institute of Export
Export House
Minerva Business Park
Lynch Wood
Peterborough PE1 6FT

Institute of Translation and Interpreting
377 City Road
London EC1 1NA

International Air Transport Association (IATA)
Route de l'Aeroport 33
BP672 1215 Geneve
Switzerland

International Chamber of Commerce
38 Cours Albert 1er
75008 Paris
France

International Maritime Organisation
4 Albert Embankment
London SE1 7SR

International Standards Organisation
Case postale 56
CH–1211 Geneve 20
Switzerland

Lloyd's Register of Quality Assurance Centre
Hiramford
Middlemarch Office Village
Siskin Drive
Coventry CV3 3FJ

London Metal Exchange
London Metal Exchange Ltd
56 Leadenhall Street
London EC3A 2DX

P&O Nedlloyd Ltd
Beagle House
Braham Street
London E1 8EP

Organisation for Economic Co-operation and Development (OECD)
2 rue Andre-Pascal
75775 Paris
France

SGS United Kingdom Ltd
SGS House
217–221 London Road
Camberley
Surrey GU15 3EY

Simple Trade Procedures Board (SITPRO)
151 Buckingham Palace Road
London SW1W 9SS

Trade Indemnity plc
12–34 Great Eastern Street
London EC2A 3AX

World Trade Organisation
Centre William Rappard
Rue de Lausanne 154
CH–1211 Geneve 21
Switzerland

Appendix B

International purchasing/ trade and shipping terms and abbreviations

Acceptance	Acceptance of an entry occurs when a valid declaration is processed by CHIEF IES (and the goods are available for inspection). This is a Customs definition.
Accepting bank	The bank which accepts a draft drawn under a documentary credit.
Ad valorem	According to value. An ad valorem freight rate is one where freight is based on the value of the goods.
AN	Arrival notice.
ANSI	American Nation Standards Institution.
ARO	Average rate option.
ASME	American Society of Mechanical Engineers.
ATA	Admission temporaire/temporary admission.
BAF	Bunker adjustment factor. Freight adjustment factor to reflect current cost of bunkers.
BIFA	British International Freight Association.
Bill of Exchange	A forward dated undertaking to pay prepared by the debtor and signed by the creditor to acknowledge debt and date payment due. Used in documentary credits to allow period of credit.
B/L	Bill of lading.
Bolero	An electronic bill of lading project.
Box	Colloquial name for a container.
Break bulk cargo	Goods shipped loose in a vessel's hold and not in a container.
BSC	British Shippers Council
BSI	British Standards Institution. The authorized body for the preparation of national standards in the UK.
CABAF	Currency and Bunker Adjustment Factor. A combination of CAF and BAF.
CAD	Cash against documents.
CAF	Currency adjustment factor. Freight adjustment factor to reflect currency exchange fluctuations.

CAP	Common Agriculture Policy.
C/B	Container base.
C&D	Collection and delivery. Carriage from or to customers premises to or from CFS.
CEN	European Committee for Standardisation
CFS	Container Freight Station. Place for packing and unpacking LCL consignments.
CFSP	Customs Freight Simplified Procedures.
CHIEF	Customs Handling of Import and Export Freight (the customs entry processing computer system).
CISG	Convention on the International Sale of Goods 1980 (Vienna Convention).
Clear/clearance	The clearance of an entry is the point at which any revenue associated with the declaration has been paid or secured and the entry can no longer be queried or amended by CHIEF. The goods can now be released into the declared customs procedure or can be removed under a transit arrangement (subject to any commercial considerations). Customs definition.
Closing date	Last date on which export goods can be accepted for a nominated sailing.
CMI	Comité Maritime International.
CMT	Cut, make and trim.
Community Transit	The procedure required for the movement of uncleared non-community goods between or through Member States of the European Community.
Confirming bank	A bank which adds its own undertaking to that of the issuing bank. The confirming bank is usually the advising bank.
COT	Customers own transport. Customer collects from/delivers to CFS/CY.
CP	Charter Party.
CRF	Clean report of findings
CT	Combined transport.
CWE	Cleared without examination (by customs).
D/A	Documents against acceptance.
DC	Documentary credit.
Declarant	The person making the customs declaration in his or her own name or the person in whose name a customs declaration is made.
Declaration	The details of a consignment of goods, imported or removed from a customs warehouse declared to customs.
Deferment account	An account underwritten by a bank or insurance company to which import duties due are posted.
Delivery order	A document authorizing delivery to a nominated party of goods in the care of a third party. Can be issued by a carrier

	on surrender of a bill of lading and then used by a merchant to transfer title by endorsement.
Detention	Charge raised for detaining a container or trailer at customer's premises for a longer period than provided in tariff.
DIN	Deutsches Instut für Normung.
DII	Direction Inter departmentale de l'Industrie.
Direct Trader Input system	A trade computer system that supports a network of trade users and provides HC1 and ED1 access to CHIEF IES. Inventory systems are usually associated with a DTI system.
D/P	Documents against payment.
Drawback	Repayment of duty upon re-exportation of goods previously imported.
Drawee	The party to whom a draft is addressed and who is expected to accept and/or pay it upon presentation.
Drawer	The party who issued a draft. Usually the beneficiary in the credit.
ECSI	Export cargo shipping instruction.
EDI	Electronic Data Interchange.
EDIFACT	EDI for Administration Commerce and Transport. Organization responsible to UN ECE for the development of standard EDI messages for Administration, Commerce and Transport.
EEA	European Economic Area.
E&CI	Excise and Inland Customs.
Endorsement	Signing of a document (e.g. a draft, insurance document or bill of lading) usually on the reverse to transfer title to another party. Documents are often endorsed in black to permit any future holder to gain title.
Entry	An entry held on CHIEF IES consists of the declaration and control information (e.g. status route). The declaration can be amended creating a new version of the entry until it is finalised. This is a customs term.
EPU	Entry processing unit.
ETA	Estimated time of arrival.
ETD	Estimated time of departure.
EU	European Union.
FAK	Freight all kinds.
Fantainer	Container with built in forced ventilation.
FCL	Full container load. Arrangement whereby shipper utilizes all the space in a container which he packs himself.
FCR	Forwarder's certificate of receipt.
FCT	Forwarder's certificate of transport.
Feeder vessel	A short sea vessel used to fetch and carry goods and containers to and from deep-sea vessels.

FFI	For further instructions. Used in place of delivery box if final destination uncertain at time of shipment.
FIATA	International Federation of Freight Forwarders Association.
FILO	Free in liner out. Freight includes cost of discharge but not loading.
FIOS	Free in out and stow. Shipper pays for loading stowing and discharging.
Force Majeure	Circumstances beyond the control of either party to a contract.
Freight broker	The carrier's agent.
Frontier	Any place where the goods are still to be notified formally to customs by placing them under a nominated customs procedure.
Groupage	Consolidation of several LCL consignments into a container.
Groupage Agent	One who consolidates LCL consignments to offer a carrier as an FCL.
GSP	Generalised system of preferences.
GVS	General valuation statement.
Hub and spoke	A modern containerized operation whereby large container ships call at a restricted number of major (hub) ports to or from whence containers are carried to or from minor ports by feeder services (spokes).
IATA	International Air Transport Association.
ICC	International Chamber of Commerce.
ICD	Inland clearance depot. A CFS with customs clearance facilities.
IEA	International Energy Association.
IFIA	International Federation of Inspection Agencies.
IMDG Code	International Maritime Dangerous Goods Code. The IMO recommendations for the carriage of dangerous goods by sea.
IMF	International Monetary Fund.
IMO	International Maritime Organisation.
Inherent vice	Those properties of certain goods which lead to their arrival in a damaged condition without accident or negligence, for example unprotected steel will 'weather', bales of rubber stick together, copra is almost invariably infested.
INRO	International Natural Rubber Organisation.
Inventory system	A (trade) computer system that controls the arrival and departure of consignments at most ports and airports in the UK.
IPO	International purchasing office.
ISO	International Standardization Organization. International organization of national standards bodies responsible for setting standards.

Latent defect	A defect not obvious from a cursory inspection.
L/C	Letter of credit. The document in which the terms of a documentary credit transaction are set out.
LIC	Local Import Control.
LCL	Less than container load. A parcel of goods too small to fill a container which is grouped by the carrier at a CFS with other compatible goods for the same destination.
Lien	A right to retain goods and documents against payment of charges, etc. due but unpaid.
LIFO	Liner in free out. Freight includes the cost of loading but not discharging.
Liner terms	Freight includes the cost of loading onto and discharging from the vessel.
Manifest	List of goods on a vessel or aircraft.
MFN	Most-favoured nation.
MMO	Multi-modal operator.
MNI	Multinational industry.
Negotiating bank	The (nominated) bank which negotiates a presentation under a documentary credit. Usually located in the country of the seller.
NNRF	Non-negotiable report of findings.
Nominated bank	The bank nominated in the documentary credit to pay, accept, negotiate or incur a deferred payment undertaking.
NSSN	National standard shipping note.
NVO(C)C	Non-vessel owning/operating (common) carrier. A carrier issuing bills of lading for carriage of goods on vessels which he or she neither owns or operates.
OPEC	Organisation of Petroleum Exporting Countries.
Paying bank	The bank which is to effect payment under the documentary credit. It can be the issuing bank itself or a nominated bank, usually the advising or confirming bank.
PIS	Pre-shipment Inspection System.
POA	Place of acceptance – where the goods are received for transit and carrier's liability commences – also termed place of receipt.
POD	Place of delivery. Where goods are delivered and carrier liability ceases.
Poincare Franc	Fictitious gold franc originally used, amongst other things, to assess a carrier's liability in an inflation proofed manner in Hague–Visby rules.
Principal carrier	The carrier using a combined transport document (regardless of whether or not goods are carried on his own, a third party's or a consortium members vessel).
Reimbursing bank	Normally a third party bank chosen by the issuing bank to honour claims made by the paying/negotiating bank under a letter of credit.

Release	Release of goods to a customs procedure either at the frontier using the simplified declaration procedure or entry in the records using the local clearance procedure.
Removal	Removal under transit to designated premises using the local clearance procedure.
Reporting period	The time after the end of an accounting period during which all transactions for that period must be finalized. This is a customs term.
SAD	Single Administrative Document (Customs Declaration).
SDR	Special drawing rights. The mean of a basket of currencies designed to 'iron out' currency exchange fluctuations in international valuations. Now used to express limitation in the Hague–Visby Rules and MSA limitation convention, etc.
Settlement payment	Deferred payment, acceptance or negotiation under a documentary credit.
SGS	Société Générale de Surveillance.
Shipper	The person tendering goods for carriage – not to be confused with the party issuing the bill of lading or the vessel operator who is the carrier.
Shut out	Goods not carried on intended vessel.
SI	International System (of measurement – metric).
Sight on demand	If a credit provides for payment or negotiation 'at sight', the issuing or confirming bank is obliged to pay or negotiate upon presentation of conforming documents.
SITPRO	Simpler Trade Procedures Board.
Slot	Space on board a vessel occupied by a container.
SME	Small and medium-sized enterprise.
SOB	Shipped on board. Endorsement on a bill of lading confirming loading on a vessel.
Straight bill of lading	A term for a non-negotiable bill of lading in the USA. The Pomerene Act governs its operation.
Stuffing/stripping	The action of packing/unpacking a container.
SWIFT	Society for Worldwide Inter-bank Financial Telecommunication.
Tariff terms	Conditions and scale of charges.
Tax point	The point in time that establishes the rate of exchange, rates of duty and tax, etc. that apply to a customs declaration.
Temporary storage	Places approved for the deposit of imported goods which have not been cleared out of customs control.
Tenor	The period of time for which a draft is drawn. The tenor may be at sight or usance.
TEU	Twenty foot equivalent unit, e.g. $1 \times 40\text{ft} = 2$ TEU, $1 \times 20\text{ft} = 1$ TEU.
THC	Terminal handling charge.

environmental management

equipment for fire protection and fire fighting

ergonomics

essential oils

fasteners

ferroalloys

ferrous metal pipes and metallic fittings

fertilisers and soil conditioners

fine ceramics

fire tests on building materials, components and structures

fluid power systems

fluorspar

freight containers

furniture

gas cylinders

gas turbines

gears

general aspects for health care products

geographic information/geomatics.

geotechnics

glass containers

glass in building

glass plant, pipeline and fittings

graphic technology

graphical symbols

gypsum, gypsum plasters and gypsum products

horology

humane animal (mammal) traps

hydrogen energy technologies

hydrometric determinations

implants for surgery

industrial automation systems and integration

industrial fans

industrial trucks

information and documentation

information technology

internal combustion engines

iron ores

jewellery

laboratory glassware and related apparatus

lac

leather

lifts, escalators, passenger conveyors

light gauge metal containers

light metals and their alloys

limits and fits

machine tools

manganese and chromium ores

masonry

materials, equipment and offshore structures for petroleum and natural gas industries

measurement of fluid flow in closed conduits

mechanical contraceptives

mechanical testing of metals

mechanical vibration and shock

medical devices for injections

metallic and other inorganic coatings

metrology and properties of surfaces

mica

microbeam analysis

mining

natural gas

natural stone

nickel and nickel alloys

non-destructive testing

nuclear energy

oil burners and associated equipment

optics and optical instruments

packaging

paints and varnishes

pallets for unit load method of materials handling

paper, board and pulps

personal safety

petroleum products and lubricants

photography

plain bearings

plastic pipes, fittings and valves for the transport of fluids

plastics

powder metallurgy

preferred numbers

products in fibre reinforced cement

prosthetics and orthotics
protective clothing and equipment
pulleys and belts (including veebelts)
pumps
quality management and quality
  assurance
quantities, units, symbols, conversion
  factors
refractories
refrigeration
road transport informatics
road vehicles
rolling bearings
round steel link chains, lifting hooks
  and accessories
rubber and rubber products
safety devices for protection against
  excessive pressure
safety of machinery
safety of toys
sawn timber and sawlogs
screw threads
semi-manufactures of timber
sewing machines
shafts for machinery and accessories
ships and marine technology
sieves, sieving and other sizing
  methods
sizing system, designations and
  marking for boots and shoes
sizing systems and designations for
  clothes
small craft
small tools
soil quality
solar energy
solid mineral fuels
solid wastes

space heating appliances
sports and recreational equipment
starch (including derivatives and by-
  products)
steel
steel and aluminium structures
steel wire ropes
sterilisation of health care products
surface active agents
surface chemical analysis
surgical instruments
technical drawings, product definition
  and related documentation
technical energy systems
technical systems and aids for disabled
  or handicapped persons
terminology (principles and
  coordination)
textile machinery and allied machinery
  and accessories
textiles
thermal insulation
thermal turbines for industrial
  application (steam turbines, gas
  expansion turbines)
timber structures
tobacco and tobacco products
tractors and machinery for agriculture
  and forestry
transfusion, infusion and injection
  equipment for medical use
tyres, rims and valves
vacuum technology
valves
water quality
welding and allied processes
wood-based panels
zinc and zinc alloys